NSC 68 and the Poli

NSC 68 and the Political Economy of the Early Cold War examines the origins and implementation of NSC 68, the massive rearmament program that the United States embarked on beginning in the summer of 1950. Curt Cardwell reinterprets the origins of NSC 68 to demonstrate that the aim of the program was less about containing communism than ensuring the survival of the nascent postwar global economy, on which rested postwar U.S. prosperity. The book challenges most studies on NSC 68 as a document of geostrategy and argues, instead, that it is more correctly understood as a document rooted in concerns for the U.S. domestic political economy.

Curt Cardwell is an assistant professor of U.S. foreign relations history at Drake University. He received a PhD in history at Rutgers, The State University of New Jersey, in 2006 and was recipient of the Harry S. Truman Library Dissertation Year Grant in 2003.

NSC 68 and the Political Economy of the Early Cold War

CURT CARDWELL
Drake University, Iowa

CAMBRIDGE
UNIVERSITY PRESS

CAMBRIDGE
UNIVERSITY PRESS

32 Avenue of the Americas, New York NY 10013-2473, USA

Cambridge University Press is part of the University of Cambridge.

It furthers the University's mission by disseminating knowledge in the pursuit of education, learning and research at the highest international levels of excellence.

www.cambridge.org
Information on this title: www.cambridge.org/9781107480957

© Curt Cardwell 2011

This publication is in copyright. Subject to statutory exception and to the provisions of relevant collective licensing agreements, no reproduction of any part may take place without the written permission of Cambridge University Press.

First published 2011
First paperback edition 2015

A catalogue record for this publication is available from the British Library

Library of Congress Cataloguing in Publication data
Cardwell, Curt.
  NSC 68 and the political economy of the early Cold War / Curt Cardwell.
  p. cm.
  Includes bibliographical references and index.
  ISBN 978-0-521-19730-4 (hardback)
  1. United States – Foreign relations – 1945–1953. 2. United States – Foreign economic relations. 3. International economic relations – History – 20th century. 4. National security – United States – History – 20th century.
  5. Cold War. I. Title.
  E744.C354 2011
  973.91 – dc22   2011000634

ISBN 978-0-521-19730-4 Hardback
ISBN 978-1-107-48095-7 Paperback

Cambridge University Press has no responsibility for the persistence or accuracy of URLs for external or third-party internet websites referred to in this publication, and does not guarantee that any content on such websites is, or will remain, accurate or appropriate.

Contents

Acknowledgments	*page* vii
Abbreviations	xi
Introduction	1
1. NSC 68 and the Problem of Origins	8
2. Multilateralism, the Soviet Threat, and the Origins of the Cold War	28
3. Multilateralism, the Dollar Gap, and the Origins of the Cold War	58
4. The Dollar Gap and Its Discontents	92
5. The British Sterling-Dollar Crisis of 1949–1950	128
6. The Origins and Development of NSC 68	160
7. The Political Economy of Rearmament	211
Conclusion	259
Select Bibliography	271
Index	289

Acknowledgments

This book was a labor of love, and many people helped me along the way, intellectually, institutionally, and emotionally. This project would never have seen the light of day had it not been for my chance encounter with Professor Frank Kofsky at California State University, Sacramento, where I began graduate studies in 1994 working toward a Master's degree. It was, truly, a chance encounter, as up to the time I enrolled in Frank's reading seminar on U.S. foreign policy I considered myself a historian of the nineteenth century American West and was preparing to go on to a PhD program in that field. Frank's was the last reading seminar I had to take to fulfill my requirements before moving on to the Master's thesis. His was the only one offered in American history that semester, so I had to take it. Upon learning what the topic of the seminar would be, my thought was "oh, how boring." Little did I know that the seminar was about to change my life in ways I could not have imagined. The first book we read was Thomas McCormick's *America's Half-Century*, and I was skeptical. The information McCormick presented was quite new to me, and it appeared a bit conspiratorial. Then, of all things, I read William Shoup's and Laurence Minter's *Imperial Brain Trust*, a study of the Council on Foreign Relations and its role in the conduct of U.S. foreign policy between roughly 1921 and the 1970s. At this point I grew even more skeptical. Their work truly seemed conspiratorial in nature. Then I read Lloyd C. Gardner's *Economic Aspects of New Deal Diplomacy*, and I was hooked. Literally, Lloyd's first book, written nearly forty years ago, changed my life. It was erudite, scholarly, and too factual not to be taken seriously. I resolved to become a diplomatic historian.

vii

I then set out to enlist Frank Kofsky as my Master's thesis adviser with the determination to get a PhD in the field. I approached him in the hall of the history department and asked him if he would consider being my thesis adviser. His response was direct and of no small significance for the book in your hands. He agreed and also gave me a topic – the British sterling-dollar crisis of 1949–1950 and the origins of NSC 68. Well, there it is. A topic was born, one that has consumed me for the better part of the last fourteen years. Little did I know then that Frank knew Lloyd Gardner and Thomas McCormick, not to mention Walter LaFeber and William Appleman Williams – the dean of revisionist historians. Next thing I knew I was in touch with Lloyd Gardner and, ultimately, became a student of his at Rutgers, The State University of New Jersey. The rest is, as the saying goes, history. Life has a way of throwing one curve balls. One just has to be ready to smack them out of the park when they come.

Many institutions and individuals have helped me along the way with generous support. I must begin with the graduate school and history department at Rutgers, where I earned my PhD in 2006. The program in history at Rutgers is outstanding in its support of graduate students. The Harry S. Truman Library and Museum in Independence, Missouri, offered me a research travel grant in 2002 that gave me the opportunity to spend ten days at the library researching their archives. More importantly, the library awarded me its annual Dissertation Year Grant for the 2003–2004 academic year, which allowed me to offset my funding from the Rutgers Graduate School for another year. A special thanks also must go to Professor Keith Wailoo of Rutgers who provided me with a year of funding as part of his research team and study group devoted to the history of science and medicine, but which allowed me to offset a year of funding from the university itself. The Drake University Center for the Humanities provided support for a research trip to the National Archives in Great Britain. I would particularly like to thank Karl Schaefer who, as director of the Center, guided me in the process. I must thank my parents, Bob and Lana Powers, who offered their generous economic and emotional support throughout my long college career.

I would like to thank specific colleagues and mentors who have helped me along the way. Jackson Lears and James Livingston, both of Rutgers University, served on my dissertation committee and offered sage advice. Jim Livingston, in particular, has been a source of great intellectual stimulus. He will be disappointed with this book because it is a radical departure from the dissertation, but his impact on my thinking and development as a historian could not be stronger. Robert Long of

Acknowledgments   ix

CSU Sacramento stepped in and served as my Master's thesis adviser when Frank Kofsky passed away. I am indebted to him for doing so and for pointing out to me that NSC 68 actually mentions the dollar gap! Fred Adams, whom I met only because he retired from Drake University when I became his successor, has been a huge factor in seeing this work through to completion, deserves great thanks for his thorough reading of the entire manuscript and suggestions he made to improve it.

I am especially indebted to Frank Costigliola, professor of history at the University of Connecticut. I met Frank in 1997 through Frank Kofsky. When Frank Kofsky died, Costigliola took me under his wing and has been a source of guidance and inspiration ever since. He is truly a remarkable individual in his devotion to his students and his love of history. A great thanks must also go out to Robert Buzzanco, professor of history at the University of Houston. Bob was an early supporter of the work currently in your hands and has been a consistent champion of it ever since. I will forever remember his influence and input to the endeavor. For giving me a hard time throughout my years at Rutgers (and to this day), thanks goes out to Warren Kimball, professor emeritus of Rutgers. Warren probably will not like the finished product, but his imprint is on it, nonetheless. Lloyd Gardner, who advised my dissertation, is a giant among giants, and although he would not like me to say that, it is true. I could not imagine a more gregarious and supportive adviser. Working with him was the pleasure of a lifetime, and I will always cherish it as the luck of the draw.

A first book, usually, is the product of a dissertation, and no dissertation gets written without the support, prodding, and commiseration of graduate colleagues. I met some really great people in my years at Rutgers. Thanks to Amy Portwood, Kate Elias, Lindsay Braun, Mark Sykes, Katherine Howey, Katie Keller, Peter Larson, Scott Bruton, Gary Darden, and Justin Hart. Among my graduate colleagues, a special thanks goes out to Joe Gabriel, a true colleague in every sense of the word. Joe has been both the most consistent critic and the most consistent champion of my work. To long nights of drinking, great conversation, and baked potatoes!

A shout out must go to the crew at the Olive Branch in New Brunswick, New Jersey, where I did more than enough studying than I should admit. To the three Nicks, Pete, Doug, Harriet, and Andy: Thanks for the hospitality, the cheap pizza, and introducing me to the New Jersey attitude. I will never forget it. I promised you all I would acknowledge you in this book, and I have made good on my promise.

Also, I would like to thank all my students at Drake who have participated over the years in my seminar on the origins of the Cold War. The seminar gave me a chance to test my ideas with some really wonderful, bright, engaging young people who were, for the most part, born near the end or after the Cold War ended and so never knew it as a daily reality. I always gave them a cross-section of readings on the origins of the Cold War. Almost to a one they generally came down on the side of the revisionist interpretation, although not without qualms, to be sure. It is folly to think that this current generation is disengaged or less intellectual than its predecessors. You all know who you are.

The most important acknowledgments must go to the two most important individuals in my life – my wife Stephanie and my daughter Lenin. Stephanie has been by far my biggest champion and supporter. Why she ever went along with my plans to become a historian, with all of the initial poverty and the moving here and there with no guarantee of a job at the end of the day, I will never know. How is that for faith and encouragement? Not only that, but without her this book, and the dissertation that preceded it, never would have been what it is. She read it over and over, edited its many editions, and listened and commented on my many qualms and concerns and observations to the point that she knows as much about this subject as I do. No person on this planet will be happier than she that this book has reached completion. If she never hears the term NSC 68 again in her life, it will not be too soon. We've been married twenty-one years as of 2010, and what a great time it has been. To many more years!

Our daughter came along in 1998, and my life has been so enriched as a result. Despite her name, she was not the inspiration for this book nor, most importantly, its interpretational stance (she's actually named after John Lennon, but that is another story altogether). She has, however, been an inspiration toward finishing the book and leaving her a legacy of a father who cherishes truth, wisdom, and serious historical study. It is my hope that she will come to appreciate that as she grows and develops her own ideas about the larger world of which she is a part. At her age, that would be too much to ask now. Of course, her love, her smiles, her quirky comments, her great sense of humor, and so much more besides have sustained me on this journey and made it all the more worthwhile.

A study of this sort, which aims to challenge conventional wisdom, is bound to be scrutinized to the hilt (and I hope it will be!). Although I have received help and advice from many individuals, all errors of either analysis or factual information are mine alone.

Curt Cardwell
Des Moines, Iowa, 2010

Abbreviations

AMP	Additional Military Production
CCP	Chinese Communist Party
CFM	Council on Foreign Ministers
CFR	Council on Foreign Relations
CIA	Central Intelligence Agency
ECA	Economic Cooperation Administration
ECSC	European Coal and Steel Community
EDC	European Defense Community
EPU	European Payments Union
ERP	European Recovery Program (Marshall Plan)
IBRD	International Bank for Reconstruction and Development
IMF	International Monetary Fund
ISAC	International Security Affairs Committee
ITO	International Trade Organization
JCS	Joint Chiefs of Staff
MAP	Military Assistance Program
MDAP	Mutual Defense Assistance Program
MSA	Mutual Security Agency
MSP	Mutual Security Program
NAC	National Advisory Council on International Monetary and Financial Problems
NATO	North Atlantic Treaty Organization
NSC	National Security Council
OEEC	Organization of European Economic Cooperation
OSD	Office of the Secretary of Defense

OSP	Offshore Procurement Program
PPS	U.S. State Department Policy Planning Staff
RTAA	Reciprocal Trade Agreements Act
SGAE	Council on Foreign Relations' Study Group on Aid to Europe
SGEP	Council on Foreign Relations' Study Group on Economic Policy
WUSB	Western Union Supply Board

Introduction

In 1994, James Baker, wealthy lawyer, scion of the Texas elite, and long-time Washington insider, delivered a speech before the Rotary Club of Washington, DC. The occasion was the club's annual foreign relations seminar, a subject on which Baker knew a great deal. Out of government in 1994, Baker had a distinguished record of public service, one that placed him at the center of the "Reagan revolution," as former Hollywood actor and California governor Ronald Reagan's victory in the 1980 presidential campaign has come to be known. A former Marine Corps officer, Baker managed Reagan's victorious 1980 presidential run, served as White House chief of staff during Reagan's first term, secretary of the treasury during his second, and also was a fixture on the National Security Council. Part of this tenure occurred at the height of the "Reagan Cold War," when tensions between the two superpowers once again rose to a fever pitch before settling into cautious coexistence. Under George Herbert Walker Bush, Baker served as secretary of state during one of the most momentous times in modern history – the collapse of the Berlin Wall and the end of the Cold War. Baker, it is fair to say, was a Cold War warrior *par excellence*, which is what makes his comments before the Rotary Club on that day in 1994 so startling. The greatest accomplishment of the period since World War II, he said, was not the defeat of Communism, not the end of the Cold War, but the creation of a "global liberal economic regime."[1]

---

[1] Quoted from Walter LaFeber, "Technology and U.S. Foreign Relations," *Diplomatic History* 24 (Winter 2000): 1.

I came across Baker's comment long after I was in the writing stages of this study, but it does convey, in many respects, what I am trying to accomplish in this book. The primary goal of United States foreign policy officials in the post–WWII era was to create an open, global, capitalist, liberal, economic order, or what in the study is referred to as multilateralism. It was *not* primarily to prevent the Soviet Union from fulfilling its alleged designs for world conquest, as convention holds. To be sure, blocking Soviet expansionist aims (insofar as they existed) was part of the larger project, but it was neither the sole goal nor the most important one. Our understanding of the immediate postwar era, the era in which the Cold War emerged, therefore, is flawed when we put the "Soviet threat" at the center of that narrative. As Baker's comment indicates, more was at stake than the "containment" of the Soviet Union and communism.

To bear upon that argument, this monograph offers a reexamination of the origins of U.S. National Security Council paper 68, or NSC 68 as it is more popularly known, the top-secret NSC paper written during the winter and spring of 1950 and presented to President Truman on April 7. The paper, written by the State Department's Policy Planning Staff (PPS) under the direction of Secretary of State Dean Acheson and Director of the Policy Planning Staff Paul Nitze, argued that the United States needed to embark on a massive rearmament program to combat what it called "the Kremlin's design for world domination," a program that subsequently was carried out beginning in the summer of 1950, forever changing the Cold War and, indeed, the course of world history.[2] That NSC 68 was a key document of the early Cold War era is now generally recognized. It has entered the pantheon of such early Cold War fundamentals as the Truman Doctrine, Winston Churchill's "Iron Curtain" speech, and the Marshall Plan, to name just some. The problem is that the traditional narrative of NSC 68's origins is deeply flawed. As such, it contributes to a false understanding of the entire origins of the Cold War. This book aims to correct that misconception.

The conclusion that this study draws, explicated in the pages that follow, is that NSC 68, or rather the massive rearmament program that it engendered, was created and implemented, not solely or even primarily to cope with the threat posed by the Soviet Union, although, again, that was part of the larger project, but to overcome the systemic problems to the international economic order posed by the "dollar gap," an international

---

[2] NSC 68, April 14, 1950, *Foreign Relations of the United States (FRUS), 1950* I (Washington, D.C: U.S. Government Printing Office, 1977): 245.

Introduction 3

balance-of-payments problem that found western Europe, Japan, and a host of other nations in the immediate postwar era incapable of earning the dollars through the normal processes of trade that they needed to purchase U.S. exports. Although seemingly benign, the problems posed by the dollar gap were, as the evidence will show, far more potentially destructive of the American way of life, at least as defined by those in charge of making U.S. foreign policy in the Truman administration, than any threat posed by communism or the Soviet Union. As such, it is the thesis of this study that the Cold War developed less to "contain" the Soviet Union than to ensure the survival of that "global liberal economic regime" of which Baker spoke so glowingly. For the fact of the matter is that in the early Cold War, the Soviet Union was "containable," whereas the dollar gap was, in effect, not.

This study is by far not the first to highlight the dollar gap as bearing upon the origins of the Cold War or NSC 68. As early as 1956 Richard N. Gardner in *Sterling-Dollar Diplomacy* demonstrated that the dollar gap, although he did not use the term, played a significant role in the way in which the Cold War moved from being a conflict over balance-of-power issues to a crusade that Americans came to believe they had to fight. Richard Freeland's *The Truman Doctrine and the Origins of McCarthyism* and Gabriel Kolko's and Joyce Kolko's *The Limits of Power*, both of 1972, also gave due recognition to the dollar gap as a driving force in early postwar U.S. foreign policy. Sociologist Fred Block, in his 1977 monograph *The Origins of International Economic Disorder*, was one of the first authors to demonstrate how rearmament under NSC 68 came along at just the right time to save the international economy from collapse. In a 1980 article, Block speculated further on the interconnection between NSC 68 and the dollar gap. Although he did not go so far as to say that rearmament was primarily aimed at the dollar gap, he concluded that the connections were too intertwined to be mere coincidence and argued the need for further research. In *The Pacific Alliance*, published in 1984, William Borden showed how NSC 68, parlayed through the Korean War, overcame Japan's dollar gap and greatly aided its economic recovery. Andrew Rotter's 1987 *The Path to Vietnam* explored the dollar gap in relation to Britain's colonies in the Far East and how it contributed to U.S. policy toward Vietnam. Thomas McCormick, in his broad survey of twentieth-century U.S. foreign policy *America's Half-Century*, places NSC 68 in the context of global economic recovery. Melvyn Leffler, in his tome *A Preponderance of Power*, still considered the definitive work on the origins of the Cold War, at least from the U.S. perspective, explores the

4   *Introduction*

dollar gap but went to considerable lengths to downplay its significance, a fact that is dealt with significantly in the study to follow. Political scientist Benjamin Fordham's 1998 book *Building the Cold War Consensus* also locates the dollar gap at the center of NSC 68, although that is not its central argument. Rather, as the title implies Fordham is interested in, from a policy standpoint, how consensus was formed on rearmament in an environment that was generally hostile to the very idea. Importantly, Fordham draws attention to one of the central issues that gave rise to this study, that the Soviet Union's acquisition of atomic power and the Communist victory in the Chinese civil war, events that occurred roughly a month a part in the late summer and early fall of 1949, did not generate that consensus as tradition holds.[3]

However, despite the efforts of these authors, the dollar gap remains an obscure topic. There are innumerable books on the origins of the Cold War that make no reference to it or that reference it so benignly that the unsuspecting would have no clue as to its significance, works that, most importantly, assume that the Cold War can be explained in its absence.[4] Such is simply not the case, as this study, building on those that came before, readily proves. Although the dollar gap was an international

---

[3] Richard N. Gardner, *Sterling-Dollar Diplomacy: Anglo-American Collaboration in the Reconstruction of Multilateral Trade* (Oxford, United Kingdom: Clarendon Press, 1956); Gabriel Kolko and Joyce Kolko, *The Limits of Power: The World and United States Foreign Policy, 1945–1954* (New York: Harper and Row, 1972); Richard Freeland, *The Truman Doctrine and the Origins of McCarthyism: Foreign Policy, Domestic Politics, and Internal Security, 1946–1948* (New York: Knopf, 1972); Fred L. Block, *The Origins of International Economic Disorder: A Study of United States International Monetary Policy from World War II to the Present* (Berkeley, California: University of California Press, 1977); Fred L. Block, "Economic Instability and Military Strength: The Paradoxes of the 1950 Rearmament Decision," *Politics and Society* 10:1 (1980): 35–58; William Borden, *The Pacific Alliance: United States Foreign Economic Policy and Japanese Trade Recovery, 1947–1955* (Madison, Wisconsin: University of Wisconsin Press, 1984); Andrew J. Rotter, *The Path to Vietnam: Origins of the American Commitment to Southeast Asia.* (Ithaca, New York: Cornell University Press, 1987); Melvyn Leffler, *A Preponderance of Power: National Security, the Truman Administration, and the Cold War* (Stanford, California: Stanford University Press, 1992); Thomas McCormick, *America's Half-Century: United States Foreign Policy in the Cold War and After* (Baltimore, Maryland: The Johns Hopkins University Press, 1995), 2nd edition; Benjamin O. Fordham, *Building the Cold War Consensus: The Political Economy of U.S. National Security Policy, 1949–1951* (Ann Arbor, Michigan: The University of Michigan Press, 1998).

[4] Examples from standard works in the field are: Daniel Yergin, *Shattered Peace: The Origins of the Cold War and the National Security State* (New York: Houghton Mifflin, 1977); John Lewis Gaddis, *Strategies of Containment: A Critical Appraisal of Postwar American National Security Policy* (New York: Oxford University Press, 1982); David McCullough, *Truman* (New York: Simon and Schuster, 1992); John Lewis Gaddis, *We Now Know: Rethinking Cold War History* (New York: Oxford University Press, 1998);

Introduction 5

phenomenon, this study's primary focus is on western Europe. Western Europe was the area of the world with which whose economic recovery Truman administration officials were most concerned. Hence, their efforts to cope with the dollar gap were most focused there. As noted previously, Borden's *The Pacific Alliance*, a book that has been far too underappreciated, wrote about the Japanese dollar gap and how it was overcome through NSC 68 and the Korean War. No similar work has been written on western Europe. My effort here is to do for western Europe what Borden did for Japan, although, admittedly, the unwieldy nature of dealing with the many countries of western Europe has not produced as succinct an analysis as Borden did. My goal has been to lay out the broad contours of the problem associated with the dollar gap crisis in western Europe. A more comprehensive history of the entirety of the dollar gap crisis in western Europe will have to await future studies.

This study falls under the category of what is often called the economic interpretation of the origins of the Cold War, which, in an earlier time, was known as revisionism. In this, it differs from other interpretive categories such as orthodoxy, realist theory, the national security thesis, postrevisionism, and neoorthodoxy, the latter of which has become particularly prominent in the wake of the Soviet Union's collapse and the supposed U.S. "victory" in the Cold War. At risk of some generalization, the economic interpretation argues that the Cold War – the containment of communism – was not the focal point of U.S. foreign policy in the postwar era but merely an offshoot, albeit a crucial one, of the larger U.S. objective of creating an open, global economy that would ensure the survival of the free enterprise system in the United States. Furthermore, it sees U.S. foreign policy as primarily growing out of domestic concerns. Hence, it takes exception with the orthodox approach to the origins of the Cold War, the approach that still most resonates with the general public, that the Cold War was simply the "brave and essential response of free men to Communist aggression," as the late historian Arthur Schlesinger Jr. so aptly put it in a 1967 essay.[5] It differs with realist theory in arguing that domestic concerns, and not balance-of-power considerations alone, have had an indelible impact on U.S. foreign policy. It also takes issue

---

Michael J. Hogan, *A Cross of Iron: Harry S. Truman and the Origins of the National Security State, 1945–1954* (New York: Cambridge University Press, 1998); Arnold Offner, *Another Such Victory: President Truman and the Cold War, 1945–1953* (Stanford, California: Stanford University Press, 2002).

[5] Quoted in Lloyd C. Gardner, *The Origins of the Cold War* (Waltham, Massachusetts: Ginn-Blaisdell, 1970).

with the national security thesis, arguably the most popular theory of the origins of the Cold War in the present day, as being too ambiguous to be an explanatory tool for how U.S. foreign policy officials acted in the crucial years in which the Cold War developed; the national security thesis has merit, but it ultimately fails because it does not choose among the various national security interests that were primary to U.S. foreign policy officials. Anything and everything becomes "national security," which turns policymakers into virtual automatons one-tracked to this nebulous thing called national security, not thinking, feeling individuals with interests who, we can expect, had differing conceptions of what constitutes national security and who acted in accordance with those interests. It also rejects postrevisionism and neoorthodoxy because, despite their acceptance of economic factors as crucial to the conduct of U.S. foreign policy, in the final analysis they merely reassert the orthodox interpretation of the origins of the Cold War as the result of Stalin's depravity and little else.

Although "revisionism" has become a historicized term, referring both to a "school" of diplomatic historians employing the economic interpretation and the individual historians who comprised that school known as "the revisionists," such that I cannot and would not claim that this study is revisionist, undoubtedly it has been most influenced by the revisionist approach to the origins of the Cold War. As I have studied U.S. foreign policy, I have found that the revisionist school offers the best analysis for making sense of it during the early Cold War period. U.S. foreign policy officials in this time period were undoubtedly concerned with the Soviet threat, and to argue otherwise would be foolhardy. But they were not concerned with the Soviet threat alone, and they were, despite what they often said publicly, aware that the Soviet Union did not pose the most significant threat to their conception of how the postwar world should be constructed. Readers will have to decide for themselves whether this study validates the revisionist approach as against other approaches. I believe that it does.

There are other ways to theorize about the origins of the Cold War, of course, such as cultural analysis, ideology, world-systems analysis, dependency theory, among others. This study has been informed by such studies, but it has not explicitly employed their theories. An earlier version of this study attempted to analyze the ways in which rearmament under NSC 68 intersected with cultural developments in the United States and the world at large, particularly in terms of the spread of consumer culture as, at least in part, an outgrowth of the "military Keynesianism"

Introduction 7

embodied in the rearmament program. In the end, that enterprise became unwieldy, and I opted just to tell the story of NSC 68's origins as a fairly standard diplomatic history so as to set the story straight, at least as I see it. Yet, in doing so, it is my firm belief that this study will serve as a bridge to such other theoretical approaches and disciplines.

This study is based on research in the U.S. National Archives, the Harry S. Truman Library, the records of the Council on Foreign Relations housed at the Seeley G. Mudd Library at Princeton University, the British National Archives, the U.S. Library of Congress, the United States' *Foreign Relations of the United States* series, and the records of the Public Advisory Board of the Mutual Security Agency, among other archives and published primary and secondary sources. One of the key contributions that this study brings to the table is crucial evidence that this author has never seen referenced before, evidence that demonstrates conclusively that the dollar gap was a significant motivation in the decision to rearm, in fact, the most significant motivation. In doing so it challenges prevailing notions, not only of NSC 68, but of how the entire Cold War developed. It is written, however, not to silence debate, but to encourage it. The history here does not claim to be the last word on the issues that it explores. I believe that the evidence contained within this book needs to be taken seriously and not merely rejected out of hand based on ideological predilections, as sadly are so many studies that run counter to the conventional wisdom. If the argument, and the evidence used to back it up, is flawed, let that be challenged. But let us stick to the evidence.

I

NSC 68 and the Problem of Origins

> If [in writing NSC 68] we made our points clearer than truth, we did not
> differ from most other educators and could hardly do otherwise.
>
> Dean Acheson, 1969

In February 1975, roughly twenty-five years after being presented to
President Harry S. Truman, National Security Council policy recommendation 68, or NSC 68 as it has come to be known, was declassified.[1]
Although the declassification was apparently an accident on the part of
then Secretary of State Henry Kissinger, NSC 68 in fact had been a part
of public discourse for years. Secretary of State Dean Acheson, one of

---

[1] Analyses of NSC 68 are numerous. Among the most important are: Dean Acheson,
Present at the Creation (New York: W. W. Norton, 1969), 373–381; Robert P. Newman,
"NSC (National Insecurity) 68: Nitze's Second Hallucination," in Matin J. Medhurst
and H. W. Brands, eds., *Critical Reflections on the Cold War: Linking Rhetoric and
History* (College Station, Texas: Texas A&M University Press, 2000), 55–94; Benjamin
O. Fordham, *Building the Cold War Consensus: The Political Economy of U.S. National
Security Policy, 1949–1951* (Ann Arbor, Michigan: University of Michigan Press, 1998);
Michael Hogan, *Cross of Iron: Harry S. Truman and the Origins of the National Security
State, 1945–1954* (New York: Cambridge University Press, 1998), 291–314; Thomas
McCormick, *America's Half-Century: United States Foreign Policy in the Cold War and
After* (Baltimore, Maryland: Johns Hopkins University Press, 1995) 2nd ed., 88–98; S.
Nelson Drew, ed., *NSC-68: Forging the Strategy of Containment* (Washington, D.C.,
National Defense University, 1994); Walter LaFeber, *The American Age: U.S. Foreign
Policy at Home and Abroad, 1750 to the Present* (New York, W. W. Norton, 1994), 2nd
ed., 504–507, 529–530; Steve Rearden, "Frustrating the Kremlin Design: Acheson and
NSC 68," in Douglas Brinkley, ed., *Dean Acheson and the Making of U.S. Foreign Policy*
(New York: St. Martin's Press, 1993), 159–175; Ernest May, ed., *American Cold War
Strategy: Interpreting NSC 68* (New York: Bedford Books of St. Martin's Press, 1993);
Melvyn Leffler, *A Preponderance of Power: National Security, the Truman Administration,*

NSC 68 and the Problem of Origins

the principal authors of the paper, began discussing its contents publicly in early 1950, even prior to its adoption as national policy, as part of his "total diplomacy" campaign to convince the American people of the need for a stepped-up Cold War.[2] In 1962, Paul Y. Hammond published a forty-thousand-word essay on NSC 68 based primarily on interviews with those who had seen it.[3] Acheson discussed NSC 68 in some detail in *Present at the Creation*, his classic autobiography of his years in the State Department, published in 1969; although its then still top-secret status

and the Origins of the Cold War (Stanford, California: Stanford University Press, 1992), 355–360; Marc Trachtenberg, "A 'Waiting Asset': American Strategy and the Shifting Nuclear Balance, 1949–1954," in Marc Trachtenberg, *History and Strategy* (Princeton, New Jersey: Princeton University Press, 1991), 100–152; Paul H. Nitze, *From Hiroshima to Glasnost: At the Center of Decision, A Memoir* (New York: Grove Wiedenfield, 1989); Walter LaFeber, "NATO and Korea: A Context," *Diplomatic History* 13 (Fall 1989): 461–477; Robert A. Pollard, "The National Security State Reconsidered: Truman and Economic Containment, 1945–1950," in Michael J. Lacey, ed., *The Truman Presidency* (New York: Cambridge University Press, 1989), 205–235; Andrew J. Rotter, *The Path to Vietnam: Origins of the American Commitment to Southeast Asia.* (Ithaca, New York: Cornell University Press, 1987); Steve Rearden, *The Evolution of American Strategic Doctrine: Paul H. Nitze and the Soviet Challenge* (Boulder, Colorado: Westview Press, 1984); Kenneth W. Condit, *The History of the Joint Chiefs of Staff: The Joint Chiefs of Staff and National Policy: Volume II, 1947–1949*, Historical Division, Joint Chiefs of Staff, Record Group 218, Records of the Joint Chiefs of Staff, National Archives II, College Park, Maryland, 271–281; William S. Borden, *Pacific Alliance: United States Foreign Economic Policy and Japanese Trade Recovery, 1947–1955* (Madison, Wisconsin: The University of Wisconsin Press, 1984), 27–29; Jerry Sanders, *Peddlers of Crisis: The Committee on the Present Danger and the Politics of Containment* (Boston: Southend Press, 1983), 23–50; John Lewis Gaddis, *Strategies of Containment: A Critical Appraisal of Postwar American National Security Policy* (New York: Oxford University Press, 1982); John Lewis Gaddis and Paul Nitze, "NSC 68 and the Threat Reconsidered," *International Security* 4 (Spring 1980): 164–176; Fred Block, "Economic Instability and Military Strength: The Paradoxes of the 1950 Rearmament Decision," *Politics and Society* 10:1 (1980): 35–58; Sam Post Brief, "Departure from Incrementalism in U.S. Strategic Planning: The Origins of NSC 68," *Naval War College Review* (March–April 1980): 34–57; Fred M. Kaplan, "Our Cold-War Policy, Circa '50," *The New York Times*, May 18, 1980, p. 34; Paul H. Nitze, "The Development of NSC 68," *International Security* 4 (Spring 1980): 170–176; Samuel F. Wells, Jr., "Sounding the Tocsin: NSC 68 and the Soviet Threat," *International Security* 4 (Fall 1979): 138–158; Fred Block, *The Origins of International Economic Disorder: A Study of United States International Monetary Policy from World War II to the Present* (Berkeley, California: University of California Press, 1977), 86–96; Gabriel Kolko and Joyce Kolko, *The Limits of Power: The World and United States Foreign Policy, 1945–1954* (New York: Harper and Row, 1972), 507–509; Paul Y. Hammond, "NSC 68: Prologue to Rearmament," in Columbia University Press, *Strategy, Politics, and Defense Budgets*, eds., Warner R. Schilling, Paul Y. Hammond, and Glenn Snyder (New York: Colia University Press, 1962), 271–378.

[2] Dean Acheson, "'Total Diplomacy' to Strengthen U.S. Leadership for Human Freedom," U.S. Department of State *Bulletin* 22 (March 20, 1950): 427–430.

[3] Hammond, "NSC 68."

prevented him from quoting from it.[4] Prior to its declassification, NSC 68 figured in the works of many historians and other scholars as well.[5] Such widespread knowledge of NSC 68 before its declassification led Acheson biographer Gaddis Smith in 1972 to label it "the most famous unread paper of its era."[6]

Today, NSC 68 is declassified and open for scholars and the general public alike to explore. In some respects it has become as much a part of the history of the origins of the Cold War as the "long telegram," the Truman Doctrine, the Berlin blockade, the Marshall Plan, and the Korean War insofar as it serves as an additional link in the chain of events that gave us the Cold War. Yet, in other respects it remains obscure. Its contents are known, a general narrative of its history has been developed, and its importance is recognized. However, in each of these aspects NSC 68 has largely been misunderstood: The focus of the content has been skewed, the standard narrative fails to explain its origins, and NSC 68's importance has been underestimated. As way of introduction to the larger argument that this book examines, this chapter explores these themes.

NSC 68: An Introduction

On April 7, 1950, NSC 68 was presented to President Truman for his perusal and, if the authors got their way, approval. NSC 68 was primarily the result of the efforts of Secretary of State Dean Acheson and Director of the State Department's Policy Planning Staff Paul Nitze to abide by a directive the president issued on January 31, 1950, much at their behest. In the directive, the president ordered "a reexamination of our objectives in peace and war and of the effect of these objectives on our strategic plans, in light of the probable fission bomb capability and possible thermonuclear bomb capability of the Soviet Union."[7] As

---

[4] Acheson, *Present at the Creation*, 373–381, passim.

[5] For example, see Richard Freeland, *The Truman Doctrine and the Origins of McCarthyism: Foreign Policy, Domestic Politics, and Internal Security, 1946–1948* (New York: Alfred Knopf, 1970), 322–324; Gabriel Kolko and Joyce Kolko, *The Limits of Power*, 507–509; Samuel P. Huntington, "The Defense Establishment: Vested Interests and the Public Interest," in Omer L. Carey, ed., *The Military-Industrial Complex and United States Foreign Policy* (Pullman, Washington: Washington States University Press, 1968), 5–7; Walter LaFeber, *America, Russia, and the Cold War, 1945–1966* (New York: Wiley, 1967), 1st edition, 90–91.

[6] Smith is quoted in Ernest May, ed., *American Cold War Strategy: Interpreting NSC 68*, (New York: Bedford Books, St. Martin's Press, 1993), 15.

[7] NSC 68, "Notes by the Executive Secretary to the National Security Council on United States Objectives and Programs for National Security," April 7, 1950, U.S. State

NSC 68 and the Problem of Origins

the directive indicates, it was ordered in response to the Soviet Union's development of atomic power, a feat the Soviets achieved in the late summer of 1949 when they detonated an atomic "device," ending the U.S. atomic monopoly. Not mentioned in the directive was the Communist victory in the Chinese civil war, an event that occurred just weeks after the Soviet test but that would, nonetheless, find its way into the traditional narrative history of NSC 68's origins (it is mentioned in the second sentence of NSC 68 itself but not thereafter). Written over the course of roughly two months in the winter and spring of 1950, in an atmosphere of utmost secrecy, the finished document came in at roughly seventy pages and had the approval of the Secretary of Defense, the Joint Chiefs of Staff (JCS), the Secretary of State, and the National Security Council (NSC). After reading the document, Truman, who had been kept abreast of its development over the course of its writing, ordered that further analysis be made of the costs involved. According to Acheson, however, the president approved the document on April 25, 1950, at which point it "became national policy." This claim is disputed, but that is to get ahead of the story.[8]

The Document Summarized

NSC 68 painted a bleak picture of a world that had so recently fought off the aggressive aims of Germany and Japan, a world that was rapidly devolving into the Cold War. The defeat of those two nations, the document stated, and the collapse of the "two major imperial systems" – the British and the French – had seen power gravitate to two power centers, the United States and the Soviet Union. The great peril in this new era came from the Soviet Union. According to the authors, the Soviet Union was an inherently expansionistic and militaristic power "animated by a new fanatic faith" – communism – that "seeks to impose its absolute authority over the rest of the world."[9] Further, they argued that "the United States, as the principal center of power in the non-Soviet world and the bulwark of opposition to Soviet expansion, is the principal enemy whose integrity and vitality must be subverted or destroyed by one means or another if the Kremlin is to achieve its fundamental design."[10] "Conflict" between

Department, *Foreign Relations of the United States* (*FRUS*), *1950* 1 (Washington, D.C.: U.S. Government Printing Office, 1977): 237.

[8] Acheson, *Present at the Creation*, 374.

[9] NSC 68, *FRUS*, *1950* 1: 237.

[10] NSC 68, *FRUS*, *1950* 1: 238.

NSC 68 and the Political Economy of the Early Cold War

the American and Soviet systems had, therefore, become "endemic." Yet, there was more. "With the development of increasingly terrifying weapons of mass destruction," the authors of NSC 68 wrote, "every individual faces the ever-present possibility of annihilation should the conflict enter the phase of total war."[11] "The issues that face us are momentous," the authors admonished, "involving the fulfillment or destruction not only of this Republic but of civilization itself."[12]

The paper resonated with moral abhorrence for the Soviet system. The Soviet Union was a "grim oligarchy" in which individual freedom had been completely destroyed.

Where the despot holds absolute power – the absolute power of the absolutely powerful will – all other wills must be subjugated in an act of willing submission, a degradation willed by the individual upon himself under the compulsion of a perverted faith. It is the first article of this faith that he finds and can only find the meaning of his existence in serving the ends of the system. The system becomes God, and submission to the will of God becomes submission to the will of the system. It is not enough to yield outwardly to the system – even Ghandhian [sic] non-violence is not acceptable – for the spirit of resistance and the devotion to a higher authority might then remain, and the individual would not be wholly submissive.[13]

Because freedom was the antithesis of submission, it followed, in the authors' estimation, that the Soviet Union could not coexist with "free" societies. "The existence and persistence of the idea of freedom," they implored, "is a permanent and continuous threat to the foundation of the slave society; and it therefore regards as intolerable the long continued existence of freedom in the world. What is new, what makes the continuing crisis, is the polarization of power which now inescapably confronts the slave society with the free."[14]

Historians have criticized NSC 68's "hyperbolic rhetoric"; indeed, one of its principal authors, Secretary of State Dean Acheson, noted years later that the paper was "clearer than truth."[15] At its core, however, NSC 68's thesis is, in fact, very clear – the United States and its allies had to embark on "a rapid build-up of political, economic and military strength in the free world" in order to prevent the Soviet Union from fulfilling its design for world conquest. The authors of NSC 68 warned that the Soviet Union was

---

[11] NSC 68, *FRUS, 1950* 1: 237.
[12] NSC 68, *FRUS, 1950* 1: 238.
[13] NSC 68, *FRUS, 1950* 1: 239–240.
[14] NSC 68, *FRUS, 1950* 1: 240.
[15] Leffler, *A Preponderance of Power*, 355; Acheson, *Present at the Creation*, 375.

NSC 68 and the Problem of Origins

steadily building up its military forces in preparation for a likely offensive against western Europe and the Middle East, after which the United States would become the target of Soviet-Communist forces. They set 1953 or 1954 as the target date for a possible Soviet attack, although they were careful to assert that this scenario was not a given.[16] By that date the Soviet Union would, the authors argued, have a stockpile of two hundred atomic bombs and the military capacity to carry out its designs. Other options, such as staying the present course, withdrawing from the world scene into isolationism, or even launching an offensive, "preventive" war against the Soviet Union, were considered but dispensed with as being inadequate to cope with the crisis. *Only* massive rearmament, the authors maintained, could ensure the viability of the "free world." The document ended with a bleak assessment, one that left no doubt as to where things stood from the authors' perspective: "The whole success of the proposed program hangs ultimately on recognition by this Government, the American people, and all free peoples, that the cold war is in fact a real war in which the survival of the free world is at stake."

That NSC 68, with its call for massive rearmament, was an important document of the post–World War II era is generally beyond dispute.[17] That said, in fact, its importance has been both underestimated and underappreciated. Prior to NSC 68's implementation, U.S. military spending was heading downward. NSC 68, after the intervention of the Korean War, dramatically reversed that trend. Under NSC 68, defense spending, inclusive of foreign military and economic aid, shot up fourfold from a projected low of $13 billion for fiscal year 1951 to more than $58 billion. In fiscal year 1952 the figure neared $70 billion before falling to a little more than $50 billion for fiscal year 1953. Thereafter, U.S. military spending would never again dip below $42 billion annually.[18] As a result, what has been termed the "military-industrial-academic complex"[19]

---

[16] Nitze would later argue that this date had been misconstrued to assume that U.S. officials expected a Soviet attack in those years. See "Nitze's Commentary," in May, *American Cold War Strategy*, 105.

[17] The historian Melvyn Leffler, whose *A Preponderance of Power* is still considered the definitive work on the origins of the Cold War from the American side, disagrees, suggesting that NSC 68 presented nothing new. See Leffler, *A Preponderance of Power*, 355–360. This book offers a direct challenge to that claim.

[18] Doris M. Condit, *History of the Office of the Secretary of Defense, Volume II, The Test of War, 1950–1953* (Washington, D.C.: Historical Office, Office of the Secretary of Defense, 1988), 241, 259, 284, 304, 422.

[19] Stuart W. Leslie, *The Cold War and American Science: The Military-Industrial-Academic Complex and MIT and Stanford* (New York: Columbia University Press, 1993).

became a permanent facet of American life, affecting the American people in profound ways, as the increasingly militarized economy spurred a host of economic, cultural, social, demographic, technological, and even geographical changes.[20]

Furthermore, after the implementation of NSC 68 the United States expanded its power abroad in ways unseen in its history outside of wartime, stationing large numbers of troops abroad with the bases and naval stations to support them, intervening in foreign countries' internal affairs, engaging in proxy wars against Soviet client states, and conducting overt and covert operations against foreign governments. NSC 68 also paved the way for an extensive military assistance program as well as for continued economic aid beyond 1952 when such aid was supposed to cease with the winding down of the European Recovery Program, or the Marshall Plan as it is more popularly known. In addition, NSC 68 contributed significantly to the conventional and nuclear arms races, primarily when Truman made the decision to pursue development of the hydrogen bomb and greatly increase the U.S. military budget. The report, moreover, laid the groundwork for the rearmament of West Germany, the final step to its full integration into the western European community as a full-fledged member, and the "reverse course" in Japan, both major redefinitions of U.S. postwar foreign policy.

Despite its tendency toward hyperbole, NSC 68 also provided the clearest expression of U.S. ideological aims in the Cold War ever extant. Although reminiscent of such earlier statements as the Clifford-Elsey Report, the Truman Doctrine, and NSC 20/4,[21] NSC 68 forged a cohesive vision within government circles, and among politically active elites more generally, of the Cold War as a contest between good and evil in which

---

[20] Works that touch on various aspects of these changes include Hogan, *Cross of Iron*; Lizabeth Cohen, *A Consumer's Republic: The Politics of Mass Consumption in Postwar America* (New York: Alfred A. Knopf, 2003); Elaine Tyler May, *Homeward Bound: American Families in the Cold War Era* (New York: Basic Books, 1999); Paul Pierpaoli, Jr., *Truman and Korea: The Political Culture of the Early Cold War* (Columbia, Missouri: University of Missouri Press, 1999); James Patterson, *Great Expectations: The United States, 1945–1971* (New York: Oxford University Press, 1996); Michael Sherry, *In the Shadow of War: The United States Since the 1930s* (New Haven, Connecticut: Yale University Press, 1995); Ann Markusen, et al., eds., *The Rise of the Gunbelt: The Military Remapping of Industrial America* (New York: Oxford University Press, 1991); David Harvey, *The Condition of Postmodernity: An Enquiry into the Origins of Cultural Change* (Cambridge, Massachusetts: Blackwell, 1990).

[21] For a discussion of these documents, see Leffler, *A Preponderance of Power*, 130–138, 142–147, 264–265.

NSC 68 and the Problem of Origins

the United States stood alone as the sole hope for saving freedom and democracy in the world. This vision, and the language that supported it, guided U.S. foreign policy throughout much of the Cold War and served as the basis for a massive propaganda campaign aimed at convincing the American people, and indeed the world, that the Soviet Union's goal was nothing less than world domination.

Robert Blackwill, a career diplomat and scholar, offers succinct evidence that NSC 68's influence ran very deep in government circles and even transcended the Truman administration:

That few, if any, of the presidents who have served after Truman and Eisenhower ever examined [NSC 68], or even knew of its existence, is both unsurprising and unimportant. Unsurprising because presidents seldom read such lengthy policy papers, including those produced in their own administrations. To imagine Kennedy, Carter, or Bush thumbing through the pages of Nitze's old paper is to misunderstand the time pressures that accompany most postwar presidential decision making. Unimportant because what really counts is not whether presidents had read or knew about NSC 68, but instead if the ideas contained in the document were specifically familiar to the occupants of the Oval Office and, more important, if those ideas have held up over the years. The answer to both these tests is an emphatic yes.[22]

All told, then, NSC 68 was an important document. But why was it written? A large consensus has emerged around a particular interpretation of how NSC 68 came to see the light of day. It is that to which we now turn.

The Conventional Interpretation of NSC 68

Since NSC 68's declassification in 1975, the historiography on NSC 68 has ranged far and wide, eliciting analyses from the document's authors; domestic and foreign policymakers; diplomatic, cultural, intellectual, and political historians; social and political scientists; and international relations theorists, bolstered by a host of interpretative genres – realism, neorealism, revisionism, corporatism, world-systems theory, postrevisionism, and what Ernest May, in his edited volume on NSC 68, termed post-postrevisionism.[23] All of these analyses have provided us with diverse ways of interpreting and understanding NSC 68. In the main, however, these studies have focused on how effective the document was as strategy against the Soviet

---

[22] Blackwill's commentary in May, *American Cold War Strategy*, 121.
[23] For a wide range of analyses incorporating all of these various genres and disciplines, see the commentaries in May, *American Cold War Strategy*.

NSC 68 and the Political Economy of the Early Cold War

Union[24] or on how accurately it depicted the Soviet threat[25] or on its binary and apocalyptic language.[26] The actual origin of NSC 68, the reason that it was created in the first place, has been far less scrutinized. Indeed, most scholars have relied virtually entirely on the authors' own explanations for why NSC 68 was written.[27] The result has been a less-than-satisfactory accounting of what NSC 68 was and why it was created.

The conventional interpretation of NSC 68 is that put forth by the creators of the document, both in the paper itself and in their memoirs, and that which has been accepted and passed on for posterity by most historians. It is this version of NSC 68 that finds its way into high school and college textbooks. It is the version one gets from reading *Truman*, David McCullough's 1992 bestseller, certainly the general public's greatest exposure to the Truman era of the last two decades, or from viewing the Cable News Network's 1998 documentary series *Cold War*, a close runner-up. It is the version that was heard after the September 11, 2001, terrorist attack on the United States, when the document resurfaced in discussions over how the United States should respond to the perceived global threat of a new era in political commentaries aired on television. In short, it is the version of NSC 68 that has become part of the national memory. But there is a problem. NSC 68 was a seminal document, but its history is askew. What purports to be *the* explanation for NSC 68 simply does not withstand sustained analysis. Given the importance of NSC 68 for shaping both the Cold War and the modern world more generally, this problem deserves investigation.[28]

---

[24] Gaddis, *Strategies of Containment*, 89–126.

[25] Wells, "Sounding the Tocsin," 138–158.

[26] See the commentaries by Bruce Kucklick, Lloyd C. Gardner, Walter McDougall, and Emily Rosenberg in May, *American Cold War Strategy*.

[27] The three classic accounts of NSC 68 all do this. They are Hammond, "Prologue to Rearmament"; Wells, "Sounding the Tocsin"; and Gaddis, *Strategies of Containment*, 90. Hammond, of course, relies on those involved in constructing NSC 68. Wells cites Acheson. And Gaddis cites Hammond and Wells. Most other scholarly accounts of NSC 68 rely on these three authors for their interpretations of the origins of NSC 68.

[28] Gary B. Nash, et al., *The American People: Creating a Nation and a Society* (New York: Harper Collins Publishers, 1990), 2nd ed., 899–900; Paul S. Boyer, et al., *The Enduring Vision: A History of the American People, Volume II*, (New York: Houghton Mifflin, 2000), 4th ed., 798; David McCullough, *Truman* (New York: Simon and Schuster, 1992), 764–765, 771–773; *CNN: Cold War*, Directed by Tessa Coombs (Atlanta, Georgia: Turner Home Entertainment, 1998). For post-9/11 references to NSC 68, see Salim Mansur, "Global Balance: America's Plan for Worldwide Freedom and Free Enterprise," September 26, 2002, *The Toronto Sun*, p. 15; Frederick W. Kagan, "The Korean Parallel: Is it June 1950 All Over Again?" October 8, 2001, *The Weekly Standard*, p. 16; Max Boot, "Hegemony Doesn't Come Cheap," October 17, 2002, *The*

NSC 68 and the Problem of Origins

Why was NSC 68 created? According to the conventional interpretation, the impetus for NSC 68 were two events that occurred in the late summer and early fall of 1949 in the context of the Cold War. In early September, a U.S. reconnaissance plane flying a routine mission over Alaska detected high levels of radiation in the atmosphere. Within days, uncertainty became reality – the Soviets had detonated an atomic device, presumably a bomb. The U.S. atomic monopoly, what Truman had in 1945 called the United States' "ace in the hole" in the emerging Cold War, was over.[29] One month later, the Communists under the direction of Mao Tse-tung reigned victorious in the decades-long Chinese civil war, seemingly turning most of Eurasia over to communism in one fell swoop. As tradition holds, these "hammer blows" quite rightly sent Washington into a panic. The Soviet Union and the communist world revolutionary movement it ruled were on the offensive, or so it seemed. U.S. officials responded in two ways. First, the president approved development of the hydrogen bomb under the premise that the Soviets would proceed to build their own regardless of whether the United States did. Second, they produced NSC 68, a policy recommendation arguing for a program of massive rearmament to stop this new, abrasive communist assault. And, as the story goes, just in the nick of time. Two months after NSC 68 went to Truman for official review, North Korea invaded South Korea, sparking the Korean War. As one student of NSC 68 has put it, in an observation that sums up the conventional view, "the real significance of NSC 68 was its timing – the tocsin sounded just before the fire."[30] The reality, however, is quite different.

Of Soviet Bombs and Chinese Communists: Problems with the Traditional Narrative

On September 20, 1949, at President Truman's request, David Lilienthal, director of the United States Atomic Energy Commission (AEC), made a hasty retreat from his annual vacation at Martha's Vineyard to return to Washington, D.C. Truman wanted to discuss with him the evident atomic

---

Times Union, Albany, New York, p. A15; "The Things They Say," December 3, 2001, *New Technology Week*, DW.

[29] Leffler, *A Preponderance of Power*, 38.

[30] For examples, see Newman, "NSC (National Insecurity) 68," 62–64; Pierpaoli, *Truman and Korea*, 23–25; May, *American Cold War Strategy*, 3–4; Rearden, "Frustrating the Kremlin Design," 160–161; Wells, "Sounding the Tocsin"; Hammond, "NSC 68," 289–290; Gaddis, *Strategies of Containment*, 89–126, esp. 113; Leffler, *A Preponderance of Power*, 355–360. The quotes are from Wells, "Sounding the Tocsin," 117, 139.

explosion that had occurred in the Soviet Union three weeks earlier. When he arrived, Lilienthal recorded in his diary, "the President was reading a copy of the *Congressional Record*, as quiet an [*sic*] composed a scene as imaginable; bright sunlight in the garden outside, the most unbusy [*sic*] of airs." According to Lilienthal, in the most casual way Truman began speaking about the Soviet detonation. He was not alarmed. He "knew about it – knew it would probably come." Maybe German scientists working in Russia were to blame, he said. However, he was not going to tell the American people just yet. Such an announcement, he hypothesized, could "cause great fears, troubles." Moreover, there was no way to substantiate that the "Russians actually had the bomb," a conjecture about which Lilienthal strenuously disagreed. Nonetheless, the Soviets had changed, Truman thought. Since the Berlin blockade crisis, they were "talking very reasonably again." Perhaps, it had something to do with the detonation – he was not sure. At any rate, he told Lilienthal, he was "not worried." Truman then directed Lilienthal's attention to a newspaper headline announcing the British devaluation of the pound, which had occurred on September 18. Perhaps, "when this … quiets down" he would go to the people, he said.[31]

And so it was with Truman and the Soviet atomic explosion. Although he did make public the news on September 23, rather than hold it back as he initially intended to do,[32] he was not unduly alarmed. He would address it when more urgent matters were settled. Accordingly, he saw no reason to modify his request for a *reduction* in military spending for the coming fiscal year. He had signaled his decision to cut military spending in a memorandum to the NSC in July. The economy had slowed and talk of a serious recession, even the long-rumored postwar depression, filled the air. "The extent to which domestic programs have been held down to minimum levels and below during the war and post-war years is not generally understood," he wrote. "Significant reductions in this area at this time, therefore, are not feasible." On the other hand, he noted, "military and international aid programs in fiscal year 1950 are substantially above the levels we can hope to maintain consistent with a sound fiscal and economic program." Therefore, he ordered a reduction in military

---

[31] David E. Lilienthal, Manuscript Journal, September 21, 1949, David E. Lilienthal Papers, Box 197, Public Policy Papers, Department of Rare Books and Collections, Princeton University Library, Princeton, New Jersey (hereinafter PUL).

[32] Acheson claims he did so in order to secure passage of the Mutual Defense Assistance Program, which was then being debated in Congress. See Acheson, *Present at the Creation*, 312–313.

NSC 68 and the Problem of Origins

spending by $1.5 billion, down from the $14.5 billion figure from the previous fiscal year.[33] Truman was not opposed to deficit spending per se, but for political purposes he needed to keep the deficit reasonable. Hence, he sought to cut funds where he felt they were most expendable. Not insignificantly, in 1949, long after the Cold War had begun, for Truman this meant cutting the military budget.[34]

On learning of the Soviet detonation, Truman did not alter his request. Nor did his position change when one month later the Communists emerged victorious in China. When he sent his budget to Congress in January 1950, four months after the Soviet bomb and three months after the Communist victory in China, the request for lowered military spending remained. However, Truman apparently was only getting started. In March 1950, he indicated his intention to cut a further $4 billion from the military budget, down to $9 billion annually. Furthermore, from January 1 to June 30, 1950, the military in fact underwent significant downsizing, so much so that when the Korean War broke out the U.S. military was severely constrained in its ability to respond. This situation, of course, developed many months after the Soviets detonated an atomic device and China went communist. Clearly, Truman was not panicked by the Sino-Soviet developments, at least not into instigating the massive rearmament program called for in NSC 68.[35]

The Joint Chiefs of Staff (JCS) expressed greater concern than Truman over the news of the Sino-Soviet successes. However, most striking is how little they were disturbed by these events, given their position in determining threats to national security. The JCS disliked Truman's reduced defense budget for fiscal year 1951, and when they read it in the summer of 1949 they complained to Secretary of Defense Louis Johnson that it would undermine national security. However, they did not openly

---

[33] Truman to Sidney Souers, Executive Secretary of the NSC, July 1, 1949, *FRUS, 1949* I (Washington D.C: U.S. Government Printing Office, 1976): 350–352; and NSC 52/1, "Governmental Programs in National Security and International Affairs for Fiscal Year 1951," July 8, 1949, *FRUS, 1949* I: 350–357; Felix Belair, Jr., "Truman Abandons His Tax Rise Plan; Urges a Return to Deficit Spending to Raise Production and Job Levels," *The New York Times*, July 12, 1949, 1.

[34] Belair, Jr., "Truman Abandons His Tax Rise Plan" 1.

[35] Austin Stevens, "Truman Submits $42 Billion Budget," *The New York Times*, January 10, 1950, 1; on the possibility of Truman seeking even further defense cuts, see Acheson memorandum, March 24, 1950, Dean Acheson Papers, Harry S. Truman Library, Independence, Missouri (hereinafter Truman Library). Information on the effects of downsizing on the Korean War response was found in "Semi-Annual Report of the Secretary of Defense for the Six Months Ending June 30th, 1950," FO 371/81702, The National Archives, Kew, England, United Kingdom (hereinafter TNA).

20   NSC 68 *and the Political Economy of the Early Cold War*

protest the move or urge Johnson to do so. More significantly, they did not change their position after the Communists' achievements. Well into 1950, the JCS offered no rebuttal to Truman's request for reduced military spending.[36] On October 10, 1949, a Special Committee of the National Security Council endorsed a JCS report from July 26, 1949, pressing for an expanded atomic energy program estimated at $314 million in initial outlay and $54 million in annual costs once the program reached "equilibrium" (relatively small amounts even in the late 1940s), to which Truman agreed.[37] Even so, this request was *not* in response to the Communist achievements, and the October 10 memorandum specifically noted this fact.[38] In January 1950, the JCS also recommended that work on the hydrogen bomb should proceed, but, significantly, they rejected a "crash" program to build it.[39] Furthermore, as historian David Rosenberg argues, "if it had been necessary to cut back on other aspects of the defense program in order to undertake the thermonuclear project, the JCS probably would have been reluctant to recommend it."[40]

In addition, in March 1950 Chairman of the JCS Omar Bradley argued before the House Appropriations Committee that the $13 billion ceiling for military spending was adequate for the nation's defense. In his testimony he made no mention of either the Soviet atomic blast or the Communist win in China. He subsequently argued that raising defense spending to "$30,000,000,000 or $40,000,000,000" would "destroy" the nation's "industrial capacity" on which the "eventual strength of our

[36] Leffler, *A Preponderance of Power*, 304–311.
[37] "Report to the President by the Special Committee of the National Security Council of the Proposed Acceleration of the Atomic Energy Program," October 10, 1949, *FRUS, 1949* I: 559–564.
[38] Ibid., 564.
[39] "Memorandum for the Secretary of Defense," January 13, 1950, Record Group 218, Records of the Joint Chiefs of Staff, 1948–1950, Central Subject File, Box 235, NAII; K. Condit, *The History of the Joint Chiefs of Staff*, 271–281.
[40] David Alan Rosenberg, "American Atomic Strategy and the Hydrogen Bomb Decision," *Journal of American History* 66: 1(June 1979): 83. In his oft-cited article, Rosenberg paints a very different picture of U.S. officials' reaction to the Soviet bomb than is depicted here, but his evidence, such as the previous statement, belies his larger conclusions. Hogan, *Cross of Iron*, 292, argues that Secretary of the Air Force Stuart Symington *did* express grave concern over the Soviet explosion, but if so his was a rather lone voice. However, Hogan fails to note that the "seventy-group air force" he cites Symington as pleading for in light of the Soviet atomic test had been his pet project ever since becoming secretary in 1947, and that this effort had as much to do with helping the civilian aircraft industry as building a modern Air Force. See Leffler, *A Preponderance of Power*, 222. It might be noted as well that Symington was not above exaggerating the Soviet threat to achieve his aims. On this point, see Frank Kofsky, *The War Scare of 1948: A Successful Campaign to Deceive the Nation* (New York: St. Martin's, 1995), 151–154, 177–181.

NSC 68 and the Problem of Origins

country depends."[41] Given such reactions, it would be a stretch to call the JCS's response to the so-called hammer blows of 1949 an alarmed one. The NSC, moreover, reacted in much the same manner. It did argue that the $1.5 billion cut suggested by Truman be routed to the Military Assistance Program, then being hammered out by the State Department; but otherwise it saw no reason not to follow the president's recommendation, a position it maintained well into 1950.[42]

Others with influence expressed similar sentiments. Secretary of State Dean Acheson, who in short order would conduct the study that became NSC 68, did not in December 1949 believe that the Soviet Union's acquisition of atomic power increased the military threat, a viewpoint shared by Paul Nitze, the State Department's new director of the Policy Planning Staff (PPS), who, along with Acheson, also became the biggest sponsor of NSC 68 and, in fact, was responsible for writing the document. "The weight of the evidence leads to the belief that the Russians will put their chief reliance on the cold war. It is here that we must meet the most pressing dangers and not from military aggression," Acheson stated four months after news of the Soviet explosion reached the administration.[43] At the Council on Foreign Relations,[44] members of a study group chaired by WWII hero General Dwight D. Eisenhower on the future course of U.S. economic and military aid programs concurred that the Soviet acquisition of atomic power did not alter the military situation. "The strategic problem of defending Western Europe in cold and hot war has not, in my opinion, changed since September 23," Colonel Gordon A. Lincoln remarked, a sentiment shared by most of the group, Eisenhower included. Eisenhower added further, "The Russians had the ability to conquer Western Europe before they had the atomic bomb, so their possession of it does not really change the basic strategic problem of defense in that area." Furthermore, when in the spring of 1950 Eisenhower heard of the rearmament program soon to be known as NSC 68, he did not believe it was warranted.[45]

---

[41] Hammond, "NSC 68," 304.

[42] NSC 52/3, September 29, 1949, *FRUS, 1949* 1: 385–398.

[43] Memorandum from the Secretary of State, December 20, 1949, *FRUS, 1949* 1: 615.

[44] The Council on Foreign Relations was founded in 1919, chartered in 1921, on the heels of the U.S. Senate's rejection of U.S. participation in the League of Nations. It is an independent, non-partisan think tank dedicated to multilateralism and an active U.S. presence in the world. The best study of the organization is Laurence H. Shoup and William Minter, *Imperial Brain Trust: The Council on Foreign Relations and United States Foreign Policy* (New York: Monthly Review Press, 1977), 11–56.

[45] Memorandum from the Secretary of State, December 20, 1949, *FRUS, 1949* 1: 615; Nitze to Acheson, December 19, 1949, ibid., 611–612; for another comment by Acheson

The controversy over whether to build the H-bomb, the "Super"[46] as it was called in government circles, offers further proof that the Sino-Soviet advances of 1949 did not cause a great degree of alarm in government circles. If either the Soviet atomic blast or the Communist victory in China threw U.S. officials into a panic out of which emerged NSC 68, then one might expect that the decision to build the hydrogen bomb would have been a foregone conclusion. It was not. Most of the top scientists sitting on the Atomic Energy Commission's General Advisory Council voted against development of the bomb on moral grounds. Lilienthal felt similarly and believed constructing the Super would end forever any chance of having peace in the world. Moreover, for Acheson, building it was at least in part forced on the administration by domestic politics – "the attack of the primitives," he called it in his memoir – not by military considerations alone. Secretary of Defense Johnson also thought it was necessary in order to "protect the President" from Republican attacks. Truman apparently believed as much as well, at least according to Lilienthal. In his diary detailing the important January 31, 1950, meeting among Truman, Lilienthal, Acheson, Johnson, Admiral Sydney Souers, consultant to the president on national security affairs, and James Lay, executive secretary of the NSC – at which time the decision to proceed with testing the feasibility of building the bomb was given the go-ahead by the president – we find the following remark: "The President [said] that we could have had all this re-examination [of whether to pursue development of the bomb] quietly if Senator Ed[ward Fuller] Johnson [of New Jersey] hadn't made that unfortunate remark about the super bomb; since that time there has been so much talk in the Congress and everywhere and people are so excited he [the President] really hasn't any alternative but to go ahead and that was what he was going to do." Furthermore, after Lilienthal resigned as chair of the AEC, the agency under whose guidance the H-bomb was to be built, effective February 15, 1950, Truman left the

around the same time, see Acheson to Averell Harriman, December 9, 1949, Averell Harriman Papers, Box 271, Library of Congress (LC), Washington, D.C. For Lincoln and Eisenhower quotes, see Fifteenth Meeting of the Study Group on Aid to Europe (SGAE), March 20, 1950, Council on Foreign Relations (CFR), 31, Box 243, Public Policy Papers, PUL. For Eisenhower's views on rearmament, see Nitze to Acheson, "General Eisenhower's Speech," March 29, 1950, Record Group 59, Records of the Policy Planning Staff (PPS), 1947–1953, Minutes of Meetings, NAII; and also Newman, "NSC (National Insecurity) 68," 66.

[46] Its code name, in fact, was Campbell, after the international soup corporation. Hence, the term "super."

NSC 68 and the Problem of Origins

position vacant for nearly six months, reflecting a lack of urgency about the bomb even after he had approved its development. Such actions and sentiments hardly comport with a sense of shock or panic.[47]

Then there is this interesting exchange between Acheson and Senator Henry Cabot Lodge at the Senate Committee on Foreign Relations' hearings on the "world situation" in January 1950. Lodge queried whether Acheson thought a preventive war against the Soviet Union was a viable option. He stated that many "thoughtful people in military and civilian life" had come to him concerned that "the Soviet Union, due to the headway that it is making in atomic weapons, is steadily increasing in total military power" and that in a short period of time "will have a clear military superiority over the United States." These people, he noted, thought a preventive war might be the answer.

SECRETARY ACHESON: I do not think that there is anything at all in this idea of a preventative war.
SENATOR LODGE: You do not?
SECRETARY ACHESON: No, I do not. I think that brings on us all the troubles we seek to avoid, and in connection with whether it is or is not true that the passage of time steadily increases the power of the Soviet Union, that is a matter about which I think there is very great doubt. That is a matter that Secretary Johnson and General [Omar] Bradley and I have met many times to discuss, to consider exactly that [what?] the military implications are in terms of policy, and I think there is a great deal to be said on the other side.[48]

The issue here is not the efficacy of preventive war; very few people thought that expedient and NSC 68 would specifically argue against it. The issue here is Acheson's take on Soviet capabilities. There was, he said, "very great doubt" that the "passage of time steadily increases the power of the Soviet Union," even though, by then, it possessed atomic power. This, it is worth repeating, he said in January 1950, even as he was beginning to write NSC 68.

---

[47] For the Advisory Committee's views, see "Memorandum for the Secretary of Defense," January 13, 1950, RG 218, Central Subject File, Box 235, NAII; Lilienthal's thoughts are from his Journal, Nov. 1, 1949, Box 197, PUL; Acheson's views are in *Present at the Creation*, 345–349, 354. For Secretary of Defense Louis Johnson's remark, see David Lilienthal, *The Journals of David E. Lilienthal, Volume Two: The Atomic Energy Years, 1945–1950* (New York: Harper and Row, 1964), 630. For Truman's views, see ibid., 632. For more on the Johnson controversy, see ibid., 601–602. On Truman leaving the AEC chairman post vacant for six months, see Leffler, *A Preponderance of Power*, 363.

[48] United States Senate, Committee on Foreign Relations, *Reviews of the World Situation, 1949–1950, Historical Series*, 81st Congress, 1st and 2nd Sessions (Washington, D.C.: U.S. Government Printing Office, 1974), 189, brackets mine.

It was George Kennan, the father of the "containment" doctrine, who best captured the most commonly held view of the end of the U.S. atomic monopoly among U.S. foreign policy officials. "Provided we keep our own atomic attack forces in a proper state of readiness and dispersal, which is not difficult to do," Kennan argued, "the damage we should be able to do in the Soviet Union is not affected by whether the Russians have the bombs themselves or not. The bomb is not a defense against the bomb except in a very limited degree." Kennan added further that "Russia has only recently been through a tremendously destructive war; that the memory of that destruction is much more vivid in Soviet minds than it is in ours; that the Soviet economy has far less that it can afford to lose than we have; and that the Soviet leaders will not inaugurate a type of warfare bound to lead to great destruction within their own country."[49]

The reaction on China was similar. Although Dean Rusk, assistant secretary of state for far eastern affairs, worried that the Chinese were now the "junior partners" of the Soviets, the general trend of thought was more cautious. As was common the lead here came from Kennan, who, according to historian Melvyn Leffler, saw little to worry about in a Communist takeover of China. "Even if the Communists consolidated their power and remained in the Soviet orbit, which [Kennan] doubted, he did not think the Kremlin would gain significantly," Leffler contends. Although Kennan's view was at the more extreme end of the debate over doing a lot or doing nothing, others were coming around to a similar position. Marshall, for instance, believed that China was "weak, impoverished, and technologically backward." Moreover, the Soviets were unlikely to be in any position to improve the situation. For Acheson, the Communists were certain to face insuperable problems trying to consolidate their control over and then to develop China. He believed that "China had neither great industrial potential nor abundant reserves of critical raw materials." As Leffler writes, "Acheson was not alarmed" by China's fall to communism. China "could turn out to be a strategic

---

[49] George Kennan to [Willis C.] Armstrong, June 20, 1950, Record Group 59, General Records of the Department of State (RG 59), Records of the Policy Planning Staff (PPS), 1947–1953, Chronological File, NAII; see also Kennan's memorandum to Acheson of February 17, 1950, in which he wrote: "The demonstration of 'atomic capability' on the part of the U.S.S.R. likewise adds no new fundamental element to the picture.... The fact that this situation became a reality a year or two before it was expected is of no fundamental significance." Kennan to Acheson, February 17, 1950, *FRUS, 1950* I: 161.

NSC 68 and the Problem of Origins

quagmire for the Kremlin," he told the Senate Committee on Foreign Relations. Furthermore, a white paper on China had been released in August 1949 all but acknowledging the "loss" of China but arguing that there was nothing that the United States could have done. U.S. leaders were not comfortable with developments in China in the fall of 1949, but they were not shocked or disturbed by them.[50]

As these reactions and discussions demonstrate, the traditional interpretation of NSC 68's origins is deeply flawed. The Soviet Union's acquisition of atomic power and the Communist victory in China were not "hammer blows" nor did they send U.S. policymakers scrambling to rearm. They were unwelcome events, to be sure, but they had been predicted and were taken in stride.

Why NSC 68, then?

It is the aim of this study to thoroughly answer that question, but we begin by noting that NSC 68 is not silent on other potential reasons that might account for it. In fact, the document is quite explicit in this regard. For instance, the authors wrote in one passage:

> Our overall policy at the present time may be described as one designed to foster a world environment in which the American system can survive and flourish.... This broad intention embraces two subsidiary policies. *One is a policy which we would probably pursue even if there were no Soviet threat. It is a policy of attempting to develop a healthy international community.* The other is the policy of "containing" the Soviet system. These two policies are closely interrelated and interact on one another. Nevertheless, *the distinction between them is basically valid* and contributes to a clearer understanding of what we are trying to do.[51]

In another passage, this statement: "Even if there were no Soviet Union we would face the great problem of the free society, accentuated many fold in this industrial age, of reconciling order, security, the need for participation, with the requirement of freedom."[52]

As these passages from NSC 68 make clear, there was more at stake than just the Soviet threat when the authors made their plea for massive rearmament. What else was it that was at stake? Again, we can turn to the authors for an answer. Introduced in this passage is the "dollar

---

[50] Leffler, *A Preponderance of Power*, 341, 250, 248, 293, 296.
[51] NSC 68, *FRUS, 1950* 1: 252 (emphasis added).
[52] NSC 68, *FRUS, 1950* 1: 262–263.

gap," a term that readers will become very familiar with over the ensuing chapters.

The *present* foreign economic policies and programs of the United States *will not* produce a solution to the problem of international economic equilibrium, notably the dollar gap, and will not create an economic base conducive to political stability in many important countries.... There are grounds for predicting that the United States and other free nations will within a period of a few years at most experience a decline in economic activity of serious proportions unless more positive government programs are developed than are now available.... *In short, as we look to the future, the programs now planned will not meet the requirements of the free nations....*[53]

Furthermore,

... Western Europe ... faces the prospect of a rapid tapering off of American assistance [through the Marshall Plan] without the possibility of achieving, by its own efforts, a satisfactory equilibrium with the dollar area. It has also made very little progress toward "economic integration," which would in the long run tend to improve productivity and to provide an economic environment conducive to political stability. In particular, the movement toward economic integration does not appear to be rapid enough to provide Western Germany with adequate economic opportunities in the West. The United Kingdom still faces economic problems which may require a moderate but politically difficult decline in the British standard of living or more American assistance than is contemplated. At the same time, a strengthening of the British position is needed if the stability of the Commonwealth is not to be impaired and if it is to be a focus of resistance to Communist expansion in South and South-East Asia. Improvement of the British position is also vital in building up the defensive capabilities of Western Europe.[54]

The authors of NSC 68 were very clear about the importance of the situation. If the United States failed to act, if it failed to be vigorous in securing its interests, they argued, the United States' "allies and potential allies" may

as a result of frustration or of Soviet intimidation drift into a course of neutrality eventually leading to Soviet domination. If this were to happen in Germany the effect upon Western Europe and eventually upon us might be catastrophic.... Should the belief or suspicion spread that the free nations are not now able to prevent the Soviet Union from taking ... military actions ... the determination of the free countries to resist probably would lessen and there would be an increasing temptation for them to seek a position of neutrality.

[53] NSC 68, *FRUS, 1950* 1: 278, 261 (emphasis added).
[54] NSC 68, *FRUS, 1950* 1: 260.

NSC 68 and the Problem of Origins

The result would be "the withdrawal of the United States from most of its present commitments in Europe and Asia and to our isolation in the Western Hemisphere and its approaches," which, as we will see, is what U.S. foreign policy leaders sought to avoid at all costs. The real story of NSC 68 is yet to be told. It is the subject of the history that follows.[55]

[55] NSC 68, *FRUS, 1950* 1: 265, 279.

2

Multilateralism, the Soviet Threat, and the Origins of the Cold War

> Even if there were no Russia, if there were no communism, we would still face very grave problems in trying to exist and strengthen those parts of the free world which have been so badly shaken by the war and its consequences, the two wars and the consequences of both of them.
>
> Dean Acheson, January 1950

The United States emerged from World War II as a global power of the first order. The depression of the 1930s, frightening in its scope and duration, and the war, traumatic and bewildering in the dimensions of its horror, lay in the past, although neither would be forgotten easily. Nonetheless, for the United States the future looked fairly bright. The war had been won, in no small part due to the United States' valiant effort; and the United Nations, which held out hope that future wars would be prevented through dialogue and collective security, had been created largely at its behest. In addition, the economy seemed to be rebounding from the long depression of the 1930s, although concern that the war's end would see depression conditions return created its share of anxiety. Perhaps more important in the immediate term, defeating fascism and Japanese militarism restored faith in the American way of life after years of collective self-doubt brought on by the depression. When in February 1941 Henry Luce, publisher of *Time*, *Life*, and *Fortune* magazines, announced the arrival of "the American century," it is unlikely that many Americans shared Luce's optimism; there was still too much of which to be wary – an ongoing depression, war raging in Europe and Asia, and a sense that the United States itself may be

Multilateralism, the Soviet Threat, and the Origins 29

threatened. By the end of the war, however, Americans were beginning to believe that Luce might be right.[1]

For foreign policy leaders in the Truman administration and other influential elites, the advent of that American century meant something that they had not seen in a long time – opportunity. The depression and the war had been staggering. The capitalist system had almost collapsed, and Europe, the cradle of democracy, had nearly fallen prey to barbarians. These realities weighed heavily on their minds as they contemplated the future. So did the lessons of Versailles. There were to be no Wilsonian blunders this time around. Now that the United States had become a global power, U.S. leaders were determined to use that power to secure a new world order that would sustain peace and provide for prosperity, especially for the United States. "There is no need to fear," U.S. diplomat, author, and educator Adolph Berle remarked in 1941. "Rather, we shall have an opportunity to create the most brilliant economic epoch the U.S. has yet seen."[2] The war, it seemed, had wiped clean the slate of the first half of the twentieth century, and the opportunities to reshape the world appeared limitless, subject only to the power that the United States was willing to expend to reshape it. Indeed, to the majority of U.S. officials it appeared as though the United States had been given a "second chance" to right the wrongs of a world gone mad.[3]

Postwar euphoria, however, ultimately gave way to postwar frustration as U.S. foreign policy objectives smashed up against two potentially calamitous threats. The first was the increased power of the Soviet Union as a result of its contribution to the victory in WWII and the fact that its massive army was sitting in the middle of Europe. The question was: Would the Soviet Union use that power to sustain peace in cooperation with its wartime allies, or would it use it to advance a worldwide communist revolution? The second threat, the result of a world torn to shreds by two world wars and a decade-long depression, was known as the dollar gap, an international balance-of-payments crisis that proved far more intractable than anyone could have imagined. Both of these

---

[1] Henry Luce, "The American Century," *Life* (February 17, 1941): 61–66. On American wariness, see William Graebner, *The Age of Doubt: American Thought and Culture in the 1940s* (Boston, Massachusetts: Twayne Publishers, 1991), 40. Although Graebner calls the decade the "age of doubt," he calls the period immediately following the war one of general optimism.

[2] Lloyd C. Gardner, *Economic Aspects of New Deal Diplomacy* (Madison, Wisconsin: University of Wisconsin Press, 1964), 174.

[3] Robert Divine, *Second Chance: The Triumph of Internationalism in America during World War II* (New York: Anthenum, 1967).

developments presented significant challenges to U.S. foreign policy goals in the immediate postwar era, and both played central roles in the development of the Cold War. The problem is that, whereas the challenge posed by the Soviet Union is well known, the dollar gap remains obscure, a reality that makes a full understanding of the true origins of the Cold War elusive. For, as will become clear in the ensuing chapters, the origins of the Cold War cannot be grasped entirely if the dollar gap is left out of the mix. This chapter will examine the Soviet threat, and Chapter 3 will address the dollar gap. First, however, we need to explore the multilateral impulse that drove the making of U.S. foreign policy in the postwar era.

The Multilateral Impulse

For the majority of U.S. foreign policy officials in the Truman administration and other politically active elites, the primary goal of U.S. foreign policy in the postwar era was the establishment of an open, global, capitalist economy, or what in this study is being referred to as multilateralism – "free trade, free capital flows, and free currency convertibility," in Thomas McCormick's apt phrasing.[4] Ensconced primarily in the State Department, these multilateralists shared the vision of, and in many respects spoke for, the internationally oriented U.S. corporations and financial institutions that had come to dominate the U.S. economy since the late-nineteenth century (many of them had come to government service out of these very institutions). The multilateralists believed that the depression and the war demonstrated the disastrous effects of a world in which protectionism and autarchy had become the operative principles in international trade. During the depression, all of the major powers adopted some form of protectionism and a few – Germany, Japan, and Great Britain – pursued autarchic policies designed to cushion them from the effects of open trade. The lesson learned was that "unhampered trade dovetails with peace; high tariffs, trade barriers, and unfair economic competition with war," as consummate multilateralist and secretary of state under President Franklin D. Roosevelt, Cordell Hull, had famously quipped at the height of the depression.[5]

In the minds of the multilateralists, WWII created an opportunity for the United States to end forever such destructive practices and to establish

[4] Thomas McCormick, *America's Half-Century: U.S. Foreign Policy in the Cold War and After* (Baltimore, Maryland: The Johns Hopkins University Press, 1995), 2nd edition, 5.
[5] Quoted in Walter LaFeber, *The American Age: U.S. Foreign Policy at Home and Abroad, Since 1896* (New York: W. W. Norton, 1994), 2nd edition, 372–373.

Multilateralism, the Soviet Threat, and the Origins 31

a multilateral, global economy that would permit the greatest freedom for capitalist institutions to function, something which they believed was the key to prosperity at home. Their goal was to end any and all attempts to restrict international trade, whether through quotas, bilateral trade agreements, trade restrictions, unduly high tariffs, currency exchange restrictions, and bartering; to quash state interference in the private economy (unless, and when, it worked to that economy's advantage); and to tame big labor both at home and abroad. They believed planned economies were anathema and that prosperity was possible only in a world constructed on multilateral lines.[6]

This multilateral impulse came from many and varied sources. In the first instance it grew out of the need to ensure prosperity for the postwar U.S. economy. "Our productive capacity was not only unimpaired but increased during the war while that of most of the other nations was injured and in some cases virtually destroyed," a State Department paper from December 1946 states. It continued:

Consequently, we are now a main source of supply for goods of all sorts and our trade is high. This fact temporarily conceals a basic problem which will soon hit us hard unless we continue pressing forward boldly to meet it, namely, that the channels of world trade are tied up in an incredible mass of obstacles and restrictions. Quotas, tariffs, discriminations, exchange controls, bilateral arrangements for balancing trade, have mined and blocked them. Unless we succeed in clearing these channels out exporters may soon find themselves in a situation where, in order to sell limited quantities of their products in foreign markets, they will

---

[6] The multilateralist outlook is captured dramatically in a speech President Truman delivered on March 6, 1947, at Baylor University in Waco, Texas, published in *Public Papers of the Presidents of the United States: Harry S. Truman, 1947* (Washington, D.C.: U.S. Government Printing Office, 1963), 168–171. Other contemporaneous views of multilateralism in the post-WWII period are Harlan Cleveland, "The Problem of Western Europe's Competitive Position in the World and Its Remedies," July 19, 1949, Office Files of Gordon Gray as Special Assistant to the President: RG286 (hereinafter Gray Papers), Cleveland, Harland, Box 18, Harry S. Truman Library, Independence, Missouri (hereinafter Truman Library) and William Diebold, "European Recovery: The Next Two Years," May 2, 1950, Gray Papers, Diebold, Jr., William, "European Recovery," Box 7, Truman Library. The best historical depictions of the multilateralists are Walter Isaacson and Evan Thomas, *The Wise Men: Six Friends and the World They Made: Acheson, Bohlen, Harriman, Kennan, Lovett, and McCloy* (New York: Simon and Schuster, 1986); Lawrence Shoup and William Minter, *Imperial Brain Trust: The Council on Foreign Relations and United States Foreign Policy* (New York: Monthly Review Press, 1977; Authors Choice Press, 2004); McCormick, *America's Half-Century*; Neil Smith, *American Empire: Roosevelt's Geographer and the Prelude to Globalization* (Berkeley, California: University of California Press, 2003); Thomas Ferguson, "Industrial Conflict and the Coming of the New Deal: The Triumph of Multinational Liberalism in America," in Steve Fraser and Gary Gerstle, eds., *The Rise and Fall of the New Deal Order, 1930–1980* (Princeton, New Jersey: Princeton University Press, 1989), 3–33.

have to accept specified products of other countries in which they have no interest. In other words the nations of the world after developing an efficient money economy for domestic purposes have regressed virtually to the point of bartering goods with each other in the manner of primitive societies. Under such circumstances world trade will be choked and throttled.... [T]he trade of all countries will be injured and ours not least of all.[7]

It grew as well out of memories of the Great Depression. The war was horrific enough, but memories of the depression also burned deeply in those responsible for making foreign policy. William Diebold, an economist who spent the bulk of his professional career at the Council on Foreign Relations, years later wrote of what he called the "spirit of the age." He was trying to convey the uncertainty and doubt that, from his perspective, characterized the policymakers' outlook. To make his point he quoted Robert Marjolin, who, according to Diebold, "played a key part on the European side of the Marshall Plan and was Secretary-General of the OEEC [Organization for European Economic Cooperation] during its first crucial years." Marjolin said:

My own testimony aims, among other things, to dispel the belief that from the beginning of this epoch we felt sure of our clear convictions, and had an unconquerable faith in the future and an optimism that could survive every test. On the contrary, what remains engraved in my memory are the doubts, the anguish felt each day, the fear of failing, the constant wish to correct what we had done in the light of experience and always – I can never say it enough – the consciousness of the crushing memories of the period between the wars.[8]

As this comment demonstrates, fear of a return to depression conditions also lay at the center of the multilateral impulse.

This multilateral impulse derived also from the way in which Americans had coped with class conflict in the late-nineteenth and early-twentieth centuries. Historian Charles Maier has argued that creating a multilateral world "arose out of the very terms in which Americans resolved their own organization of economic power. Americans asked foreigners in the postwar era to subordinate their domestic and international conflicts for the sake of higher tonnage or kilowatt hours precisely because agreement on production and efficiency had helped to bridge deep divisions at home." Furthermore, Maier writes, "the emphasis on

---

[7] "International Economic Relations," December 30, 1946, Walter Salant Papers, Truman Library.

[8] William Diebold, Jr., "Foreign Economic Policy in Dean Acheson's Time and Ours," in Douglas Brinkley, ed., *Dean Acheson and the Making of U.S. Foreign Policy* (New York: St. Martin's Press, 1993), 242.

Multilateralism, the Soviet Threat, and the Origins 33

output and growth emerged as a logical result of the New Deal and wartime controversies, just as earlier it had arisen out of inconclusive reform movements." Indeed, mass production and consumption (what Maier calls "production and efficiency") helped alleviate class conflict during the period following depression in the 1890s without resorting to full-blown socialism, that is, a planned economy. The multilateralists believed that if the nations of the world would adopt the same practice of mass production and consumption it could do for them what it had done for the United States.[9]

However, the multilateral impulse had an even deeper source of domestic breeding. It developed out of the historical experience of Americans' own nation building. The United States had formed out of thirteen independent colonies. Although those colonies ultimately joined together in the Revolution, after victory was won they retained, as states, their independent status under the Articles of Confederation. In short order, however, some of the more well-to-do of the new republic came to the conclusion that the arrangement was unworkable and needed to be changed. Each state retained the right to make its own laws, coin its own money, and set its own trade policies. Congress had little ability to tax, no way to standardize commercial policy, and no way to force the states to comply with treaties. The U.S. Constitution was born out of the failure of this system to function. Although the Constitution did not aim solely to overcome economic difficulties, when it was adopted it ushered in perhaps the first multilateral economy in world history. It took time, but the independent states were integrated into a single economic and political unit. Trade and commercial policies were standardized. A shared currency was introduced. Trade between the states flowed unrestricted. Over the course of the next nearly two hundred years the U.S. grew into the most prosperous, productive economy ever known, not least by expanding west and conquering a continent and the people who resided in it.[10] That this policy could not claim to have prevented either war, most notably between the states themselves, or depression, the multilateralists seemed capable

[9] Charles Maier, "The Politics of Productivity: Foundations of American International Economic Policy after World War II," in Charles Maier, *In Search of Stability: Explorations in Historical Political Economy* (New York: Cambridge University Press, 1987), 121–152. See also Martin J. Sklar, *The Corporate Reconstruction of American Capitalism: The Market, the Law, and Politics* (New York: Cambridge University Press, 1988) and Alan Brinkley, *The End of Reform: American Liberalism in Depression and War* (New York: Alfred Knopf, 1994).

[10] On these points see H. W. Brands, *The Devil We Knew: Americans and the Cold War* (New York: Oxford University Press, 1993), 16.

of forgetting. They fully believed that their own country offered undeniable proof of the efficacy of multilateralism, and they called on the world to take notice of their updated version of the "city on a hill." [11]

Important as these domestic sources of the multilateral impulse were, U.S. leaders focused less on these than on the benefits to be derived from multilateralism internationally. To the world they argued that multilateralism would prevent the kind of dog-eat-dog competition for markets and resources that had seen the world devolve into warring factions in the late 1930s. It also would raise standards of living across the globe so that nations would not feel compelled to seek either autarchic or expansionistic policies to ensure their livelihoods, such as Germany and Japan had done in the 1930s and 1940s. This, in turn, would make possible the spread of democracy, for, in U.S. thinking, political freedom grew naturally from economic freedom. [12]

In their initial hubris, U.S. leaders believed that if nations would simply adopt multilateralism the problems of the world would be solved. They blamed protectionism and autarchy for the long duration of the depression and the war that followed. In other words, they blamed governments making choices for two of the greatest catastrophes of the twentieth century. From their perspective, multilateralism, therefore, was a choice. Nations that chose not to adopt multilateral policies were being obstinate or even outright hostile. Over time, U.S. leaders would recognize that the issue was not as simple as this, but in the flush of victory such introspection was nowhere to be found.

In their quest to build a multilateral world, however, the multilateralists faced many obstacles. For one, their European allies were less enthusiastic about the fruits of multilateralism than they were. As one British official noted in 1947: "the U.S. . . . stands virtually alone in the world in its belief that free enterprise can be a wise or even a major rule for the conduct of economic affairs." [13] Western European governments

---

[11] See Paul Hoffman testimony House of Representatives, Committee on Foreign Affairs, *To Amend the Economic Cooperation Act of 1948, as Amended* (Washington, U.S. Government Printing Office, 1950), 81st Sess., 2nd Cong., 74; "The Position of the United States in the World Economy," [n.d.], RG59, Records of the PPS, 1947–1953, PPS Members – Chronological File, Robert W. Tufts, National Archives II, College Park, Maryland (hereinafter NAII).

[12] Representative examples of these popular appeals are found in the Atlantic Charter (1941) and Truman's Navy Day Celebration Speech (October 27, 1945).

[13] Memorandum of Conversation, Mr. William Adams Brown, staff member of the Brookings Institute and informal observer of the Geneva conference, May 9, 1947, *Foreign Relations of the United States* (hereinafter *FRUS*), 1947 1 (Washington, D.C.: U.S. Government Printing Office, 1973): 941.

Multilateralism, the Soviet Threat, and the Origins

35

faced a war-weary public that demanded change. The people wanted full employment, universal health care, decent housing, and other social programs, all of which their governments had promised to them for their sacrifices in the war. With strong Communist and Socialist parties in virtually all of these countries, state planning alternatives to multilateralism carried strong support. Nonetheless, western European governments, desperate for U.S. imports, were at least nominally committed to multilateralism; indeed, some within those governments were staunch multilateralists. However, they always had to walk a fine line between pushing their nations toward greater multilateralism and retaining the welfare state so many people demanded. This reality meant that any sign that multilateralism was not living up to its promise would force them to opt out of the system.[14]

Multilateralism, insofar as it required a strong U.S. presence in the world, also found little support among the American people. Most Americans looked on WWII, much as they had WWI, as a great crusade that they and their nation had selflessly undertaken to beat back the forces of tyranny in support of democracy. Having fought two wars to save Europe from its own destruction, most Americans expected the United States to return to its traditional policy of limited involvement with the world outside its borders. Furthermore, U.S. officials had touted U.S. participation in the newly created United Nations and the Bretton Woods institutions, which established the International Monetary Fund and the International Bank for Reconstruction and Development, as all the international involvement that was needed. They could not fathom that the U.S. would keep its armed forces in Europe or Asia once the war ended. Many Americans, as well, were concerned with reconversion, bringing the boys home, and avoiding a postwar depression, concerns that focused their attention, where it traditionally was, on domestic affairs and away from international ones. Convincing the American people that the United States needed to stay active in world affairs would be no easy obstacle to overcome.

Then there was the U.S. Congress. Congress's control of the budget, its position as the final arbiter of U.S. involvement in foreign alliances, and its power to set tariff policy gave it great control over U.S. foreign policy. Moreover, the immediate postwar Congress, especially its Republican

---

[14] McCormick, *America's Half-Century*, 53–55; Fred L. Block, *The Origins of International Economic Disorder: A Study of United States International Monetary Policy from World War II to the Present* (Berkeley, California: University of California Press, 1977), 77–79.

members, favored economic nationalism over multilateralism, reflecting the fact that the majority of U.S. businesses and corporations found their customer base primarily within U.S. borders. Although the economic nationalists in Congress were by no means isolationists, they supported high tariffs to protect U.S. industries from foreign competition and were generally distrustful of the multilateralists' agenda, which they suspected at times of being elitist, anti-American, and sometimes even pro-communist. They were strong supporters of capitalism and market economies and, in time, would become reliable anti-communists. Nevertheless, they were a constant thorn in the side of the multilateralists. They were also, for the most part, strict opponents of the New Deal and were ever leery that the Democrats' true agenda was to create a new New Deal at home and, perhaps, even one abroad, which, as we will see, boded ill for the multilateralists once foreign economic aid became a necessity.[15]

There were also the progressive internationalists, liberals who had risen to power during Roosevelt's tenure as president and, due to the depression, garnered more influence than they likely otherwise would have. They were internationalists in that they supported a positive U.S. presence in the world where, they believed, America's trade, technological prowess, and moral guidance could engender a world community built on the common goals of peace and prosperity. They believed that U.S. exports could help raise the standard of living for people the world over, not least in the United States, and, in the process, foster good faith and lasting friends. The progressive internationalists, however, were not advocates of unregulated free trade like the multilateralists were. They believed that the depression proved that the proponents of multilateralism had gotten it wrong. Capitalism needed government to save it from itself. Against multilateralism, they envisioned a world built on a system of regional trade blocs that would practice economic planning to ensure full employment and economic stability. Furthermore, they were proponents

---

[15] The best depiction of the economic nationalists remains Richard Freeland's *The Truman Doctrine and the Origins of McCarthyism: Foreign Policy, Domestic Politics, and Internal Security, 1946–1948* (New York: Schocken Books, 1974), passim. See also Michael J. Hogan, *A Cross of Iron: Harry S. Truman and the Origins of the National Security State, 1945–1954* (New York: Cambridge University Press, 1998), 17–21, 99–101, 325–329; Block, *International Economic Disorder*, 33–38, 71–73; Richard N. Gardner, *Sterling-Dollar Diplomacy: The Origins and Prospects of Our International Economic Order* (New York: McGraw-Hill, 1969), 236–248; John Lewis Gaddis, *The United States and the Origins of the Cold War, 1941–1947* (New York: Columbia University Press, 1972), 344–346, 357; Alonzo Hamby, *Beyond the New Deal: Harry S. Truman and American Liberalism* (New York: Columbia University Press, 1973), 180, passim.

Multilateralism, the Soviet Threat, and the Origins 37

of a policy of peace and cooperation with the Soviet Union, which pitted them against both the multilateralist and the economic nationalist factions. Although largely swept aside in the wake of Roosevelt's death, they presented problems for the multilateralists because they continued to push their agenda publicly and found a prominent spokesman in the form of Secretary of Commerce and former Vice President Henry Wallace, potentially weakening support for multilateralism at a time when its success was far from certain.[16]

The Soviet Union's newfound power after World War II posed an additional problem. The Soviet Union took a tremendous beating during the war, but it had been one of the victors and had gained much prestige in the international arena as a result. Its occupation of eastern Europe and its place as an arbiter of Germany's future meant that it would no longer be isolated, as it had for most of its brief history. Furthermore, it had the largest army in Europe, though like the West's forces, it too had undergone downsizing after the war. That was troubling enough, but the greatest threat posed by the Soviet Union was that it stood as the champion of socialist, or planned, economies at a time when U.S. leaders were attempting with all their might to forge a free market, multilateral world. Any effort to make multilateralism a reality meant dealing with the Soviet Union in one way or another.[17]

By far the greatest obstacle to the creation of a multilateral world, however, was the sheer fact of the world's destruction and the need to reconstruct it. As we will see, U.S. leaders were somewhat slow to realize just how much the war had disrupted the pre-war system. So convinced were they of the rightness of their cause, they failed to see weaknesses lying just below the surface. Rather, they believed that if the world merely adopted multilateral principles all would be made well. The fact is that European nations could not even begin to think about multilateralism when they had barely enough food to feed their own citizens.[18] In spite

---

[16] On the progressive internationalists, see Melvyn Leffler, *A Preponderance of Power: National Security, the Truman Administration, and the Cold War* (Stanford, California: Stanford University Press, 1992), 32–33, 50, 138–140; Carolyn Eisenberg, *Drawing the Line: The American Decision to Divide Germnay, 1944–1949* (Cambridge, United Kingdom: Cambridge University Press, 1996), 32–51; Freeland, *The Truman Doctrine and the Origins of McCarthyism*, 179, 184, 216, 225, 298–306; Hamby, *Beyond the New Deal*, 203–204, 215–218, 232, 245–246.

[17] Paul Kennedy, *The Rise and Fall of the Great Powers: Economic Change and Military Conflict from 1500 to 2000* (New York: Random House, 1987), 361–365; McCormick, *America's Half-Century*, 58–64.

[18] Kennedy, *Great Powers*, 357–372.

of these significant challenges, the multilateralists marched resolutely forward, confident that history was on their side. Soon, however, that confidence was to be sorely tested.

Enter the Soviet Union

It is generally accepted, at least in the United States, that the Cold War was the inevitable result of the clash between the two major powers, each possessing vastly different social and economic systems, that emerged in the wake of World War II – the United States and the Soviet Union. In the familiar story, the Soviet Union caused the Cold War by reneging on war and postwar agreements made at the Tehran, Yalta, and Potsdam conferences held among the Big Three and by embarking on a policy of expansion, intimidation, and deceit designed, ultimately, to communize the world. In response the United States instituted the policy of "containment" aimed at preventing the Soviet Union from succeeding in its nefarious plans. Although historians have, over the more than forty years that the Cold War existed and in the twenty years since it has ended, whittled away at that traditional perspective, primarily by demonstrating that the United States was not simply an innocent in the origins of the Cold War, it is still generally believed that the Soviet threat, at least for the United States, was the primary cause of the Cold War, whether because U.S. officials simply believed that the Soviet Union harbored expansionist aims and acted accordingly or because, as John Lewis Gaddis has argued, "as long as Stalin was running the Soviet Union a cold war was unavoidable."[19] But are such positions sustainable? Were the issues of conflict between the United States and the Soviet Union sufficient to bring on the Cold War? What was the Soviet threat in reality and how did U.S. officials perceive it? Answering these questions is crucial to a true understanding of the origins of the Cold War and, in the long run, NSC 68.

Any inquiry into the origins of the Cold War must begin with the conditions of the Soviet Union after WWII. The United States emerged from the war better and stronger than it was before the war. The same cannot be said of the Soviet Union. At the end of the war, the Soviet Union lay in ruins virtually unimaginable to anyone who did not live through it. An estimated twenty-five million Soviet citizens and soldiers lost their lives fighting the invading Germans. Most of those fatalities

---

[19] John Lewis Gaddis, *We Now Know: Rethinking Cold War History* (New York: Oxford University Press, 1997), 292.

Multilateralism, the Soviet Threat, and the Origins

were men, meaning that the Soviet Union faced not only an immediate manpower shortage but one in the future as well, and in the first years after the war the birth rate plunged to record lows. Physical destruction in the areas occupied by Germany and its allied troops was devastating. The Soviets saw damage to 39,000 miles of railroad track, which greatly hampered transportation. The loss of some seven million horses made transportation problems worse and exacerbated the reduction in agricultural production as well. Tractors, wagons, grain combines, river boats, trains, livestock, all were destroyed in mass numbers. Some 70,000 Soviet villages and towns were obliterated. At war's end, twenty-five million Soviets suffered from inadequate food, clothing, and shelter. According to one historian, "people lived in holes in the ground." The Soviet Union suffered more damage than any other country in the war. Even Germany and Japan, two of the war's antagonists, fared better.[20]

Making matters worse, concentration on military production in order to defeat Germany left the Soviet Union strong militarily, vis-à-vis the countries of Europe (though not the United States), but weak internally. At war's end, the Soviet Union was still employing horse power and steam engines in many of its factories and farms. When Soviet troops removed anything that was transportable from defeated Germany – machines, railroad track, iron and steel in whatever form – they did so, not as plunderers, but in desperation to rebuild their shattered country.[21]

To rebuild, the Soviets had to resort to the five-year plans reminiscent of the 1920s and 1930s. These were austerity measures of forced industrialization devised to increase output of "producer goods (heavy industry, coal, electricity, cement) and transport to the detriment of consumer goods and agriculture ... *with a natural reduction in military expenditures from their wartime levels*," as historian Paul Kennedy puts it.[22] In his famed February 9, 1946, "election" speech, Stalin predicted it would take "three or more new five-year plans ... to guarantee [the Soviet Union] against 'all contingencies,'" a prognosis that, if true, meant the Soviet Union would not be rebuilt, in Soviet terms, until at least 1961.[23]

---

[20] Kennedy, *Great Powers*, 362–363; LaFeber, *The American Age*, 440.
[21] Kennedy, *Great Powers*, 362–363.
[22] Kennedy, *Great Powers*, 363, emphasis added.
[23] Joseph Stalin's pre-election speech of February 1946 as reported by George Kennan, U.S. *Charge de Affaires* in the Soviet Union, to the Secretary of State James Byrnes, February 12, 1946, *FRUS, 1946* 6 (Washington, D.C.: U.S. Government Printing Office, 1969): 695.

The Soviet people suffered greatly under these programs as the standard of living barely reached subsistence levels. Nonetheless, they had been successful in the 1930s and were again in the immediate postwar era.[24] Success, however, is relative. Through its first postwar five-year plan, the Soviet Union managed merely to achieve, by 1950, *pre-war* levels of production that, though high, never neared even the United States's pre-war, depression-plagued levels, let alone its postwar ones.[25]

It should be noted, as preeminent historian of the Soviet Union Geoffrey Roberts has pointed out, that despite the heavy destruction the Soviet Union endured during the war, its leaders, especially Stalin, were not demoralized by the beating but came out of the war believing that it had proved the Soviet Union to be a bonafide country that had secured a spot in the category of great nations that would determine the future course of the postwar world. The Cold War emerged, according to Roberts, in part because the United States refused to accord the Soviet Union what its leaders believed was its hard-earned legitimacy and rightful place as one of those nations.[26]

If Soviet capabilities made military invasions to secure Soviet interests unlikely, what about its intentions? Or, because intentions are difficult to prove even if they are stated baldly, what can Soviet actions in the immediate postwar years tell us about their intentions? It is to an analysis of Soviet actions in the immediate postwar era that we must now turn.

The Soviet Union is often blamed for instigating the Cold War because of its subjugation of the peoples of eastern Europe. According to the conventional interpretation, the Soviets made promises to conduct "free and unfettered elections" throughout the liberated territories at Yalta in February 1945 in the Declaration on Liberated Europe but then reneged on that pledge and communized them. That the Soviet Union did communize eastern Europe cannot be denied. The question is when and why? Tradition holds that communization occurred in Poland, Rumania, and Bulgaria even before the war ended and was secured throughout eastern Europe by early 1948 when Czechoslovakia, the most democratic of

[24] LaFeber, *American Age*, 381.
[25] Kennedy, *Great Powers*, 363. On the fact that U.S. leaders did not believe the Soviet Union would strike militarily against western Europe, see Leffler, *A Preponderance of Power*, 111, 124–125, 149–151, 209–210, 305–308, passim. Although Leffler cites many a CIA or Joint Chiefs of Staff document detailing worst-case scenarios about the Soviets, he is consistent in claiming that they never really believed in a military strike.
[26] Geoffrey Roberts, *Stalin's Wars: From World War to Cold War, 1939–1953* (New Haven, Connecticut: Yale University Press, 2006), 296–320, 329–332.

Multilateralism, the Soviet Threat, and the Origins 41

all the east European countries, fell to a Communist coup. As to why, the common belief is that Stalin intended all along to communize eastern Europe as part of his plan to spread communist revolution, and that the pledge for free elections had merely been a smokescreen. However, the evidence, including new evidence emerging from former Soviet bloc countries, does not support this conclusion.

Whereas the Soviet Union did communize eastern Europe, it is certainly the case that Stalin's policies there developed over time and were from the start about security not expansion of the Soviet empire in order to export communist revolution. It is this last point that is the most important. At Yalta, both Churchill and Roosevelt confirmed their earlier agreements that the Soviet Union had legitimate security concerns that required it making a sphere of influence out of eastern Europe, although what that precisely meant was left undefined.[27] Unfortunately, they were less forthcoming about this issue with the peoples of their respective countries. At Yalta, FDR persuaded Stalin to sign the Declaration on Liberated Europe, but it was clear to all the major participants that the Declaration really meant nothing. It was filled with enough loopholes and lack of enforcement mechanisms to make it worthless. Roosevelt frankly admitted, if James Byrnes can be believed, that the Declaration was mostly for domestic political purposes, not a statement of true intention. As historian John Lewis Gaddis has written, "Roosevelt's reluctance to apply the declaration less than two weeks after Yalta when the Russians imposed a puppet government on Rumania doubtless indicated to Moscow that the President did not expect literal compliance with the terms of the agreement."[28] Although it remains a source of bitter contention what Roosevelt would have done about eastern Europe had he outlived the war, the initial U.S. position under President Truman largely was to accept Soviet domination of eastern Europe, subject to nominal inclusion of a few pro-Western, even anti-Soviet, members into the governments formed there. Stalin's security concerns were authentic; the communization of eastern Europe was not initially the primary goal except insofar as Soviet security was an issue.[29]

---

[27] On this point, see Warren Kimball, *The Juggler: Franklin Roosevelt as Wartime Statesman* (Princeton, New Jersey: Princeton University Press, 1991), 171–176. Kimball tells me that Roosevelt "would have quailed at the phrase 'spheres of influence'" and "would have preferred the term 'sphere of responsibility.'" E-mail to author, April 22, 2010.

[28] Gaddis, *The United States and the Origins of the Cold War*, 163–164.

[29] The following works all concede as much even as their authors come from very different political persuasions: Lloyd C. Gardner, *Spheres of Influence: The Great Powers Partition*

This interpretation remains true even as new evidence has emerged that Stalin intended the communization of eastern Europe once it became clear that the Germans would be defeated, ending, seemingly, one the Cold War's most burning questions – did Stalin seek the communization of eastern Europe all along or was his action a reactive measure against hostile actions taken by the United States? The issue is a source of debate because we know that Stalin did not immediately communize all of eastern Europe. In Poland, Rumania, and Bulgaria, he essentially did, but in Hungary, Czechoslovakia, east Germany, and the Soviet zone of occupation in Austria, free elections were held. In Hungary and Austria the Communists were routed, whereas in Czechoslovakia they won handily. In years past, some historians have used this evidence to argue that Stalin only communized all of eastern Europe once the United States and Britain provoked him into doing so through actions perceived by him to be hostile to Soviet interests.[30] The new evidence, however, purports to demonstrate that Stalin did intend the communization of eastern Europe all along (although "socialization" would be a better term) and continued to work toward this end through the respective nations' Communist parties even after closing down the Comintern in 1943. This evidence is supposed to prove, once and for all, that Stalin was indeed to blame for the Cold War.[31] Even if true, however, such moves are hardly inconsistent with Stalin's security concerns. Furthermore, U.S. officials acquiesced in the communization of Poland, Bulgaria, and Rumania, as Marc Trachtenberg has shown, such that it can hardly be argued that this action greatly disturbed administration officials.[32] Moreover, the fact remains that Stalin did not

---

Europe, From Munich to Yalta (New York: Ivan Dee Publishers, 1993); Diane Clemens, *Yalta* (New York: Oxford University Press, 1970); Gaddis, *The United States and the Origins of the Cold War*; Vojtech Mastny, *The Cold War and Soviet Insecurity: The Stalin Years* (New York: Columbia University Press, 1996); Vladislov Zubok, *Inside the Kremlin's Cold War: From Stalin to Khrushchev* (Cambridge, Massachusetts: Harvard University Press, 1996); Roberts, *Stalin's Wars*; Marc Trachtenberg, "The United States and Eastern Europe in 1945: A Reassessment," *Journal of Cold War Studies* 10:4 (Fall 2008): 94–132.

[30] Barton J. Bernstein, "American Foreign Policy and the Origins of the Cold War," in Thomas Paterson, ed., *The Origins of the Cold War* (Lexington, Massachusetts; D.C. Heath and Company, 1974), 2nd edition, 89–99.

[31] Eduard Mark, "Revolution by Degrees: Stalin's National-Front Strategy for Europe, 1941–1947," Cold War International History Project (CWIHP), Working Paper no. 31, Woodrow Wilson International Center for Scholars, Washington, D.C.; Vladislov Zubok, *A Failed Empire: The Soviet Union and the Cold War from Stalin to Gorbachev* (Chapel Hill: The University of North Carolina Press, 2007).

[32] Marc Trachtenberg, "The United States and Eastern Europe in 1945: A Reassessment," *Journal of Cold War Studies* 10:4 (Fall 2008): 94–132.

Multilateralism, the Soviet Threat, and the Origins

immediately communize all of eastern Europe, which leaves open the possibility that he believed he could live with friendly, non-Communist governments in some cases. Stalin believed, as Geoffrey Roberts has argued, that both eastern and western Europe eventually would be socialized, but how and when did not seem to particularly concern him. Roberts also astutely points out that "at the end of the Second World War Stalin was already in his mid-sixties and could not expect to live to see the long-term outcome" of the transition to socialism. The main point is that Stalin hardly was driven by the sinister goal of communizing eastern Europe, as tradition holds. In the initial stages of what became the Cold War, Soviet actions in eastern Europe were not particularly hostile and conformed to the Yalta and, later, the Potsdam agreements.[33]

That such evidence holds true is further borne out by the fact that Stalin did not initially force eastern Europe into an autarchic bloc designed to serve the ends of the Soviet Union.[34] For instance, on January 4, 1949, Poland signed trade agreements with Britain, Albania, Austria, Finland, Denmark, Argentina, Romania, France, and western Germany. Of those agreements, Britain's and Argentina's, countries outside the "iron curtain," were the largest, nearing some $600 million. These agreements occurred despite the fact that Poland was the country that Stalin most sought to keep in the Soviet orbit. The reason Poland sought trade with these other nations? The Soviet Union had reduced its trade with that country because it needed the goods at home to aid the reconstruction effort there. Much the same was true of Czechoslovakia. On January 12, 1949, the Czechoslovakian government hosted a Czechoslovak Industries Fair in New York City in order to promote its goods in the United States. Dr. Karel Fink of the Czechoslovak embassy was quoted as saying: "Czechoslovakia is not a country that wants only trade with the East. Today Czechoslovak industries are coming to New York, for Czechoslovakia has always been willing to trade with all the countries of the world." This happened after the 1948 coup that brought the Communists to power.[35]

Further evidence that Stalin was concerned foremost with security and not exporting communism through expansion is demonstrated by his lack

---

[33] Roberts, *Stalin's Wars*, 245–253, the quote is on 249.

[34] See, for instance, Robert Service, *Stalin: A Biography* (Cambridge, Massachusetts: Belknap Press, 2004), 516–517.

[35] Sydney Gruson, "Britain and Poland to Sign $600,000,000 Trade Pact," *The New York Times*, January 4, 1949, 1; "Czech Fair Opening Here to Aid Trade," *The New York Times*, January 12, 1949, 39.

of support for communist revolutions around the globe or even near to him at home. In all nations where Communist parties had the chance to assume power in the immediate postwar era – Greece, China, Italy, France – Stalin worked against them or stayed neutral. When civil war broke out between Greek Communists and the British-backed Monarchist Party in 1944, he refused to get involved. Rather, "he had promised Churchill in 1944 to stay out of Greek affairs and had kept the promise, as even Churchill admitted," notes historian Walter LaFeber.[36] Stalin's refusal to aid the Greek Communists ultimately caused a split with Marshall Josep Broz Tito of Yugoslavia, who wanted to aid them aggressively in the hopes of building a socialist Balkan Federation. When the Soviet leader could not be persuaded, Tito "defected" from the Soviet camp. Stalin did virtually nothing to counter Tito, a rather odd reaction for a man supposedly hell-bent on world, or even just European, conquest. As historian Thomas McCormick remarks, in a sentiment that is becoming increasingly clearer, Soviet "foreign policy was more utilitarian than doctrinaire."[37]

Nor did Stalin support Mao Zedong's Chinese Communist Party (CCP) in its battle with U.S.-backed Chiang Kai-shek's Kuomintang for control of China. Rather, as he told Milovan Dijlas, the Yugoslavian Communist leader, in 1948, "when the war with Japan ended, we invited the Chinese comrades to reach an agreement as to how a modus vivendi with Chiang Kai-shek might be found. They agreed with us in word, but in deed they did it their own way when they got home: they mustered their forces and struck."[38] As McCormick puts it, Stalin "discourage[d] the CCP from a revolutionary attempt to seize power," believing, as many U.S. officials did, "that a unified China, even a communist one, might be more of a danger than an aid to Russian interests in Asia."[39] Only after "Mao's military fortunes began to develop 'in a direction favorable to the people,'" write three historians utilizing newly opened Soviet archives, "did Stalin begin to support the [CCP]."[40]

Stalin was equally unsupportive of the desires of Communists to acquire power in France and Italy, where they held popular support due to their

---

[36] LaFeber, *American Age*, 477; Milovan Dijlas, *Conversations with Stalin* (New York: Harcourt, Brace, and World, 1962), 182–183.

[37] Dijlas, *Conversations with Stalin*, 182–183; McCormick, *America's Half-Century*, 65; Roberts, *Stalin's Wars*, 348–350.

[38] Dijlas, *Conversations with Stalin*, 182.

[39] McCormick, *America's Half-Century*, 58.

[40] Sergei Goncharov, John Lewis, and Xue Litai, *Stalin, Mao, and the Korean War* (Stanford, Calif.: Stanford University Press, 1993), 1, 24. For another account using newly opened

Multilateralism, the Soviet Threat, and the Origins   45

valiant fight against the Nazi scourge. Communists in these countries certainly looked to the Soviet Union for support in their efforts to reform their societies. Nevertheless, they found the Soviet leader very unresponsive. For instance, he did not speak to French Communist leader Maurice Thorez once between November 1944 and November 1947. Rather than attempting to assume power either through revolutionary or democratic means, Stalin cautioned local Communist leaders to work within the existing bourgeois governments, which he knew were hostile to the Communists. His motivation apparently was due to his desire, first, to keep the Grand Alliance alive by not antagonizing the allies, and, second, by his belief that, in the long run, socialism would win out in these countries so that there was no need to create antagonism. That changed as the Cold War began to harden in 1947, and it became apparent to Stalin that the United States was determined to rebuild western Germany as well as to create an anti-Soviet bloc out of western Europe through the Marshall Plan. In September 1947 the Soviet Union created the Communist Information Bureau, known as the Cominform, a successor to the Comintern that had been officially dissolved in 1943. Although the Cominform mostly focused on eastern Europe, the leaders of the Communist parties in France and Italy were invited to its inauguration. However, the invitation came, supposedly, because they had failed to inform Stalin of their expulsion from the governing coalitions in their countries in May 1947, a reflection of just how distant they had become from him. Thereafter, the Communist parties of those countries began a concerted campaign to undermine the Marshall Plan, though they met with very little success. By then, most western Europeans were looking West for their future. Stalin, meanwhile, cracked down on eastern Europe but did nothing substantial to help the Communist parties in western Europe.[41]

A few "hot spots" developed. In Iran in 1945–1946, for instance, the Soviets refused to disengage from the northern section of the country where they had control per wartime agreements. Northern Iran held rich oil fields that the Soviet Union hoped to develop for domestic consumption. The United States and Britain also wanted access to Iranian oil. U.S. officials, however, wondered if the Soviet refusal to leave was an indication that they were bent on territorial expansion. Secretary of State James Byrnes went to the United Nations claiming

archives, see Brian Murray, "Stalin, the Cold War, and the Division of China: A Multi-Archival Mystery," CWIHP, Working Paper no. 12.

[41] Roberts, *Stalin's Wars*, 317–320; Mark, "Revolution by Degrees," 33–38; Gonchorav, et al., 28.

46   *NSC 68 and the Political Economy of the Early Cold War*

as much.[42] Nevertheless, crisis was avoided when the Soviets suddenly removed their troops after receiving assurance of oil concessions. These failed to materialize and the Soviet Union did nothing in response. As one historian studying recently opened Soviet archives has concluded: "Soviet goals in Iran were limited to concrete demands and, despite the U.S.S.R.'s aggressive behavior during the 'Iranian crisis,' did not include territorial aggrandizement."[43]

In Turkey a crisis emerged in mid-1946 when the Soviets asked for a redrawing of the Montreux treaty of 1936 governing ship movements through the Dardanelles Straits. The Soviets complained that the treaty had proved ineffective in protecting the Soviet Union during the war, although certainly it also reflected a long-term Russian desire for a warm water port leading to the Mediterranean. They asked for a conference among the Black Sea states to rewrite the treaty. As with the Iran crisis, some U.S. officials thought this was further proof of Soviet expansionist aims. At an August 15, 1946, cabinet meeting, Truman made plain that he intended to stop the Soviets in Turkey. When Dean Acheson asked if the president understood that such a position might mean war, Truman concurred, arguing that "we might as well find out whether the Russians were bent on world conquest now as in five or ten years."[44] However, whether Truman's claim meant that he truly believed the Turkish "crisis" would go that far has been called into question. As historian Melvyn Leffler has shown, neither of the two highest ranking foreign service officers assigned to the Soviet Union believed Soviet moves were aggressive, and Truman made comments around the same time that downplayed Soviet actions.[45] A more realistic portrayal of both the Iranian and Turkish "crises" is that put forth by Geoffrey Roberts, whose recent *Stalin's Wars*, is one of the most comprehensive books written about Stalin utilizing Soviet

---

[42] Leffler, *A Preponderance of Power*, 110.

[43] Natalia Yegorova, "The 'Iranian Crisis' of 1945–46: A View from the Russian Archives," CWIHP, Working Paper no. 15. See also Roberts, *Stalin's Wars*, 308–309.

[44] Acheson, *Present at the Creation*, 195–196; Truman is quoted from Wilson D. Miscamble, C.S.C, *From Roosevelt to Truman: Potsdam, Hiroshima, and the Cold War* (New York: Cambridge University Press, 2007), 295. See also Eduard Mark, "The War Scare of 1946 and Its Consequences," *Diplomatic History* 21:3 (Summer 1997): 383–416. Acheson claims in *Present at the Creation* that Eisenhower prompted the question, but Eisenhower was not at the meeting. See Jonathan Knight, "American Statecraft and the 1946 Black Sea Straits Controversy," *Political Science Quarterly* 90:3 (Autumn, 1975): 463–464, fn. 27.

[45] Leffler, *A Preponderance of Power*, 123–125; Melvyn Leffler, "The War Scare of 1946," July 18, 1997, H-Diplo Discussion List, http://www.h-net.org/~diplo.

Multilateralism, the Soviet Threat, and the Origins   47

archives. He writes: "What the Iranian and Turkish incidents showed was that Stalin was prepared to push hard for strategic gains but not at the expense of a break in relations with Britain and the United States." We are left with a picture of Stalin as being far more flexible than tradition would have it.[46]

One incident that many historians consider to be the final break from the wartime alliance to the Cold War was the Soviet refusal to participate in the Marshall Plan and, more importantly, to drive other east European nations to refuse to participate as well. There is no doubt that the Soviets did do these things. However, it is arguable whether this was a case of the Soviets acting aggressively. They had agreed to attend the conference held to work out the details of the proposed program. What they did not know was that the Americans had written the proposal in such a way that they fully expected and hoped to receive a Soviet refusal. The desire for such a refusal arose because U.S. officials feared Congress would never accept the program if it aided communists, a reflection of how the domestic political tide was flowing in an anti-Soviet direction, in no small part due to the Truman administration's own actions, as we will see. The proposal stipulated that the United States would determine what the aid was allocated for, which would have meant intervening in Soviet internal affairs, as, in fact, was the case for the countries that accepted the aid. The Soviets could never have agreed to such a trampling of their sovereignty, especially given their own belief in their newly found status as a great world power. So they walked out. However, this was hardly an instance of Soviet perfidy.[47]

The division of Germany, one of the Cold War's most enduring symbols, has been laid at the feet of the Soviets as well. The claim is very dubious, however. Although settling the German issue was certain to be difficult, the image of the Soviet Union cutting Germany in two to serve its expansionist aims is wrong. As historian Carolyn Eisenberg has shown, multilateralists in the State Department, backed by supporters in the war department, took the lead in dividing Germany virtually from the end of WWII when they surreptitiously reversed Joint Chiefs of

---

[46] Robert's, *Stalin's Wars*, 311.

[47] George Kennan, *Memoirs* (Boston, Massachusetts: Little, Brown, 1972), 342; Charles Bohlen, *Witness to History* (New York: W. W. Norton, 1973), 263ff.; Dean Acheson's comments from the Princeton Seminar, July 8–9, 1953, add considerable weight to the thinking that went into the problems associated with Soviet participation in the Marshall Plan. See Princeton Seminars, Dean Acheson Papers, Reading Copy III, Princeton Seminar Participants, May 15–16, 1954, folder 2, reel 5, track 1, Box 98, Truman Library, 15–16.

Staff order 1067. This order, signed by Truman on May 10, 1945, had called for tough measures against Germany. Germany was to be limited in terms of its rehabilitation. It was to be punished for its transgressions. However, State Department officials, and their friends in the war department, realized early on that the rehabilitation of western Europe as a whole, necessary if multilateralism were to function globally, required the rehabilitation of German heavy industry. Slowly they then began the process of rebuilding the western portion of the country, against Allied agreements, all the while claiming that the Soviets were the ones being nefarious over Germany. Finally, on June 7, 1948, the three western powers announced their intention to create a separate West German state and several days later instituted a shared currency for their zones in direct violation of the Potsdam accords.[48]

The decision to create a separate West German state and the announcement of a new currency for it precipitated one of the early Cold War's most memorable events – the Soviet blockade of Berlin. The German capital of Berlin sat inside the Soviet zone of occupation and was itself divided into four zones among the four powers – Britain, France, the United States, and the Soviet Union – just as Germany itself was. Access to Berlin from the western zones occurred along several heavily guarded roads and rail lines. In June 1948, Stalin ordered these closed in what appeared to be an attempt to take over the city. Long viewed as a pristine example of Soviet aggression, it is now recognized that, although not the wisest move Stalin ever made, it was undertaken, not to seize Berlin, but in an attempt to get the three western powers back to the negotiating table. In other words, it was instigated to encourage them to keep the four-power alliance together. If this was the goal, however, it failed miserably. In response to the blockade, the United States and Britain instituted the famed Berlin airlift, in which aircraft flew supplies into the city to keep the population of western Berlin fed and clothed. The airlift served as a great propaganda tool for the United States and Britain, and it painted the Soviets as heartless aggressors. A year later, Stalin lifted the blockade.[49]

In February 1948, Czechoslovakia, one of the most democratic nations within the Soviet sphere in eastern Europe, fell to an alleged communist "coup." However, let's review the facts. As early as July 1947, eight months before the coup, U.S. Ambassador to Czechoslovakia Laurence

---

[48] Eisenberg, *Drawing the Line*, passim; Roberts, *Stalin's Wars*, 354–355.
[49] Eisenberg, *Drawing the Line*, 379–394, 411–476; Roberts, *Stalin's Wars*, 354–355.

Multilateralism, the Soviet Threat, and the Origins · 49

A. Steinhardt cabled his superiors in Washington with the news that Czech Communists had control of "Interior, Finance, Agriculture, Labor, Information and Internal Trade and substantial ... control of Ministries of Foreign Affairs and National Defence," "effective control of police," "preponderant influence in trade union organizations," "substantial control [of] 5 out of 10 daily Praha [Prague] newspapers with nation-wide circulation," "increasing economic dependence of Czechoslovakia on Soviets," and "strong Czechoslovak feeling of dependence on Soviet[s] for future protection against a resurgent Germany."[50] More importantly, after the coup, Steinhardt reported that there was "no direct evidence of Soviet interference."[51] In the coup's aftermath, the U.S. Central Intelligence Agency (CIA) made this observation:

> The Kremlin for some time has had the capability of consolidating its position in Czechoslovakia. The coup was precipitated by the stubborn resistance of Czech moderates to continued Communist control of the police force.... The Czech coup and the demands on Finland, moreover, do not preclude the possibility of Soviet efforts to effect a rapprochement with the West.... In fact, the Kremlin would undoubtedly consider the consolidation of its position in the border states as a necessary prerequisite to any such agreement.
>
> In Western Europe, the Communists continue to concentrate on legal means to gain their objectives rather than on violence and direct action.... The Communists could not at this time carry out a similar coup in either Italy or France, as they do not have control of the police or the armed forces.[52]

In fact, the seizure of power by the Czech Communists occurred "legally," historian Melvyn Leffler tells us, after twelve ministers from other democratic parties quit their posts.[53] To be sure, thereafter the Communists established a Communist dictatorship along Stalinist lines completely loyal to Moscow. However, hardly can this turn of events be called an unexpected power grab that reflected yet another Soviet move to further its conquest of Europe, as it is so often portrayed.[54] Rather, it was consistent with Stalin's increasing consolidation of Soviet control over eastern Europe in light of the breakdown of the Grand Alliance that was occurring

---

[50] Steinhardt to Secretary of State George Marshall, July 15, 1947, quoted in Frank Kofsky, *The War Scare of 1948: A Successful Campaign to Deceive the Nation* (New York: St Martin's, 1995), 93–94.

[51] Steinhardt to Secretary of Sate George Marshall, April 30, 1948, quoted in Kofsky, *War Scare*, 95.

[52] CIA 3–48, March 10, 1948, quoted in Kofsky, *War Scare*, 96–97.

[53] Leffler, *A Preponderance of Power*, 205.

[54] For a recent example, see Miscamble, *From Roosevelt to Truman*, 312.

over U.S., British, and French policy over Germany. Even then, it was *not* carried out at Stalin's behest.

A common Cold War refrain is that, although the Soviet Union may not have been willing to risk a military conquest of western Europe, which would hardly gain it friends there and would potentially do more harm than good to the regime, it was hoping for the economic collapse of the region, which would pave the way for communism to take hold there, as communism feeds off of economic destitution. To that end, it is argued, the Soviet Union took steps that would bring about western Europe's downfall, such as refusing to cooperate over Germany or to participate in the Marshall Plan.[55] This view, in fact, was encouraged by U.S. officials such as U.S. Ambassador to the Soviet Union Walter Bedell Smith and Secretary of State George Marshall, but there is very little truth in it.[56] As regards Germany, the simple fact is that the Soviets were not willing to compromise the political and economic objectives agreed to at Yalta and Potsdam, whereas by the end of the war the Americans had come to find them deplorable and wanted them revised. Even so, the Soviets pressed for reparations but ultimately agreed to the U.S. effort to raise Germany's level of industrial production so that, in part, it could pay reparations out of current production; the Soviets had refused such increases in the initial deliberation stages over Germany's future. Furthermore, the Soviet Union expected four-power cooperation to keep Germany in check and devise a plan for its future, a position that belies the argument that the Soviets were trying ruin the German economy. The Berlin blockade, as we have seen, was instituted to "force the western powers to resume negotiations with the Soviet Union about the future of Germany."[57] As Geoffrey Roberts has argued, Stalin never gave up his belief that German unification under four-power auspices could be achieved and went to his grave believing so. These actions hardly comport with a desire to undermine the German economy in order to bring western Europe to its knees. We also have already seen that U.S. officials devised the Marshall Plan in such a way that they hoped the Soviet Union would reject participation in it, which the Soviets did. They then turned around and blamed the Soviets for being obstructionists, when clearly that is not the case at all. Furthermore, rejecting its own participation in the Marshall Plan

---

[55] Miscamble, *From Roosevelt to Truman*, 310–312.

[56] On the efforts of these individuals to construct such an image, see Eisenberg, *Drawing the Line*, 277–317.

[57] Roberts, *Stalin's Wars*, 350.

Multilateralism, the Soviet Threat, and the Origins 51

and forcing the other eastern European states to follow suit was hardly the best way for the Soviets to undermine the west European economy. Agreeing to the aid, which would have involved the Soviets in deliberations concerning the allocation of funds both for western and eastern Europe, would have been far more effective if that was their true goal. Then they truly could have been obstructionist. The argument that the Soviets sought to destroy the western European economy as a way to communize it simply does not square with the facts.

Of course, what matters is less what Soviet intentions and capabilities actually were than what U.S. officials believed they were. What did they believe? There can be no doubt that top-level U.S. officials thought that the Soviet Union posed the greatest real and potential threat to U.S. security in the immediate postwar era. Nonetheless, as top-level memoranda show, U.S. officials did not believe that the Soviet Union would use military force to achieve its goals, an essential point because if it was not willing to use force, and U.S. officials believed as much, then all the Soviets had was propaganda and the hope of a western economic collapse, which hardly can be considered "offensive" means to world domination.

Several examples will suffice to make the case. "The Soviet Union will not resort to direct military action against the West in the near future and expects and counts on a period of several years of peace," stated a report from the Department of Eastern European Affairs dated May 4, 1949.[58] "Is war inevitable?" George H. Butler, deputy director of the State Department's Policy Planning Staff (PPS), asked in a June 9, 1949, memorandum then answered: "The public statements of the highest responsible U.S. government officials indicate that the U.S. answer at the present time is in the negative."[59] In a memorandum to Dean Acheson dated January 6, 1950, George Kennan, former director of the State Department's PPS, laid out what in memorandum after memorandum was standard opinion among top-level government officials concerning the Soviet Union's intentions:

Most recent indications are that Soviet attention is shifting to Germany and China, with reduced hopes for accomplishments of western European [Communist] parties. If this is true, it would indicate no Soviet intention of attacking in west at this juncture; and indeed there are no indications that Soviet leaders are intending to resort to war at this stage to achieve objectives.[60]

[58] Frederick G. Reinhardt to George Kennan, May 4, 1949, *FRUS, 1949* 1 (Washington, D.C.: U.S. Government Printing Office, 1976): 293–294.
[59] Memorandum by George H. Butler, June 9, 1949, *FRUS, 1949* 1:327.
[60] George Kennan to Dean Acheson, January 6, 1950, *FRUS, 1950* 1 (Washington, D.C.: U.S. Government Printing Office, 1977): 128.

NSC 68 and the Political Economy of the Early Cold War

On July 15, 1948, a memorandum noted the following comments from State Department Counselor and Soviet expert Charles E. Bohlen:

> Mr. Bohlen said that as an aftermath of the war Europe had been left in a dangerous state of unbalance…. He had concluded, moreover, that the most dangerous period had been in the immediate postwar years, 1945–1947, when the U.S. military establishment was rapidly disintegrating and the American public had not yet been alerted to the Russian peril; yet *it was significant that the Soviet Army did not move during this period. Furthermore, it should be remembered that the Russian Army had not moved beyond the line which we now refer to as the "iron curtain."*[61]

Bohlen's comments are especially important as Soviet forces in Europe at that time were far superior to the West's and, more importantly, were believed to be. A State Department assessment of Soviet and Western strength in 1947 put Soviet forces in eastern Europe at 1,110,000 and combined British, French, and U.S. forces at 529,000 in western Europe.[62] When the West was most vulnerable, having demilitarized after the war, the Soviet Union did not take advantage of the situation and U.S. officials acknowledged as much. Although the United States alone possessed atomic capabilities, something that may account for Soviet behavior, Bohlen never mentioned this point.

There also is this statement that U.S. Ambassador to the Soviet Union Admiral Alan G. Kirk made at the meeting of the U.S. ambassadors at Rome from March 22–24, 1950. Commenting on "Soviet objectives and tactics in Europe," Kirk noted,

> [T]here were certain weaknesses in the Soviet Union which should be considered. The two basic shortages in terms of raw materials were those of rubber and petroleum. It was generally believed that there were no more large unexploited oil reserves available to the Russians. The other important weakness was that of the transportation system which in all respects, rail, highway, and water, was not highly developed in a modern sense.[63]

Furthermore, in September 1948 Colonel Robert P. Landry made this observation in a memorandum to President Truman:

> Because the Russians have assembled a formidable fighting force in Germany, they will require a tremendous logistical effort in order to launch any large-scale

---

[61] Charles Bohlen's remarks before the third meeting of the working group participating in the Washington Exploratory Talks on Security, July 15, 1948, quoted in Kofsky, *War Scare*, 287 (emphasis added).

[62] Memorandum from the Secretary of War Robert P. Patterson to the Assistant Secretary of State for Occupied Areas Major General John H. Hilldring, February 26, 1947, *FRUS, 1947* 1:718.

[63] *FRUS, 1950* 3:822–823.

Multilateralism, the Soviet Threat, and the Origins 53

and sustained offensive. Lines of communication to the Eastward are essential to its success. I was told at the G-2 [intelligence] briefing that the Russians have dismantled hundreds of miles of railroads in Germany and sent the rails and ties back to Russia. There remains, at the present time, so I was told, only a single track railroad running Eastward out of the Berlin area and upon which the Russians must surely depend for their logistical support. This same railroad line changes from a standard gage, going Eastward, to a Russian wide gage in Poland, which further complicates the problem of moving supplies and equipment forward.[64]

The final item is from Dean Acheson, who made the following observations about the Soviet Union in discussing whether the United States should pursue development of the hydrogen bomb in light of the acquisition of the atomic bomb by the Soviet Union in the summer of 1949.

Russian history is divided, but Soviet history seems to be against military adventures which entail any risk.... The Crimean war, the Russo-Japanese war and World War I show tendencies toward aggressive adventure. But these latter may be said to have involved no great risk and to have lessons that risk is hard to estimate. The great care to escape involvement in the "capitalist" war of 1939 supports the thesis that the lesson was learned.[65]

This from a man who, in a little more than a month, would begin concocting the shockingly exaggerated depiction of the Soviet threat found in NSC 68.

As these reports and memoranda demonstrate, there existed plenty of doubt and ambiguity about the nature of the Soviet threat within *top circles* of the Truman administration in the years in which the Cold War emerged. Not only did officials express their belief that the Soviet Union was likely incapable of successfully achieving its alleged goals of communist expansion through military means, but they also argued that it did not exhibit behavior that demonstrated any inclination to do so.[66]

---

[64] Colonel Robert P. Landry to the President, September 28, 1948, quoted in Kofsky, *War Scare*, 294–295.

[65] Memorandum by the Secretary of State, December 20, 1949, *FRUS, 1949* 1:614.

[66] To be sure, there exists in the archives a plethora of intelligence reports and security assessment documents drawn up by those agencies charged with analyzing the nation's national security – the Central Intelligence Agency, the National Security Council, the Joint Chiefs of Staff, the Department of Defense, the Joint Intelligence Committee, the individual armed services, and the like – documents that offer a depiction of the Soviet threat very different from that portrayed in this chapter. As the these documents have been declassified over the last thirty years, some historians have used them to argue that (1) the Soviet Union was in fact the expansionist, threatening menace that U.S. officials often portrayed it as; or (2) that they at least believed that it was, and so cannot be faulted for acting on that belief; or (3) that the Soviet Union was the only potential threat

It is not being argued here that the Soviet threat was nonexistent or that the Soviet Union had no culpability in starting the Cold War. The threat was real insofar as the Soviet Union was the only nation capable of challenging the U.S. militarily, ideologically, and politically in the immediate postwar era. It did, for instance, have the largest army in the world, and that army was sitting in the middle of Europe. That fact could hardly be ignored. Had it wanted to, it likely could have conquered western Europe, absent Spain, Portugal, and Great Britain, and perhaps even moved on the Middle East, although holding on to these areas would have been extremely difficult and augured against such a move. It also posed an ideological challenge in that it offered an alterative to free-market capitalism as a way of life that also promised freedom and prosperity to the disinherited and disparaged masses, however empty the promise may have been in reality. Furthermore, U.S. officials certainly believed that the Soviet Union constituted the gravest possible threat to U.S. national security and, undoubtedly, filtered their views about virtually every foreign policy maneuver through that prism.

Nonetheless, as the evidence put forth in this chapter demonstrates, in its actions the Soviet Union did not present the kind of threat that would justify laying blame for the Cold War solely at its feet. Not only was it highly improbable that it would undertake to attempt the conquest of Europe, let alone the world, an absurdity of the highest order, given the destruction it suffered during the war and its relatively slow reconstruction effort, but it also showed itself very reluctant to engage in revolutionary activity and repeatedly proved itself accommodating in its relations with the United States and the other allies, subject to its security concerns (for instance, over Turkey and Iran and many issues related to Germany's future). Furthermore, U.S. officials did not believe that the Soviet Union would use military force to achieve its goals, whatever those goals were.[67]

to the nation's "national security" in a world in which national security had become the focal point of official thinking about the world. The problem with the use of such documents is that they generally reflect worst-case scenarios about the Soviet threat because it is the job of such agencies to produce such analyses. What matters is less the documents themselves, however intriguing they may be, and more what those top officials responsible with conducting the nation's foreign policy do with them. Furthermore, when comparing conflicting documents, such as those depicting a very dire Soviet threat and those depicting a much less ominous one, we can fairly assume that the less ominous ones are more accurate, for why would any U.S. officials lie or distort the Soviet threat to make it appear less threatening?

[67] New evidence coming out of the Soviet and former Communist-bloc archives confirms this assessment even if the authors often come to different conclusions. The CWIHP has put out a number of studies that reveal Stalin as cautious and driven far more by

Multilateralism, the Soviet Threat, and the Origins

What, then, was the Soviet contribution to the origins of the Cold War? The primary contribution that the Soviet Union made to the origins of the Cold War was that it simply refused to bow down to U.S. demands or go along with its prescriptions when they conflicted with vital Soviet interests. This scenario played itself out most obviously in Germany, where, against the Yalta and Potsdam Accords, the United States chose to reconstruct the European war's main belligerent and the Soviet Union's mortal enemy to full industrial status, including, ultimately, its remilitarization. This, against the Soviet Union's desire to maintain quadripartite control until an agreed upon peace treaty could be actualized. It occurred over eastern Europe, Iran, and Turkey (although in the case of the latter two the Soviet Union ultimately, and rather quickly, backed down), over international control of atomic energy, in the negotiations over the Marshall Plan, and in other areas as well. Given this, probably the only way the Cold War could have been prevented would have been for the Soviet Union to retreat back behind its borders, in effect removing itself from world affairs much as it had done for its brief existence. However, Stalin and his officials were unwilling to do so, and for good

---

Soviet security concerns than ideology or world domination. Among these are Katherine Weathersby, "'Should We Fear This?' Stalin and the Danger of War with America," Working Paper No. 39, July 2002; Vojtech Mastny, "NATO in the Beholder's Eye: Soviet Perceptions and Policies, 1949–1956, Working Paper No. 35, March 2002; Ethan Pollock, "Conversations with Stalin on Questions of Political Economy," Working Paper No. 33, July 2001; Vladimir O. Pechatov, "'The Allies are Pressing on You to Break Your Will...' Foreign Policy Correspondence between Stalin and Molotov and Other Politburo Members, September 1945–December 1946," Working Paper No. 26, September 1999; Natalia Yegorova, "The 'Iran Crisis' of 1945–46: A View from the Russian Archives," Working Paper No. 15, May 1996; Norman M. Naimark, "'To Know Everything and To Report Everything Worth Knowing': Building the East German Police State, 1945–49," Working Paper No. 10, August 1994; Scott D. Parrish and Mikhail M. Narinsky, "New Evidence on the Soviet Rejection of the Marshall Plan, 1947: Two Reports," Working Paper No. 9, March 1994; Kathryn Weathersby, "Soviet Aims in Korea and the Origins of the Korean War, 1945–1950: New Evidence from the Russian Archives," Working Paper No. 8, November 1993. The exception is Eduard Mark, "Revolution By Degrees: Stalin's National-Front Strategy For Europe, 1941–1947," Working Paper No. 31, February 2001. These articles can be accessed online at: http://wilsoncenter.org/index.cfm?topic_id=1409&fuseaction=topics.publications&group_id=11901. See also Roberts, *Stalin's Wars*; Vladislav Zubok and Constantine Pleshakov, *Inside the Kremlin's Cold War: From Stalin to Khrushchev* (Cambridge, Massachusetts: Harvard University Press, 1997); Norman Naimark and Lenoid Gibianski, *The Establishment of Communist Regimes in Eastern Europe, 1944–1949* (Boulder, Colorado: Westview Press, 1998); and Norman Naimark, *The Russians in Germany: A History of the Soviet Zone of Occupation, 1945–1949* (Cambridge, Massachusetts: Belknap Press, 1997); Melvyn Leffler, "Inside Enemy Archives: The Cold War Reopened," *Foreign Affairs* 75 (July/August 1996): 120–135.

reasons. They had fought too hard for their nation's (and their regime's) survival. They had justly won a say in Germany's future, and they were not about to trust the West to guarantee that it could keep Germany from rising up a third time and make another go at conquering Mother Russia. Perhaps most importantly, as Geoffrey Roberts has emphasized, they had achieved great power status, in fact, arguably, more so than any other regime in Russian history. Understandably, they intended both to maintain that status and use it to their advantage. In doing so, they were merely acting as we would expect the leaders of any great power to act. They pressed their issues and they took chances, but not to the point of risking war. They believed in the ultimate triumph of communism over capitalism, but they had no time table for when that would occur, and they did not believe that they had to bring it about through force of arms or by stealthily undermining the economy of western Europe. To argue as much is to assign far too much zeal for Marxist-Leninist ideology to Soviet leaders, especially Stalin, than they could possibly have mustered at a time when their primary concern was rebuilding their war-ravaged country and maintaining their prestige in the international arena. The Soviet Union contributed to the origins of the Cold War, but not because it harbored some design for world conquest. It did so, rather, because its leaders were determined to fight for vital interests.

Here is the reality. As judged by those responsible for constructing U.S. foreign policy in the immediate postwar era, which is to say the multilateralists, the Soviet Union posed a threat to the United States and its allies primarily insofar as that if the United States failed to foster a viable economic and political system for the "free world," then and only then might communism advance and the Soviet Union's power increase as a result, although even that was not a certainty. The fact of the matter is that the United States commanded overwhelming economic power, it dominated the sea and the air militarily, it alone possessed the atomic bomb, and it had garnered significant leadership authority. In essence, the postwar world was its to win or to lose. A State Department paper from 1949 told it straight:

The challenge to the U.S. and other free nations is this: can free men successfully organize themselves in free institutions so that they can realize their potentialities, thus meeting and containing the Soviet threat and fulfilling their own aspirations[?] The resources of the free world vastly exceed those of the Soviet world. If the free world is unable to develop its resources successfully – to summon up the courage and determination and to draw upon the intelligence of free men to build up adequate defense, to achieve a workable economy, and to establish

Multilateralism, the Soviet Threat, and the Origins

stable political conditions – then the eventual defeat of the free world will be in a sense deserved.[68]

And yet, the Cold War did emerge, and the justification for it, as promulgated by Truman administration officials, was that the Soviet Union was hell-bent on world domination to which the United States, as the principal defender of the "free world," had no choice but to respond. To understand why, we need to explore the dollar gap crisis and its implications for U.S. foreign policy in the immediate postwar era.

[68] "The American Problem and the Legislative Problem," [1949], RG 59, Records of the PPS, Policy Planning Staff Members – Chronological File, Robert W. Tufts, Box 52, NAII.

3

Multilateralism, the Dollar Gap, and the Origins of the Cold War

> Western Europe's exports to North America have nearly reached, in physical volume, the 1938 level. But the 1938 level, or for that matter any pre-war level, is not a relevant target.... Europe can no longer finance a large surplus of dollar imports; the dollar trade deficit must be drastically narrowed. If for the near future this must be done primarily by a reduction in Europe's dollar imports, this is obviously no real or permanent solution. Somehow, both Europe's dollar earnings from exports, and the availability of non-dollar supplies of food and raw materials, must be enormously increased, as compared with both present and pre-war volumes, if there is again to be a strong and prosperous Western Europe and a functioning world economy.
>
> Harland B. Cleveland, 1949

For U.S. foreign policy officials committed to creating a multilateral economy in the aftermath of WWII, the Soviet Union presented a formidable obstacle. As we have seen, however, the Soviet Union was not a hostile power against which the United States simply had no choice but to respond defensively. In fact, given the evidence presented in Chapter 2, it is difficult to contend that the Cold War can be laid at the feet of the Soviets. That said, if there were no other explanation that might account for the origins of the Cold War it would have to be conceded that, even given the relatively benign nature of the Soviet threat in the immediate postwar period, it nonetheless sits at the heart of the Cold War. In such an event, this study would never have seen the light of day. However, in fact, there is another explanation, one that must be taken into account to fully understand the origins of the Cold War. It was called the dollar gap.

The dollar gap was the shorthand phrase for an international balance-of-payments crisis that emerged with full force in the postwar

58

Multilateralism, the Dollar Gap, and the Origins 59

era, threatening to destroy the nascent global economy that the multilateralists in the Truman administration were trying so desperately to construct. To cope with the crisis, the multilateralists formulated three foreign policy actions that are some of the most important in the nation's history – the British loan, the Greco-Turkish aid bill, and the European Recovery Program, more popularly known as the Marshall Plan. However, in pushing these endeavors the multilateralists discovered that they did not have the support of the U.S. Congress, many of whose members were not keen on the idea of providing either loans or grants to foreign nations, some of whom were the United States' foremost competitors in world trade. In their efforts to sell Congress on these programs, the multilateralists found that although Congress was not persuaded by the purely economic arguments associated with failing to pass them, it responded favorably when they cast them as moves aimed at stopping the Soviet Union from fulfilling its design for world conquest.

Hence, the effort to gain Congress's approval of the administration's plans for contending with the dollar gap led to a dynamic that put the Soviet threat at the forefront of U.S. foreign policy, even as that threat was not, in fact, much of threat at all, at least not in the way that convention holds. Stating as much is not to argue that the Soviet Union posed no threat or that U.S. officials believed that it did not. Rather, it is to argue that the Soviet threat cannot alone explain the origins of the Cold War. To that end, this chapter explores the dollar gap and the role it played in how the Cold War developed.

The Dollar Gap

Writing about the dollar gap in 1984, historian William Borden noted that "few non economists understood it [at the end of World War II] and not all historians have understood it subsequently."[1] Today, little has changed. Pick up any standard history of the Cold War and one would be wont to find any mention of the dollar gap. It rarely finds its way into college or high school text books. The acclaimed CNN documentary *Cold War*, released in 1998, made no reference to it.[2] Though a few, more

---

[1] William Borden, *The Pacific Alliance: United States Foreign Economic Policy and Japanese Trade Recovery, 1947–1955* (Madison, Wisconsin: University of Wisconsin Press, 1984), 23.

[2] Episode three, "The Marshall Plan: 1947–1952," ignores the dollar gap, a huge oversight because the Marshall Plan was put forward in large measure to deal with the dollar

specialized studies have acknowledged and analyzed the dollar gap, it has been woefully understood and understudied.[3] Yet, from the perspective of U.S. foreign policy officials committed to creating a multilateral economy, the dollar gap posed a threat to the American way of life in the immediate postwar era that rivaled any threat posed by communism and the Soviet Union. Comprehending that threat, and the way it intersected with the Cold War, are central to the core objective of this study – understanding the origins of NSC 68.

WWII saved the United States from economic morass and turned the country into an economic powerhouse unmatched in the annals of human history. For the nations of Europe and Asia, however, the war had the opposite effect. Their countries were very nearly obliterated. Their cities lay in shambles, and their rural areas fared no better. Millions of their citizens were dead or maimed. Germany and Japan, the "workshops" of Europe and Asia, lay dormant. The great empires of Britain and France were shaken to their core, as colonized peoples began clamoring for freedom; whether they would survive intact remained to be seen. The Soviet Union, which experienced the brunt of the fighting against Nazi Germany, was "blown back to the stone age," as the saying goes. China had been ravaged by Japan and was again on the verge of falling into civil war. In essence, virtually the entire world outside of the western hemisphere had collapsed or was undergoing dramatic change. The result

gap. Watching *Cold War* would make one none the wiser where the dollar gap is concerned, even though an understanding of it is essential to understanding the origins of the Cold War. Jeremy Isaacs, *Cold War*, Episode III, *The Marshall Plan: 1947–1952* (Atlanta, Georgia: Cable News Network, 1998).

[3] Works that discuss the dollar gap include: Richard N. Gardner, *Sterling-Dollar Diplomacy: Anglo-American Collaboration in the Reconstruction of Multilateral Trade* (New York: Oxford University Press, 1956); Gabriel Kolko and Joyce Kolko, *The Limits of Power: The World and United States Foreign Policy, 1945–1954* (New York: Harper and Row, 1972); Richard Freeland, *The Truman Doctrine and the Origins of McCarthyism: Foreign Policy, Domestic Politics, and Internal Security, 1946–1948* (New York; Schocken Books, 1974); Fred L. Block, *The Origins of International Economic Disorder: A Study of United States International Monetary Policy from World War II to the Present* (Berkeley, California: University of California Press, 1977); Fred L. Block, "Economic Instability and Military Strength: The Paradoxes of the 1950 Rearmament Decision," *Politics and Society* 10: 1 (1980): 35–58; Borden, *The Pacific Alliance*; Andrew J. Rotter, *The Path to Vietnam: Origins of the American Commitment to Southeast Asia* (Ithaca, New York: Cornell University Press, 1987); Melvyn Leffler, *A Preponderance of Power: National Security, the Truman Administration, and the Cold War* (Stanford, California: Stanford University Press, 1992); Thomas McCormick, *America's Half-Century: United States Foreign Policy in the Cold War and After* (Baltimore, Maryland: The Johns Hopkins University Press, 1995), 2nd edition.

Multilateralism, the Dollar Gap, and the Origins

was the emergence of a massive balance-of-payments crisis between the United States and most of the world, a crisis that came to be called the dollar gap.

The dollar gap referred to the fact that in the postwar era the demand for U.S. exports far exceeded the world's capacity to pay for those exports. It had first emerged in the interwar period, principally with Europe, when the United States moved from being a debtor to a creditor nation, as a result of the loans it provided to the Associated Powers during WWI, even as it retained a large export surplus. Being a creditor nation meant that the United States invested more abroad than all countries combined invested in it, such that its net balance on investments was positive; possessing an export surplus meant that the United States exported more than it imported, providing a positive balance on trade. However, this situation was unusual because a creditor nation usually would be expected to import more than it exported as a means of offsetting the imbalance of its investments as a way of ensuring an overall balance of payments among nations, as Britain had done in the nineteenth century. What this unique circumstance meant for Europe is that after WWI, Europe found itself both in debt to the United States *and* running a trade deficit with it, such that its ability to earn dollars was seriously compromised. Exacerbating matters, the U.S. Congress saw fit to increase import duties under the Fordney-McCumber Tariff of 1922, thus making it more difficult for Europe to penetrate the already virtually impenetrable U.S. market. It would do the same in the 1930s during the Great Depression with the Smoot-Hawley Tariff, the largest tariff in U.S. history up to that time.

Prior to the onset of the Great Depression, the dollar gap was closed through (1) U.S. private foreign investments and loans (especially the Dawes and Young plans, which gave loans to Germany that it then used to pay reparations to Britain and France who, in turn, used those dollars to purchase U.S. exports); (2) triangular trade (whereby dollars earned by Latin America and European colonies in Asia from U.S. raw material purchases would be used to purchase manufactured goods from Europe, thereby providing Europe dollars to purchase U.S. goods); and (3) so-called invisible transactions such as shipping, tourism, and overseas investments (they were "invisible" because they could be neither predicted nor tracked with any certainty but did add dollars to the European purse). However, this way of covering the dollar gap only survived as long as the global economy and U.S. economic

NSC 68 and the Political Economy of the Early Cold War

power survived. The Great Depression brought the whole enterprise crashing down.[4]

As a result, during the 1930s the dollar gap effectively disappeared as nations across the globe turned their backs on multilateralism and pursued policies of economic nationalism – bilateral trade arrangements, high tariffs, quotas, currency inconvertibility, trade restrictions, import substitution, and bartering – to ensure their livelihoods. The British Imperial Preference system, Nazi Germany's "thousand-year" Reich, Japan's Greater East Asian Co-Prosperity Sphere, the Soviet Union's policy of "socialism in one country," and, to a lesser extent, the United States' New Deal, were all reflections of this move. By 1933, world trade had dropped 40 percent. Although the United States sought to keep multilateralism afloat through creation of the Export-Import Bank and the Reciprocal Trade Agreements Act, both of 1934, it took WWII to put the United States in a position to try to reestablish multilateralism as the guiding principle in world trade, a position only achieved through the blood, sweat, and tears of war.[5]

The problem at the end of the war was that the dollar gap still existed, exacerbated now by wartime destruction, but all of the earlier mechanisms for closing it had been destroyed. The loans had dried up with the onset of the Great Depression, and private foreign investment was slow to materialize in the aftermath of the war as would-be investors proved unwilling to risk their capital in unstable regions. Triangular trade also came crashing down. In Asia, it first had been blocked by Japanese occupation of most European colonies during the war, and then by independence

[4] For the dollar gap in the 1920s, see Block, *The Origins of International Economic Disorder*, 17–22; Frederick C. Adams, *Economic Diplomacy: The Export-Import Bank and American Foreign Policy, 1934–1939* (Columbia, Missouri: University of Missouri Press, 1976), 1–41; Frank Costigliola, *Awkward Dominion: American Political, Economic, and Cultural Relations with Europe, 1919–1933* (Ithaca, New York: Cornell University Press, 1984), 140–166; Melvyn Leffler, *The Elusive Quest: America's Pursuit of European Stability and French Security, 1919–1933* (Chapel Hill, North Carolina: University of North Carolina Press, 1979), passim; Alfred E. Eckes, Jr., *A Search For Solvency: Bretton Woods and the International Monetary System, 1941–1971* (Austin, Texas: University of Texas Press, 1975), 6–15.

[5] On the move toward protectionism, see Block, *The Origins of International Economic Disorder*, 25–31; Eckes, *A Search for Solvency*, 15–31; Lloyd C. Gardner, *Economic Aspects of New Deal Diplomacy* (Madison, Wisconsin: University of Wisconsin Press, 1964), 3–24, passim; McCormick, *America's Half-Century*, 17–42; Patrick Hearden, *Roosevelt Confronts Hitler: America's Entry into World War II* (DeKalb, Illinois: Northern Illinois University Press, 1987. On the Export-Import Bank and the Reciprocal Trade Agreements Act, see Adams, *Economic Diplomacy*, passim.

Multilateralism, the Dollar Gap, and the Origins 63

movements in these colonies after the war. With regard to Latin America, the western Europeans were simply too broke to produce goods for sale in the region. In addition, to pay for the war, especially Britain, but other western European nations as well, had been forced to sell their foreign investments and to reduce their share of world shipping. For obvious reasons, tourism had virtually ceased and would not recover for many years. A further problem was that the United States had developed synthetic materials to replace raw ones unobtainable during the war, such as rubber, which the U.S. traditionally had purchased from European colonies in Asia, cutting off another source of dollars. Yet another problem was that in the aftermath of the war the demand for U.S. imports in Europe increased far above pre-war levels while European imports to the United States slowed to a trickle. Lastly, Europe's industries were largely destroyed, which made filling domestic production needs difficult enough without also having to concern themselves with production for exports to the dollar area. Thus, at the end of the war western Europe did not possess the means to earn the dollars that it needed to conduct trade with the United States. Its only other option was to dip into its gold and dollar reserves, which were finite and, therefore, not a solution to the dilemma.[6]

The dollar gap was not confined to western Europe. Japan also experienced a huge dollar gap with the United States, a problem that became critical once it was apparent that the Communists would be victorious in the Chinese civil war. With China potentially moving out of the global economy, U.S. officials determined that Japan would have to take its place as the "workshop" of Asia, the great producer and consumer that would be developed to serve as the engine of capitalism in the region. Suffering from low production levels and war destruction (like western Europe), Japan also had difficulty finding trading partners in traditional sectors. Its neighbors held great contempt for the Rising Sun Empire because of its wartime conduct and refused to trade. Given this reality, Japan had to rely on the United States for virtually all of its import and export trade. In the late 1940s, however, the United States found little need for Japanese products, which denied Japan the dollars needed to pay for U.S. imports. A huge dollar gap began to emerge, one that threatened to force Japan to

---

[6] Harlan B. Cleveland, "Dollar Shortage: Causes and Remedies," the Harry S. Truman Library, Independence, Missouri (hereafter Truman Library), 2. See also Kolko and Kolko, *The Limits of Power*, 56–90; Block, *The Origins of International Economic Disorder*, 82–86; Borden, *The Pacific Alliance*, 18–60; Rotter, *The Path to Vietnam*, 49–69; Leffler, *A Preponderance of Power*, 159–164, 314–317.

64 NSC 68 and the Political Economy of the Early Cold War

break its trade with the United States and look for other means to satisfy its economic needs.[7]

The dollar gap touched many areas of the globe as well. Although Europe and Japan were of greatest concern, many nations suffered from an inability to earn sufficient dollars to trade with the United States. In January 1949, the *New York Times* noted severe dollar gaps with the following countries and regions: the nations of Latin America, the Philippines, Egypt, Sweden, Israel, South Africa, and even Czechoslovakia and Poland, the latter of which continued vigorous trade with the West despite being within the Soviet bloc. The problem with these nations was less destruction and disruption caused by the war, although this was a factor, and more the fact that they had very little to offer the United States in the way of exports even as they wanted to purchase U.S. products that they could not procure elsewhere. Bringing these nations into the capitalist fold would become part of a larger U.S.-led agenda to "modernize" countries that were allegedly "backwards," leading to a host of problems that the United States is still contending with today.[8]

The enormity of the crisis can be seen in the numbers. For the period July 1, 1945, to June 30, 1949, the United States exported $67.4 billion worth of goods and services. For the same period it imported $35.3 billion worth of goods and services, leaving a balance-of-payments deficit of $32.1 billion. Of that $32.1 billion, more than 70 percent, or roughly $25.5 billion, was financed by U.S. government aid, that is, U.S. taxpayer dollars through such means as the United Nations Relief and Rehabilitation Administration and the Marshall Plan. This amount, in

---

[7] Borden, *The Pacific Alliance*, 61–143. "Post-ERP Prospects and Aid Programs," June 19, 1950, Office Files of Gordon Gray as Special Assistant to the President (hereinafter Gray Papers), Record Group 286, Records of the Agency for International Development (RG 286), Post-ERP Economic Projections, Box 9, Harry S. Truman Library, Independence, Missouri (hereinafter Truman Library).

[8] Thomas Conroy, "World's Basic Ills in Sharper Focus," January 4, 1950, *The New York Times*, 50; "Egypt a Big Buyer of U.S. Goods in '49," *The New York Times*, January 4, 1950, 77; "South Africa Hit by Dollar Famine," *The New York Times*, January 4, 1950, 72; "Philippines Turns To Hard Austerity," January 4, 1949, *The New York Times*, 75. For evidence that the dollar gap was a worldwide phenomenon, see "International Economic Policy," December 23, 1949, Walter Salant Papers, International Relations, 1950, Box 2, Truman Library. On Czechoslovakia and Poland specifically, see Address Delivered by Paul H. Nitze, Department of State, at the Naval War College on October 21, 1949, RG 59, Records of the Department of State, Records of the Policy Planning Staff, 1947–1953, Policy Planning Staff Members, Chronological File – Nitze, 3, National Archives II, College Park, Maryland (hereinafter NAII).

Multilateralism, the Dollar Gap, and the Origins

essence, represented the dollar "gap" because it was the amount above which nations, through their own capabilities, actually could pay to settle their balance of payments with the United States. The remaining $6.6 billion was paid for through these nations' gold reserves (which, as noted, were finite) and what meager exports they could sell to the United States, mostly luxury goods that had a small consumer base.[9] As these figures demonstrate, foreign trade was greatly important to the United States in the postwar era. Not only did the United States sell $67.4 billion in goods abroad for the period, helping to fuel prosperity at home, but faced with the potential loss of that trade and the consequences to the domestic economy that might accrue therefrom, it paid for a good portion of those exports itself. This situation places the dollar gap at the heart of the postwar history of the United States and, given the global role that the United States played in the postwar era, the world.[10]

The great problem that the dollar gap posed was this: If the dollar gap could not be closed at a level of international trade sufficient to maintain the high level of U.S. exports necessary for free market capitalism to function at home, then the open, global, capitalist economy Truman administration officials were determined to create in the postwar era had next to no chance of succeeding. Bereft of dollars or the means to earn them, the nations of the world eventually would have had no choice but to cease or greatly reduce their trade with the United States. They would have had to pursue either socialist economies based on, in Borden's phrasing, "planned state-to-state trading," or economic nationalist (autarchic) policies designed to promote self-sufficiency, much as in the 1930s.[11] It is important to stress that such moves would have been out of necessity, not choice, which is what made the dollar gap so dangerous. For the dollar gap reflected a structural imbalance in the global economy that, as U.S. officials were to find out, had no easy solution.

For U.S. foreign policy officials and other elites committed to multilateralism, the dollar gap was a wholly unexpected albatross that threatened to undermine, not only the free enterprise system at home and abroad, but

---

[9] "Statistical Survey of United States Government Postwar Foreign Aid," December 16, 1949, *Foreign Relations of the United States* (hereinafter *FRUS*), *1950* 1 (Washington, D.C.: U.S. Government Printing Office, 1977): 810–813.

[10] "International Economic Relations," December 30, 1946, Salant Papers, International Relations, 1946–1947, Box 2, Truman Library; "Foreign Aid and the United States Balance of Payments," May 29, 1951, ibid.

[11] Borden, *The Pacific Alliance*, 24.

66   *NSC 68 and the Political Economy of the Early Cold War*

their entire foreign policy agenda. As they viewed the matter, if the world could not purchase U.S. exports due to lack of dollars, the free enterprise system was doomed. Lacking export markets, the U.S. economy would most assuredly stagnate – repeating the 1930s. If the past was any indicator, social unrest was sure to follow. If the trend could not be reversed, greater state control of the economy undoubtedly would become necessary. What would happen then? For a variety of reasons, the New Deal had not sufficed in the 1930s to end the depression. Only world war had released the United States from its grip. If the United States found itself in a severe depression in the postwar era, as the isolation of the United States to the western hemisphere would certainly evoke, what then? Another New Deal or, perhaps, something far more socialistic? A garrison state led by a commander-in-chief with dictatorial powers? Either of these alternatives would spell the end of the free enterprise system that these officials were trying so desperately to maintain, and it was that outcome that they were determined to prevent at all costs.[12]

Nowhere were these sentiments more clearly expressed than in a speech President Truman delivered in March 1947 at Baylor University in Waco, Texas. The purpose of the speech was to push for U.S. participation in the International Trade Organization (ITO), which was to be the subject of meetings held in Geneva, Switzerland beginning the following April. To that end, the bulk of the speech was devoted to warning Americans against the perils of economic warfare, which, he averred, had lengthened the Great Depression and, he implied, had led to WWII (he stopped just sort of actually making that last claim). The speech was taken right out of the multilateralists' play book, touting as it did "free enterprise" as the trade system "most conducive to freedom," which "Americans value even more than peace," as opposed to "pattern[s] of trade," in which "decisions are made by governments." The world was in economic turmoil, not unlike after WWI, he argued, and the United States – "the economic giant of the world" – had to lead by pushing the world to "reduc[e] barriers

---

[12] See "Decline in US Economy Would Have Far Reaching Effects," *Current Economic Developments*, 1945–1972 (hereinafter CED), RG 59, 6–8, NAII; Paul Nitze, "A Program for Resolving the Balance of Payments Problem of the United States," Gray Papers, Working Papers; Executive Departments; Department of the Interior – General – Working Papers – Miscellaneous, Box 22, Department of State, Folder 2, esp. 4–5, Truman Library; John M. Leddy, Oral History, June 15, 1973, 66–67, Truman Library. See also R. Gardner, *Sterling-Dollar Diplomacy* (1956), 1–23; Michael J. Hogan, *Cross of Iron: Harry S. Truman and the Origins of the National Security State, 1945–1954* (New York: Cambridge University Press, 1998), 69–118, passim.

Multilateralism, the Dollar Gap, and the Origins

to trade." "We must not go through the thirties [*sic*] again," he implored with a solemnity that is apparent even in the written text of the speech.

It is in the middle of the speech that the dollar gap makes its appearance, although the president did not use the term. "The products of some countries are in great demand," he began, by which he principally meant the United States and Canada, which ran a trade surplus with Europe, although a meager one in comparison to the United States. "But buyers outside of their borders do not hold the money of these countries in quantities large enough to enable them to pay for the goods they want. And they find these moneys difficult to earn." As a result, he conjectured, they turn to restrictive trade practices – quotas, high tariffs, bilateral agreements, and the like – designed to discriminate against those countries for the simple reason that they lacked the currencies or the ability to obtain them that they would need to continue trading with those countries. Then, he said:

If this trend is not reversed, the Government of the United States will be under pressure, sooner or later, to use [restrictive trade] devices to fight for markets and raw materials. And if the Government were to yield to this pressure, it would shortly find itself in the business of allocating foreign goods among importers and foreign markets among exporters and telling every trader what he could buy or sell, and how much, and when, and where. This is precisely what we have been trying to get away from, as rapidly as possible, ever since the war. It is not the American way. It is not the way to peace.

As the president indicated, it is for this reason that the dollar gap was of such concern to the multilateralists. If it could not be overcome, state economic planning was certain to become a necessity in the United States itself.[13]

The issue, however, was more complicated even than Truman suggested. It was not that foreign markets in and of themselves would stop the downward trend toward state planning. Rather, according to these officials, markets capable of absorbing a *high level* of U.S. exports were needed. William Clayton, assistant secretary of state for economic affairs and part owner of Anderson, Clayton, Inc., the largest cotton-marketing firm in the world, made the point in 1945:

Today we are exporting $14 billion worth of goods a year. We simply can't afford after this war to let our trade drop off to the two or three billion figure it hit in 1932 during the depression.... Some of our best economists estimate that we will

---

[13] *Public Papers of the Presidents of the United States: Harry S. Truman, 1947* (Washington, D.C.: U.S. Government Printing Office, 1963), 168–171. This speech is significant not only for its content but because it shows that Truman understood clearly the problems posed by the dollar gap and that he shared the multilateralists' views on the necessity for overcoming it.

probably have to sell $10 billion worth of goods abroad if we want to have relatively high level employment and a national income in the neighborhood of $150 billion. In other words, we have got to export three times as much as we exported just before the war if we want to keep our industry running at somewhere near capacity.[14]

As Clayton's comments reflect, when U.S. leaders spoke of a dollar *gap*, they meant the amount of dollars nations were capable of earning, through imports to the United States or other means, *below* the minimum level of exports it was believed that the United States needed to maintain prosperity. In 1945, that level stood at $10 billion and in 1950 at $13 billion, at least according to the multilateralists. At then-current levels of world production, those figures were impossible to meet. At best, the rest of the world could sell the United States a mere $6 billion in imports, leaving a huge dollar gap. In this situation, the United States had only two choices: (1) it could settle for a lower level of global trade, a level that would effectively condemn the U.S. economy to stagnation and state planning; or (2) it could finance the gap. Of course, it chose the latter, primarily by implementing the Marshall Plan, the massive economic aid program instituted in 1948 to contend with the dollar gap.[15]

As it was, the only way the dollar gap was met in the period 1949–1950 was because of the Marshall Plan, which provided western Europe free U.S. exports, which it otherwise could not pay for, while western Europe set out to rebuild its shattered economy. As Paul Hoffman, head of the Economic Cooperation Administration (ECA), the U.S. side of the Marshall Plan's administrative apparatus, told the Senate Committee on Foreign Relations in September 1949:

There is only one restriction now on the amount of trade that Europe gives America, and that is the limit on the dollars they can earn or we will give them.

---

[14] Quoted in Block, *The Origins of International Economic Disorder*, 41.

[15] Cleveland, "Dollar Shortage"; First Meeting of the Study Group on Economic Policy, November 1, 1949, Gray Papers, Council on Foreign Relations – Study Group Reports, Box 6, 1, Truman Library; Consultation on Trade Arrangements with Great Britain, September 20, 1949, U.S. Senate, Committee on Foreign Relations, *Reviews of the World Situation, 1949–1950* (Washington, D.C.: U.S. Government Printing Office, 1974), 51–70, esp. 60; Testimonies of Paul Hoffman, Dean Acheson, and Averell Harriman, February 21–22, 1950, U.S. House, Committee on Foreign Affairs, *To Amend the Economic Cooperation Act of 1948* (Washington, DC: U.S. Government Printing Office, 1950); Fifth Meeting of the Study Group on Aid to Europe (hereinafter SGAE), May 18, 1949, Council on Foreign Relations (CFR), 30, Box 242, Public Policy Papers, Department of Rare Books and Special Collections, Princeton University Libraries, Princeton, New Jersey (hereinafter PUL).

Multilateralism, the Dollar Gap, and the Origins 69

The practical limit today is how many dollars we will give them.... The limit is not ... anything in the way of restrictions in these countries against American goods. That has no application at all to this present situation. The limit is the number of dollars practically that Congress wants to give them.[16]

Without the Marshall Plan, the dollar gap would have closed but not in a way that U.S. leaders committed to multilateralism found desirable. Left to run its natural course in a free market economy, trade would have balanced out at whatever level western Europe and other nations could afford. As Hoffman told the House Committee on Foreign Affairs in February 1950, "The task is not merely closing Europe's dollar gap at any level of trade. The gap could be closed tomorrow if exports from the dollar area to Europe were reduced to what Europe can now earn. That would call for a reduction in exports of more than $3,000,000,000. The effect of such a drastic reduction would obviously mean catastrophe for Europe and severe dislocation of our own economy."[17]

As this evidence bears out, the Marshall Plan was, therefore, at least in part, driven by the demands of the U.S. economy. A memorandum released from the White House on April 3, 1950, makes this point crystal clear. "The European Recovery Program [Marshall Plan] will come to an end at the close of 1952. The reduction and eventual termination of foreign assistance will create tremendous economic problems at home and abroad unless vigorous steps are taken both by us and foreign countries. If no off-setting measures are worked out, it may well be that United States exports will be sharply reduced, with serious repercussions on our domestic economy, and with equally serious effects on friendly areas of the world which are dependent on our goods."[18] Contrary to popular belief, the Marshall Plan was not solely a humanitarian relief effort nor was it aimed solely at preventing communism from taking over Europe. By 1949, it had become a U.S. aid program as much as a western European one.[19]

---

[16] Paul Hoffman testimony, U.S. Senate, *Reviews of the World Situation*, 60.

[17] Paul Hoffman testimony, February 21, 1950, *To Amend the Economic Cooperation Act of 1948*, 6.

[18] Anthony Leviero, "President Directs Gray to Formulate World Trade Drive," April 3, 1950, *The New York Times*, 3. The British made note of these comments as well. See Oliver Franks to Ernest Bevin, April 11, 1950, Foreign Office (FO), 371/86974, The National Archives, Kew, England, United Kingdom (hereinafter TNA).

[19] See "Effect of the European Recovery Program on the United States Economy in 1949," February 28, 1950, Salant Papers, International Relations, Box 2; "The Problem of the Dollar Gap," March 20, 1950, CED, 1–3; Testimonies of Hoffman, Acheson, and Harriman, February 21–22, 1950, *To Amend the Economic Cooperation Act of 1948*; Diebold, "European Recovery: The Next Two Years," May 2, 1950, Gray Papers,

NSC 68 and the Political Economy of the Early Cold War

However, from the perspective of U.S. foreign policy officials committed to multilateralism, the dollar gap was not solely an economic issue but had major political ramifications as well. Because the nations of the world were in desperate need of goods of all kinds, and because the United States was virtually the only nation capable of providing them, the United States garnered a degree of power and influence in the immediate postwar era that it otherwise would not have had.[20] Such power and influence, however, only existed so long as U.S. *economic* power remained dominant. If the dollar gap could not be overcome and the nations of the world turned away from multilateralism, for lack of dollars or the means to earn them, U.S. influence in the world would have been greatly weakened. A State Department briefing paper in the summer of 1949 made the point clearly:

> An almost certain result of even a modest decline in dollar availabilities would be the strengthening and perhaps entrenchment of restrictive and discriminatory trade and payments arrangements.... A business depression might reduce the willingness of Congress to provide funds for foreign lending. Many countries cannot hope to recover without the reconstruction and development programs.... These developments would play into Communist hands. Our international prestige and influence would undoubtedly suffer. Communist party membership and influence could be expected to increase, and moderate and liberal governments would have difficulty remaining in office. Many governments which have based their foreign policies largely on cooperation with the US would be weakened or overthrown. In their search for markets and supplies, other countries would look more sympathetically toward sales of goods of military as well as general economic significance to the Soviet bloc.[21]

What influence would the United States have had in the world if trade slowed to levels approaching those of the 1930s? If that decade is any indicator, the answer clearly is: not very much. The United States' economic power was central to its ability to lead the world in the direction the multilateralists wanted it to go. If that power had dwindled due to the demise of global trade, occasioned by an inability to find a solution for the dollar gap, nations that otherwise wanted to ally themselves with the United States would have surely, and in many respects without any other choice, turned their backs on the United States and its multilateral agenda. Once they had started down that path, it would have been very

---

Economic Cooperation Administration, Series of Policy Statements, Box 7, 4, Truman Library.

[20] R. Gardner, *Sterling-Dollar Diplomacy* (1956), 313–325.

[21] "Decline in US Economy Would Have Far Reaching Effects," July 25, 1949, CED, 7–8.

Multilateralism, the Dollar Gap, and the Origins

difficult to affect a reverse course. Thus, the dollar gap had the potential to undermine, not only the United States' foreign policy objectives as laid out by the multilateralists, but its new found role as a world power par excellence as well.[22]

It is important to stress that the problems posed by the dollar gap had no intrinsic relationship to the Soviet Union and, therefore, to the Cold War. Take the Soviet Union out of the picture and the dollar gap still would have existed. Of course, the Soviet Union cannot be taken out of the picture and, for that reason, it undoubtedly exacerbated an already volatile situation. Yet, it is worth noting that Truman administration officials made this claim when arguing before Congress about the seriousness of the dollar gap and that they also did so in NSC 68.[23] The fact of the matter is that the dollar gap and the difficulties it presented would have existed whether the Soviet Union did or not.[24] The reader should keep this point in mind as we turn to a brief examination of three of the most important foreign policy moves undertaken by the Truman administration in the immediate postwar era: the British loan of 1946, the Greco Turkish Aid Bill of 1947 (in the context of the Truman Doctrine), and the Marshall Plan inaugurated in 1948. First, however, it is necessary to call attention to the fact that, even as these developments took shape, Truman administration officials remained ambivalent about the threat posed by the Soviet Union, a not inconsequential point considering what, in fact, happened.

Ambivalence and Frustration in Making Sense of the Soviet Threat

At the end of WWII and well into 1946 few U.S. officials talked about the Soviet Union as a hostile nation determined to take over and communize the world. In 1945, Averell Harriman had referred to the Red Army's

[22] On these points, see "Notes on Discussion at PPS Meeting," May 20, 1949, RG 59, Records of the PPS, Minutes of Meetings, 1947–1952, Box 32, 2, NAII; "Foreign Effects of a U.S. Depression," July 1, 1949, Gray Papers, Working Papers, Executive Departments; Department of the Interior – General – Working Papers – Miscellaneous, Box 22, Folder 2, Truman Library; Frank Altschul, "America's New Economic Role," *Foreign Affairs* 31 (October 1952–July 1953): 393–404; and "Decline in US Economy Would Have Far Reaching Effects," CED, 6–8.

[23] See, for instance, the Acheson quote at the beginning of Chapter 2. NSC 68 also makes this observation twice. NSC 68, in Ernest May, ed., *American Cold War Strategy: Interpreting NSC 68* (New York: Bedford Books of St. Martin's Press, 1993), 41, 52.

[24] See, for instance, "Suggestions for Discussion with Gordon Gray," April 14, 1950, George Elsey Papers, Box 59, 2, Truman Library; "European Integration," November 11, 1949, RG 59, Records of the PPS, Country and Area Files: Europe, NAII.

advance into western Europe as a "barbarian invasion of Europe," but even he thought a deal still could be worked out with the Soviets.[25] Harriman's views eventually caught the ear of Secretary of the Navy James Forrestal, who would go on to become one of the most virulent, and most paranoid, anti-communists in the U.S. government. However, except for Forrestal and a few others, the notion that the Soviets harbored some plan for world domination, or even domination of Europe, was not the common perception.[26]

In fact, initial U.S. policy toward the Soviet Union was fraught with ambiguity and frustration. Although Truman allegedly got tough with Soviet Foreign Minister Vyacheslav Molotov when he first met him in April 1945,[27] in the months after he waffled considerably. In late May he dispatched Harry Hopkins, Franklin Delano Roosevelt's trusted friend and personal envoy, to meet with Stalin and smooth things over. In early July he recognized the reorganized Polish government on the basis of the Soviet understanding of the Yalta Accords, subject to free elections to be held at an unspecified date. He also expressed great satisfaction that the success of the atomic bomb test carried out on July 16, 1945, in New Mexico meant that the United States no longer needed the Soviets to enter the war against Japan. At times, as Melvyn Leffler has noted, he worried that the Soviets had expansionist goals in the Near and Far East. However, he also told Henry Wallace that the Soviets had legitimate security concerns along its borders and that he was committed to cooperating with them. Yet, Truman was outraged when Secretary of State James Byrnes worked out a compromise with the Soviets on the governments of Bulgaria and Rumania at the Moscow meeting of the Council of Foreign Ministers (CFM) held in December 1945 and set up to work out peace treaties with the former Nazi satellite states, a compromise that quite possibly could have seen Soviet troop withdrawals from the Balkans and perhaps all of

---

[25] Lloyd C. Gardner, *Spheres of Influence: The Great Powers Partition Europe, From Munich to Yalta* (New York: Ivan Dee Publishers, 1993), 255.

[26] Leffler, *A Preponderance of Power*, 46. Leffler maintains that such prominent figures as Eisenhower, Marshall, and Clay, not to mention Truman himself, disagreed with alarmists such as Forrestal.

[27] The well-known story that Truman gave Molotov a dressing down has now been called into question. The source for the story is Truman's own memoirs, but neither the American nor Soviet record of the talks record the exchange. Furthermore, the records suggest that the meeting ended in an amicable interchange. See Geoffrey Robert's *Stalin's Wars: From World War to Cold War, 1939–1953* (New Haven, Connecticut: Yale University Press, 2006), 268–269; and Geoffrey Roberts, "Sexing up the Cold War: New Evidence on the Molotov-Truman Talks of April 1945," *Cold War History* 4: 3 (April 2004): 105–125.

eastern Europe. Although Byrnes remained secretary of state for another year, his influence on the president waned.

On February 9, 1946, Stalin delivered a so-called election speech, in which he seemed to suggest that war between the capitalist and communist worlds was likely inevitable. Some U.S. officials viewed the speech as nothing less than a declaration of World War III. Not Truman, however. He viewed the speech as harmless, as, indeed, a careful reading of it bears out. Furthermore, in March 1946 former British Prime Minister Winston Churchill delivered his famed "iron curtain" speech at Fulton, Missouri, with Truman sitting at center stage. Truman had read the speech beforehand and expressed his wholehearted support for its contents. When the press began to demure, however, Truman back peddled and tried to distance himself from it, lest he be seen as inimical to cooperation with the Soviets. He did the same in September 1946 when his Secretary of Commerce Henry Wallace, a leading voice of the progressive internationalists, approached him about a speech he was to deliver at Madison Square Garden in New York City reproaching the way that U.S. policy toward the Soviets was developing. Wallace supported cooperation with the Soviets in the interest of international peace. According to Wallace, Truman spent over an hour discussing the speech with him, at one point exclaiming that it perfectly captured U.S. foreign policy goals. When the speech began to be criticized by others in the administration, however, Truman did an about-face and said he had not read it and had approved it hastily. Wallace was subsequently fired. Truman's ambivalent attitude toward the Soviets, shared by many other influential leaders, was characteristic of the U.S. position throughout the early stages of what became the Cold War.

If there was ambivalence, however, there was also frustration. The frustration stemmed from the simple fact that the Soviet Union was unwilling to kowtow to the demands of the United States as defined by the multilateralists in the Truman administration. The multilateralists believed that the war had provided the United States with a mandate to assume the mantle of world leadership and end the cycle of depression and war that had brought so much hardship in the past. It was not turning out that way, however. The Soviet Union apparently had not received word of the mandate. Yet, as their inability to force the Soviets' hand in eastern Europe and elsewhere showed, they were really helpless to do anything about it but protest. They had assumed U.S. power and good intentions would be enough to rule the day. Their assessment, however, was wrong. Stalin was not playing ball, but neither was he

74   *NSC 68 and the Political Economy of the Early Cold War*

breaking the Yalta Accords. Nor was he impressed by either "atomic" or "dollar" diplomacy, at least not into giving up his security zone.[28]

Part of the frustration was relieved by George Kennan, minister-counselor to the U.S. embassy in Moscow. In early 1946, Kennan was asked to write a memorandum on his views of the Soviet Union's postwar behavior. A career diplomat who had risen through the ranks of the diplomatic corps following in his father's footsteps, Kennan was not a foreign policy elite along the order of Averell Harriman or Dean Acheson, who made their way into government via the private sector. Because of this background, most historians agree that Kennan considered himself an outsider and felt that his talents were insufficiently recognized and underappreciated, which caused him a great deal of anguish. Apparently, he was on the verge of resigning his position when he was asked to provide the assessment of Soviet behavior that would ensure his place in history. It is likely that he viewed the request as his swan song, which might account for its length and verbosity (it came in at 8,000 words and subsequently became known as the "Long Telegram").[29] Kennan described the Soviet Union as a nation driven both by concerns for its security and its determination to expand communism as the vanguard of the communist movement. He argued that it was pointless to try to negotiate with Soviet leaders as they were incapable of compromise. Nonetheless, he insisted that the Soviet Union was relatively weak and would respond to force. Thus, the United States needed to keep a careful eye on Soviet actions and respond with a show of power wherever and whenever the USSR sought to expand.[30] Kennan's policy recommendation came to be known

[28] See Roberts, *Stalin's Wars*, 267–279, 290–293, 305–312, 313–314, 328–329, 352–354; Leffler, *A Preponderance of Power*, 30–40, 44–54, 103, 107–110, 138–140; Daniel Yergin, *Shattered Peace: The Origins of the Cold War and the National Security State* (New York: Houghton-Mifflin, 1977), 80–81, 93, 101–104, 115, 147–152, 166–167, 174–177, 249–256; John Lewis Gaddis, *The United States and the Origins of the Cold War, 1941–1947* (New York: Columbia University Press, 1972), 198–315; Kolko and Kolko, *The Limits of Power*, 40–42, 53–57; Wilson Miscamble, *From Roosevelt to Truman: Potsdam, Hiroshima, and the Cold War* (New York: Cambridge University Press, 2007), 114–115, 143–148, 197–202, 251–254, 270–276, 278–287, 299–301; Lloyd C. Gardner, *The Origins of the Cold War* (Waltham, Massachusetts: Ginn-Balisdell, 1970), 1–44; Alonzo Hamby, *Beyond the New Deal: Harry S. Truman and American Liberalism* (New York: Columbia University Press, 1973), 102–106, 113–119, 127–133.

[29] I am using Leffler's figure here. Some say it came in at far less. See Fabian Hilfrich, "George Kennan," in Ruud van Dijk, ed., *Encyclopedia of the Cold War, Volume 2* (New York: Routledge, 2008), 487. Hilfrich says it came in at 5,300 words.

[30] Leffler, *A Preponderance of Power*, 108–109; John Lewis Gaddis, *Strategies of Containment: A Critical Appraisal of Postwar American National Security Policy* (New York: Oxford University Press, 1982), 25–53; Yergin, *Shattered Peace*, 168–171.

Multilateralism, the Dollar Gap, and the Origins

as "containment," and it was quickly adopted by the multilateralists as their answer to the Soviet conundrum. Containment had existed before Kennan wrote his famed telegram, to be sure, but it was he who articulated the policy in a concrete and discernible way. As Melvyn Leffler writes, "Kennan's analysis was appealing because it provided a unifying theme to U.S. foreign policy. Kennan urged policymakers to view Soviet Russia as their enemy and to approach all other issues from the viewpoint of competition with the Kremlin."[31]

As some saw it, however, Kennan's analysis was deeply flawed. In July 1947, *Foreign Affairs*, the Council on Foreign Relations' organ of record, published a shortened version of the Long Telegram under the authorship of a "Mr. X" titled "The Sources of Soviet Conduct," although the real author – Kennan – was quickly acknowledged as such. Shortly thereafter, Walter Lippman, the esteemed journalist and social commentator, attacked the containment idea as ineffectual. It essentially put U.S. foreign policy in Soviet hands, he argued, because that country could then dictate when and where the United States needed to engage. Plus, it committed the United States to an impossible extension of its power. It was an inane conception, in Lippman's estimation.[32] Apparently, Kennan was taken aback by Lippman's attack, even admitting that the criticisms were essentially valid, although he believed his policy had been misunderstood. Kennan had argued that the Soviet Union was inherently expansionist and that there was no use in trying to negotiate with it. But he had also argued that the Soviet Union was weak and would remain so, and that all the United States had to do was show resolve and the Soviet Union could be contained "easily." What happened, however, was that U.S. officials latched on to the first aspect of Kennan's theory and not the second. They chose to make the Soviets into giants, whereas Kennan saw them as proverbial bullies on the school yard who, once stood up to, would retreat. Consequently, Kennan disowned what became containment even as the multilateralists, and just about everybody else, came to embrace it. Hence, although "containment" became official U.S. policy in 1946, it would be mistaken to argue that it reflected reality.[33]

[31] Leffler, *A Preponderance of Power*, 108.
[32] Mr. X, "The Sources of Soviet Conduct," *Foreign Affairs* 25: 4 (July, 1947): 566–582; Walter Lippman, *The Cold War: A Study in U.S. Foreign Policy* (New York: Harper, 1947).
[33] George Kennan, *Memoirs, 1925–1950* (New York: Bantam, 1967), 373–387; Williams Appleman Williams, *America Confronts a Revolutionary World, 1776–1976* (New York: William Morrow, 1976), 175–177.

76   NSC 68 and the Political Economy of the Early Cold War

In addition to Kennan's prognosis in the summer of 1946, the Clifford-Elsey report appeared. Instigated by a frustrated Truman, who had discovered that American power was not omnipotent in light of a Soviet Union determined to call its own shots, the report was another attempt, similar to the Long Telegram, by the U.S. government to assess the Soviet Union's behavior. The report described the Soviet Union in the darkest of terms. The Soviet Union was trying to conquer the world. Its war preparations had not ceased after the war and were continuing apace. It was building an alliance with the Chinese Communists, penetrating the Middle East, and even making inroads into South America. If the United States did not act decisively, the report argued, it would shortly find itself encircled by Communist states. Written primarily by Clark Clifford and George Elsey, it received suggestions and backing from the State, War, and Navy departments, the Central Intelligence Group (the Central Intelligence Agency had not yet been created), the Joint Chiefs of Staff (JCS) and the U.S. Attorney General, which is to say it had high-level backing.[34]

However, the Clifford-Elsey report, for all of its dark imagery and dire predictions, was ridiculous on its face. Here is how one of the foremost students of the Truman administration's foreign policy describes it:

Clifford and Elsey ignored actions that might have injected hues of gray into their black-and-white characterization of Soviet foreign policy. They neglected to mention that the Kremlin made no objection to the entry of U.S. troops in South Korea, pretty much accepted American domination of postwar Japan, and only feebly protested the American military presence in northern China. They were uninterested in the fact that Soviet armies had withdrawn from Manchuria and that there was scant evidence of any ongoing Soviet assistance to the CCP [Chinese Communist Party]. They overlooked the free elections that were held in Hungary and Czechoslovakia and the relatively representative governments that were established in Austria and Finland. They disregarded the intelligence reports detailing the partial withdrawal of Soviet armies from occupied areas, the large-scale demobilization of Russian troops within the Soviet Union, and the departure of Russian forces from northern Norway and from Bornholm. They failed to acknowledge that Stalin discouraged insurrectionary activity in Europe, offered no leadership to Communist revolutionaries in Southeast Asia, failed to exploit opportunities in Arab lands, and straddled sides between the Nationalists and the Communists in China.

In addition, they "presented a totally misleading rendition of Soviet capabilities." And, finally, the report was replete with "double standards and

---

[34] The full report is in Arthur Krock, *Memoirs: Sixty Years on the Firing Line* (New York: Funk and Wagnalls, 1968), 417–482. See also Leffler, *A Preponderance of Power*, 130–138.

Multilateralism, the Dollar Gap, and the Origins

self-deception." After reading it, Truman ordered it held "under lock and key" for fear it would leak out and destroy any attempt to work with the Soviets. More importantly, he did not act on its recommendations, except insofar as they merely restated already existing plans.[35]

As these points demonstrate, well into 1946 there was great uncertainty about the exact nature of the Soviet threat among U.S. officials, coupled with frustration about their own impotency in dealing with the Soviets. This outlook reflected the reality that the Soviets were not being particularly hostile, except insofar as they would not simply bow to U.S. demands. Yet, in short order a new conception of the Soviet Union would begin to emerge, one that painted it as a power determined to take over the world, which left the United States with no choice but to respond – hence, the Cold War. What needs explaining is why this new conception emerged. It is here that the dollar gap and the Soviet threat begin to intersect.

The Dollar Gap, the Soviet Threat, and the Origins of the Cold War

The British Loan of 1946

United States efforts to establish a postwar, multilateral world economy began in earnest in 1941 when the United States demanded that Britain agree to multilateral principles in clause four of the Atlantic Charter agreement, much to the consternation of Winston Churchill. Churchill managed to weaken the commitment by inserting the well-known caveat "with regards to existing obligations," which effectively safeguarded Imperial Preference, the autarchic bloc set up in 1931 to counter the effects of the global depression, for the time being. Furthermore, during WWII the United States used the Lend-Lease program, created to supply Britain with war material and other goods in its effort to stave off the German assault, to "manipulate" Britain's dollar reserves in its favor as a means to counteract British autarchy in the postwar era. The effort to bring Britain around to multilateralism was furthered in 1944 with the Bretton Woods Agreement, which established the International Monetary Fund (IMF) and the International Bank for Reconstruction and Development (the World Bank). Britain, both the United States' strongest ally and toughest competitor, reluctantly agreed to dismantle Imperial Preference at Bretton Woods once the war was over and recovery had begun. However, no enforcement mechanism was established, a fact

---

[35] Leffler, *A Preponderance of Power*, 132–133; David McCullough, *Truman* (New York: Simon and Schuster, 1992), 543–545.

78 NSC 68 and the Political Economy of the Early Cold War

that dismayed the multilateralists in the State Department, who wanted Britain to adopt multilateralism at once. Although there is no reason to believe that the abrupt termination of Lend-Lease once the war ended was other than, as Truman would later say, a mistake, it set the stage for the British loan of 1946.[36]

The British had hoped that Lend-Lease would continue after the war and were shocked that the United States ended it so quickly (as were the Soviets). Bereft of other means for obtaining the dollars they needed to purchase badly needed U.S. goods (the IMF and the World Bank were not yet operational), the British asked for a loan. Their request was for $6 billion. U.S. officials balked at that amount as politically unfeasible but agreed to a $3.75 billion loan. The intent of the loan was to allow Britain to continue purchasing vital imports from the United States while it rebuilt its shattered nation and empire. In exchange, the British agreed to dismantle a key component of Imperial Preference – currency inconvertibility – effective one year from the date of the signing of the loan agreement, which, as it turned out, was July 15, 1947. In this regard, the loan was a boon for the multilateralists as it forced Britain to begin adopting multilateral principles far sooner than Bretton Woods called for. [37]

Truman administration officials were anxious to aid the British because without Britain on board multilateralism had little chance of succeeding. Though badly shaken by both world wars, Britain remained a formidable force in world affairs. It held great political, strategic, and economic influence over vast regions of the globe – India, Malaysia, Canada, much of the Middle East, Hong Kong, Argentina, Egypt, the Sudan, South Africa, and Australia. The British pound sterling was still the world's most used currency. If Britain opted out and continued its autarchic ways, many of these countries would have no choice but to follow suit. In addition, Britain and the Commonwealth bought more goods from the United States than any other region of the world outside of the western hemisphere, making Britain's ability to continue purchasing U.S. exports crucial to the success

---

[36] Block, *The Origins of International Economic Disorder*, 32–69; R. Gardner, *Sterling-Dollar Diplomacy: The Origins and Prospects of Our International Economic Order* (New York: McGraw-Hill, 1969), 257–268. On Truman, see Dean Acheson, *Present at the Creation: My Years in the State Department* (New York: W. W. Norton, 1969), 122.

[37] R. Gardner, *Sterling-Dollar Diplomacy* (1956), 180–224; Walter Isaacson and Evan Thomas, *The Wise Men: Six Friends and the World They Made, Acheson, Bohlen, Harriman, Kennan, Lovett, and McCloy* (New York: Simon and Schuster, 1986), 362–365.

Multilateralism, the Dollar Gap, and the Origins

of the United States' domestic economic needs. Simply put, if Britain refused or was incapable of going along with multilateralism, the policy was doomed.[38]

Britain wanted the loan because it did not have the machines, raw materials, and food stuffs necessary to provide its citizens with a decent standard of living or to maintain its operations with the empire. Although British officials were very reluctant to sign away Imperial Preference in return for the loan, they clearly felt that they had little choice. As Chancellor of the Exchequer Hugh Dalton noted, without the loan "we should have to undergo greater hardships and privations *than even during the war*; and all those hopes of better times, to follow in the wake of victory, would be dissipated in despair and disillusion."[39]

The U.S. Congress was another matter altogether. Congress did not favor the idea of economic aid for the British "empire." It had not forgotten how during the Great Depression the British Imperial Preference system, according to many of its members, had robbed Americans of access to the vast sterling area, thereby perpetuating the depression in the United States. As a result, Congress stonewalled on passing the loan, which led to the first of the great *domestic* crises that would challenge U.S. officials in their pursuit of a multilateral world. The Truman administration had hoped to get the British loan approved by March 1946, but by May Congress still had not acted. However, what in 1956 historian Richard Gardner called the "new factor in American policy" came to the rescue at just the right moment.[40]

Initially, top-level foreign policy officials in the Truman administration told the truth in their support of the loan, which is to say that they tied it to the need to create a multilateral world economy. For instance, as Secretary of State James Byrnes said, "If we fail to make this loan, Britain will be forced to do business by barter with a bloc of nations. These nations will be forced to do business with Britain in preference to other nations, which means dividing the world into economic blocs, thereby endangering the peace of the world." Secretary of the Treasury Fred Vinson argued, "Two rival blocs [American and British] would mean economic warfare ... world trade would be destroyed.... We would find our trade decreased, and our people unemployed. England would find her

---

[38] "Essential Elements of US–UK Relations," April 19, 1950, *FRUS, 1950* 3 (Washington, D.C.: U.S. Government Printing Office, 1977): 870.

[39] Quoted in R. Gardner, *Sterling-Dollar Diplomacy* (1956), 232, emphasis added.

[40] R. Gardner, *Sterling-Dollar Diplomacy* (1956), 248.

80   *NSC 68 and the Political Economy of the Early Cold War*

standard of living deteriorated and impoverished. . . . The consequences to world prosperity and to world peace would be disastrous."[41] Congress, however, was not buying the argument. Congress had been led to believe that Bretton Woods would provide the economic means to rebuild the world economy. Now it was being asked to give a loan outside of the Bretton Woods institution. In addition, many congressmen felt that the generous Lend-Lease settlement, which forgave Britain's $20 billion wartime debt, was enough of a giveaway. Key congressmen wondered what sort of precedent the British loan was setting. What assurances were there that the loan would work? How was Congress to be certain that the administration would not be before it in another week, month, or year asking for more? Under such criticisms, approval for the loan stagnated.[42]

It was in this context that the British loan suddenly and dramatically became crucial to preventing communism from rolling over Britain. Senator Arthur Vandenberg, one of the few Republican senators support-ive of the administration's foreign economic goals, did not mention the Soviet Union in his sudden plea for the loan, but he left little doubt as to his reference. Taking the floor, he argued, "If we do not lead some other great and powerful nation will capitalize [on] our failure and we shall pay the price of our default." In the House, witness Charles S. Dewey, a Republican banker, asked for passage of the loan on the grounds that "certain conditions exist in the world today which we did not foresee when the war terminated. . . . This loan, to me, will be the means, and probably the last chance we have, of bringing back to our side very will-ing nations who might, due to force of circumstances and difficulties, slip under the general influence of the Russian ideology of government."[43] Speaker of the House Sam Rayburn, one of the last to speak on the floor of the House after a sixteen-hour debate over the loan, chimed in, telling his colleagues, "I do not want Western Europe, England, and all the rest pushed toward an ideology that I despise. I fear if we do not cooperate with our great natural ally that is what will happen."[44] Under these per-suasive arguments, *and only under them*, the loan to Britain passed and an important lesson was learned – Congress tended to be resistant to

---

[41] Quoted in R. Gardner, ibid., 242–243.
[42] R. Gardner, *Sterling-Dollar Diplomacy* (1956), 236–248; Freeland, *The Truman Doctrine and the Origins of McCarthyism*, 62–69.
[43] Quoted in R. Gardner, *Sterling-Dollar Diplomacy* (1956), 250.
[44] John Crider, "Nonpartisan Vote," *The New York Times*, July 14, 1946, 1.

Multilateralism, the Dollar Gap, and the Origins 81

foreign economic aid but was willing to fund programs in the name of fighting communism.[45]

The rub is that Britain was the last nation in Europe that faced a communist takeover. The Communist Party in Britain was virtually nonexistent. The British people were not disposed to communism and would not have been even without the loan. The real threat was autarchy, not communism.

The Greco-Turkish Aid Bill of 1947

Although the need for the British loan was an indication that the transition to multilateralism would not be smooth, it was not until early 1947 that what came to be known as the dollar gap first arose as a distinct problem. Not surprisingly, the problem began with Great Britain. The loan to Britain was supposed to smooth the initial transition from a depression-wartime economy based on autarchic policies to a multilateral one. The loan proved inadequate; it was supposed to last four years, but Britain blew through it in six months. Devastated by the war, Britain was unable to generate enough production to get out of its quagmire, even with the new assistance. Along with the rest of Europe, Britain's position deteriorated rapidly during the particularly harsh winter of 1946–1947, which created both a significant drain on the loan and the potential that Britain would have to dip into its gold and dollar reserves to continue purchasing U.S. exports.[46]

Attempting to head off the worst, in February 1947 Britain informed the United States that it no longer could afford to provide aid to Greece and Turkey. By jettisoning the $400-million-a-year obligation, the British could relieve the immediate drain. Greece was then in the midst of a civil war between communist rebels and the British-backed Monarchist Party. Turkey, although relatively stable by Western terms, nonetheless was feeling pressure from the Soviet Union to allow it access to the Dardanelles Straits, a historic Russian demand. When British officials notified U.S. officials that it would stop aid to Greece and Turkey effective April 1, 1947, they expected that the United States would desire to hold on to these areas as much as they did. The two nations stood at the gateway

---

[45] R. Gardner, *Sterling-Dollar Diplomacy* (1956), 248–253; Freeland, *The Truman Doctrine and the Origins of McCarthyism*, 47–69.

[46] R. Gardner, *Sterling-Dollar Diplomacy* (1956), 306–347; Freeland, *The Truman Doctrine and the Origins of McCarthyism*, 70–81.

82   *NSC 68 and the Political Economy of the Early Cold War*

to the oil of the Middle East, which both the Americans and British had come to see as key to world economic recovery in general as well as of strategic importance. What is less understood is that Britain's dollar gap led to this situation, which shows the significant role that the dollar gap played in one of the key events in the origins of the Cold War – the pronouncement of the Truman Doctrine.[47]

In attempting to secure aid for Greece and Turkey, the great obstacle, once again, proved to be Congress – whose job it was to appropriate the funds – and, by extension, the American people. Both of these bodies had been led to believe that the British loan would be the last offer of foreign economic aid needed to spur recovery. The newly elected majority Republican Congress of 1946 had campaigned on cutting taxes, not raising them. Such dislike for high taxes translated into dislike for foreign aid, which they felt only brought undue competition on U.S. exporters.[48]

As with the British loan, when U.S. officials approached Congress with their request they initially told the truth. In a February 27 meeting at the White House among congressional leaders, President Truman, Secretary of State George C. Marshall, and Undersecretary of State Dean Acheson, Marshall explained that aid to Greece and Turkey was necessary for humanitarian reasons and to help the British. Congressional leaders did not like what they were hearing. "Isn't this pulling British chestnuts out of the fire?" they asked; and, "how much is it going to cost?" Acheson, sensing things were not going well, asked if he could jump into the "fight." Then, in words that would essentially become doctrine to U.S. foreign policymakers for years to come, Acheson postulated that if the United States did not step in now to "contain" the communist threat in Greece "like apples in a barrel infected by one rotten one, the corruption of Greece would infect Iran and all to the east. It would also carry infection to Africa through Asia Minor and Egypt, and to Europe through Italy and France, already threatened by the strongest domestic Communist parties in Western Europe." Communism would spread over the whole globe, Acheson warned, unless the United States took a decisive stand in Greece and Turkey. With that, congressional leaders changed their attitude dramatically. A deafening silence fell over the room. Then, Senator Arthur Vandenberg turned to the president and

---

[47] R. Gardner, *Sterling-Dollar Diplomacy* (1956), 306–347; Freeland, *The Truman Doctrine and the Origins of McCarthyism*, 82–87.

[48] R. Gardner, *Sterling-Dollar Diplomacy* (1956), 236–253; Freeland; *The Truman Doctrine and the Origins of McCarthyism*, 94–96.

Multilateralism, the Dollar Gap, and the Origins 83

said: "Mr. President, if you will say that to the Congress and the country, I will support you and I believe that most of its members will do the same."[49] Days later, President Truman delivered his famous Truman Doctrine speech, in which he divided the world between "'free peoples' and governments that relied on 'terror and oppression,'" and in the process committed the United States to checking communism wherever it reared its ugly head.

Yet, the truth of the matter is that the Greek civil war had nothing to do with a Soviet-led Communist advance. Stalin turned his back on the Greek Communists in keeping with the October 1944 agreement, which he had worked out with Churchill and had solidified at Yalta, over spheres of influence in eastern Europe. Though publicly fostering the notion of a Soviet advance in Greece, U.S. officials, Leffler writes, believed that "right-wing officials bore substantial responsibility for the turmoil in Greece. The government had failed to foster economic recovery. Instead it tried to suppress the Communist party, discredit all its opponents, and conduct a plebiscite on whether or not to retain the monarchy." "There was," Leffler informs us, "little evidence that the Soviets were fomenting trouble." Nonetheless, the Truman administration, including President Truman himself, used the rhetoric of Soviet expansion to push its agenda. Not about to appear soft on communism, Congress, as with the British loan, okayed the funds.[50]

On the heels of the Greco-Turkish aid bill, Britain went ahead with its pledge to suspend nonconvertibility of sterling on July 15, 1947. The move was a disaster. Free to exchange their sterling holdings into dollars without first having to obtain London's approval, the nations of Europe and the Commonwealth revealed their distrust of sterling and began exchanging it at a faster-than-expected rate. Two weeks later Britain called a halt to convertibility. The economic, not to mention psychological, impact of this brief, failed experiment with multilateralism was devastating to the British. Never again would Britain place multilateralism above imperial concerns, a fact that would be all too clear when the British sterling-dollar crisis of 1949–1950 erupted.[51]

The two crises of 1947 effectively ended Great Britain's role as a major world power. When first informed of Britain's inability to continue

---

[49] Acheson, *Present at the Creation*, 219.
[50] Freeland, *The Truman Doctrine and the Origins of McCarthyism*, 88–101, Truman quoted on 85; Leffler, *A Preponderance of Power*, 125–127, 142–144.
[51] R. Gardner, *Sterling-Dollar Diplomacy* (1956), 313–325.

84   NSC 68 and the Political Economy of the Early Cold War

supplying aid to Greece and Turkey, Acheson remarked, "there are only two powers in the world now," by which he meant the United States and the Soviet Union. By this, as historian Bruce Cumings observes, "Acheson did not mean that an era of bipolarity had dawned, although he meant that as well; he meant something much deeper – the substitution of American for British leadership." The period from February 1947 to July 1950, filtered through the Truman Doctrine, the Marshall Plan, North Atlantic Treaty Organization (NATO), and culminating with implementation of NSC 68, comprised the United States' search for the means to actualize the path to hegemony that the British decline had left open.[52]

The Marshall Plan of 1948

Britain's economic crises in 1947 and worsening conditions in western Europe brought home to U.S. officials that western Europe's economic problems in relation to the dollar area were much worse than initially thought. It was this recognition by U.S. leaders that saw the emergence of the United States' grand plan for overcoming the dollar gap – the Marshall Plan, named after former Army Chief of Staff during WWII and Secretary of State from late 1947 to early 1949 George Marshall, who initiated the program at a June 5, 1947, commencement address at Harvard. The creation of the Marshall Plan in the spring of 1948 represents how much the dollar gap had moved to center stage with the Truman administration. Paul Nitze, an investment banker who had entered government service during the war and who worked extensively on the Marshall Plan (and who was to become the primary author of NSC 68), thought that western Europe needed $8 billion immediately. The threat, he said, was not of a Soviet invasion but of economic collapse that would push western European nations toward socialism. The U.S. economy, he argued, would be greatly damaged and the capitalist system itself imperiled.[53]

U.S. officials were concerned that if Europe turned to socialism it could potentially be co-opted by the Soviet Union, but that concern was only one of the forces behind the Marshall Plan and not necessarily the most important. The problems that the Marshall Plan sought to overcome – economic

[52] Bruce Cumings, "The American Century and the Third World," *Diplomatic History* 23: 2 (Spring 1999): 360; McCormick, *America's Half-Century*, 72.
[53] Walter LaFeber, *The American Age: U.S. Foreign Policy at Home and Abroad, 1750 to the Present* (New York: W. W. Norton, 1994), 2nd edition, 479.

Multilateralism, the Dollar Gap, and the Origins 85

destitution, low productivity, and the dollar gap – would have existed whether the Soviet Union did or not and, therefore, would have been in need of remedy if a multilateral world were to take shape. The presence of the Soviets mattered little in this situation. To be sure, intelligence reports and national security assessments emanating from such agencies as the JCS, the State-War-Navy Coordinating Committee, and the Joint Intelligence Committee warned that if the Soviets gained control of western Europe's resources their military capacity to wage war against the United States would be greatly enhanced. However, top-level civilian officials, whose job it was to determine final policy, most often worried about the effects of a European collapse on the domestic economy and acted on that premise, not the military considerations.[54] Furthermore, as the historian Alan Milward has argued, western Europe had greatly improved its position by mid-1947 when the Americans first began speaking publicly about an aid program. Left to their own devices, the western Europeans, Milward contends, would have recovered on their own and – here is the important point – not succumbed to Soviet dominance. Thus, if Milward is correct, there is very little to the argument that the Marshall Plan saved western Europe from communism, as is so often claimed. What would not have occurred in the absence of the Marshall Plan was a solution for the dollar gap, which is to say that western Europe likely would have survived but would have done so independently of the United States, a most unwelcome outcome for those U.S. officials and other elites who believed prosperity at home depended on multilateralism abroad. It is in this context that the Marshall Plan was devised.[55]

Set up as a four-year program at the cost of $17 billion,[56] the Marshall Plan gave the western Europeans U.S. exports that they otherwise could

---

[54] Leffler, *A Preponderance of Power*, 157–164. Leffler contends that "the economic motivations behind the Marshall Plan were secondary," but the evidence he provides belies his own argument. For instance, he quotes Harriman on page 162 arguing that the Marshall Plan's failure to be enacted "would endanger the survival of the American system of free enterprise." To suggest that "the survival of the American system of free enterprise" did not weigh more heavily on the mind of Harriman than the Soviet threat, given all we know about the state of that threat at that time, is curious, given a historian of Leffler's caliber. See also Michael J. Hogan, *The Marshall Plan: America, Britain, and Reconstruction of Western Europe, 1947–1952* (New York: Cambridge University Press, 1987), 51–52.

[55] Alan S. Milward, *The Reconstruction of Western Europe, 1945–51* (Berkeley, California: University of California Press, 1984). See also Leffler, *A Preponderance of Power*, 159–160.

[56] The Europeans asked for a $27 million program. The actual amount spent over the four years, according to Walter LaFeber, was $13 billion. LaFeber, *The American Age*, 480.

86   *NSC 68 and the Political Economy of the Early Cold War*

not pay for while they worked to rebuild their shattered economies. It was a brilliant plan. Funding western European import purchases from the United States kept the foreign markets open for U.S. exporters, thereby staving off potential depression at home, while at the same time providing western Europe its needed imports to help rebuild its industry so that ultimately it could become "self-supportive," i.e., capable of earning dollars through the normal processes of trade. Perhaps most importantly, it kept western Europe, at least for the time being, firmly in the U.S. camp, for without the Marshall Plan western Europe, including Great Britain, would have had little choice but to cease purchasing U.S. goods and devise other means to sustain itself.[57]

The lesson learned by playing the communist card to gain passage of the British loan and the Greco-Turkish aid bill was not lost on administration officials when they sought to sell Congress on the Marshall Plan. In fact, their initial efforts went too far in this direction, causing at least one senator to privately tell the administration that many in Congress felt that the Truman Doctrine had been a form of manipulation and that they were not about to be cajoled by such antics again.[58] Nevertheless, when Congress began to stall on passing the legislation, as Frank Kofsky and Richard Freeland have shown, the administration fomented a "war scare" in order to secure passage of it before the Italian general elections to be held on April 18, 1948, in which it was believed that the Italian Communists would likely win a majority.[59]

There were really two war scares, or one with two relatively independent parts. The first centered on Czechoslovakia and the alleged Communist coup that occurred there in February 1948; the second on a telegram sent from General Lucius D. Clay, military governor for the U.S. zone in Germany, to Washington, D.C., on March 5, 1948, that bespoke of an imminent attack by the Soviet Union on western Europe. As regards Czechoslovakia, as we saw in Chapter 2, it is difficult to describe what occurred there in February 1948 as truly a coup, given that the Czech Communists were already in control of most departments of the government prior to it and that the Soviet Union was not directly involved. Nevertheless, publicly Truman administration officials held up the Czech coup as evidence that the Soviet Union was on the move.

---

[57] McCormick, *America's Half-Century*, 72–88; LaFeber, *The American Age*, 479–482.
[58] Freeland, *The Truman Doctrine and the Origins of McCarthyism*, 252–257.
[59] Frank Kofsky, *The War Scare of 1948: A Successful Campaign to Deceive the Nation* (New York: St. Martin's Press, 1995), 83–168; Freeland, *The Truman Doctrine and the Origins of McCarthyism*, 264–287.

Multilateralism, the Dollar Gap, and the Origins

Clay provided the other part of the war scare. In the telegram, which was sent on March 5, 1948, he wrote:

For many months, based on logical analysis, I have felt and held that war was unlikely for at least ten years. Within the last few weeks, I have felt a subtle change in Soviet attitude which I cannot define but which now gives me a feeling that it may come with dramatic suddenness. I cannot support this change in my own thinking with any data or outward evidence in relationships other than to describe it as a feeling of a new tenseness in every Soviet individual with whom we have official relations. I am unable to submit any official report in the absence of supporting data but my feeling is real. You may advise the chief of staff of this for whatever it may be worth if you feel it advisable.[60]

Although this memorandum hardly presents the necessity for a call to arms, based as it is on a "feeling," the Truman administration seized on it to argue before Congress and the American people that a war with the Soviet Union was imminent unless Congress passed the Marshall Plan, which it subsequently did.[61]

Yet, as Kofsky astutely points out, as soon as the war scare served its purpose, securing congressional approval for the Marshall Plan, Marshall immediately departed for a six-week sojourn to South America, as if passage of the Marshall Plan had somehow stopped the Soviet Union from its plans for an invasion. As Congressman Harold Knutson, chair of the House Ways and Means Committee, remarked at the time: "Things can't be very serious when Secretary of State Marshall goes to Bogota for six weeks."[62] Indeed. Once again, the Truman administration used an exaggerated notion of the Soviet threat to push through legislation that had everything to do with the dollar gap but very little to do with the Soviet Union. And once again, it worked.

Why the Soviet Threat Worked

Why did the Soviet threat work so well in bringing Congress, and by inference the American people, around to the administration's goals? Three things need to be kept in mind in attempting to answer that question.

---

[60] Kofsky, *War Scare*, 104; Freeland, *The Truman Doctrine and the Origins of McCarthyism*, 284–285.

[61] Kofsky, *War Scare*, 140–141; Freeland, *The Truman Doctrine and the Origins of McCarthyism*, 284–287. See also Carolyn Eisenberg, *Drawing the Line: The American Decision to Divide Germany, 1944–1949* (New York: Cambridge University Press, 1996), 387–389.

[62] Quoted in Kofsky, *War Scare*, 141.

First, it does not stand the test of legitimacy to contend that the Soviet threat was a sham that the administration waved before Congress every time it faced an uphill battle over this or that legislation. That argument fails the test of plausibility, lest we believe members of Congress were (are) unintelligent dupes. Second, and yet it remains a fact that, in our three examples – the British loan, the Greco-Turkish aid bill, and the Marshall Plan – the administration initially told the truth in their pleas for economic aid and the truth did not work. It was only after the administration evoked the Soviet threat that Congress gave its consent. Third, there was a prevailing counterargument to the administration's scare tactics pushed by the progressive internationalists such as Henry Wallace, which means that it cannot be argued that the people and the Congress had no alternative but to believe the administration. So what is going on here?

One answer is that administration officials were telling the truth when they argued that a given piece of legislation was necessary lest the situation redound to the Soviet's advantage. Although the administration, at times, did exaggerate the Soviet threat and was not above fomenting a war scare to achieve its goals, its members certainly believed that the Soviet Union posed a threat, insofar as it had the biggest army in Europe and stood for a contrary way of life. Furthermore, if the United States had failed to achieve its goal of creating a successfully functioning, multilateral world economy and had found itself isolated to the western hemisphere, then the Soviet Union's influence would undoubtedly have grown, though to what extent is far from clear. Preventing such an occurrence was *not* the administration's first goal, primarily because the Soviet Union was weak and had no interest in military conflict with the United States. Nonetheless, in evoking the Soviet threat there is no reason to suggest that the administration lied; it did not have to.[63]

Another answer is that in the postwar era the U.S. Congress and the American people already were predisposed to viewing the Soviet Union in a negative light. Given the decades-long campaign to convince them that the Bolshevik revolution in Russia was illegitimate, dangerous, and evil, this fact is not very surprising. The United States had waited nearly sixteen years after the October 1917 revolution to recognize the Soviet Union, ten after the end of the Russian civil war that saw the Bolsheviks emerge victorious. Furthermore, in 1919 and 1920, a "red scare" gripped

---

[63] H. W. Brands, *The Devil We Knew: Americans and the Cold War* (New York: Oxford University Press, 1993), 34.

Multilateralism, the Dollar Gap, and the Origins

the nation on the heels of the American Communist Party's declaration of loyalty to Moscow. Thousands of communists and suspected communists were harassed, arrested, and, in the case of foreigners, often deported. The notion that communists under the direction of Russian Bolsheviks were seeking to take over the United States entered the public's consciousness. Although such views toward the Soviet Union and communism were somewhat tempered during the 1930s, the signing of the Nazi-Soviet Non-Aggression Pact in August 1939 blurred the differences between Hitler and Stalin in the minds of Americans. So-called red fascism, the belief that communism under Stalin and fascism under Hitler were really just two sides of the same coin, was born. When the Nazis attacked the Soviet Union in the summer of 1941, instantly making it an ally of the United States and Great Britain, expediency required that negative views of the Soviet Union and communism be relaxed. The American people were treated to a heavy propaganda campaign during the war designed to improve the Soviet Union's image. It was all a mirage, however, and most Americans knew it. Once things began to go awry between the United States and the Soviet Union after the war, it took no special pleading to convince them that the Soviets were the bad guys and the Americans the good. Not that either the American people or the Congress merely rolled over and played dead. They did not. When push came to shove, however, it was obvious which side they would choose.[64]

Moreover, the national press, popular pundits, and Congress itself often took the lead in pushing anti-communism, quite independently of the administration. As historian Mark Selverstone has argued, the administration did not need to cajole either the press or the pundits to adopt an anti-communist stance. Often, in fact, they cajoled the administration to take a harder line, accusing the administration of being too soft on communism or of not being well enough on top of the threat.[65] As for Congress, the most obvious example is Senator Joseph McCarthy of Wisconsin who spawned the phenomenon – McCarthyism – that bears

[64] On red fascism, see Les K. Adler and Thomas G. Patterson, "Red Fascism: The Merger of Nazi Germany and Soviet Russia in the American Image of Totalitarianism," *American Historical Review* 75 (April 1970): 1046–1064. On tempered views of the Soviet Union during WWII, see Gaddis, *The United States and the Origins of the Cold War*, 32–62. On the transition to anti-communism, see Stephen J. Whitfield, *The Culture of the Cold War* (Baltimore, Maryland: Johns Hopkins University Press, 1996), 2nd edition, passim.

[65] Mark Selverstone, *Constructing the Monolith: The United States, Great Britain, and International Communism, 1945–1950* (Cambridge, Massachusetts: Harvard University Press, 2009), passim; Gaddis, *The United States and the Origins of the Cold War*, 282–315. Leffler disagrees, *A Preponderance of Power*, 106–107, 144–146.

90   NSC 68 and the Political Economy of the Early Cold War

his name. Well before McCarthy began issuing forth his accusations in February 1950, however, Congress had got on board the anti-communist bandwagon, particularly its Republican members who saw it as a vehicle for rolling back the New Deal and its alleged leftist supporters.[66] This is not to absolve the administration for knowingly using the politics of anti-communism, as some historians have attempted to do.[67] Rather, it is to argue that anti-communism was already in the air. It was so thick it was palpable. In such an environment, any foreign policy legislation that did not make use of it made little sense, as the administration found out all too well. Use of the Soviet threat, even exaggeration of it, was not about duping the Congress and the people that it served so much as it was about giving the people what they wanted.

This, too, in an environment in which the American people's trust in their government had not yet been polluted by the Vietnam debacle and the Watergate scandal, the latter forcing the resignation of President Richard Nixon in 1974. Americans were far more trustful of their government at that time than they came to be later on. Hence, they had little reason to question the administration's propagandistic arguments.

Another factor was Soviet behavior. C. Tyler Wood, who was assistant to the deputy administrator of the ECA in 1948 and 1949, put the matter this way in a 1971 interview. He was speaking about the Marshall Plan legislation, but his comments have wider implications:

It was interesting that every time we seemed to be getting into trouble with our legislation, and things looked a little less sure, Mr. Stalin ... would come forward with some action to scare the hell out of the United States and the United States Congress, and the boys would flock in and vote for the appropriations. It was absolutely amazing. It almost seemed to me at times that Stalin ... [was] all part of the Marshall Plan in order to keep appropriations going, because [the Soviets] were a great help with that.[68]

To be sure, Soviet actions did often appear hostile. However, given the atmosphere, any moves the Soviets made, short of packing up their troops from eastern Europe and heading home, dismantling the Soviet Union, and, one imagines, disinterring Lenin from his tomb in Red Square, were

---

[66] The best book on this subject remains Freeland, *The Truman Doctrine and the Origins of McCarthyism*.

[67] Gaddis, *The United States and the Origins of the Cold War, 1941–1947*, 254–263, 290–296, makes this claim in an attempt to counter the hypothesis that the Truman administration did, in fact, exaggerate the Soviet threat to get foreign economic aid bills through Congress.

[68] C. Tyler Wood, Oral History, June 18, 1971, 76–77, Truman Library.

Multilateralism, the Dollar Gap, and the Origins

destined to appear ominous, especially with the administration, often with the aid of the national press, encouraging that view. In this sense Wood is right – Stalin did help the administration.

Still, it is important to stress that the administration did not set out to use the politics of anti-communism as a way of overcoming congressional opposition to their aid programs. That was a development that administration officials latched on to as they watched the debate over the British loan unfold, when the evocation of the Soviet threat proved critical to getting the loan through a reluctant Congress. The same held true for the Greco-Turkish aid bill and the Marshall Plan. This fact is important to stress because it offers further evidence that the Soviet threat was not the primary issue. Given this, it might be fairly argued that the Congress essentially forced the administration to adopt a far greater anti-communist stance than it intended to in order to get what it wanted. Considering what was at stake – the collapse of nascent global economy and the American free enterprise system with it – administration officials were hardly about to let Congress stand in the way. If Congress wanted or needed some greater justification, the administration would supply it.

Thus, in effect, were two Cold Wars born – the real one, which concerned Soviet and American differences over the future course of Europe, especially Germany and, to a lesser extent, the Far East, in which the Soviet Union was clearly the weaker of the two powers and concerned primarily with ensuring its security; and the exaggerated one, that the goal of the Soviet Union was nothing less than world conquest over which the United States had no choice but to respond to defend the free world. The first was the result of the geopolitical realities of, arguably, the inevitable conflict between two rival systems that WWII left in its wake, but which carried within it the possibility of turning out differently than it did, for instance, if the two nations had managed to cooperate over Germany. The second was the result of the postwar, domestic, political environment in the United States in which anti-New Deal, economic nationally oriented Republicans faced off against a Democratic administration committed to multilateralism at all costs, which made bipartisanship in foreign policy virtually impossible without resorting to the politics of anti-communism. Once the genie was unleashed, however, it never was possible to put it back in the bottle, and very few people even tried.

4

The Dollar Gap and Its Discontents

> It is all too easy to see what would happen if aid were cut off in the middle of the [Marshall Plan] program. The European countries would simply have to slash drastically their imports from us.
>
> > Averell Harriman testimony before the House Committee on Foreign Affairs, February 22, 1950

> MR. MANSFIELD: Is it the contention of the State Department that by 1952 western Europe ... would be in a position to stand on its own feet and carry on economic relations with the rest of the world?
> SECRETARY ACHESON: No; I do not think I would say that it is the contention that that would be so. As I said, it all depends upon the success which we will have in dealing with the dollar-gap problem.
>
> > Dean Acheson testimony before the House Committee on Foreign Affairs, February 21, 1950

As we saw in Chapter 3, in the immediate postwar years Truman administration foreign policy officials' efforts to cope with the dollar gap focused on providing loans and grants to cover the gap on the premise that such aid would buy time for western Europe to recover to the point that it could earn dollars at a high level of trade through the normal processes of trade. The European Recovery Program (ERP), or the Marshall Plan, was the principal program set up to accomplish this goal. However, even as the first shipments of Marshall Plan aid reached western Europe in May–June 1948, U.S. officials and their friends in high places were acknowledging, privately, that the Marshall Plan would not succeed in ending the dollar gap by 1952, the end year of the program, and that something needed to be done to contend with that reality. They hid this information from the U.S. Congress and the American people, both of whom had been

The Dollar Gap and Its Discontents

led to believe the Marshall Plan would be the last program of economic aid that western Europe would need to make a full recovery. In the meantime, they set out to find a permanent solution for the dollar gap. In this chapter, we analyze that search.[1]

Throughout 1949 and into 1950, American elites in and out of government theorized, analyzed, debated, and recommended solutions about and for overcoming the dollar gap. Their ideas ran the gamut from encouraging, if not forcing, European economic integration to lowering the U.S. tariff to developing Africa for "use" by western Europe to utilizing some of Winston Churchill's paintings in British trade exhibits promoting the sale of British products in the United States, to everything in between. Analyzing the various solutions these elites contemplated is essential for understanding the magnitude of the crisis. Only then can we begin to see how such a radical idea as rearmament might have been used to overcome it.

On the one hand, what emerges from such an analysis is an interesting foray into the mindset of these elites as they tackled the problem of creating a world structured on multilateralism. Fascinating in itself, it provides a window into a world the general public did (and does) not inhabit. On the other hand, what emerges is the reality that all solutions for the dollar gap extent simply would not suffice to overcome it, given the time frame occasioned by the impending end of the Marshall Plan in 1952. This reality makes clear that the dollar gap was no sideshow crisis in comparison to the threat posed by the Soviet Union.

The "Mystery" of the Dollar Gap

Speaking before the House Committee on Foreign Affairs in February 1950, Paul Hoffman, head of the Economic Cooperation Administration (ECA), the agency primarily responsible for administering ERP aid, made the following observation: "Such technical phrases as 'dollar gap' and 'balance of payments deficits' may seem mysterious, but there is no mystery in the facts they describe."[2] That Hoffman felt the need to describe the dollar

---

[1] Frank Lindsay to Allen Dulles, May 1, 1948, Study Group on Aid to Europe (SGAE), Council on Foreign Relations (CFR), 30, Box 242, Public Policy Papers, Department of Rare Books and Special Collections, Princeton University Libraries, Princeton, New Jersey (hereinafter PUL); Allen Dulles to Paul Hoffman, June 15, 1948, ibid.; Hoffman to Dulles, June 22, 1948, ibid.

[2] U.S. House of Representatives, *To Amend the Economic Cooperation Act of 1948: Part One*, 81st Cong., 2nd Session (Washington, D.C.: US Government Printing Office, 1950), 5.

gap or, more amazingly, the term "balance of payments deficits" as "mysterious" illustrates an important fact: In the period under discussion, very few people knew, and even fewer understood, what the dollar gap even was. This reality appears to answer for what otherwise would be a potentially damaging conundrum for the thesis at hand – if the dollar gap was such a critical issue, one that threatened to destroy the American way of life every bit as much as, say, a Soviet victory in the Cold War, then why has it wallowed in obscurity? Why is it not more known? And more importantly, why, if this was so, did U.S. officials not make a greater case for their foreign policy based on the threat posed by the dollar gap?

The answers, in part, lie in Hoffman's use of the term "mysterious" to describe the dollar gap. If administration officials felt the need to call the dollar gap mysterious before the House Committee on Foreign Affairs, then clearly they believed that they faced an uphill battle with Congress, and no less so with the American people, where the dollar gap was concerned. In retrospect, the dollar gap is not all that difficult to understand. The nations of the world could not buy U.S. goods, or the goods from other countries whose currency was pegged to the dollar, if they did not have the dollars to do so. Moreover, in the postwar era, most of those nations lacked the means to earn dollars in sufficient amounts. Given that situation, the United States had four options: (1) offer loans to foreign nations through private banks, either directly or through investment; (2) provide dollars (or the goods) as grants, which is what the Marshall Plan did; (3) import more from dollar-starved nations so that they could earn dollars; or (4) limit trade to the level of dollars those nations could earn on their own, which was imponderable for the multilateralists in the Truman administration because it would have meant a level of global trade far too low for the U.S. economy to prosper along free-market lines.

For Congress, whose primary constituents were generally far more concerned with domestic than foreign affairs and did not always share the long view of the multilateralists, the dollar gap sounded a bit like hocus-pocus. The very term itself had an esoteric quality to it, as if it was something only those "in the know" could truly understand. Furthermore, giving U.S. goods to competitors as grants, such as under the Marshall Plan, did not appear to make logical economic sense, whatever the justification. Increasing imports, however desirable that was from the standpoint of the multilateralists, proved problematic as well, as such imports were certain to compete with domestic industries; at any rate, increasing imports was a debate of epic proportions in American history that was not likely to be overcome before 1952. Although loans were probably the

The Dollar Gap and Its Discontents

most acceptable method, they had very little practical value, as we will shortly see. That all of these options were being suggested by the multilateralists, whom the more economically nationalist-based members of Congress generally distrusted, only made matters worse.

To get a sense of Congress's reticence about the administration's explanations of the dollar gap, we can turn to the same hearings at which Hoffman described it as mysterious. Congressman John M. Vorys wanted to know why further economic assistance, as was being asked for, was being offered as a grant rather than a loan, especially if western European recovery was moving forward rapidly, as the administration had stated in its effort to show that progress had, in fact, been made. When Hoffman, clearly exasperated by the question, explained that loans were impractical because they could not be repaid due to the western Europeans' lack of dollars, Vorys would not back down.

MR.VORYS: If we are going to borrow from the American people for [the continuation of the Marshall Plan], it is going to be a loan to those who get it....

MR.HOFFMAN: We do not want to make bad loans and I do not know where they will get these dollar earnings for a long time ahead.

MR.VORYS: We will wait.

MR.HOFFMAN: Will you wait 100 years? It will take 50 years for Europe to come back, in my opinion to where she is earning enough to handle what she needs in a given year and service the debt she now has.

MR.VORYS: If Europe is in that bad shape I am wondering whether this is a recovery or a relief program we are dealing with.[3]

Given such sentiments, it becomes clear why focusing on the dollar gap alone proved problematic for the administration.

The primary reason that U.S. officials did not place greater emphasis on the dollar gap in selling their foreign policy to Congress and the American people, however, is that they had done so in the past, and the results had been severely disappointing. Each time the administration had gone before Congress to make a case for economic aid – for the British loan, for the Greco-Turkish aid bill, and for the Marshall Plan – it forthrightly discussed them in terms of the dollar gap even though they did not use the phrase itself. In each instance the response had been lukewarm at best. Instead, the administration, as we have seen, found that the only way it could sell its economic foreign policy agenda was to play up the Soviet menace.[4] The result is that, to this day, the dollar gap remains mysterious, even to most historians.

[3] Ibid., 77–78.
[4] For a contemporaneous view expressing this sentiment, see Calvin B. Hoover, "Foreign Economic Aid and Communism," *The Journal of Political Economy* 54 (February 1951),

NSC 68 and the Political Economy of the Early Cold War

However mysterious the dollar gap was, there can be no doubt that those who understood it and its implications fretted about it considerably. Consider, for instance, the following excerpt of a letter from Secretary of State Dean Acheson to Congressman Philip J. Philbin from November 1949, which further demonstrates both Congress's lack of understanding of the threat posed by the dollar gap and how some in the administration understood it all too well:

It cannot be too strongly emphasized that our exports must be maintained at the highest possible level. The prosperity of many American industries depends directly on the maintenance of our export trade. When those industries are prosperous, their contribution to the domestic economy directly benefits all other industries, raising living standards and improving the economic situation generally. As was clearly demonstrated in the 1930's, a decline in exports and imports causes far-reaching damage to the entire economy. As export producers lose their markets and curtail their production, their workers have to cut down on their own purchases at home, and the vicious spiral of depression is intensified.[5]

There are still scholars who maintain that as U.S. leaders formulated foreign policy in the early postwar era, "not much stress was placed on the relationship of U.S. exports to domestic prosperity." As the comment by Acheson demonstrates, however, that is simply untrue.[6]

2–3. The literature on this crosses biases. Both Richard Freeland, *The Truman Doctrine and the Origins of McCarthyism: Foreign Policy, Domestic Politics, and Internal Security, 1946–1948* (New York: Schocken Books, 1974), and John Lewis Gaddis, *The United States and the Origins of the Cold War, 1941–1947* (New York: Columbia University Press, 1972), argue that Congressional obstinacy shaped U.S. foreign policy in the years in which the Cold War began, even as they come to very different conclusions as to what it all means. Richard N. Gardner, *Sterling-Dollar Diplomacy: Anglo-American Collaboration in the Reconstruction of Multilateral Trade* (New York: Oxford University Press, 1956), offers a conclusion similar to Freeland's.

[5] Acheson to Congressman Philip J. Philbin, November 25, 1949, RG 59, Central Decimal File, 1945–1949, Great Britain-Trade, 841.5151, National Archives II, College Park, Maryland (hereinafter NAII). I have never seen this piece of evidence cited before, but the importance of it cannot be overstated. Since the publication of William Appleman Williams' *The Tragedy of American Diplomacy* in 1959, and especially after the second edition appeared in 1962, historians have been trying to debunk his thesis that the driving force behind U.S. foreign policy since at least the 1890s had been the creation of an economic "open door" for the world to ensure social stability and the survival of the free enterprise system at home. Comments such as this one by Acheson virtually single-handedly belie such efforts.

[6] The quote is from Melvyn Leffler, *A Preponderance of Power: National Security, the Truman Administration, and the Cold War* (Stanford, California: Stanford University Press, 1992), 316. Leffler, of course, does not cite the previous letter from Acheson to Philbin.

The Dollar Gap: Solutions and Realities

Beginning in late 1948, U.S. public and private elites searched for solutions that would end the dollar gap. In examining the various solutions that these individuals explored, we can identify five categories that within them contained one or more solutions. The first was to increase western Europe's productivity and consumption to levels at which it could trade with the United States at a level consistent with the export demands of the U.S. economy, which, according to these individuals, required western European economic and political integration. The second concerned increasing U.S. imports so that other nations could earn dollars, which, among other things, meant lowering the U.S. tariff. The third was the continuance of economic aid beyond 1952, when the Marshall Plan was scheduled to end. The fourth was finding ways to increase western European dollar earnings through sources other than direct trade. Finally, there were a number of radical schemes that were bandied about that show the depth to which the crisis spawned some really creative thinking over how to solve it. As we will see, none of these solutions proved viable for ending the dollar gap crisis by 1952 or, in fact, beyond.

Increasing Western European Production and Consumption

From the perspective of U.S. foreign policy officials and other elites committed to multilateralism, the ultimate solution to overcoming the dollar gap with western Europe was to increase European productivity and, by virtue of that, European consumption.[7] "The Europeans must not only expand their productive capacities but must, through greater efficiency, through lower costs and improved marketing methods, improve the competitive position of their products in the markets of the United States and

---

[7] Harlan Cleveland, "The Problem of Western Europe's Competitive Position in the World Economy and Its Remedies," July 19, 1949, Office Files of Gordon Gray as Special Assistant to the President (hereinafter Gray Papers), Record Group 286, Records of the Agency for International Development Working Papers (RG 286), Dollar Gap Correspondence; Bureau of the Budget; Dollar Gap Reports, Box 18, Correspondence on Dollar Gap, Harland B. Cleveland, Harry S. Truman Library, Independence, Missouri (hereinafter Truman Library); 6th Meeting of the Study Group on Aid to Europe (SGAE), June 27, 1949, CFR, 30, Box 242, 2, PUL; "Summary," July 18, 1949, SGAE, ibid.; "European Integration," November 7, 1949, Record Group 59, General Records of the Department of State (RG 59), Records of the Policy Planning Staff (PPS), 1947–1953, Country and Area Files – Europe, 2, NAII; Acheson testimony, U.S. Senate, Senate Committee on Foreign Relations, *Reviews of the World Situation 1949–1950*, *Historical Series*, 81st Cong., 1st and 2nd sess. (Washington, DC: U.S. Government Printing Office, 1974), 288.

98   *NSC 68 and the Political Economy of the Early Cold War*

the rest of the world," Secretary of State Dean Acheson told the House Committee on Foreign Affairs in February 1950. However, that was easier said than done. As Hoffman testified at the same hearing, "The United States, with 150,000,000 people, turned out in 1949 a gross national product of about $260,000,000,000. Western Europe, with 270,000,000 people, had a gross national product of $160,000,000,000."[8] Even with the Marshall Plan, western Europe was incapable of achieving parity with the dollar area at a high rate of trade.

To shed light on western Europe's "competitive problem," we can turn to a report from July 1949 written by Harlan Cleveland, an administration official working on the Marshall Plan who spent considerable time studying the dollar-gap crisis in 1949. His views offer a keen insight into the problem of western European production and how U.S. elites perceived it.

Cleveland began the report by juxtaposing the effects of the Industrial Revolution on western Europe and the United States. "Although the industrial revolution was in origin a European phenomenon, its effects were by no means as revolutionary in the old world as in the new. In both hemispheres, the advances in production techniques and methods were accompanied by changes in the relationships between labor and capital, between agriculture and industry, and between producers and the market on the one hand and consumers and the market on the other." However, in Europe the process was, Cleveland espoused, "incomplete." Not so in the United States. "Between the Civil War and the first World War every phase and type of American production, distribution and consumption was drawn into and intimately bound up with an all pervasive domestic market which stretched without barriers from ocean to ocean and embraced the entire population." This was due to "an endowment of freely available natural resources" and a "social psychology ... which militated against social castes with fixed standards of consumption appropriate for each." Because this was not the case in Europe, and because "social castes" were fixed there, "neither in depth nor in breadth were the nations [of Europe] ever able to develop fully the potentialities of the internal European market or to draw their population into the vortex of the marketplace to the same extent as in the United States." Given this, "it is not surprising," Cleveland wrote, "that by the end of the nineteenth century Western Europe's rate of economic growth was definitely beginning to decline." Then, in an observation with which Marx and Lenin would have concurred, he wrote, "It

---

[8] Dean Acheson testimony, February 21, 1950, *To Amend the ECA of 1948*, 14–15; Hoffman testimony, February 21, 1950, ibid., 8.

The Dollar Gap and Its Discontents

is against this background that late nineteenth century imperialism [*sic*] can be understood. As the internal capacity for growth became less and less, the possibilities for expansion in other parts of the world became more attractive." Thus, "Western European capital accumulations tended more and more to be invested at higher rates of return abroad rather than in modernization and improved efficiency of industrial production at home," with a subsequent decline in western European productivity overall. The long-term result of this, of course, shaped incontrovertibly by World War I and the Great Depression, "was a noticeable increase in the disparities in the economic growth of the United States as compared with Western Europe." Additionally, he noted, "this can be seen most clearly in the rates of productivity increase." Western Europe's productivity declined steadily, while the United States' rose exponentially, especially after World War II broke out. Long before that, however, the Europeans responded by adopting "monopoly and restrictionism," which, Cleveland opined, "was consistent with the European economic tradition...." Hence, the autarchy of the 1930s, of which Hitler was the foremost example.

Autarchy, Cleveland argued, only perpetuated the cycle of decline. "In 1913," he wrote, "Western Europe supplied at least 80% of the manu-factured goods entering into world trade while the United States supplied about 10%; by 1938, Western Europe's share had fallen to 53% and the United States had increased its share to 21%." Clearly, autarchy was not beneficial, went the implication. There was a further problem. "One of the basic factors which historically has limited Western Europe's eco-nomic growth was greatly modified by World War II," Cleveland argued. "Under the impact of the growth of communism, the corroding effects of the war and the Nazi occupation, and the increased knowledge of the American standard of living disseminated by American troops and American movies, the traditional caste attitude towards appropriate con-sumption expectations and tastes has finally been swept away." Yet, he noted with concern, "this breaking of psychological and social barriers has occurred precisely at a time when Western Europe lacks the resources even to restore the pre-war standard of living."

What was to be done? How could western Europe get out of this quagmire and increase its productivity so as to be able to "compete" with the United States at a high level of trade? Cleveland's answer was as follows:

To achieve a rate of growth of productivity in Western Europe greater than pre-war and comparable to that in the United States implies a major structural change in the characteristics of the Western European market, particularly the market

NSC 68 and the Political Economy of the Early Cold War

for manufactures. Structural change in effect implies the reversal of the historical tendencies which have characterized the development of modern capitalism in Europe. *Basically, this means the formation of a single, pervasive and highly competitive domestic market in Western Europe of sufficient size and scope to support mass production and consumption. It requires the final conquest of non-commercial production and consumption by the market. It entails the abandonment of governmental and private restrictionist and protectionist practices and the end of open or covert autarchies of a local and national character.*[9]

Here, then, was one potential solution for overcoming western Europe's dollar gap – western European economic integration.

There was a great deal of support for such integration among U.S. officials and other elites.[10] ECA head Paul Hoffman argued before the House Committee on Foreign Affairs in February 1950 that what was needed in western Europe was the "creation of a single, large market, to be brought about by (1) the removal of all quantitative restrictions on the movement of goods, (2) the elimination of monetary barriers to intra-European trade [i.e., currency inconvertibility], and (3) the progressive reduction of tariffs among the participating countries."[11] The State Department's Policy Planning Staff (PPS) took the issue even further. Italy, the argument was made in an October 1949 meeting, had an excess of workers; France had a deficit. Unemployed Italians, therefore, should be able to find employment in France. This objective was not merely for economic gain. "Freedom of movement of people is awfully important from [a] political standpoint," PPS Director George Kennan noted. "There is no question about it," Richard M. Scammon, State Department director of research for Europe, offered. "Consider the question of what Oklahoma would have done if people from the dust bowl couldn't move to California. The idea of a new start, [of a] new place to go, has a psychological

---

[9] Cleveland, "The Problem of Western Europe's Competitive Position in the World Economy and Its Remedies" (emphasis added), Truman Library.

[10] 84th Meeting of the PPS, May 25, 1949, RG 59, Records of the PPS, 1947–1953, Minutes of Meetings, 1947–1952, Box 32, NAII; Kennan to Acheson and Webb, August 22, 1949, RG 59, Records of the PPS, 1947–1953, Country and Area Files – Europe, 1948–1949, 1, NAII; Memorandum for Perkins, October 17, 1949, RG 59, Records of the PPS, 1947–1953, Country and Area Files – Europe, 1948–1949, Box 27, NAII; "European Integration," November 7, 1949, RG 59, Records of the PPS, 1947–1953, Country and Area Files – Europe, 1948–1949, 2–3, NAII; Arthur Smithies, "European Unification and the Dollar Problem," Gray Papers, Working Papers, Intra-European Cooperation Administration, "Recovery Guides," Trade Liberalization in Europe, Box 19, Truman Library; 11th Meeting of the SGAE, December 20, 1949, CFR, 30, Box 242, 9–10, passim, PUL; Hoffman testimony, February 21, 1950, *To Amend the ECA of 1948*, 8–10.

[11] Hoffman testimony, February 21, 1950, ibid., 9.

The Dollar Gap and Its Discontents

aspect." Western European industry, too, needed to be more logically dispersed. There was "little practicality" in the Italians developing their steel industries, Paul Nitze commented, when France and Germany were better suited for such enterprises.[12] The *New York Times* argued that a "complete currency union" was necessary – "not just removing exchange controls and restoring the pre-war freedom of convertibility but literally having the same colored paper, bearing the same pictures, circulating throughout the area." Some individuals, such as Hans Morgenthau, dean of the "realist school" of diplomatic history, imagined a Europe "fashioned after the model of the United States of America," what he called a "United States of Europe."[13]

Paul Hoffman was so adamant that the western European nations integrate economically that he appeared ready to force it on them.[14] In an October 31, 1949, speech before the Organization of European Economic Cooperation (OEEC), the administrative agency for the Marshall Plan on the European side, he demanded that the ERP nations take greater strides toward economic integration or face a drastic reduction, if not elimination, of future Marshall Plan funding. Whether Hoffman truly believed that integration should be forced in this fashion was a source of debate, although his public statements on the matter appear to have been sincere.[15] Nonetheless, there is little reason to doubt that he had acted when he did largely because he felt coerced by Congress, where some members were making such demands. When push came to shove, Hoffman knew well where he had to make haste. Still, Hoffman, a businessman of the first rank who intimately understood the workings of the corporate world, had great faith in large markets as a progressive force, and integration clearly fit that criterion.[16]

For all of economic integration's potential as a solution for the dollar gap, however, it was fraught with difficulties. On the one hand,

---

[12] 152nd Meeting of the PPS, October 18, 1949, RG 59, Records of the PPS, 1947–1953, Country and Area Files – Europe, Box 27, 2–3, NAII.

[13] Hans Morgenthau to Kennan, June 10, 1949, RG 59, Records of the PPS, 1947–1953, Country and Area Files – Europe, Box 27, NAII.

[14] Hoffman to Harriman, April 21, 1949, U.S. Department of State, *Foreign Relations of the United States, 1949* (Washington, D.C.: U.S. Government Printing Office, 1975), 4: 383–385; Hoffman testimony, February 24, 1950, *To Amend the ECA of 1948*, 69–73.

[15] 2nd Meeting of the Study Group on Economic Policy (SGEP), December 1, 1949, Council on Foreign Relations, 35, Box 243, 5, PUL; Hoffman testimony, February 21, 1950, *To Amend the ECA of 1948*, 8.

[16] See, for instance, the 152nd Meeting of the PPS, October 18, 1949, RG 59, Records of the PPS, 1947–1953, Country and Area Files – Europe, Box 27, NAII.

nationalism still exhibited strong tendencies in western Europe. "It is nonsense to say there can be closer association in economic matters unless you get into the currency field, which leads to abandonment of sovereignty. And that is not for this decade," Kennan opined in June 1949.[17] Even if nationalism could be circumvented, as R. C. Leffingwell, chairman of the board of the J. P. Morgan Company and member of the Council on Foreign Relations' Study Group on Aid to Europe (SGAE), noted in *Foreign Affairs*, "too much intra-European trade may divert needed labor and materials from the necessary task of making exports to the outer world, and leave a yawning dollar gap."[18] Averell Harriman, then roving ambassador for the ERP, noted an even deeper problem. "Competition," he remarked before the same study group, "has never been known in Europe."[19]

At the PPS, Robert Tufts, who would work extensively on NSC 68, wondered whether "union on the continent might in effect intensify the dollar problem." He added: "I am a little worried ECA wants to advocate unification as a solution to the dollar problem. I don't feel it is. If we persuade Congress that's what's needed to solve the dollar problem we might be in a very bad position." Kennan responded that "it depends on whether you can increase food and raw material production so you can take off some of the demand for those from the dollar area. It wouldn't do to increase dollar goods." Kennan then added the following interesting observation:

The Germans, during the war, did come very close to making Europe self-supporting, without any substantial foreign trade. They had eastern Europe to draw on. They had really many of the things we are now talking about; ... they ran combined boards for distribution of raw materials for the whole area dominated by the Germans, and the same thing with banks and financial matters. I must say they kept up production very well, and they managed to get food distributed pretty well. If not faced with military operations, they would have made a go of it. What I am driving at is that they solved the dollar problem by not importing anything from the dollar area but still kept people employed.

[17] Meeting of the PPS, June 8, 1949, RG 59, Records of the PPS, 1947–1953, Country and Area Files – Europe, Box 27, 2, NAII.

[18] R. C. Leffingwell, "Devaluation and European Recovery," *Foreign Affairs* 28 (October 1949), 210–211; Harriman's comment is in 16th Meeting of the SGAE, April 24, 1950, CFR, 31, Box 243, 12, PUL; Michael L. Hoffman, "ERP Goal Shifted to Economic Union," *The New York Times*, April 7, 1949, 1.

[19] R. C. Leffingwell, "Devaluation and European Recovery," *Foreign Affairs* 28 (October 1949), 210–211; Harriman's comment is in 16th Meeting of the SGAE, April 24, 1950, CFR, 31, Box 243, 12, PUL; Michael L. Hoffman, "ERP Goal Shifted to Economic Union," *The New York Times*, April 7, 1949, 1.

The Dollar Gap and Its Discontents

This prompted Acheson to ask whether economic union might, in fact, find Europe "worse off than before." Nitze did not think so. "I wouldn't think it would have a bearing one way or another on the dollar deficit. Europe might be more self-sufficient – our exports to Europe decline. Some of the pressure of sales to the dollar area would also be diminished." Lest the import of Nitze's comment be missed, his point was not that such a development would be acceptable or desirable but that, in his estimation, integration would not make much of a difference on the dollar gap. It simply was not the answer.[20]

At the Council on Foreign Relations (CFR) Study Group on Economic Policy (SGEP), members concurred that economic integration was not feasible. ECA economist Harold Stein wanted it clearly stated that "the discussion group did not feel that [Paul] Hoffman's policy of pushing European integration [is] ... particularly realistic." Princeton economist Gardner Patterson added that "the integration program tends to require that each European country achieve net balance with Europe, and that Europe balance with the U.S., both of which do not make economic sense." Group member J. J. Kaplan questioned "how large" the savings would be. "And," he asked, "how long will it take before we see them?"[21]

Much the same could be found at the meeting of the SGAE in December 1949. Economist William Diebold remarked that in his "speech [before the OEEC on October 31, 1949] Mr. Hoffman was putting integration too far." Diebold especially took exception with the speech's "'or else' character" and suggested it "may raise serious difficulties in the future." He cautioned against placing too much significance on integration. There were "many significant obstacles to overcome," and "Congress will insist on seeing concrete manifestations before appropriating more aid." He suggested that "Hoffman may be creating additional hurdles" rather than solving matters. Alan Dulles, international corporate lawyer and soon-to-be director of the Central Intelligence Agency (CIA), pointed up the problem by noting that "each economic crisis has in the past immediately led to the resumption of national barriers, as self-preservation became the watchword." Council member Walter Mallory responded that he "was convinced that nothing like the requisite amount of cooperation will be achieved" for integration. To which University of Chicago economist Jacob Viner responded: "Only a 'hot' Russian threat could lead Western Europe to integrate

---

[20] 152nd Meeting of the PPS, October 18, 1949, RG 59, Records of the PPS, 1947–1953, Country and Area Files – Europe, Box 27, 4, NAII.

[21] 7th Meeting of the SGEP, April 17, 1950, CFR, 30, Box 242, 2, PUL.

effectively; short of that ... the evolution of history was the only means." Mallory then suggested that any "real accomplishment in this field would require the various states to give up a great deal of sovereignty." Viner agreed, "They would have to give up a lot of sovereignty for relatively small economic gain."[22]

Emile Despres, economist at the College of William and Mary, thinking of Hoffman's speech, commented that "dangers did exist if we pushed integration too hard," although he added that "there might be military or political reasons for greater integration, economic factors apart." Howard Ellis, economics professor at the University of California, thought that perhaps the group was setting its sights too high. He said that "it was important to distinguish an ambitious scheme for the thorough integration of the Western European economy from the lesser aim of getting an effective utilization of existing plant. The latter task was manageable," he remarked. Agreeing with Ellis, Viner noted that "even the United States had paid a long-run price for its unity, and that the result had not been all gain." General Dwight Eisenhower interjected that "our Constitutional Convention had also had hard words and found the going difficult." It is not, he felt, "particularly dangerous politically to press hard for integration." Despres, however, opined that "there was only one possible benefit to be gained by pushing integration so hard, namely that if we think there is no possibility of European viability by 1952 [the end year of the Marshall Plan] and we want to blame Europe, this is a good way to do it for political reasons."

The group generally agreed that "the various barriers to freer trade in Europe (including tariffs) were very important as a cause of low efficiency and productivity." There could be no doubt that "economies of large scale production and the movements toward lower costs ... could be expected to result from freer trade within Europe." Nonetheless, they were doubtful that "viability will result from greater integration alone."

The question was raised as to "how much the integration of Western Europe would reduce the dollar gap." Diebold offered that "it would assist either by leading to new sources of supply with Europe or by making European goods competitive in the rest of the world by helping to lower costs of production." Dulles further suggested that "the economies stemming from large markets would be a most important factor in raising productivity." However, Ellis noted that he had talked to "an eminent French economist" – a Mr. Uri – about "what lines would be favorably

---

[22] 11th Meeting of the SGAE, December 20, 1949, CFR, 30, Box 242, 2, PUL.

The Dollar Gap and Its Discontents

affected if Europe became a large free trade area." The Frenchmen had told him, Diebold said, that such a development would "mean economies of large scale for only automobiles and perhaps radios." Hamilton Fish Armstrong, editor of *Foreign Affairs*, suggested that it was the obvious belief of the group that "integration would not greatly affect the dollar gap." He added that "overemphasis on integration would be a serious mistake. Failure would be very disappointing in that case. If the public believes in the emphasis, failure might lead them to wash their hands of Europe." Eisenhower argued that "this conclusion was a most important one ... success or failure of the Marshall Plan is not dependent upon economic integration." Viner commented that "economic integration was a particularly difficult approach." To which Eisenhower responded, "The State Department's view had consistently been that real economic union was impossible but terribly important."

This group also took up the issue of what "American policy [should] be with regard to possible intra-European integration which would not include Britain or the Sterling Area." Viner suggested that "our policies with respect to the British Empire and the regional approach within Europe are in conflict. For years we have been attempting to break up the Ottawa Agreements [on Imperial Preference] between England and rest of the Commonwealth. Now we are encouraging precisely this sort of thing within Western Europe." Viner complained that "these are inconsistent policies unless proximity makes a difference in the latter case." Armstrong responded that "proximity did make the cases different because, in the case of Europe, it had a strategic significance." "So has the British Empire," Viner noted.[23]

Devaluation of the British pound figured into the discussion over western European integration as well, and was a source of great debate.[24] The British devalued the pound on September 18, 1949, in an effort to make its products more saleable in dollar areas. The devaluation came as a response to a renewed dollar gap crisis that the British experienced beginning in the summer of 1949 (chronicled in Chapter 5). Debates about the efficacy of the devaluation raged before and after that date. Some, such as the Treasury Department, believing devaluation was necessary "to shake out high costs," supported it right away. Others came along slowly. At the SGAE, Walter Mallory remarked that he "did not see how devaluation of

---

[23] 11th Meeting of the SGAE, December 20, 1949, CFR, 30, Box 242, 20, PUL.
[24] 6th Meeting of the SGAE, June 27, 1949, CFR, 30, Box 242, 9, PUL; Smithies, "European Unification and the Dollar Problem," Truman Library.

NSC 68 and the Political Economy of the Early Cold War

the pound could help Britain so long as she buys more in the dollar area than she sells here. Would not the dollars gained by larger export sales be more than offset by the higher cost of imports?" Columbia economist Ragnar Nurske responded that "devaluation would increase British sales to the United States, thus increasing dollar earnings." However, Viner was "skeptical whether we would actually permit them to expand their exports to this market very greatly." He noted that "scotch is probably an exception; but on the other major trade items, such as woolens, cotton, textiles, and pottery, there would be strong pressure in this country for higher tariffs." Viner further stated, "Unless the problem of devaluation can be dealt with on a broad front, it had better be left alone."[25]

And so it went. Although there existed general agreement that western European economic integration was key to raising productivity, viewed as necessary for closing the dollar gap, as U.S. officials and other elites studied the issue in the fall of 1949 it became increasingly clear that integration was fraught with too many difficulties to be a viable solution in the *immediate* term. As Acheson noted in October 1949, "While recognizing that economic integration should greatly assist necessary economic adjustments, I believe that this argument should not be misinterpreted to mean that the solution of the dollar payments problem lies solely or necessarily primarily in integration."[26] Or as Hoffman told the House Committee on Foreign Affairs, "[Economic integration] would have little immediate effect in closing the dollar gap and reducing the amount of American aid required by Europe."[27] Economic integration was, in and of itself, clearly not a viable solution to ending the dollar gap by 1952.

Increasing U.S. Imports

Another possible way to overcome the dollar gap was to increase U.S. imports. If western European and other nations could sell more to the United States, then they could earn more dollars. This course of action,

---

[25] 6th Meeting of the SGAE, June 27, 1949, CFR, 30, Box 242, PUL; R. C. Leffingwell memorandum, SGAE, May 24, 1949, CFR, 30, Box 242, 18, PUL; U.S. Secretary of the Treasury John Snyder to Acheson, July 9, 1949, *Foreign Relations of the United States (FRUS)*, 1949 4 (Washington, D.C.: U.S. Government Printing Office, 1976): 800; Harriman to Acheson, June 25, 1949, *FRUS, 1949* 4: 792.
[26] Memorandum for Perkins, October 19, 1949, RG 59, Records of the PPS, 1947–1953, Country and Area Files – Europe, Box 27, 2–3, NAII.
[27] Hoffman testimony, February 21, 1950, *To Amend the ECA of 1948*, 8.

The Dollar Gap and Its Discontents   107

however, also produced a number of obstacles. In the first instance, in order to increase imports, the U.S. economy had to continue to operate at a high level of prosperity. This condition was necessary: (1) to ensure that the U.S. would continue to purchase foreign products and thereby keep dollars flowing abroad; (2) to maintain prosperity at home; and (3) for propaganda value vis-à-vis its ideological and political conflict with communism.[28] "The economy of Western Europe can only be brought into reasonable balance with the hard currency area on the basis of a considerable expansion in the total volume of world trade," Frank Altschul, attorney for Lehman Brothers, wrote in a memorandum offering his thoughts during the first meeting of the SGEP, and "this expansion can only take place if there is a vigorous forward thrust, or at least stability at a very high level, in business activity in the United States."[29] "If there is a recession here our imports will fall sharply and we will be very conservative about expenditures," noted R. C. Leffingwell at the fourth meeting of the SGAE. "Thus a recession here would be the greatest threat to both recovery and defense, so it is important to realize that [the] underpinning of the whole program is American prosperity."[30] Council member John Williams noted, "The present improvement does owe a great deal to present prosperity of the United States, and its continuance will depend considerably on our prosperity in the future."[31] Or as a State Department paper from July 1949 put it: "Reductions in U.S. imports would almost certainly give rise to depression and unemployment in the foreign industries producing these goods. The depressing effects would spread in some degree throughout the national economies [of many nations]. There would also be secondary depressing effects on third countries.... These dislocations would

---

[28] 2nd Meeting of the SGEP, December 1, 1949, CFR, 35, 1–3, PUL; "Memorandum for the Discussion Group on Economic Policy," January 24, 1950, Gray Papers, Working Papers, CFR – Study Group Reports, Box 6, 1, Truman Library; SGAE, April 4, 1949, CFR, 30, Box 242, 15, PUL; SGAE, "Summary," July 18, 1949, CFR, 30, Box 242, 2–3, PUL; "Suggestions for Discussion with Gordon Gray," April 14, 1950, George Elsey Papers, Box 59, 2, Truman Library; Department of State, Office of the Assistant Secretary for Economic Affairs, "Foreign Effects of a U.S. Depression," July 1, 1949, Gray Papers, Working Papers; Executive Departments; Department of Interior, General, Working Papers, Miscellaneous, Department of State, folder 2, Box 22, Truman Library; "European Integration," November 7, 1949, RG 59, Records of the PPS, Country File – Europe, 2, NAII; Diebold, "European Recovery: The Next Two Years," 3, 6, Truman Library.
[29] "Memorandum to Members of the Study Group on Economic Policy," November 21, 1949, Gray Papers, CFR – Study Group Reports, Box 6, Truman Library.
[30] 4th Meeting of the SGAE, April 4, 1949, CFR, 30, Box 242, 15, PUL.
[31] 7th Meeting of the SGAE, May 24, 1950, CFR, 30, Box 242, 1, PUL.

NSC 68 and the Political Economy of the Early Cold War

stem from reductions in U.S. purchases, even though financial aid from the United States continued at substantially the present level."[32]

Maintaining a high level of foreign trade was also necessary for the U.S. economy. "If we ... push exports down to the present level of imports," Acheson remarked before the House Committee on Foreign Affairs, "I think we have to reach the conclusion that certain other things may be impractical which we would not really like to contemplate. This is a very, very serious question. There is no more serious question than this before us at the present time."[33] At the CFR, Frank Altschul offered a similar conclusion: "It is my conviction that we cannot under present circumstances maintain what has come to be called full employment – which is today an accepted objective of national economic policy – if there is a material decrease in our export trade."[34]

Finally, economic downturn in the United States would once again bring into question capitalism's viability for modern industrial societies; the propaganda gains for the communists of such a downturn might well be fatal. A paper drawn up by the assistant secretary of state for economic affairs in July 1949 noted that

No development could play more into the hands of the Soviet Union than a U.S. depression. The Soviet Union and the Communist parties throughout the world would have concrete evidence in support of their propaganda that the United States and the capitalist system generally brought unemployment and insecurity, if not misery. Fulfillment of the predictions of the Communists would offer them the initiative among the workers of the world. It would be a grave mistake for the United States to under-estimate the effects in many countries of Communist propaganda, or perhaps more properly, psychological warfare. The answer to the Communist countries, as well as those advocating extensive economic planning in non-Communist countries, is the maintenance of high levels of production and employment in the United States.[35]

Or, as Viner put it, "a depression here would seem to justify communist arguments that the United States could not sustain prosperity." He added: "Our maintenance of a high standard of living is a major factor in our foreign policy."[36] The issue was particularly sensitive where the ERP was concerned. As Diebold noted: "It is of considerable importance

[32] "Foreign Effects of a U.S. Depression," 2, Truman Library.
[33] Acheson testimony, February 21, 1950, *To Amend the ECA of 1948*, 23.
[34] Frank Altschul, "Memorandum for the Discussion Group on Economic Policy," January 24, 1950, Gray Papers, Working Papers, CFR – Study Group Reports, Box 6, 1, Truman Library.
[35] "Foreign Effect of a U.S. Depression," 4–5, Truman Library.
[36] SGAE, September 26, 1949, CFR, 30, Box 242, 17, PUL.

The Dollar Gap and Its Discontents

to the political and economic success of American policy in Europe that the Communist claim – plainly false when it was made – that the aid program was primarily a device to sustain the American economy should not be given substance during the last half of the program." But, he added, "This also means that Congress and the Administration must continue to resist efforts to give particular domestic groups special treatment in the aid program, thus turning it into a form of taxpayer subsidy to American producers."[37]

If there was agreement that the U.S. economy had to function at a high level of prosperity as an upward pull on all economies of the non-Communist world, how exactly to achieve that pull was not clear.

One of the greatest problems that U.S. and western European officials had to face was how to achieve an increase in imports into the United States for western European, Japanese, and other nations' products. Long before Americans had ever heard of the Beatles or, by American standards, of a go-cart-like vehicle called a Datsun (now Nissan), U.S. consumers had little interest in foreign products, save for luxury items, which generally only the rich could afford. The United States' hyper-productive, ultra-modernized economy was producing the goods Americans wanted, not Europe and certainly not Japan.[38]

The issue was taken up at a meeting of the CFR's SGAE held on May 18, 1949. The issue, put in the form of a question by Ragnar Nurske, was: "Assuming that American aid will come to an end, how is Europe to achieve a balance in its foreign accounts?" He noted that "the United States is one of the most important potential markets, because Europe has a special need for dollars and because the European share of the United States market is negligible." But then came the problems. "Our job is to accept a larger flow of European goods," Nurske contended, but "to do it will hurt some sectors of the economy and lead to strong pressure to use the escape clauses in our trade agreements." Eisenhower noted another problem: "European exports to the United States depend heavily on prosperity in this country because they are so largely composed of luxury goods." Nurske agreed but argued that "Europe also produces items of mass consumption for which there could be a market here if we would lower our tariffs and if European sales techniques improved." He argued: "We have prosperity now and European imports

---

[37] Diebold, "European Recovery: The Next Two Years," 6, Truman Library.
[38] SGAE, May 18, CFR, 30, Box 242, 9–10, PUL; SGAE, September 26, 1949, CFR, 30, Box 242, 19, PUL; 9th Meeting of the SGEP, May 8, 1950, CFR, 35, 25, PUL.

are a smaller proportion of our national income than in 1928." Isidor Rabi, the esteemed atomic scientist, wanted to know "if Europe could now supply enough additional goods to improve [its] position." Nurske answered affirmatively, but pointed out that "we are not concerned with securing equilibrium now.... The crucial period is after the end of the Marshall Plan." Viner, "doubted Europe's ability to supply large quantities of additional goods for the American market at present. Last year," he noted, "England sold all the woolens it produced; its total production of consumer goods was less than in 1928."

Then, Viner got to the heart of the matter: "What are the items which Europe can hope to export here in quantity? ... The drift in world trade has been in favor of a larger share for the United States and against the rest of the world which is another reason for pessimism.... Changes in technology and fashions have also worked against European exports to the United States. For instance, silk and rubber will never again have the commanding position they once did; the trend away from cigar-smoking reduces tobacco imports; domestic wines and liquors can compete with imported varieties; the shift away from linens also has trade consequences." Viner stated that he "could think of no commodity in which import prospects had improved expect perhaps iron ore." "And uranium," Hanson Baldwin added.[39] Thus, even had western Europe and Britain been in a position to produce more, they had little to sell. Overcoming the dollar gap, then, required finding something the Europeans could produce that the Americans would buy. But how to do that?

Any effort to increase U.S. imports meant lowering the high U.S. tariffs.[40] "A direct attack by Western Europe on the American market must form a major part of the solution for Europe's dollar problem," a paper discussed in the SGAE declared.[41] As Hoffman told the National

---

[39] 5th Meeting of the SGAE, May 18, 1950, CFR, 30, Box 242, 8–9, PUL; "Future Problems for United States Foreign Economic Policy," [n.d.], Elsey papers, Foreign Relations, Economic Policy, Box 59, 16–17, Truman Library.

[40] Walter Salant, "International Economic Policy"; "Basic Foreign and Domestic Economic Problems Involved in Adjusting the Balance of Payments of the United States," Walter Salant Papers, International Relations, 1950, Box 2, 2, Truman Library; Salant to the Stabilization Devices Committee, April 20, 1948, ibid.; Joseph M. Jones to Clark Clifford, November 23, 1949, Elsey Papers, Foreign Relations, Economic Policy, Box 59, 2, Truman Library; Paul Hoffman, Address before the World Affairs Council and the National Association of Manufacturers, April 20, 1950, ibid.; Acheson testimony, February 21, 1950, *To Amend the ECA of 1948*, 15–16, 23.

[41] "Summary," July 18, 1949, CFR, 30, Box 242, PUL.

The Dollar Gap and Its Discontents

Association of Manufactures, "We must sell less to and buy more from Europe." He conceded that "there is little appeal in such a program, but if we do not sell less and buy more, we must either continue our aid or see the European economy placed in grave danger, which, in turn, would seriously endanger our own prosperity and security."[42] "If the United States is to exercise leadership in dealing with the world's economic problems, [tariff reduction] may be one of the best ways," John Kenneth Galbraith offered in the SGEP's first meeting on November 1, 1949. At the same meeting, R. Gordon Watson remarked that "he had felt for sometime that it might be wise for the United States to become a free trade country," as Britain had been in the nineteenth century. He added that, if it did, "we shall at last [least?] be paid for more of the goods we are shipping abroad." Altschul, chairman of the study group, "thought there would be some political advantage in presenting a tariff cut as a condition to end the spending of money abroad."[43] What, however, were the chances Congress would lower tariffs?

The answer was: not likely. Tariffs have famously pitted industry against agriculture, city against farm, and party against party in American history. The late 1940s proved no exception. Economic nationalist-oriented Republicans, led by Senator Robert Taft of Ohio, consistently sought to raise tariffs or block them from being lowered. For Taft, tariffs were, along with creeping socialism, softness on communism, and deficit spending, political hot potatoes to pull out at election time. Try as administration officials did to explain that to sell abroad the United States had to buy from abroad, the Republicans stood their ground and the tariff remained high well into the 1950s. Such tactics proved a consistent source of headache for the multilateralists as they attempted to promote their agenda because the high U.S. tariff made an easy target when Europeans and other nations felt pressed to pull back from embracing the policy. Elite internationalists attending the CFR's Study Group on Aid to Europe worried that Congress was simply uneducated when it came to the realities of international trade. For instance, Isador Lubin, economist and special assistant to the secretary of state in 1949 and 1950, wondered "how far the idea had permeated Congress that today the problem is different

---

[42] Address by Paul Hoffman before the National Association of Manufactures, April 20, 1950, Elsey Papers, Box 59, Truman Library.

[43] 1st Meeting of the SGEP, November 1, 1949, Gray Papers, Council on Foreign Relations – Study Group Reports, Box 6, Truman Library.

NSC 68 and the Political Economy of the Early Cold War

from what it was in 1948," while Diebold suggested that the "next stage in Congress' *education* might be the lesson that total imports do not tell the whole story. A country's whole economy must be considered." That Congress appeared to need an education in such fundamentals makes clear that tariff reduction was no easy matter.[44]

The primary vehicle for tariff reduction had been devised in 1934 by Secretary of State Cordell Hull and Franklin Roosevelt. The Reciprocal Trade Agreements Act (RTAA), more known for the "most favored nation" clause embodied in it, gave the president the power to unilaterally (that is, without congressional approval) enter into trade agreements with foreign countries that reduced their tariffs on U.S. imports in exchange for reduced tariffs on their imports to the United States. However, even the RTAA proved difficult. Generally, Congress passed the RTAA for two years at a time and then reviewed it and brought it up for a renewal vote. This made the issue a constant source of tension, for the Republicans always made an issue of it. In the sixteen years between its first passage in 1934 and 1950, the Republicans had only twice put forward a majority in support of it in both houses – 1943 and 1948 – the former during the wartime emergency and the latter when they succeeded in placing limits on the president's powers. Given all of this, the probability that tariff reduction could suffice as a solution for the dollar gap appeared a long shot at best. Indeed, as late as May 1950, the ECA would complain in its final quarter report for fiscal year 1949 that despite positive efforts on the part of the western Europeans to increase their imports to the United Sates, the U.S. tariff was still too high and was proving an obstacle for said increase.[45]

Continued Economic Assistance Beyond 1952

Virtually all of those individuals involved in trying to find a solution for the dollar gap agreed that continued economic aid beyond 1952, the end year for the Marshall Plan, would be necessary.[46] "Congress must get over

[44] Freeland, *The Truman Doctrine*, 325–334; CFR, SGEP Dec 1, 1949, 4–5, PUL, emphasis added.
[45] James Reston, "Economic Strength, Too, for Atlantic Defense," *The New York Times*, June 11, 1950, 127; Felix Belair, Jr., "U.S. Import Bars Decried by E.C.A.," *The New York Times*, May 9, 1950, 15.
[46] "Post-ERP Prospects and Aid Programs," June 19, 1950, Gray Papers, Post-ERP Economic Projections, Box 9, Truman Library; Acheson testimony, February 21, 1950, *To Amend the ECA of 1948*, 19–20. For a dissenting view see Ernest T. Weir, "Notes on a Trip to Europe," Averell Harriman Papers, Marshall Plan, 1948–1950, General Correspondence – W, Box 268, Library of Congress (hereinafter LC), Washington, D.C.

The Dollar Gap and Its Discontents

the idea that everything is over by 1952," Kennan remarked in an October 1949 meeting of the PPS devoted to the issue of western European integration. "That is true irrespective of whether you get union or not," Nitze interjected.[47] Eisenhower noted before the SGAE in May 1949 that "1952 has no significance as a cut-off date and aid may have to be extended past that time."[48] "The 1952 date was an impossible target for the achievement of equilibrium," economist Harold Stein observed at the SGEP in December 1949, although, as George Ball, international lawyer and diplomat, responded, "the 1952 date had the advantage of providing a stimulus to the Europeans." Stein concurred, adding nonetheless that "the 1952 date was necessary nonsense."[49] "It had been assumed at the outset that the need for dollars would not be fully met at the end of the Marshall Plan," Altschul commented at the same study group in January 1950. The task of the group, Altschul then stated, was to "find a new scheme under which the U.S. Government could supply dollars after 1952."[50] President Truman said so publicly in June 1950 in an address before the University of Missouri when he made the observation, "Our vital national interest in a healthy world economy will not end in 1952."[51]

The issue was of utmost importance because if 1952 arrived and no program of continued economic aid were in place, western Europe would immediately suffer a cutoff of an estimated $2 billion to $2.5 billion in aid, sending their imports plunging. Then, western Europe would have no choice but to pursue autarchy. "In the absence of direct or indirect post-ERP U.S. aid," a State Department working group on the dollar gap wrote in a June 1950 report, "Western Europe might restrict its export production to somewhat less than maximum levels and would probably try to carry out even more autarchic domestic programs."[52]

Once again the problem was Congress, as well the American people it represented. Having been assured by the administration in 1948 that the Marshall Plan would be the last aid package needed to get western Europe up and running again, Congress was not likely to look too favorably on any extension of the ERP past 1952. In fact, there was concern

---

[47] 152nd Meeting of the PPS, October 18, 1949, RG 59, Records of the PPS, 1947–1953, Country and Area Files – Europe, Box 27, 12, NAII.

[48] 5th Meeting of the SGAE, May 18, 1949, CFR, 30, Box 242, 12, PUL.

[49] 2nd Meeting of the SGEP, December 1, 1949, CFR, 35, 7, PUL.

[50] 3rd Meeting of the SGEP, January 4, 1949, CFR, 35, 8, PUL.

[51] "Text of Truman's Address at University of Missouri," June 10, 1950, *The New York Times*, 2.

[52] "Post-ERP Prospects and Aid Programs," 3, Truman Library.

that Congress would not even fund the last year, or would reduce drastically the allotment and make it ineffective. "There was no doubt that the program would have trouble in Congress," Frank Altschul remarked at a meeting of the SGEP. It was his opinion that "the more emphasis placed upon a plan for beyond 1952, the more chance there will be that Congress will implement the measures required until 1952."[53] Altschul made a good point. At a meeting with the economist and banker Lord Thomas Walter Brand, Senator William Fulbright "doubted[ed] whether there would in fact be any more appropriations for the third and fourth year of ERP." He stated that "there was a general impression in the Congress that the end to be accomplished by such appropriations was the unification of Europe; and that Congressmen reasoned that if this does represent the end which our Government intends ... and if unification is not in fact being accomplished, then the conclusion seems clear to the average Congressman that there is no point in wasting any more funds in ECA appropriations destined to serve a futile purpose."[54]

Beginning in 1950, administration officials began floating the idea that some form of aid would have to continue beyond 1952. However, they were adamant that the Marshall Plan itself would end in that year and that any continuation of economic aid such as might be requested would come under a different program.[55] Given Congress's attitude, however, that was bound to be a long and nasty battle. Certainly, the administration could not afford to wait and see what Congress might do. It goes without saying, 1952 would wait for no one.

Increasing Dollar Earnings through Means Other Than Direct Trade

Another avenue that U.S. officials and other elites considered for easing the dollar gap was to find other means than direct trade through which to get dollars into the hands of western Europeans and other nations. Three solutions generally accepted as essential to any long-term solution to the dollar gap were stockpiling, greater investment in "backward" areas, and the resumption of triangular trade. Although separate issues, they represented parts of a greater whole and they were never really separated

---

[53] 2nd Meeting of the SGEP, December 1, 1949, Gray Papers, CFR – Study Group Reports, Box 6, 4, Truman Library.

[54] Memorandum of Conversation, October 13, 1949, RG 59, Records of the PPS, 1947–1953, Country and Area Files – Europe, Box 27, Truman Library.

[55] Hoffman testimony, February 24, 1950, *To Amend the ECA of 1948*, 92, passim.

The Dollar Gap and Its Discontents

out in the minds of U.S. leaders. Discussion of one inevitably led to a discussion of the others.

Stockpiling strategic materials would see the United States purchase raw materials from many of Europe's colonies, which, as Eisenhower remarked, "might lead to dollars reaching Europe indirectly," that is, through triangular trade.[56] Precisely the point, but as another meeting participant noted, most of our "stockpiling purchases are subject to the 'Buy American' clause which gives preference to domestic suppliers, a most unstrategic arrangement."[57] Actually, by 1949 stockpiling had already become crucial to aiding the dollar gap. A panicked Acheson wrote John R. Steelman, chief of the National Security Resources Board, on July 29, 1949, concerned about the "developing situation in stockpile policies and programs." Congress, at Truman's request, was considering a $300 million reduction in the coming fiscal year's appropriation and was also seeking domestic over foreign suppliers of strategic materials.[58] This move would be "unfortunate," Acheson wrote, "in light of our security requirements." As well, he added, "a decision to reduce foreign buying in favor of domestic procurement would simultaneously impair our efforts to solve the current dollar difficulties which vitally affect United States interests abroad."[59] The NSC also reacted negatively to the rescission for reasons of the dollar gap. "From the standpoint of the important secondary benefit of stockpiling, as a stimulus to foreign economies, the proposed limit would reduce stockpile purchases during FY 1951 in areas which are presently receiving substantial dollar aid from the United States by as much as $100 million."[60]

As for "investment in backward areas," here the lead was the Point Four Program announced by President Truman in his inaugural speech in 1949. The objective of Point Four was to provide technical assistance to "under-developed" regions, which would enable them to build up their infrastructures, increase productivity, and become consumers. It also aimed at making these areas more attractive to private investors so that U.S. governmental aid would have a shelf life. Moreover, it was seen as

---

[56] 5th Meeting of the SGAE, May 18, 1949, CFR, Box 242, 10, PUL.

[57] Ibid.; Memorandum for Mr. Kermit Gordon, White House Staff, July 20, 1950, Elsey Papers, Stockpiling, Box 11, Truman Library.

[58] "Extracts from Letters Prepared by the Director of the Bureau of the Budget," July 8, 1949, *FRUS, 1949* I (Washington, D.C.: U.S. Government Printing Office, 1976): 355–356.

[59] Acheson to John R. Steelman, July 29, 1949, *FRUS, 1949* I: 364.

[60] "Governmental Programs in National Security and International Affairs for the Fiscal Year 1951," September 29, 1949, *FRUS, 1949* I: 385.

a way to channel dollars to Europeans. Through Point Four, said one participant of the SGAE, "we may not only help to keep our own economy at a high-level of activity; we may also help incidentally to promote Europe's dollar balance of payments."[61] Another participant, however, noted that "Point Four [was] of dubious value since it points toward backward areas and that is exactly not the place that Americans will want to build factories abroad."[62] Indeed, according to an ECA report of June 1950, "U.S. private investment abroad, except in the petroleum industry, has been reduced to a trickle," and the "burden of financing the dollar gap ... has fallen in recent years largely and increasingly on direct U.S. grants and loans."[63] Nor were the Export-Import Bank or the International Bank for Reconstruction and Development, more popularly known as the World Bank, in much position to help, being that they were "handicapped by the limited ability of these countries to meet local development costs or to service dollar loans."[64]

The ECA produced a report on the subject on March 29, 1950, and the State Department discussed it in an interdepartmental meeting on May 16, 1950. At issue was "the attainment of European and Japanese viability" after 1952. In the ECA scheme, the United States would import more from western Europe and export less to western Europe (what applied to western Europe applied to Japan as well). Western Europe's decrease in dollar imports would be made up through trade with the "under-developed" world; western Europe would buy commodities from these countries, which relieved them of spending dollars, and turn around and sell back to them the manufactures constructed from those commodities. However, this was dependent on "induc[ing] under-developed areas of the world to forego plans for industrialization and self-sufficiency and rather expand exports to Europe in two-way mutually advantageous trade."[65] The feasibility of that, however, was not clear.

A State Department working group on the dollar gap also pushed for investment in less-developed countries as a way of recommencing triangular trade. "The present rate of development in the under-developed

---

[61] 5th Meeting of the SGAE, May 18, 1949, CFR, 30, Box 242, 4, PUL.
[62] Ibid., 12.
[63] Economic Cooperation Administration Staff, "The Dollar Shortage," June 12, 1950, Gray Papers, Economic Cooperation Administration, Series of Policy Statements, Box 7, 2, Truman Library.
[64] "Post-ERP Prospects and Aid Programs," 5, Truman Library.
[65] "Comments on ECA Memorandum Entitled 'The Way Out for Europe: A Projection of World-Wide Trade and Payments Adjustments to Declining Marshall Plan Aid,'" May 19, 1950, Gray Papers, Post ERP Economic Projections, Box 9, 2, Truman Library.

The Dollar Gap and Its Discontents

areas must be accelerated, not only to maintain stability in these areas but also to promote economic viability in Europe and Japan." The problem was that although western Europe had saleable goods, it could only sell about 10 percent to the United States and 10 percent to eastern Europe. Moreover, although less-developed countries had a need for the goods, they did not have the means for developing the industries necessary to produce the commodities that would put them in a position of being able to buy such goods. The working group came up with an ambitious plan. It proposed "the formulation of a new U.S. program which will enable the under-developed areas to receive a considerable volume of net imports through grants and through long-term loans that do not require dollar repayment." How were they going to accomplish this? "Under this proposal, Japan would begin in FY 1952 to pay the U.S. Government in yen for its U.S. aid imports, which consist chiefly of wheat and cotton. The U.S. Government would then grant these yen to countries in South and Southeast Asia to support development projects that the [World] Bank would not finance and that would promote these under-developed countries' stability and increase their production of primary commodities needed by Japan." This would have the benefit of not "increas[ing] trade discrimination in the under-developed countries, since the European and Japanese unrequited exports to these countries would be additional to, rather than in substitution for, U.S. and other manufactures that these countries are now buying out of their own resources." The report urged that the program could be applied to western Europe as well.[66]

However, it was all theory. George Ball reported to the CFR that the Europeans were not very favorable to the investment idea. "Some Frenchmen have felt that their situation is such that investment in under-developed areas (India, etc.)," Ball remarked, "will not contribute anything quickly (within the next five or ten years)." Rather, "these men feel, an injection of a certain number of dollars into the continent directly would do the job."[67]

A few observers noted that western Europe may be encouraged to develop Africa as a means of remaining viable. George Kennan was particularly keen to this idea. If the "European[s] collaborat[ed] in the development of Africa," Kennan explained, they "might find a better field for merging [their] interests than in affairs at home." In addition to serving

---

[66] "Post-ERP Prospects and Aid Programs," 9, Truman Library.
[67] 9th Meeting of the SGEP, May 8, 1950, CFR, 30, Box 242, 3, PUL (brackets in the original).

as "a source of raw materials," Africa could provide "a market for their products which would take their trade out of the dollar areas and might relieve their dollar position."[68] Of course, that might have been a solution for the dollar gap but not one that would have solved the problem of trade between western Europe and the dollar area. But, then, Kennan never did see eye to eye with the multilateralists.

This interest in Africa was part of a larger idea of funneling dollars to Europe via "third countries" taken up by the PPS. The idea had close parallels to the Point Four Program but was distinct from it. At a June 1949 meeting of the PPS, Harlan Cleveland suggested "putting dollars elsewhere in the world and letting Europe earn the dollars out of a Point 4 sort of thing." Kennan wanted to know "whether anything is spelled out on the question." Henry LaBouisse, State Department coordinator of foreign aid and assistance for the Marshall Plan, mentioned that a report by the ECA had discussed it in terms of the "surplus in this country." This remark prompted Cleveland to offer that the "U.S., from its own economic standpoint, is going to have to cover its own export surplus with gifts to somebody.... Assuming you have to give money away in the world," perhaps "it is better to put dollars where they will not result in immediate recovery in U.S. but where they will take a circuitous route home." Perhaps, "we should buy our own exports for years[,]" Kennan interjected. To which Cleveland said, "That is [the] standard view in Europe. The Russians have said we must."[69]

Cleveland was also a participant in the SGEP. At the February 23, 1950, meeting of the group the discussion centered in part on Altschul's suggestion, written up in a memorandum of January 24, 1950, that an International Investment Authority be set up to enable the western European countries to invest abroad, which would ultimately "contribute mightily to the restoration of equilibrium in the free world." It would do so by raising production levels across the globe, or at least the "free world." Under the heading "approaches to a solution," Altschul laid out his reasoning for the Investment Authority. "On the economic side, the following suggestions have been touched upon at our previous meetings: (1) The stimulation of imports through tariff reduction and the revision of Customs regulations which handicap the free flow of goods to

[68] 84th Meeting of the PPS, May 25, 1949, RG 59, Records of the PPS, 1947–1953, Minutes of Meetings, 1947–1952, Box 32, 15, NAII; Meeting of the PPS, June 3, 1949, RG 59, Records of the PPS, 1947–1953, Minutes of Meetings, 1947–1952, Box 32, 2, NAII, for Kennan quote; 3–4.

[69] Meeting of the PPS, June 3, 1949, RG 59, Records of the PPS, 1947–1953, Minutes of Meetings, 1947–1952, Box 32, 8–9, NAII.

The Dollar Gap and Its Discontents

the United States[;] (2) Increased stockpiling of strategic and other raw materials[;] (3) Revision of our agricultural policy[; and] (4) The assumption by the United States of some of the British Sterling debt." Then he made this observation:

> No attempt has been made to estimate the extent to which any or all of these measures might reduce the dollar gap.... However, I believe it is the sense of the group that the practical political difficulties which are likely to be encountered in connection with pursuing each of these suggestions are such that on the most optimistic basis one cannot expect that measures taken in respect to all of them together would not measurably close the dollar gap.[70]

Restarting triangular trade was another potential remedy. Triangular trade was the process whereby Europe's colonies and protectorates sold raw materials to the United States and then spent the dollars they earned in Europe for manufactures, thus providing Europe dollars to spend in the United States. The practice had been key in getting dollars to Europe in the pre-war period; if it could be resurrected a similar benefit might accrue. Restarting triangular trade was welcomed by many in the CFR. "However, there are serious limitations to that development *at present*," Viner noted. "Canada, for instance, has lots of sterling but has been unable to find all the goods she wants in the United Kingdom and so has had to buy them here." Viner further felt that "we would get nowhere until we showed the Europeans what goods they could hope to export here, especially in the face of our long history of trying to keep out their products."[71] There were other problems with triangular trade as well. As Hoffman explained to the House Committee on Foreign Affairs, "European nations which were able to earn dollars [through triangular trade] up until the war now find that in the case of those dollars ... earned through triangular trade the people who earn them want to keep them to use themselves for buying in the United States." Hoffman elaborated: "The Indonesians no longer want to pay their dollars to Holland for imports from Holland so the Dutch can buy from us. They want to buy from us direct. The Malayans want to buy from us direct. The Indians are independent now, and they do not want to siphon all their trade through Great Britain. They do not want the British to get dollars they earn selling jute to us by selling cloth to them."[72] Restarting

[70] Frank Altschul, "Memorandum for the Discussion Group on Economic Policy," January 24, 1950, Gray Papers, CFR-Study Group Reports, 2, Truman Library.
[71] 5th Meeting of the SGAE, May 18, 1949, CFR, 30, Box 242, 10–11, PUL (emphasis added).
[72] Hoffman testimony, February 24, 1950, *To Amend the ECA of 1948*, 78.

triangular trade was essential and became the foreign policy of the United States toward Southeast Asia and other regions, which contributed to initial U.S. involvement in Vietnam and elsewhere in the "Third World." However, in the fall of 1949 and well into 1950, how to get it going again was plagued with seemingly intractable problems.

Additional solutions for getting dollars into the hands of the Europeans through means other than direct trade were also discussed. One focused on encouraging tourism, which was a form of "invisible items in Europe's balance of payments." (By "invisible" income is meant sources of income that are largely hidden because they cannot be predicted or tracked with any degree of certainty.) Members of the SGAE thought "a great deal could be accomplished in expanding American travel to Europe if the US government tried to help in this matter." More "facilities," that is, housing, had to be built if Europe were to "absorb another 100,000 summer tourists." The suggestion was made that "perhaps the ECA counterpart funds could be used for this purpose." (Counterpart funds were national currencies equal to the amount of ERP dollars a nation received that the United States required ERP recipients to put aside for uses to be determined at another date.) Another answer was to send more students and teachers abroad. Viner offered that "the last few summers everyone has gone to Europe who could get passage; ... Perhaps the US government could help by making more ships available; the British could do the same thing." Henry Wriston, president of Brown University, added that "over half the travellers [sic] last year had gone by airlines." Ellis agreed that "improved facilities, sending students abroad, and other measures to develop tourism" were important, and he added that they would have the additional benefit of not "coming under the heading 'aid to Europe.'"[73] The British were thinking along the same lines. In particular, U.S. student tourists were seen as ripe for coddling. "My colleague, the Minister of State," an unknown author of a memorandum from October 1949 wrote, "put up an idea for the student class.... He suggested that we could use troop-ships, or ships of that class. The students would have rather longer than three or four weeks [stay in Britain], and they would be extremely useful from the point of view of Anglo-American relations. They would also be useful from the point of view of dollar income."[74]

Still another avenue along these lines considered was importing unemployed laborers as domestic servants. Rabi noted that "when in Japan he

---

[73] "Consideration of the Effect of Declining American Aid Upon Western European Recovery," SGAE, September 26, 1949, CFR, 30, Box 242, 20–21, PUL.

[74] "Matters to be Discussed with the Chancellor of the Exchequer and the President of the Board of Trade in Connexion with the Dollar Problem," [October 15, 1949], FO 371/82943, The National Archives, Kew, England, United Kingdom (hereinafter TNA).

The Dollar Gap and Its Discontents

had become impressed with the possibilities of helping out foreign balances of payments while at the same time meeting a US problem by importing domestic servants for limited periods." Wriston added that the issue had been raised before the OEEC, "particularly as a means to absorbing surplus Italian labor." "Domestic servants would be non-competitive," Rabi offered. The problem, however, was the immigration laws. No one in the group "expected any important changes ... in our immigration laws" that would allow such a practice to occur. Besides, as academician Edward Mead Earle argued, "bringing over the DPs [Displaced Persons] will not contribute much to Europe's balance of payments whereas Italians or Japanese working in this country would swell the immigrant remittances."[75]

There were two further schemes put forth that are worthy of mention if only for their imaginative qualities. The first was to develop a market for British toys in the United States. In a letter to Averell Harriman from January 1950, Charles Churan of Graham & Childes, Ltd., informed Harriman that the company was sending "Charles Creed's famous private collection of model soldiers (15,000 strong) on a department store tour of the U.S. and Canada" as a way of stimulating interest in British toys. The soldiers themselves were not toys. "They are gems," Churan wrote, "collector's pieces; with uniforms entirely authoritative down to the tiniest detail. Napoleon even *looks* like Napoleon!" Continuing on, Churan got more to the point: "The Creed Army is the spear-head – the task force – of our exhibition of modern toy soldiers – tanks, radar, British and American troops in snow suits and gamma ray capes, model planes, miniature petrol driven racing cars, model yachts, doll's prams – all types of quality toys which, though they must buck our tariff in the U.S., do not really up-set the £300,000 domestic market the American toy manufacturers aim at each year." Churan then offered this interesting observation:

Now, inasmuch as Charles Creed *is* in Paris, ... and his army is European – International, and the fact that he is *lending* his army to aid sales (largely British, but orders will be taken for *any* European model makers who come up to standard) would you consider this effort an example of O.E.E.C.? If this promotion exhibition were taken to South America, for instance, does it follow the Marshall Gospel according to Paul Hoffman? Is it, in its small but spectacular way (the publicity the American department stores will unleash for their own benefit will be terrific!) an example of a co-operative effort?[76]

[75] "Consideration of the Effect of Declining American Aid Upon Western European Recovery," SGAE, September 26, 1949, CFR, 30, Box 242, 21, PUL.

[76] Charles Churan to Harriman, January 10, 1950, Marshall Plan, General Correspondence – C, Box 266, Harriman Papers, LC (italics and parentheses are all in the original).

The second scheme was to use the paintings of Winston Churchill as an attention-getter for an exhibit of British goods in the United States. In a letter to Andrew Berding from Roscoe Drummond, chief European information officer of the ECA, dated June 1, 1950, sent to Harriman via Berding, Drummond wrote that "we feel that if an exhibit of Churchill's paintings were held at the same time it would serve to dramatize the trade exhibit and bring many tens of thousands of people to the department store sponsoring it." Once Churchill had pledged his cooperation, Drummond stated, the search will go out to "find outstanding department stores in major American cities to sponsor and pay for both exhibits." Drummond was soliciting Harriman's help because Churchill was a personal friend of Harriman. Drummond was certain that "Mr. Churchill, himself a great patriot, will agree to the idea as one means of bringing perhaps many millions of dollars into British hands." He added that, "there is nothing, of course, to prevent Mr. Churchill's painting[s] themselves from being sold during the trade exhibit if Mr. Churchill is willing." Drummond closed his note by remarking that "this idea comes to us from Bill Howlett, of the Byoir Advertising Agency in Chicago, who has come to us as a consultant to assist us with the information side of the dollar gap problem."[77] None of these schemes, however, were likely to resolve the gap problem by 1952.

"Radical Schemes" Contemplated

Given the growing sense of potential catastrophe, a number of unorthodox solutions were put forward as means for dealing with the crisis. One such solution pushed by George Kennan saw Britain, the United States, and Canada forming a closer union, leaving the continent to form its own economic union with France leading the charge. Paul Nitze would refer to this idea as among a number of "radical schemes" the PPS contemplated in the heady months of the fall of 1949 as a means of curing the dollar crisis. The scheme grew out of a series of meetings held in May and June 1949 in the PPS. Gladwyn Jebb, Kennan's counterpart in the British Foreign Office, had written to Kennan on April 7, 1949, requesting that Kennan come to Britain to discuss informally the long-term future of British involvement on the continent, particularly in regard

---

[77] Roscoe Drummond to Andrew Berding, June 1, 1950, Marshall Plan, General Correspondence – B, Box 266, Harriman Papers, LC; Berding to Harriman, June 7, 1950, ibid.

The Dollar Gap and Its Discontents

to the effects of European integration. The meetings were held in preparation for Kennan's travels to Britain.[78]

The idea of the United States, Britain, and Canada forming a closer union and leaving the continent to go its own way, at least economically, emerged as a response to the realization that western European integration necessitated British involvement but that Britain was unwilling to accept the kind of involvement that would make integration efficacious. Britain was simply unwilling to commit beyond a certain point. That being the case, Kennan was looking for alternatives that would both aid Britain and move western Europe forward. Initially, the scheme was not given much weight by Kennan. It fell into the category of Kennan's penchant for ruminating about ideas, however fantastic, in the hopes of gaining clarity. However, the British sterling-dollar crisis of 1949–1950 changed that. In August 1949, Kennan wrote Acheson to indicate his belief that an association between the United States, Britain, and Canada was the only way to solve the "pound-dollar problem." Britain had to readjust its economy to that of North America's, he argued. He suggested that the British should be told that "we are prepared to contemplate a closer relationship with them and the Canadians to the extent that this is needed to facilitate the economic adjustment that must be made."[79]

In retrospect the plan does indeed seem fantastic. Although it called only for the United States to disassociate economically from the continent, it is difficult to see how this would not have led to a great weakening of U.S. political and even military involvement on the continent as well, a most unwelcome scenario. Nonetheless, the PPS continued to push the idea throughout the late summer and into the fall of 1949. For instance, Nitze suggested that an "informal British-U.S.-Canadian working group" be set up to analyze the feasibility of them forming a closer union. In addition, the issue was discussed at a meeting of the American members of the Combined Policy Committee on cooperation over atomic energy among the United States, Canada, and the United Kingdom.[80]

---

[78] Nitze is quoted in the Princeton Seminars, October 10, 1953, Dean Acheson Papers, reel 1, track 2, Box 97, 6, 3, Truman Library; Gladwyn Jebb to Kennan, April 7, 1949, RG 59, Records of the PPS, 1947–1953, Country and Area Files: Europe, 1948–1949, NAII; Kennan to Charles Bohlen, October 12, 1949, ibid.

[79] Kennan to Webb and Acheson, August 22, 1949, RG 59, Records of the PPS, 1947–1953, Country and Area Files – Europe, NAII.

[80] 6th Meeting of the PPS, August 15, 1949, RG 59, Records of the PPS, 1947–1953, Country and Area Files – Europe, 2, NAII; Minutes of the Meeting of the American Members of the Combined Policy Committee, September 13, 1949, *FRUS, 1949* 4: 520–522. See also the very interesting letter and memorandum sent by Kennan to Bohlen on

In connection with this idea, it became necessary to consider what would be done with the "sterling balances." These were pound sterling debts Britain owed to many sterling-area countries as a result of the war. Short of dollars during the war, Britain had to obtain goods and raw materials from the sterling area on promise of repayment at a future date. At war's end the debt stood at $13 billion. The debt was a bane because paying it down shuttled British products into the sterling area rather than the dollar area where they could have aided in decreasing the dollar gap. In other words, they added nothing to the British purse. Any closer association among Britain, the United States, and Canada would necessitate paying off these balances, and the United States would likely have to pick up the tab. It would be an unprecedented undertaking, and no one seriously believed Congress would approve. Plus, the plan's success depended on Britain's agreement. That proved problematic, as Britain throughout the fall of 1949 and into 1950 continued to shy away from firm commitments even as it pursued a more autarchic course.[81]

The obstacle that ultimately made such a proposal impossible was Germany. Kennan alone seemed capable of imagining a world in which Germany was free to go neutral. In an interesting exchange with Robert Oppenheimer, in which "Oppie" expressed his fear of Germany looking east rather than west, Kennan amazingly remarked that "[e]veryone would agree with you about that in France and England, and probably here in Washington. I am not sure it is [the] most hair-raising thing, where consequences of not allowing for the inevitable tendency of that area of Europe to form third force will not be unfortunate."[82] However, as Acheson made clear, "the character of Western Germany and of its relations to its neighbors is rapidly being molded. There are signs that it is already taking a familiar and dangerous nationalist turn. This trend must be expected to continue unless German resources and energies can be harnessed to the security and welfare of Western Europe as a whole. The danger is that the time to arrest and reverse this trend is already

---

October 12, 1949, RG 59, Records of the PPS, 1947–1953, Country and Area Files – Europe, NAII.

[81] 4th Meeting of the SGEP, January 25, 1950, Gray Papers, Working Papers, General File, Balance of Payments Records – U.K. 1948–1949, Currency Convertibility – Sterling Area, CFR – Study Group Reports, Box 6, 1, Truman Library.

[82] 97th Meeting of the PPS, June 8, 1949, RG 59, Records of the PPS, 1947–1953, Minutes of Meetings, 12, NAII.

The Dollar Gap and Its Discontents

very short. This consideration weighs heavily in our thinking."[83] By November Nitze had abandoned any notions of a U.S.-U.K.-Canada alliance, if indeed he had ever taken them seriously.[84] Thus, Kennan's ideas ultimately went nowhere.

Finally, there were the two most radical schemes to contemplate. Despite the problems with all of the previously mentioned "solutions" to the dollar gap, there remained two possibilities that were viable and would have closed the dollar gap rather quickly. First, the United States simply could have stopped funding the gap. In truth, the dollar gap was a creation. It only existed because the United States chose to fund it. Had the United States ceased doing so, the gap would have closed at whatever level the market dictated. "The dollar gap could, of course, be closed tomorrow if exports from the dollar area to Europe were reduced to what Europe can now pay with her present earnings," Hoffman told the National Association of Manufacturers in an April 1950 address. However, "that would call for a reduction in exports of more than $3 billion. Such a quick and drastic reduction would obviously mean catastrophe for Europe because her very life depends on maintaining a huge flow of food and raw material imports, as well as certain tools and equipment which can be obtained only in the United States." And he added: "Such a reduction would also result in a severe dislocation of our own economy." However, for political and economic reasons, such a breakdown in trade and money transfers was what U.S. officials were trying to prevent.[85] "It depends on where you want to balance," Acheson told the House Committee on Foreign Affairs in February 1950. "Our total balance of payments now is somewhere over $16,000,000,000. You can always balance your payments somewhere, but if you balance them at the level

---

[83] Memorandum for Perkins, October 19, 1949, RG 59, Records of the PPS, 1947–1953, Country and Area Files – Europe, Box 27, 2, NAII.

[84] See Nitze to Webb, November 16, 1949, RG 59, Records of the PPS, 1947–1953, Country and Area Files – Europe, Box 27, NAII; "Outline of Work Program on Western European Economic Integration," ibid.

[85] Address by Paul Hoffman before the National Association of Manufactures, April 20, 1950, Elsey Papers, Box 59, Truman Library (emphasis added). See also 1st Meeting of the SGEP, November 1, 1949, CFR, 35, Box 243, 2, PUL; "European Integration," November 7, 1949, RG 59, Records of the PPS, Country and Area Files – Europe, Box 27, NAII; "Summary Outline of Discussion of Long Term Problems for January 1950 Economic Report," November 17, 1949, Elsey Papers, Box 59, Truman Library; Hoffman testimony, February 21, 1950, *To Amend the ECA of 1948*, 6; ECA Staff, "The Dollar Shortage," Truman Library; Diebold, "European Recovery: The Next Two Years," 4, Truman Library.

of our imports at the present time, I think both the free world and the United States would suffer considerable shocks in the whole struggle that we now are having with another point of view."[86]

The other solution was for western Europe to increase greatly its trading relations with eastern Europe and, by implication, the Soviet Union. Traditionally, trade between eastern and western Europe had been quite extensive. Eastern Europe was western Europe's bread basket as well as an outlet for its manufactured goods. This traditional pattern of trade, however, had been broken by the war and the subsequent Soviet domination of the region. If it could be reestablished, Europe as a whole could be made viable. The problem was that this pattern of trade would also make European nations more autarchic even as they cut imports from the United States because of their lack of dollars, a most undesirable outcome. There were geopolitical concerns in any such development as well. If western Europe increased its trade with eastern Europe, it was likely to go neutral in the Cold War or even side with the Soviets.

Such was the topic of discussion at the June 1949 meeting of the SGAE. Debating whether western Europe had the capability of going neutral, virtually all members were in agreement that western European neutrality was likely impossible to achieve, but, should it be achieved, would be disastrous for the United States. For the time being, western Europe would be "dependent," as McGeorge Bundy, then a Harvard professor of international relations, put it, on either the United States or on the Soviet Union. He could not envision that "a Third Force of the sort advocated by writers in *The New Statesman* and *The Nation* was possible." This reality meant western Europe had to be tied to the United States. Summing up the general attitude, Eisenhower noted that: "The United States could not remain an island of freedom and democracy if the rest of the world were dominated by Communism." East-west trade, therefore, had to be contained, however traditional it may have been.[87]

As things were at the time, keeping such trade contained was proving difficult. U.S. officials tried to curb the trade on the grounds that it was, in effect, arming the enemy. However, that did not always prove a persuasive argument with the western European nations, even though they faced the Soviets directly. At a meeting of the Foreign Ministers from September 18, 1950, Acheson complained to British Foreign Minister

---

[86] Acheson testimony, February 21, 1950, *To Amend the ECA of 1948*, 20.

[87] 6th Meeting of the SGAE, June 27, 1949, CFR, 30, Box 242, 10, PUL; Meeting of the U.S. Ambassadors at Paris, October 21–22, 1949, *FRUS, 1949* 4: 481–82.

The Dollar Gap and Its Discontents

Ernest Bevin and French Foreign Minister Robert Schuman that the western Europeans were selling strategic materials to the Soviet Union that U.S. producers were kept from doing because they were obeying the embargo on sensitive materials. Moreover, exports of strategic materials earmarked for western Europe under the Mutual Defense Assistance Program were being shipped to the Soviet Union. Furthermore, there was lack of agreement over what constituted adding the word strategic to any particular export. Moreover, some nations were simply ignoring the ban altogether and thus reaping the rewards of the Americans' folly. The members of the SGAE left off by merely agreeing that more work would have to be done on the issue. Indeed, U.S. officials would continue to be agitated over east-west trade for years to come.[88]

No Way Out

This examination detailing the various problems and possible solutions associated with developing a permanent answer to the dollar gap has been necessary to make a fundamental point – despite great effort aimed at finding a solution to the dollar gap well into 1950, no viable solution presented itself, especially given the time frame allotted by the impending end of the Marshall Plan in 1952. Such was the topic of a question put to Secretary of State Dean Acheson by Congressman Chester Merrow at hearings on whether to amend the ECA act held in early 1950. Questioned by Congressman Merrow as to whether there is "any planning at the moment for any type of an organization to continue aid to the OEEC countries after [the ERP] is finished," Acheson responded simply by saying "No."[89] Acheson was a master of political manipulation. He was being honest when he responded in the negative to the query whether there was any plan to "continue aid" to western Europe when the ERP ended. There was not. But something *was* in the works – NSC 68. Before we turn to it, however, we need to examine the British sterling-dollar crisis of 1949–1950.

---

[88] 5th Meeting of the Foreign Ministers, September 18, 1950, *FRUS, 1950* 3 (Washington, D.C.: U.S. Government Printing Office, 1977): 1234–1238; Comment of Colonel Charles B. Bonesteel, Meeting of the U.S. Ambassadors at Paris, October 21–22, 1949, *FRUS, 1949* 4: 482.

[89] Acheson testimony, February 21, 1950, *To Amend the ECA of 1948*, 36.

5

The British Sterling-Dollar Crisis of 1949–1950

> The UK's collapse is one of the most dramatic events of recent history and the suddenness of that collapse has demonstrated the extent and depth of her former close association in the business and financial structure of Europe.
>
> David K. E. Bruce, U.S. Ambassador to France, 1949

United States foreign policy officials and other elites committed to multilateralism viewed the European Recovery Program (ERP), or the Marshall Plan, as a stop-gap measure designed to ease western Europe's dollar gap while more permanent solutions to it could be found. In the summer of 1949, however, it became clear to them that the Marshall Plan was not achieving its desired end as the dollar gap hit Britain with renewed force, causing it to dip into its gold and dollar reserves to purchase badly needed imports and, ultimately, to place trade restrictions on U.S. and other dollar area imports and begin contemplating autarchic solutions to overcome its economic woes. This, even as it was receiving Marshall Plan aid. The British crisis of 1949–1950 served as a wake-up call to Truman administration officials and their British counterparts that the dollar gap was a far more serious crisis than they had realized initially and that if something were not done to overcome it by 1952, the end year of the Marshall Plan, the western world would likely collapse. Whereas U.S. foreign policymakers knew that the Marshall Plan would not in and of itself fix the dollar gap, they at least thought it would be sufficient to provide time to find a more permanent solution. Seen in this light, the crisis was wholly unexpected. Its unexpectedness, however, is precisely what made it so important. The objective of this chapter is to analyze

128

The British Sterling-Dollar Crisis of 1949–1950   129

in depth the British crisis of 1949–1950. The British crisis did not alone lead to NSC 68, but it is unlikely that NSC 68 would have been created in its absence.

The Marshall Plan and Its Discontents

The Marshall Plan was sold to both Congress and the American people on the promise that by 1952 it would restore the participating nations to a level at which they would be able to earn dollars through the normal processes of trade and therefore not need to rely on U.S. aid. Initially, the Marshall Plan proved a great success. "ERP Winning Aims, Its Chiefs Report," a *New York Times* headline on February 9, 1949, expounded. Paul Hoffman, head of the Economic Cooperation Administration (ECA), the agency primarily responsible for administering ERP funds, called the Marshall Plan the "greatest bargain the American people ever had."[1] Speaking in April 1949, Hoffman noted seven achievements that the Marshall Plan had accomplished in its first ten months including "increased [industrial] production to virtually the prewar level"; "steel ... output ... [of] 40,000,000 tons, or 30 per cent more than 1947"; "exports ... 21 per cent higher than in 1947"; and "crop production ... about one-fourth higher than the poor crop year of 1947, and about equal to the pre-war levels."[2] In May 1949, the ECA noted in a report to Congress that Europe's industrial output equaled the 1938 level and that its dollar deficit, or gap, had been slashed 30 percent.[3]

Britain, which was the primary benefactor of the Marshall Plan, also showed encouraging signs of recovery.[4] "British Export Soaring," the *New York Times* noted on February 9, 1949.[5] The February 23, 1949, issue of the *Times* also reported that "Britain's trading deficit with the United States was £113,600,000 (about $454,400,000).... This compares with a deficit of £235,800,000 in 1947." In addition, "British exports to the United States rose from £61,300,000 in 1947 to

---

[1] C. P. Trussell, *The New York Times*, February 9, 1949, 12.
[2] "ERP at Mid-Mark, Hoffman Asserts," *The New York Times*, April 3, 1949, 12.
[3] "ECA Finds Europe's Output at '38 Level; Foresees a 30% Decline in Dollar Deficit," *The New York Times*, May 17, 1949, 13.
[4] A diagram in *The New York Times*, February 13, 1949, 5(E), divides ERP funds for 1948–1949 as follows: Britain 26.1%, France 20.7%, Benelux 15.1%, Italy 12.1%, with the remainder at 26%. See also Andrew Rotter, *The Path to Vietnam: Origins of the American Commitment to Southeast Asia* (Ithaca, New York: Cornell University Press, 1987), 52.
[5] *The New York Times*, February 9, 1949, 4.

£70,800,000 in 1948, while imports were reduced from £297,100,000 to £184,400,000."[6] The glee, however, masked a harsh reality. Britain's productivity was up, but its dollar gap remained. In early 1949, the only thing keeping the British economically tied to the United States was George Marshall's dollars.[7]

Successful as the Marshall Plan was in its first year, running alongside it were trends that began to undermine it. In late 1948, the U.S. economy slipped into a recession. Business slowdowns were reported for each of the first six months of 1949, except in April when a slight rise attributed to "seasonal" changes occurred. In the four years since the end of the war, the fear had been that inflation would run amok due to a scarcity of goods. Not only was there pent-up demand not being serviced at home, due to the lengthy time it took to convert from a war to a peacetime economy, but a large quantity of U.S. goods were being sent abroad to supply a destitute world. By 1949 production had caught up with demand and had begun to surpass it. As the *New York Times* reported: "The story that the recent Christmas shopping season revealed is that war-time shortages of almost everything but automobiles and housing are over. The pipe-lines of supply are full and, in some cases, overflowing. The long-predicted buyer's market is at hand."[8] By 1948, fears of inflation were giving way to fears of deflation. The gross national product fell 1.5 percent. Industrial production dropped 8.8 percent. By July 1949, 4.1 million people, the highest number since the end of the war, were unemployed.[9]

---

[6] "British Slash Trade Deficit In Trade With U.S.," *The New York Times*, February 23, 1949, 37.

[7] "Britain Close to Trade Balance Except with Respect to Dollars," *The New York Times*, March 12, 1949, 6; "Aim of Britain Set as Dollar-Gap Cut," ibid., March 29, 1949, 37; Fred L. Block, *The Origins of International Economic Disorder: A Study of United States International Monetary Policy from World War II to the Present* (Berkeley, California: University of California Press, 1977), 86–96; William Borden, *The Pacific Alliance: United States Foreign Economic Policy and Japanese Trade Recovery, 1947–1955* (Madison, Wisconsin: University of Wisconsin Press, 1984), 27–29.

[8] C. F. Hughes, "Boom is Leveling Off, Most Businessmen Feel; Readjustment Awaited," *The New York Times*, January 3, 1949, 41(L).

[9] Council of Economic Advisors, *The Economic Report to the President: 1949* (Washington, DC: U.S. Government Printing Office, 1949), 13, passim; Council of Economic Advisors, *The Economic Report to the President: 1950* (Washington, DC: U.S. Government Printing Office, 1950), 3–5, 25–29, passim; "Continued Decline Noted in January," *The New York Times*, February 13, 1949, 10(F); "February Output Shows New Drop," *The New York Times*, March 26, 1949, 20; "Survey Shows Rise in April Business," *The New York Times*, May 1, 1949, 1(F); "Business Decline Continued in May," *The New York Times*, June 22, 1949, 48; "Business Decline Continues in June," *The New York Times*, June 26, 1949, 1(F); "Financial Week," *The New York Times*, February 13, 1949, 1(F); "Surplus Declared Replacing Deficit," *The New York Times*, May 10, 1949, 35.

The British Sterling-Dollar Crisis of 1949–1950

In the long run, the recession was mild in the United States. The great demand for goods abroad and at home, government subsidies for domestic producers, Marshall Plan and other foreign aid that paid for exports, and military expenditures made a serious recession or depression a near impossibility, a relief to those who had worried that a postwar depression was certain in the United States. However, the recession wreaked havoc on Europe and especially on Great Britain. The result in Britain was the sterling-dollar crisis of 1949–1950.[10]

The British "Empire" in the Postwar Era

Before proceeding to examine the crisis in detail, it is necessary to gain a fuller understanding of Great Britain at the close of the war. Britain's "empire" had been dying a slow death since the turn of the century. World War I, the worldwide depression of the 1930s, and World War II hastened that decline. For instance, in 1948 Britain produced less consumer goods than in 1928.[11] Nonetheless, in the post–World War II era Britain still held on to several colonies and protectorates, especially in Southeast Asia and, more importantly, served as banker for the vast sterling area, a region that included the United Kingdom, the Commonwealth dominions (excluding Canada), the British colonies, and several non-British countries that used sterling as their currency, including Egypt and Sweden.[12] To gain a sense of the size of the sterling area, in 1950 sterling financed roughly 36 percent of all *world* trade.[13] The sterling area was a shadow of Britain's once immense empire. Nonetheless, it retained Britain's standing as a major world power. What this meant in ultimate terms was that Britain would try to hold on to the sterling area at any cost.

During the 1930s, Britain had demonstrated just how far it was willing to go to keep hold of the sterling area. In response to the Great Depression, and more specifically to the Smoot-Hawley tariff instituted by the United States in 1930, Britain formed the Imperial Preference system.[14] Imperial

---

[10] CEA, *The Economic Report to the President: 1950*, 29–30.
[11] Comment by economist Jacob Viner, Fifth Meeting of the Study Group on Aid to Europe, May 18, 1949, Council on Foreign Relations (CFR), 30, 9, Public Policy Papers, Department of Rare Books and Special Collections, Princeton University Libraries, Princeton, New Jersey (hereinafter PUL).
[12] "Ten-Word Lexicon of Foreign-Trade Terms," *The New York Times*, July 10, 1949, 5(E).
[13] Edward H. Collins, "Economics and Finance: 'The Dollar Gap' – Gone or Just Obscured?" *The New York Times*, November 27, 1950, 45.
[14] Block, *The Origins of International Economic Disorder*, 25–31; Walter LaFeber, *The American Age: U.S. Foreign Policy at Home and Abroad, 1750 to the Present* (New York: W. W. Norton and Company, 1994), 2nd edition, 350.

Preference created a sterling "bloc" out of the sterling area, in effect making it autarchic, or self-sufficient. Trade among sterling area nations remained duty free, whereas high tariffs were set against all imports produced outside the sterling area. By giving a preferential position to British and other sterling nations, this system created a large trading bloc that discriminated against the trade of nonsterling nations. The Imperial Preference system was especially hard on the United States, which could produce goods at far cheaper rates than any other nation in the world and thus constituted Britain's principal competitor in world trade. Imperial Preference did not preclude sterling nations from trading with the dollar area, which consisted of the western hemisphere, the United States possessions, and the Philippines. Nonetheless, the high tariff placed on dollar goods made them too expensive and thus limited their sales with the sterling area. The demise of Imperial Preference was the focus of U.S. efforts to get Britain to adopt multilateral trading policies in exchange for Lend-Lease during WWII and for the British loan of 1946.[15]

Besides Imperial Preference, Britain established two other trade policies during the war that made the sterling area more autarchic. The first was the dollar pool. Not all sterling nations participated in the dollar pool. Those that did were required to remit all of their dollar earnings to Britain, at which time they would receive sterling credits or promises on future manufactured goods. When dollar pool nations wanted to buy from the United States, for instance, they would apply to Britain for the dollars needed to purchase the goods. Although the point of the pool was to conserve dollars for the war effort, it continued operating in the postwar era, giving Britain great control over the dollar purchases of a sizeable number of sterling-area countries. The second move was nonconvertibility. Prior to the war, sterling had been freely convertible. Outside of dollar pool nations, those nations holding sterling could exchange it for dollars or any other currency. Under nonconvertibility, France, for instance, could only spend its sterling in the sterling area. Nonconvertibility forced holders of sterling into bilateral trade arrangements with Britain and away from the multilateralism that U.S. officials sought.[16]

Prior to WWII, Britain's means for earning dollars came from three sources: (1) through direct trade with the dollar area; (2) through export

[15] Richard N. Gardner, *Sterling-Dollar Diplomacy: Anglo-American Collaboration in the Reconstruction of Multilateral Trade* (Oxford, United Kingdom: Claredon Press, 1956), 18–19, 31–34, 64–68; Block, *The Origins of International Economic Disorder*, 14–31; Rotter, *The Path to Vietnam*, 49–50.

[16] R. Gardner, *Sterling-Dollar Diplomacy* (1956), 55, 214–215, 330; Block, *The Origins of International Economic Disorder*, 65; Rotter, *The Path to Vietnam*, 49–50.

The British Sterling-Dollar Crisis of 1949–1950

of raw materials from its colonies – Malaysia, for example, would sell rubber to the United States and would then buy finished products from Britain with the dollars it earned; and (3) through "invisible income" – overseas investments, shipping, and tourism. By these latter two means especially, Britain was able to obtain a rough balance of payments with the dollar area in the pre-WWII period, though, as we have seen, at a greatly reduced level of trade between the two areas.[17] WWII, however, greatly disrupted Britain's whole economic system, making these invisible incomes less viable. Britain relinquished nearly all of its overseas investments to finance the war, and its share of world shipping declined precipitously. Moreover, many of its colonies were occupied by the Japanese during the war and were either in shambles or making moves toward independence, which made them precarious as sources of raw materials to sell to the dollar area. The United States also, to give just one example, developed synthetic rubber during the war, because it could not obtain any from Japanese-controlled Malaysia. This action further burdened Britain once peace came, because synthetic rubber made the natural variety virtually unnecessary. Finally, British industry simply was not productive enough to produce goods both for the home market, the first priority, as well as for export, which is one reason that the Marshall Plan was so necessary.[18]

In addition to these structural problems, one of the gravest problems Britain faced in the postwar era was acquiring the means to settle its debt with the sterling-area nations. To pay for the war, Britain borrowed heavily from the sterling area in the form of raw materials and goods based on credit and through the means of the dollar pool. To give an indication of how the war affected Britain, in the span of five years Britain went from being a creditor to a debtor within the sterling area itself.[19] At war's end, Britain owed the sterling-area nations the equivalent of about $13.5 billion.[20] There were two ways to settle the balances. First, those nations holding sterling credits could exchange them in Britain for dollars for use in the dollar area. This was the favored method, as many of the goods these nations sought could only be found in the United

---

[17] Borden, *The Pacific Alliance*, 21–22; Rotter, *The Path to Vietnam*, 55–60.

[18] "Britain Sees Peril to Rubber Trade: Resents Effect Our Synthetic Industry is Having on Her Natural Product," *The New York Times*, May 12, 1949, 43; Borden, *The Pacific Alliance*, 21–22; Rotter, *The Path to Vietnam*, 58.

[19] Rotter, *The Path to Vietnam*, 50.

[20] Consultation on Trade Arrangements with Great Britain, September 20, 1949, Committee on Foreign Relations, U.S. Senate, *Reviews of the World Situation: 1949–1950* (Washington, D.C.: U.S. Government Printing Office, 1974), 51.

134 NSC 68 and the Political Economy of the Early Cold War

States and other dollar markets. However, this taxed Britain's already precarious dollar earnings. Second, the credits could be used to purchase manufactured goods in Britain. Two problems came in conjunction with this method. One was that it did not add anything to national wealth in Britain; the British manufacturer was merely paid out of the British Treasury. The second was that the method made the area more autarchic because through credit purchasing, British manufacturers were assured a buyer for their goods in the sterling area, whereas in the dollar area they faced competition. Thus, trade tended to gravitate toward the sterling area and away from the dollar area, further widening the dollar gap. In the same vein, the sterling nations were assured a market for their raw materials in Britain, which simply added to the autarchic nature of the sterling area.[21]

The core of Britain's problem in the immediate postwar era was primarily one of insufficient production. Britain needed to produce a sufficient amount of goods so that it could earn enough dollars to simultaneously maintain gold and dollar reserves, which it set at a minimum of $2 billion, pay off its debt to the sterling area, and provide needed dollar goods both for its own people and the rest of the sterling area through its role as banker for the area. This problem came at a time when some of Britain's traditional means for earning dollars had ceased to exist, such as foreign investments and profits from world shipping. If Britain had been as "hyper"-productive as the United States was after the war, the problem may have been solved.[22] However, Britain was not. The only thing keeping Britain tied to the dollar area by 1948 was the Marshall Plan. Thus, Britain was walking on a slippery slope in late 1948 and early 1949. Any downward trend was likely to push Britain over the edge into economic chaos.

The Crisis Begins

That push began in February 1949. "Britain Reports Drop in February Exports," the *New York Times* reported on March 22.[23] In early April,

---

[21] On these points, see "The Sterling Balance Problem," March 27, 1950, Current Economic Developments, 1945–1972 (hereinafter CED), Record Group 59, General Records of the Department of State (RG 59), National Archives II, College Park, Maryland, (hereinafter NAII), 4–5; and Raymond Daniel, "London Renewing Commonwealth Tie," *The New York Times*, May 1, 1949, 5(E).

[22] "Britain Suspends Dollar Purchasing," July 25, 1949, CED, 2, NAII.

[23] *The New York Times*, March 22, 1949, 12; see also, "Sterling Area has Deficit: $328,000,000 Shortage Incurred in First Quarter of 1949," *The New York Times*, April 7, 1949, 10.

The British Sterling-Dollar Crisis of 1949–1950   135

the *New York Times* reported that Britain accrued a $328 million debt in the first quarter of the year. The primary cause for Britain's export decline was the recession that began in the United States in late 1948.[24] When the recession hit, American demand for British goods declined. Compounding matters, once the recession began in earnest, word emerged that Britain was about to devalue the pound.[25] Even though British officials stead-fastly denied this, U.S. importers responded by slowing their buying from Britain under the premise that they would be able to buy cheaper once devaluation occurred. The overall result of this drop in exports was a contraction of Britain's already meager dollar earnings. The dollar gap was back.[26]

Britain's initial reaction to its export decline was to put forward a plan for all of the ERP nations to cut their dollar imports by 10 percent and to secure outside sources for the goods they traditionally bought from the dollar area. Britain suggested the new approach at a meeting of the Organization for European Economic Cooperation (OEEC), the organization set up on the European side to manage the Marshall Plan, on March 5 and 6, 1949. France and Belgium both balked. French offi-cials said it "amounted to an effort to impose British austerity upon the continent and to limit European economic cooperation."[27] Faced with opposition from the other ERP nations, the British recanted their push for a "non-selective" 10 percent cut in dollar imports. However, reflecting the influence it still retained, Britain secured agreement from the other Marshall Plan states to reduce their dollar imports, though at no set fig-ure, and to concentrate efforts on securing imports from outside the dol-lar area.[28]

U.S. officials had not been asked to sit in on the discussions from the beginning, a situation that considerably irked roving U.S. ambassador

---

[24] Willard Thorp to Dean Acheson, June 27, 1949, *Foreign Relations of the United States* (hereinafter *FRUS*), *1949* 4 (Washington, D.C.: U.S. Government Printing Office, 1975): 794.

[25] Sir Oliver Franks, British ambassador to the U.S., to the Secretary of State, May 20, 1949, FO 371/75577, UE 3176, The National Archives, Kew, England, United Kingdom (hereinafter TNA); Clifton Daniel, "Talk of Devaluation Still Frets British," *The New York Times*, May 4, 1949, 17; "Devaluation Talk Sets Back Sterling," ibid., May 18, 1949, 41.

[26] "Implications of the Sterling Area Crisis to the U.K. and the U.S.," August 18, 1949, *FRUS, 1949* 4: 806–820.

[27] Harold Callender, "ERP Nations Split on Austerity Cuts," *The New York Times*, March 6, 1949, 22.

[28] Harriman to Hoffman, April 12, 1949, *FRUS, 1949* 4:374–377; Harold Callender, "Europeans to Drop ERP 'Master' Plan," *The New York Times*, March 7, 1949, 6.

for the Marshall Plan Averell Harriman. However, on March 7 and 8, Harriman was asked to join the meetings and present the U.S. point of view about the new trade policy being considered. His remarks provide key insight into the thinking among U.S. foreign policy officials in the early months of 1949.

By his own account, Harriman began his discussion by stressing to the group the negative reception the policy would have on U.S. public opinion. The policy being considered would be "extremely dangerous in its potential effects on ... [a] very important segment of American public opinion desiring [a] sound trade relationship between United States and Europe [that is] to be achieved through [the] Marshall Plan, and ... [on] less important but vocal elements of American public opinion which were opposed to [the] Marshall Plan and would gladly misinterpret [the] OEEC attitude." He reiterated that the goal of the ERP was European self-support by 1952, a goal that he stated would require the efforts of all concerned nations, the United States included. To this end, he argued, the United States had shown itself willing to do its part by its promotion of the ITO (International Trade Organization) and its support for the "progressive lowering of the barriers leading to expanded world trade." Responding directly to the initiative before the meeting, Harriman said: "We are opposed to restrictive policies and especially to [the] creation of [an] autarchic Europe."[29]

Autarchy – this was something to fear. It was, according to Truman administration officials committed to multilateralism, the autarchy of the 1930s that had prolonged the depression. It was also, they believed, the autarchy of the 1930s that had precipitated a second world war. Virtually, the entire postwar foreign policy of the United States was in one way or another aimed at destroying the forces of autarchy. In the summer of 1949, with Britain on the verge of economic collapse, autarchy was, once again, precisely what they were facing.[30]

[29] Harriman to Hoffman, April 12, 1949, *FRUS, 1949* 4: 375–376.
[30] See, for instance, Laurence Shoup and William Minter, *Imperial Brain Trust: The Council on Foreign Relations and United States Foreign Policy* (New York: Monthly Review Press, 1977), passim; Melvyn Leffler, *A Preponderance of Power: The Truman Administration, National Security, and the Cold War* (Stanford, California: Stanford University Press, 1992), 8–15. There is disagreement on this score. The reasons for the depression's long duration and what effects it had on the road to war have long been a source of debate. Current thinking, particularly in economic circles, is that its duration can be tied to deflationary monetary policies used to maintain fixed exchange rates, as economist Barry Eichengreen has argued. See his *Elusive Stability: Essays in the History of International Finance, 1919–1939* (New York: Cambridge University Press, 1990), esp. 215–270. However, as it has taken the advent of time and available sources to come

The British Sterling-Dollar Crisis of 1949–1950   137

Harriman stressed that "United States productivity per inhabitant was three or four times that of Europe and that a basic new approach to the problem of European productivity and hence of European contribution to world trade was essential."[31] Harriman pointed to what was fast becoming conventional thinking among U.S. officials and what had led them to call for greater western European economic unity under what they termed the "second phase" of the Marshall Plan – the need to increase western European productivity to match United States levels. As we saw in Chapter 3, the only thing keeping western Europe tied to the United States in 1949 was the Marshall Plan. If the gap could not be bridged at the level of exports the United States was generating, it would be bridged at the level western Europeans were capable of generating, which, in the view of most U.S. officials, would prove devastating to the U.S. economy as then constituted. Closing the gap at a low level likely would also mean a low standard of living for western Europe, leaving the region potentially vulnerable to communist penetration or at least neutrality in the Cold War, both prospects being anathema to Truman administration leaders. Raising productivity and consumption would solve the issue, just as a rising tide lifts all boats, or so they believed.

Harriman continued: "I laid particular emphasis upon [the] need for [a] realistic examination of European costs and pricing policies. I said we could not accept [the] thesis apparently advocated by Cripps to [the] effect that new non-dollar sources of supply should be developed regardless of cost or effect on trade with [the] dollar area." Sir Stafford Cripps, British Secretary of the Exchequer, responded "that there would be still [an] important dollar deficit in 1952 and that consequently drastic measures would be needed." In 1952, the Marshall Plan was scheduled to end. Cripps was attempting to ensure that Britain could survive economically independent of the United States after that date, if such a need arose. For U.S. officials, Cripps's sentiments merely represented a return to the economic nationalism they blamed for the Great Depression. They saw Britain's move as the all-too typical reaction of Europeans to turn to protectionism whenever the going got rough. "Our congress and people expected [that] they would by 1952 have contributed to [the] creation of world trade conditions and particularly [of] European trade conditions

---

to this conclusion, U.S. leaders at the time clearly did not view the debacle in the same light. They were multilateralists, and they saw autarchy as a direct threat to their world view. As to the role of autarchy in leading to WWII, it is necessary to state only that from the perspective of 1949, autarchy very much seemed to have been what led to war.

[31] Harriman to Hoffman, April 12, 1949, *FRUS, 1949* 4: 376.

considerably less restrictive than those existing at [the] time [ERP?] was initiated," Harriman stated.[32]

Harriman urged the group to develop plans to increase dollar earnings. "With regard to colonial and backward area development," he said, "emphasis should be on developing new sources of exports to increase dollar earnings rather than on finding substitute sources of supply to avoid dollar spending." Ultimately, Harriman noted that, in light of his comments, several changes to the working paper before the group had been made, the most important of which he said was "measures to increase productivity [so as] to reduce or eliminate trade barriers."[33]

Although, the final document reflected Harriman's influence, it ultimately remained a British directive. As reported by the *New York Times*, the finished plan called for a "reduction of dollar imports without fixing a figure, to urge financial stabilization but without insisting upon exchange or other controls in all cases, to recommend expansion of trade among Marshall Plan nations by using their overseas as well as their metropolitan resources, [and] *to propose seeking imports from South America and Eastern Europe to replace those payable in dollars.*"[34] British officials knew their nation's financial future was bleak. They were prepared to take whatever measures were necessary to correct it.

By June, Britain had suffered four consecutive months of export declines to the United States and was beginning to get desperate.[35] One indication of that desperation comes from the relationship it formed with newly independent India. Free to go its own way after 1948, the question was, would it? In May 1949, as Britain was becoming painfully aware of its dire position, Britain managed to keep India in the British Commonwealth as an independent nation in what the *New York Times* noted was "the first time in history [Britain] will include among its members a republic which refuses to pledge allegiance to the Crown." The *Times* pointed to several reasons why India may have wished to remain a part of the Commonwealth even though it recently had fought

---

[32] Harriman to Hoffman, April 12, 1949, *FRUS, 1949* 4: 376. The block and question mark here are in the original.

[33] Ibid., 376–377.

[34] Harold Callender, "ERP 'Cabinet' Balks at British Policy," *The New York Times*, March 8, 1949, 7 (emphasis added).

[35] "Britain Reports Drop in February Exports," *The New York Times*, March 22, 1949, 12; "British Export Dip Inflates Deficit," *The New York Times*, May 21, 1949, 4; Clifton Daniel, "British Now Alarmed by Economic Situation," *The New York Times*, May 29, 1949, 4(E); "Britain's Exports to U.S. in May Show Big Decline," *The New York Times*, June 17, 1949, 3.

The British Sterling-Dollar Crisis of 1949–1950

so hard for its independence. Among these were the sterling balances it held and could use to obtain manufactured goods and dollars, a fear of Communist agitation, and Imperial Preference, which assured India a market in Britain for its raw materials. As for Britain's reasons for wanting to keep India in the fold, the *Times* reported: "Whatever problems remain it is generally recognized that greater difficulties would have confronted the Commonwealth with India out. Not only would it have strengthened the tendencies toward [sterling area] disintegration had she cut herself adrift, but the formula for inclusion of republics within the family, hitherto held together by the Crown, is seen as a means of *future expansion* and *strengthening* of the Commonwealth." Britain was taking no chances.[36]

An even more drastic measure was the trade pact Britain agreed to with Argentina on June 8, 1949. The pact called for Britain to supply Argentina with agricultural equipment, fuel oil, and other petroleum products. In return, Argentina would supply Britain with an equal value amount of beef and other foodstuffs. This bartering arrangement was necessary "because of dollar shortages," the *New York Times* reported. The United States protested the agreement on the grounds that it violated the General Agreement on Tariffs and Trade signed both by Britain and the United States in 1947. U.S. officials argued that the Anglo-Argentine agreement represented trade discrimination, because it effectively shut the United States and other nations out of the Argentine market for the duration of the pact, which was to be five years. Equally, because it locked a portion of Britain's export trade into a barter arrangement, it diverted British exports from the dollar area and thus further exacerbated Britain's ability to earn dollars.[37]

In light of the United States' protest, the "pro-Peron" Argentine newspaper *Democracia* pointed to the "skillful policy of President [Juan Domingo] Peron [in] remov[ing] his country from the capitalist influence of Wall Street, which on a grudge basis seeks a retaliatory financial policy against Buenos Aires." *Democracia* further noted that "the Anglo-Argentine pact was the strongest blow yet struck at the 'great plutocracy' of the North."[38] As such sentiments indicate, U.S. efforts to forge a multilateral economy were under great assault all over the world in 1949.

---

[36] Raymond Daniel, "London Renewing Commonwealth Tie," *The New York Times*, May 1, 1949, 5(E), emphasis added.

[37] "Britain-Latin Pact Protested by U.S.," *The New York Times*, June 10, 1949, 3.

[38] Virginia Lee Warren, "Pro-Peron Paper Hits U.S. Protest," *The New York Times*, June 14, 1949, 19.

140   *NSC 68 and the Political Economy of the Early Cold War*

The Anglo-Argentine trade agreement created quite an uproar both in Congress and with the Truman administration. As the Senate saw things, "the [Anglo-Argentine] arrangement put this country in the position of financing a British monopoly of the Argentine machinery market through [ERP financing], while abetting Britain's discrimination against American agricultural exports." Hoffman noted that the "proposed trade agreement was a 'dreadful' departure from the kind of multilateral trading system the Marshall Plan was intended to recreate," the *New York Times* reported. "I have no defense for that type of trading," Hoffman asserted. "It is the wrong kind of bilateral agreement for bringing about the type of trade world we want." Stressing just how much the administration objected to the pact, Hoffman suggested: "We could cancel the [Marshall Plan] program [to Britain] if we thought it was justified by [the Anglo-Argentine] agreement."[39] Despite U.S. protestations, however, the trade pact went through. U.S. officials, in the end, could do little to prevent it, short of ending ERP aid to Britain, as Hoffman had threatened. That, however, was the last thing they wanted to do. The Marshall Plan was the only thing keeping Britain and the sterling area tied to the United States, a reality that was becoming increasingly clearer every day.[40]

U.S. opposition to the Anglo-Argentine trade agreement brought to light underlying misunderstandings that existed between Britain and the United States concerning economic policy. According to the *New York Times*, the stern response to the trade pact from Paul Hoffman caught Britain off guard. "As recently as this week," the *Times* reported,

the [British] Foreign Office and Treasury circles remained of the view that United States pressure for abandonment of the bilateral trade system reflected the opinion of a small section of the State Department and was actually being opposed by the [ECA].... Realization that the United States is deadly serious about bringing the system of controlled bilateral and discriminatory trade to an end is spreading over London like an epidemic of summer flu.

The *Times* noted that the technical matters of multilateralism, such as currency convertibility and nondiscrimination, which were the focus of the European Payments Union Averell Harriman was devoting so much time to, did not put food on the average Briton's table. The Anglo-Argentine trade pact was an example. "One-third of Britain's meat comes from

[39] Felix Belair, Jr., "Hoffman Suggests Ending British Aid," *The New York Times*, June 18, 1949, 6.
[40] Virginia Lee Warren, "Britain, Argentina Sign Trade Accord," *The New York Times*, June 28, 1949, 2.

The British Sterling-Dollar Crisis of 1949–1950

Argentina. *There are no dollars to buy it anywhere else.* The British meat ration is now 20 cents' worth weekly. Here that's about two small lamb chops or two-thirds of a pound of stew beef." British officials were confounded that the United States would consider ending ERP aid to Britain for attempting to secure a higher standard of living for the average Briton. "To argue against an agreement providing five years' meat supply in exchange for oil and British manufactures is to argue either that British consumption must drop or that the Government must abandon altogether its system of conducting foreign trade and return it to private enterprise," the *New York Times* reported. Perhaps, the latter was what American officials wanted, though, as we will see, Britain was not about to let that happen. Britain and the United States were at crossroads. Into this environment, like a perfect storm, came the British sterling-dollar crisis of 1949.[41]

The Crisis

Britain's emerging new dollar gap, coming as it did despite Marshall Plan aid, was staggering in its severity. The drain on dollars occurred with rapid and disconcerting speed. In the twelve months prior to April 1949, Britain's gold and dollar reserves had fallen about $362 million before being bolstered by the Marshall Plan. In the second quarter of 1949 (April–July) the reserves fell $262 million alone, reducing them by June 30 to roughly $1.6 billion, well below the set minimum of $2 billion, with no signs of slowing.[42]

On June 16, 1949, United States Ambassador to Britain Lewis Douglas cabled Secretary of State Dean Acheson with the following: "This is to alert you to the possibility that [Britain] may be confronted this summer with a major financial crisis not unlike that which developed in 1947." Douglas added, "The economic consequences would almost certainly precipitate a political crisis as well." The gold-dollar drain on British reserves had risen from £82 million in the first quarter of 1949 to £150 million for the April–June quarter. "After allowance for ECA, IMF [International Monetary Fund], and Canadian contributions total reserves [are] expected to fall to pounds 400 million end of June compared [with] pounds 471

[41] Michael L. Hoffman, "U.S., Britain Near Trade Showdown," *The New York Times,* June 19, 1949, 5, emphasis added.
[42] "Implications of the Sterling Area Crisis to the U.K. and the U.S.," August 18, 1949, *FRUS, 1949* 4: 809; "Devaluation of Currencies Follows Financial Talks," September 19, 1949, CED, 1.

million end of March and pounds 552 million [at the] beginning of ERP," Douglas said. Several factors attributed to the drain were laid out, all but one attributed to the U.S. recession and the rumor of impending devaluation of the pound by Britain. Douglas suggested that "while some of these adverse factors may not continue to operate so strongly in the immediate future, there seems to be little prospect for [a] sufficient degree of improvement, except in [the] unlikely event of [a] strong reversal of recent trends in [the] US economy." Douglas noted further that release of Britain's recent export-import figures scheduled for June 30 would almost certainly have an adverse effect and would probably constitute a further downward spiral.

Britain was likely to take drastic measures to "arrest the rot," Douglas said. Among the measures Britain might be forced to make were "drastic cuts in UK dollar imports"; "shedding more military and political commitments abroad"; "increasing pressure on the sterling area to reduce its dollar drain"; and "tightening [the] bonds between sterling and certain other currencies, perhaps even trying to rivet them to sterling." He admonished that Britain's problems could have horrific consequences for the United States:

> Since many other countries would be affected by a British collapse it seems to us that the logic of the situation would compel Britain and other nations to move toward the development of at least a quasi autarchic sterling area, embracing as many countries as could be brought or forced into it. Also, with the probable shrinkage of trade with the dollar area, would not these countries eventually have to consider a reorientation of their trade toward Eastern Europe and Russia?

Douglas said he had been "informed from wholly authentic sources that [the British government] had developed a program which, if necessary to adopt, 'will insulate the UK from strong American pressure to devalue sterling and which the US will not like.'" He believed that devaluation of sterling, which was fast becoming the short-term American prescription for easing Britain's dollar gap, would be "resisted to the end." He also worried that the political crisis the economic crisis was likely to create in Britain would cause the British government to blame the United States for Britain's economic woes. "If such a crisis develops," Douglas wrote, "we must anticipate a difficult period in Anglo-American relations."[43]

---

[43] United States ambassador to Britain Lewis Douglas to Acheson, June 16, 1949, *FRUS, 1949* 4: 784–786; see also Michael L. Hoffman, "Britons Fear New Economic Crisis as Dollar Earnings Stay Too Low," *The New York Times*, June 16, 1949, 8; and "Britain's Exports to U.S. in May Show Big Decline," *The New York Times*, June 17, 1949, 3. For

The British Sterling-Dollar Crisis of 1949–1950

Writing to Acheson on June 22, the ambassador continued his analysis of the crisis. There were four "methods," he wrote, for "attacking" Britain's dollar gap, only one of which he considered viable – devaluation. The others were (1) "a drastic reduction in direct costs"; (2) "to convince the public that the present value of sterling can and will be maintained"; and (3) creation of a "protected autarchic trading area, centered on London and using sterling as its basic currency." Of the latter, Douglas continued: "We fully appreciate what this would entail in damage to the US economy, in frustration of political and strategic objectives in Europe and in effects on Canada." Although the British knew such an outcome was likely, he asserted, "We anticipate that, in its efforts to deal with the imminent crisis, the UK will take many steps which would be consistent with the ultimate creation of such an area, especially if [it] continued for a long time." Douglas was not convinced, however, that such an area could be sustained. "The dollar economy is so important in the economic life of the western world that it would be impossible to isolate a sterling hegemony completely." In addition, he went on, "attempts to create such a bloc would cut across so many opposing national interests on the continent and even in the sterling area that it would be impossible to hold the group together." He also believed that "the creation of such an isolated sphere would take too long to provide a sufficiently prompt answer to the present problem."[44]

Such thoughts were wishful thinking on Douglas' part. It is true that the British did not want to pursue autarchy. The pursuit of autarchy, a Foreign Office paper from late June 1949 commented, would create "complete and utter conflict between our political and strategic aims on the one hand and our economic aims on the other hand." But neither would they take unacceptable risks. "We cannot again be forced into the situation of 1945," the paper continued, "when, against our better judgement, we were compelled to accept policy obligations on convertibility and non-discrimination as the price of obtaining essential short-term financial assistance" (i.e., the British loan discussed in Chapter 3). "We cannot afford another 1947," the paper stated, when Britain saw a major run on sterling after enacting convertibility per the loan agreement. Hence, though they wanted to avoid autarchy, the paper made clear that "if we can see no outlet" from our troubles we would have to "give up the

---

the British perspective, see "The Dollar Situation," June 27, 1949, FO 371/75578, UE 1949, TNA.

[44] Douglas to Acheson, June 22, 1949, *FRUS, 1949* 4: 787; "Implications of the Sterling Area Crisis to the U.K. and the U.S.," August 18, 1949, *FRUS, 1949* 4: 806–820.

Marshall Plan attempt to secure dollar viability by 1952" and pursue "self-sufficiency based upon intensified controls and bilateralism."[45]

Just how bad things were getting became apparent when Harriman met with Cripps on June 21, 1949, to discuss the evolving crisis. Harriman was convinced that Britain's only hope of getting out of its predicament was to allow sterling to be freely convertible into other currencies; at the time all sterling transactions had to be cleared by the bank of England. As Harriman saw it, convertibility would introduce competition into the continent and drive prices down. Cripps did not agree. For him, convertibility meant Britain would lose control of sterling and with that its initiative. Cripps' main concern was saving dollars. After his conversation with Cripps, Harriman wrote to ECA chief Paul Hoffman: "Abandonment steps toward liberalization trade and introduction competition would mean complete loss of perspective. We must keep our eye on the real dangers among which perhaps none is more serious than consolidation of present bilateralism into an autarchic system."[46]

As if this were not enough, Douglas cabled Harriman in late June about a conversation he had with British Foreign Secretary Ernest Bevin. "Ruminating on the danger which confront[s] us, and the importance of Anglo-American collaboration, Bevin remarked that he had reliable indications from Communist sources that the Kremlin is currently jubilant over impending conflict between dollar and sterling interests. The word is being passed to the faithful that a breakdown of Western solidarity is imminent and that the setbacks heretofore suffered by Communist forces will soon be a thing of the past."[47]

Secretary of State Dean Acheson, who among U.S. officials always seemed to be thinking ahead, put the British crisis in the larger context of the ERP in a telegram to Douglas on June 30, 1949. "Since continued Eur[opean] imports of substantial quantities of basic foods and raw materials from Canada, and US after 1952 will be a desirable and economic pattern of trade," Acheson wrote, "[the] overriding objective of US and Eur[opean] policy sh[oul]d be to remove present dependence of Eur[opean] countries upon extraordinary dollar assistance, especially by

---

[45] "The Dollar Shortage: Forthcoming Discussions with the USA and Canada," June 30, 1949, FO 371/75579, UE 4189, TNA.

[46] Memorandum by Averell Harriman, June 21, 1949, Averell Harriman Papers, Truman Administration, Marshall Plan, 1947–1951, John W. Snyder trip, July 1949, Box 272, Library of Congress, Washington, D.C. (hereinafter LC), 4.

[47] Douglas to Harriman, June 29, 1949, Harriman Papers, Marshall Plan, John Snyder Trip, July 1949, Box 272, 2, (LC).

The British Sterling-Dollar Crisis of 1949–1950

expansion of sales from UK, other Eur[opean] countries and sterling area to Canada, US and Latin America during [the] years 1949–52." Acheson was thinking ahead to when ERP dollars would stop flowing to Britain. If Britain was already having problems, what would happen then? As we will see, it would not be the last time Acheson would evoke the year 1952 as the critical year of decision.[48]

U.S. concerns about British moves were confirmed when in early July British officials began talking of pursuing an autarchic course. At a meeting between Douglas and Bevin, Bevin told Douglas that "we were now confronted with the issue [of whether there should] be two economies in the world, i.e., the Soviet and that of the Western world; or should there be three, i.e., [a] Soviet [area], [a] Sterling area and [a] dollar area." "The future," he said, "would depend very largely on the extent to which the US would be willing to go to meet the UK." Asked by Douglas what he meant, Bevin replied that he meant "how far the US would go toward pretty far-reaching state planning." Bevin then made mention of the current U.S. recession as a major factor in Britain's problems. Douglas countered that it was not fair to call the recession "an American recession." Rather, it "was more of a world-wide adjustment following a tremendous war time inflation." But Bevin, Douglas wrote in his cable, "was not inclined to accept this view of the matter." Bevin told Douglas that autarchy was not what Britain was seeking, but Douglas was not so sure. He ended his memorandum with the comment that he was "disquieted [by] ... the implications of [his] conversation with Bevin."[49]

Douglas had reason to be disquieted. In response to the mounting crisis, the British announced to the Americans in early July that they intended to cut dollar expenditures by $400 million, or 25 percent, the amount that represented the drop in their reserves below the required $2 billion mark.[50] Such a move was a step toward autarchy. Nevertheless, recognizing that the British were determined to enact the restriction, which

---

[48] Acheson to Douglas, June 30, 1949, *FRUS, 1949* 4: 797–798; "Devaluation of Currencies Follows Financial Talks," September 19, 1949, CED, 3.

[49] Louis Douglas to Harriman, July 4, 1949, Harriman Papers, Truman Administration, Marshall Plan, 1947–1951, John W. Snyder trip, July 1949, Box 272, LC. For the British position, see "The Dollar Shortage: Forthcoming Discussions with the USA and Canada," FO 371/75579, UE 4189, TNA.

[50] Assistant Secretary of State for Economic Affairs Willard Thorp to Acheson, June 27, 1949, *FRUS, 1949* 4: 793–796; "Britain Facing Serious Financial Difficulties," July 25, 1949, CED; "Sydney Gruson, "Britain to Cut Dollar Buying by $400,000,000 in a Year," *The New York Times*, July 15, 1949, 1; Felix Belair Jr., "$397,000,000 is Held British Dollar Gap," *The New York Times*, 51.

in effect reneged on Article Nine of the Anglo-American loan agreement of 1945, U.S. officials had little choice but to accept it.[51] They remained adamant, however, that "we must receive assurances, and the public must be advised, that this action is not a reversal of policy into the line of complete restrictionism."[52] Such assurances were necessary because, if Congress and the American people came to believe that Britain was pursuing a policy of autarchy while taking freely of the generosity of the United States through the Marshall Plan, there was likely to be a severe backlash against future Marshall Plan aid, and without it, Britain would have no choice but to pursue autarchy.

Britain's decision to restrict U.S. imports came as quite a shock to U.S. leaders, and they began to wake up to the severity of the crisis.[53] In the first instance, they determined to move with great caution. They would make their position clear and try to bring British officials around to their line of thinking. They would be especially careful, however, not to appear to be meddling in British internal affairs. Douglas noted: "If the British people come to believe that ... the US interfered with or attempted to dictate internal British policies, the British people will unit[sic] wholeheartedly in opposition to the US.... It is essential, therefore, that the US not only avoid telling the British what they should do in their internal affairs, but also avoid giving any impression that we have done so."[54] As to fixing Britain's dollar gap, they recognized the problem as a deep-seeded one that would require long-term solutions. In the short-term, they determined that devaluation of the pound against the dollar as the only viable course of action.[55]

Meanwhile, British officials made public the mounting dollar-gap crisis on July 5, 1949, and announced that Britain had entered into a barter-trade deal with the Soviet Union, similar to the Anglo-Argentine trade agreement, for one million tons of Soviet coarse grains in exchange for British machinery. In reporting the trade pact, the *New York Times* noted

---

[51] For the administration's debate with Congress on Britain's failure to adhere to article nine of the loan agreement, see Consultation on Trade Arrangements with Great Britain, September 20, 1949, *Reviews of the World Situation*, 51–70.

[52] Thorp to Acheson, June 27, 1949, *FRUS, 1949* 4: 793–796; Acheson to the American embassy in Britain, June 27, 1949, *FRUS, 1949* 4: 796–797.

[53] "Devaluation of Currencies Follows Financial Talks," September 19, 1949, CED, 1.

[54] "Implications of the Sterling Area Crisis to the U.K. and the U.S.," August 18, 1949, *FRUS, 1949* 4: 807.

[55] Douglas to Acheson, June 22, 1949, *FRUS, 1949* 4: 787–790; Harriman to Acheson, June 25, 1949, *FRUS, 1949* 4: 792–793; Thorp to Acheson, June 27, 1949, *FRUS, 1949* 4: 793–796; "Britain Suspends Dollar Purchasing," July 25, 1949, CED, 2.

The British Sterling-Dollar Crisis of 1949–1950

that "the British [normally] buy wheat for dollars from the United States and Canada."[56]

On July 9, 10, and 11, 1949, British and American officials held meetings to explore Britain's sterling-dollar crisis. The meetings proved disheartening for American officials. The conversations, according to conference participant U.S. Secretary of the Treasury John Snyder, "confirmed [the] impression gained from Douglas [in his] conversations with Bevin, i.e., that we now seemed to be facing squarely a fundamental difference between US and UK in [the] approach to [the] problem of [British] economic recovery and stability." Cripps recognized that Britain "had to make greater efforts to become competitive," though he saw this need in terms of "selected industries ... not [as] an over-all problem." However, he was adamant against devaluation of the pound. In fact, he attempted to insert into the communiqué issued forth from the meetings wording that suggested that both the United States and Canada had agreed that devaluation was wholly unnecessary, a move that was successfully deflected by Snyder. What Cripps wanted to employ, Snyder reported, was "international planning to ensure stability on a *status quo* basis, rather than the kind of flexibility required to shake out high costs and restrictive elements which contribute to [Britain's] present difficulties." Once again, the point is made that Britain and the United States came at the problem of economic policy from different perspectives. Britain was most concerned with the immediate survival of its livelihood, and thus was willing to implement autarchic policies to secure that end, whereas the United States, though seeking the same end, looked to the implementation of multilateralism as the sound path to take. This reflected each nation's domestic political economy. Snyder's final memorandum on the conference reflected this reality: "While [the British] purport to be striving toward multilateral trade and non-discrimination, it is apparent that they consider attainment of these objectives to be subservient to requirements of maintaining stability and thus protecting rigidities not only of [the] UK but, now, of sterling area as a whole."[57]

Nonetheless, the talks were not wholly unfruitful. The communiqué issued from the meetings noted that the three nations still held great faith in "a single multilateral system of trade in which dollar and non-dollar

---

[56] Sydney Gruson, "U.S.-British Talks Held Exploratory; Cripps Airs Plight," *The New York Times*, July 9, 1949, 1.

[57] U.S. Secretary of the Treasury John Snyder to Acheson, July 9, 1949, *FRUS, 1949* 4: 799–801; John Snyder to Dean Acheson, July 10, 1949, *FRUS, 1949* 4: 801–802.

148   *NSC 68 and the Political Economy of the Early Cold War*

countries could operate together." In addition, they agreed to September talks at the ministerial level to further discussion of long-term solutions to Britain's sterling-dollar crisis. The communiqué, however, also laid bare the dire realities of the situation – no long-term solution had yet been found, including, it needs emphasizing, the Marshall Plan. "The communiqué conspicuously failed ... to suggest any new plan or proposals for tackling the problems of establishing a system in which dollars and sterling could meet as equals, which the communiqué said was the aim of the three countries for the future pattern of world trade," the *New York Times* noted. Echoing these thoughts, the communiqué urged that "remedies other than financial assistance such as that provided by the United States and Canada must be explored."[58]

On July 15, 1949, Britain publicly announced its intention to restrict $400 million in American exports to Britain.[59] Then, in talks held among the finance ministers of the British Commonwealth countries July 17–19, 1949, the sterling-area nations all agreed to match the British reduction. Sir Stafford Cripps, who had hoped at best for the sterling countries to meet Britain half way, called their parley "one of the most successful Commonwealth conferences we have ever had." Cripps, the *New York Times* reported, "said the aim of the Commonwealth Finance Ministers was to maintain the sterling area in such a position as to be able to take advantage of any long-term solution [to the dollar gap] that might materialize." In other words, Britain was taking no chances. It would continue to operate under the assumption that U.S.-UK good relations and a one-world economy were the principal goals, but in the meantime it would shore up its strength with the sterling area just in case that economy failed to materialize any time soon and alleviate Britain's chronic dollar problem.[60]

Nonetheless, much to U.S. dismay, the British did begin to contemplate that perhaps the solution was for Britain to develop an independent sterling area, which would mark a return to the closed trade world of the 1930s. The House of Commons took up the issue on July 18, 1949. As that body understood it, the world would be divided into three economic areas – a dollar area, a sterling area, and a ruble area. Bevin, testifying

---

[58] Snyder to Acheson, July 9, 1949, *FRUS*, 1949 4: 799–801; Sydney Gruson, "Three Powers Map September Parley on Sterling Crisis," *The New York Times*, July 11, 1949, 1.

[59] Sydney Gruson, "Britain to Cut Dollar Buying by $400,000,000 in a Year," *The New York Times*, July 15, 1949, 1.

[60] Harriman to Hoffman, June 21, 1949, Harriman Papers, Marshall Plan, Box 272, John Snyder Trip to Europe, 1949, LC.

The British Sterling-Dollar Crisis of 1949–1950

before the Commons, argued sternly against such a proposal. "I confess that I have been tempted in that direction.... [However,] the best contribution which we can make to the world is to reduce the number at least to two, because if we try to develop the three I can see one of the most terrible conflicts arising."[61] The very fact, however, that such a proposal was even being considered by the House of Commons shows the extent to which such a policy was seriously being contemplated.

While Cripps was informing reporters about the Commonwealth parley, Ernest Bevin was speaking before the House of Commons about the Washington conference of July 9–11. There, Bevin hinted at a possible long-term solution to the British dollar problem. He said: "If we can bring the dollar area and the sterling area together and produce the right cooperation we can make President's Truman's fourth point a living reality in helping to lift the standards of life throughout that great area." By "fourth point," Bevin meant Truman's Point Four Program, announced at the state of the union address of 1950, which was designed to bring the Third World into the fold of the capitalist nations by offering them technical and financial assistance to help them build up their fledgling economies. Point Four never received the kind of attention that the ERP did. The administration knew that Congress would not support anymore Marshall Plans and never even considered asking for Point Four as a financial program. Ultimately, Point Four became a program geared to offer technical assistance alone, which could not do the sort of thing Bevin was referring to. Nonetheless, Point Four was important for another reason: The ideas postulated in it would become important in the formulation of NSC 68.[62]

By August the crisis had reached a fever pitch. "The situation is so grave," noted Douglas, "that if the drain on the sterling area gold and dollar reserves cannot be shortly halted, the UK government, in our opinion, will be faced with one overriding necessity – to stop the drain at all costs." This could induce the British to contemplate "further cuts in UK dollar expenditures which go beyond those contemplated in July, and [possibly] extend [those cuts] to such important US exports as tobacco, cotton, oil and films." In addition, the UK government could put "pressure

---

[61] Alan Bullock, *Ernest Bevin: Foreign Secretary, 1945–1951* (London: William Heinemann Ltd., 1983), 710.

[62] Clifton Daniel, "Sterling Nations Decide to Curtail Dollar Purchases," *The New York Times*, July 19, 1949, 1; C. P. Trussell, "Point Four Bills Sent to Congress by the President," *The New York Times*, July 2, 1949, 1; Walter Salant, Ph.D., Oral History, March 30, 1970, 36–43, Truman Library; Rotter, *The Path to Vietnam*, 18–22; Borden, *The Pacific Alliance*, 42.

on sterling area countries to take additional measures beyond those contemplated in July to cut their dollar expenditures" and undertake "a search for non-dollar sources of supply even if this involves discrimination against the US, high costs, and, in the case of Russia and Eastern Europe, political risks." What is more, Britain might "refus[e] to make any new commitments which involve the risk of payment in gold and dollars." Finally, Douglas wrote, Britain could encourage "Canada to modify the existing wheat agreement [between Britain and Canada] in favor of payment in sterling, and ultimately to other hard currency countries to arrange trade on the basis of bilateral agreements involving no payment in gold or dollars." Though the British did not harbor a desire to implement these policies, Douglas proffered, "the British situation is such that they may be compelled, however reluctantly, to adopt such measures in order to bring their dollar deficit under control."[63]

According to Douglas, the effects of the British crisis on the United States were potentially disastrous. "Continued economic difficulties in the UK and sterling area[,] which induce difficulties in other countries[,] could make impossible the successful achievement of our ECA objectives by 1952, as well as have effects on the level of US economic activity." If Britain instituted a rigid autarchy in the sterling area, western European nations might follow suit. They might opt to join with the British or, as likely, orient their trade toward eastern Europe where markets were readily available. Foremost, a British ascension from the multilateral schematic would signal to other nations that multilateralism was unwise.

Britain's problems cannot be isolated from other countries. Sterling area countries would be compelled to follow in the wake of the UK's [restriction on dollar imports] and pursue similar policies, particularly such heavy dollar users as India and Australia.... There would also be strains on the cohesion of the sterling area and the British Commonwealth (the two are not identical).... Should an economic recession occur in the UK and [the] sterling area, it would affect other, particularly OEEC, countries, for it would tend to reduce their level of economic activity, jeopardize their recovery programs, and drive them to restrictive policies. Moreover, such countries as France and Italy with major Communist movements might be faced with intensified political difficulties.

"The crux of the problem," Douglas wrote, "is the ability of the UK through economic production to compete successfully in world markets. Without this the UK will not be able to avoid continued dollar crises." He recommended that the United States take concrete measures to increase

[63] "Implications of the Sterling Area Crisis to the U.K. and the U.S.," August 18, 1949, *FRUS, 1949* 4: 806–820.

The British Sterling-Dollar Crisis of 1949–1950

dollar earnings for Britain, including "resumption and regularization of ... strategic material buying," reduction of tariffs in the United States, and, a more striking proposal, "increase the tempo of our educational campaign to teach the American people the connection between tariff policy, world economic well-being and our national security."

Douglas ended his memorandum by stating that Britain's problems were intrinsic and that any solution must be far-reaching. He cautioned that direct dollar aid was not the course to take, that a permanent way of bolstering British productive capacity so as to compete in world markets was the only acceptable course of action.[64]

A solemn Truman told his cabinet on August 26: "We are faced with a terribly serious world situation, a world financial situation." Britain "is practically 'busted' ... and unless a solution to the problem is found our world recovery program is going to smash up and all our post-war efforts will go to pieces." Acheson cabled his friend Sir Oliver Franks to query "whether the British wished to work towards a free world in which exchanges between [the] dollar and the sterling areas were at a high level, or whether they wished to build up a soft currency world centered round the sterling area and cut themselves off from North America." Things were looking bleak.[65]

Britain's flirtation with autarchy in the summer of 1949 has long been forgotten. For reasons not entirely discernible, scholars who have studied the period with particular attention to Britain's woes have generally been silent on the matter.[66] Perhaps this is because, in the long run, Britain did not choose the autarchic route. How important could it have been if it was not chosen? Yet for those U.S. officials committed to multilateralism, the prospect that Britain might pursue a "third way" was imponderable.[67]

---

[64] "Implications of the Sterling Area Crisis to the U.K. and the U.S.," 806–820, emphasis added; "Decline in US Economy Would Have Far Reaching Effects," CED, 6–8.

[65] Eban A. Ayers diary entry, August 26, 1949, quoted in Walter LaFeber, "NATO and Korea: A Context," *Diplomatic History* 13 (Fall 1989): 461–477; Acheson quoted in Robin Edmonds, *Setting the Mould: The United States and Britain, 1945–1950* (Oxford, UK: Clarendon Press, 1986), 108–109, brackets in original.

[66] See, for instance, John Killick, *The United States and European Reconstruction, 1945–1960* (Edinburgh, United Kingdom: Keele University Press, 1997). In all fairness to Killick, he does speak about autarchy; the word can even be found in the index. But he does not speak of the autarchic moves Britain made in 1949, except in the most roundabout way. Nonetheless, he acknowledges that the likely outcome of an unfixed dollar gap was the "continuation of the European autarchy of the 1930s" (184); Leffler calls attention to the concern over autarchy, or "closed trading blocs," as he describes it, but does not draw the same conclusions I do from these concerns. *A Preponderance of Power*, 314–315, passim.

[67] "Decline in US Economy Would Have Far Reaching Effects," CED, NAII, 6–8.

It needs to be stressed, nevertheless, that the British government generally did not want an autarchic outcome, although some committed socialists did.[68] The situation such as it evolved was not an issue of choosing between two ways of life. Rather, such an outcome was inevitable if the dollar gap could not be fixed. This point is made clear when Bevin met reporters on his arrival in the United States to begin high-level talks with the Americans about the crisis. After being asked by the swarm of reporters that confronted him at the dock where he landed if he was in the United States to ask for more money, he replied that he was not. Clearly exasperated by the question, he admonished the reporters to look at all the good things that had been accomplished in the last year and a half. He mentioned specifically the Brussels Pact,[69] the seating of the OEEC, the implementation of the Marshall Plan and the North Atlantic Treaty Organization (NATO), and British steps toward dismantling its colonial holdings by virtue of the independence given recently to India, Pakistan, and Ceylon. Then, he said: "The worry we now have is: We are afraid that this will all be frustrated if we cannot settle the economic maladjustment.... We cannot have one democratic world politically, if it is to be based on two worlds economically. We must harmonize our affairs." How precisely to do that, however, was the great question.[70]

In September things took a change for the better, at least in the immediate sense, when the British devalued the pound by more than 30 percent from £4.08 to £2.80.[71] Although both nations realized devaluation alone would not solve Britain's dollar gap, they now agreed prices in the sterling area had to come down if it were ever to be competitive. This was an important correction for Britain's dollar crisis. For their part, U.S. officials pledged to help Britain ease its dollar gap through such means as stockpiling, offshore procurement, lowering of tariffs, and the implementation of the Point Four Program for development of "backwards" areas, which President Truman had introduced in his 1949 inaugural address, although at this juncture no means for securing these measures were discernible.[72]

[68] See, for instance, Thomas Balogh, *The Dollar Gap: Causes and Cures* (London: Oxford University Press, 1950).
[69] The Brussels Pact, formerly the Treaty of Brussels, was signed by Britain, France, the Netherlands, Belgium, and Luxembourg on March 17, 1948. It was the staging ground for both NATO and the Western European Union. However, it was aimed at Germany, not the Soviet Union.
[70] Bullock, *Bevin*, 716.
[71] Raymond Daniel, "Britain Cuts Pound 30% to $2.80 to Spur Exports to the Dollar Area; 8 Sterling Nations Follow Suit," *The New York Times*, September 19, 1949, 1.
[72] Walter Salant to the Council of Economic Advisors, September 29, 1949, Salant Papers, Truman Library.

The British Sterling-Dollar Crisis of 1949–1950

Perhaps for that reason, most importantly Britain's devaluation of the pound proved to U.S. leaders that Britain was not deliberately pursuing a policy of autarchy. The $400 million restriction imposed on U.S. imports in the summer had left U.S. officials wondering exactly what British intentions were. By deciding to devalue, the British convinced U.S. officials they wanted to work together. The road ahead would hardly be smooth, but both nations would face it with the knowledge that they needed one another and that bringing the sterling and dollar areas into rough balance was their common goal. How that was to be achieved, however, remained unsolved.[73]

Meanwhile, the problems continued to mount. French officials had not been asked to sit in on the September talks between Britain, Canada, and the United States. Thus, they did not learn of the devaluation beforehand, as it was now generally assumed that Canada and the United States had. The secrecy surrounding the devaluation angered the French considerably, especially as devaluation of the pound forced devaluation of the French franc. Failure to consult them was, the French argued, a direct affront to the idea of European cooperation, economic or otherwise. They wondered whether Britain and the United States desired to form an alliance independent of the continent. For French officials, such an alliance would constitute the abandonment of their country, because the continent free of British and American involvement, they believed, could only mean a Europe dominated by Germany. The French debacle caused Dean Acheson to ask: "Where did we go wrong? ... Did [the British] take advantage of us? ... What do we learn from this?"[74]

---

[73] Raymond Daniel, "Britain Cuts Pound 30% to $2.80 to Spur Exports to the Dollar Area; 8 Sterling Nations Follow Suit," *The New York Times*, September 19, 1949, 1; "Joint Communique," John Ohly Papers, Foreign Aid file, Individual Regions, Countries – United Kingdom, Box 118, Truman Library; "Tripartite Financial Discussions," September 19, 1949, RG 59, Current Economic Developments," 1945–1972, 2, NAII; "Position Paper for the Discussions with the British and Canadians on Pound-Dollar Problems, Prepared by the Policy Planning Staff," September 3, 1949, *FRUS, 1949* 4: 822–830; Acheson to the U.S. embassy in Britain, September 12, 1949, *FRUS, 1949* 4: 833–839; for Cripps' views, see Douglas to Acheson, September 27, 1949, RG 59, Central Decimal File, 1945–1949, Great Britain – Trade, 841.5151, NAII; for the U.S. view of devaluation, see Acheson to Senator Alexander Wiley, November 23, 1949, RG 59, Central Decimal File, 1945–1949, Great Britain – Trade, 841.5151, NAII.

[74] Acheson memorandum, October 19, 1949, *FRUS, 1949* 4: 847–849; U.S. ambassador to France David K. E. Bruce to Acheson, October 22, 1949, *FRUS, 1949* 4: 343; "Effects of Currency Devaluation Reported," September 26, 1949, CED, NAII, 7; Harold Callender, "French Tie Crisis to Slash in Pound," *The New York Times*, October, 6, 1949, 7; Harold Callender, "Fear of Germany Rules French Policy in Europe," *The New York Times*, August 21, 1949, 4(E).

NSC 68 and the Political Economy of the Early Cold War

Congress, as usual, created problems for the Truman administration as well. The need to obtain annual approval for Marshall Plan funding from Congress gave Congress great influence in affecting the course of U.S. foreign policy in Europe. In July 1949, Congress cut $299,871,420 from the 1950 installment of ERP, even though the administration had lobbied that the full amount be allotted. Further, it warned western Europe that the Marshall Plan would be canceled the following year if steps toward greater European unity were not made soon. Both Congress and the administration had expected that devaluation would coincide with immediate steps toward currency convertibility. When Britain balked, Congress grew restless. Administration officials pleaded with the British throughout the last week of October 1949 to take some further action that would assure Congress before it adjourned for the year that western Europe was making greater progress toward unity. U.S. officials wanted it to approve the selection of a head chief, or president, who could coordinate the actions of their various countries. The U.S. choice was Paul-Henri Spaak, former prime minister of Belgium. British officials would have none of it. Approving Spaak, or any other person, head of a European *union* was tantamount to throwing away the empire, in their estimation. For, it would signal to the sterling area that Britain was abandoning it in favor of the continent. Anyway, what Congress and Truman administration officials really wanted was currency convertibility, a step that the British refused to take for the same reason that they opposed a European union. Currency convertibility meant tying Britain more closely to the continent and potentially away from the sterling area. Britain was not about to surrender this area under any conditions. As Ernest Bevin put it: "[Britain] was ... a world power ... not merely a European power."[75]

By the end of October it was apparent that whatever benefits were expected to come from devaluation were not materializing. Rather than spur exports to the dollar area, it actually made for a more autarchic sterling area. Devaluation was supposed to make dollar goods more expensive in Britain and sterling goods cheaper in the United States. It was believed the currency adjustment would spur British goods to

---

[75] "ERP Nations Get Senate Warning," *The New York Times*, July 14, 1949, 6; Acheson to the U.S. embassy in Britain, October 14, 1949, *FRUS, 1949* 4: 429–430; Douglas to Acheson, October 18, 1949, *FRUS, 1949* 4: 430–431; Memorandum of Conversation, October 21, 1949, Dean Acheson Papers, Box 65, Truman Library; Douglas to Acheson, October 26, 1949, *FRUS, 1949* 4: 435–437.

The British Sterling-Dollar Crisis of 1949–1950 155

the dollar area while contracting American goods to the sterling area. However, per the demands of British labor, devaluation was accompanied by wage increases to compensate for the increased cost of imported goods, which tended to negate the effects of more expensive U.S. goods and thus of the devaluation. In addition, because the devaluation made U.S. goods more expensive, the sterling-area nations began trying even harder to obtain British goods, the effect being that British goods that should have been going to the dollar area instead found their way to the sterling area, chasing easy money. As most of the goods sold from Britain to the sterling area were done on credit, Britain's economy received no monetary benefit in return; the individual producer was simply paid out of the British purse. The *New York Times* noted the crux of the problem: "Until steps are taken to deflate the sterling area and particularly to deflate sterling balances (which still total nearly $12 billion) establishment of convertibility of sterling currencies is impossible. Without convertibility the great chance to wipe the barriers threatening to create a permanent two-price, two-bloc world in the West that was offered by devaluation will be lost."[76]

Britain's dire predicament was the subject of a speech by Cripps at the opening session of the House of Commons on October 27, 1949. As the *New York Times* reported, Cripps declared: "The only way that Britain and the sterling area had been able to make ends meet since the war had been through loans, Marshall Plan aid and the steady diminution of Britain's gold and dollar reserves." "What is to happen when Marshall aid comes to an end?" he asked. "How, then, are we to get the cotton, the non-ferrous metals and other raw materials and food stuffs, without which most of production must stop?" His answer: "Only by earning dollars that had previously been supplied without toil on Britain's part, could it be done," the *Times* reported. "Exports must be increased and diverted from the soft currency area to dollar markets." Cripps took up the sterling balances problem and revealed that Britain would have to begin restricting the credits on account that the sterling nations used to obtain goods from Britain. "In these new circumstances we cannot afford to export largely without getting anything by way of return," he said. Nor, he added, could Britain continue "repaying sterling debts to the same extent as hitherto." "We must go slower, whether we like it or not," Cripps stated firmly. He "acknowledged," according to the *Times*, "that

---

[76] Michael L. Hoffman, "Devaluation Benefits are Seen in Jeopardy," *The New York Times*, October 23, 1949, 4(E).

the Labor Government (his own) had been able to maintain its social services and full employment largely because of outside help."

How grave and difficult our situation is will be realized when it is appreciated that even this reduced program (of imports), which barely supplies our raw materials needs, is only possible with the assistance of the European Recovery Program and the Canadian dollar loan and that both of these forms of special assistance must before long disappear.... If Britain, for lack of dollars, had to curtail imports still further, it would be impossible to maintain the flow of raw materials needed for full employment and for full production.

Cripps concluded by admonishing that "it was up to the British people to increase productivity and exports to places where dollars could be earned if they wanted to keep the welfare state that socialism was building."[77]

With the date for Congress's adjournment fast approaching and no new progress made with Britain, ECA chief Paul Hoffman geared up for an emergency trip to Europe to attempt to persuade the OEEC nations that some greater moves toward unity had to be made. Hoffman wanted to tell Britain its days of stalling were up. If he had his way, Britain would have to agree to certain policies, one of which was the appointment of Spaak as head of an as-yet-undefined European union, or the United States would pull the plug on foreign aid and other assistance. In a meeting between Acheson, Secretary of the Treasury John Snyder, and Hoffman on October 25, 1949, Hoffman had to be persuaded against taking such a strong position. Acheson expressed his concern about using the term "unification" in any discussion with the OEEC nations. He noted further that "the question of surrender of sovereignty was inevitably involved in the establishment of any central banking structure." Hoffman was not easily persuaded, however. After the meeting adjourned, he requested to meet with Acheson and Deputy Undersecretary of State James Webb. Pressing his case again, he stated that "he would not be able to successfully present further appropriation requests on behalf of ECA unless he could be assured of very substantial progress within the immediate future, and that he felt it his duty to make this clear to the Europeans." Webb protested that it would be extremely unwise to "place the U.S. Government in the position of foreclosing fund requests to continue the ECA except on performance of certain conditions which might prove on analysis and discussion to be

[77] Raymond Daniel, "Cripps Again Asks Export Diversion," *The New York Times*, October 27, 1949, 3.

The British Sterling-Dollar Crisis of 1949–1950

impossible of achievement." This would, he argued, be tantamount to "abandon[ing] the European Recovery Program." Webb finished off by saying to Hoffman that "the requirements for the so-called unification of Europe were by no means [as] clear in the minds of the State Department policy and economic staffs as they appeared to be in his." Acheson buttressed Webb's position, albeit, as Webb wrote in his memorandum, in a more "diplomatic way," noting that "he would be quite concerned about pressing for action at this time which involved political and sovereignty decisions which could not possibly be made on short notice." "What we needed most," Acheson remarked, "was an assurance that steady progress would be made along the lines of freeing up trade, introducing competition over wider markets, etc."[78]

In his speech before the OEEC in Paris, delivered on October 31, 1949, Hoffman heeded Acheson's advice and urged the OEEC nations to move quickly, not to unify, but to integrate their economies. Urgency was necessary because the Marshall Plan was fast coming to a close and unless something was done the dollar gap would remain in 1952, with disastrous consequences for both western Europe and the United States. Congress's dissatisfaction also demanded urgency, Hoffman stressed. He pleaded with the OEEC nations to "have ready early in 1950 a record of accomplishment and a program which together will take Europe well along the road toward economic integration." The next day, the continental nations, absent Britain, agreed to adopt some measure of currency convertibility by January 15, 1950. Neither Congress nor the administration was appeased, however. The *New York Times* reported that the administration would not even ask for the third annual installment of the Marshall Plan if some plans were not adopted by January. Although this is hardly what the administration wanted – it would have preferred that Congress just stayed out of discussions over the Marshall Plan – political expediency dictated otherwise. Thus, as 1950 opened, Marshall Plan aid for 1951 was in serious jeopardy.[79]

The real blow, however, came from Britain. In response to Hoffman's speech the British announced that their country could not and would

---

[78] Acheson to the U.S. embassy in Britain, October 24, 1949, *FRUS, 1949* 4: 434; Memorandum of Conversation, October 25, 1949, Acheson Papers, Box 65, Truman Library.

[79] *FRUS, 1949* 4: 438–440; Harold Callender, "Hoffman Demands Action by Europe on Economic Unity," *The New York Times*, November 1, 1949, 1; Felix Belair, Jr., "Marshall Aid End Threatened by U.S.," *The New York Times*, November 1, 1949, 22; Harold Callender, "Cripps Limits Ties to Europe's Trade," *The New York Times*, November 2, 1949, 1.

not integrate economically with the continent. As the *New York Times* reported, Cripps "stressed the difficulties of European integration – a word he placed in quotation marks in the typed text of his speech, evidently to show that it was Mr. Hoffman's, not his. He contended that the sterling area was a 'well-integrated group' of nations that maintained a wide system of multilateral trade." Cripps did, nevertheless, welcome such measures as would lead to greater economic integration on the continent. Britain, though, was staying out.[80]

Thus, in late 1949 the British sterling-dollar crisis threatened to blow apart U.S. officials' efforts to construct that multilateral economy that they had deemed so necessary to the well-being and security of the United States. In the long run, devaluation did pay off in terms of increasing British dollar reserves, although it did not end the dollar gap.[81] However, that should not blind us to the fact that in late 1949 those developments could not have been predicted. When we analyze U.S. policymakers' actions during this time we need to keep that in mind. For instance, in candid talks conducted in 1953 and 1954 with the associates Acheson had served with in the Truman years, in what came to be known as the Princeton Seminars, Acheson remembered being "scared to death" by the British crisis, a position, however, he did not take when he wrote his memoirs some years later. Paul Nitze, who would go on to become the primary author of NSC 68, in the same session, may have provided a reason why, when he noted that:

[The] British financial crisis looked even more serious than it, in the event, turned out to be.... None of us were sure that the difficulty with the sterling area wasn't really much more deep seated ... and we did discuss at that time, at least at lower levels in the State Department, Treasury and ECA, much more radical schemes to try to meet the long-term weakness of the British financial position, such as refunding the sterling obligations around the world; such as some scheme really for the US taking an entirely different relationship to the sterling area, bolstered by the political arrangements between the United States and Canada and the British Commonwealth in general.[82]

Nitze was speaking in 1953, long after any such need for "radical schemes" had been obviated. We cannot let the outcome determine our

---

[80] Harold Callender, "Cripps Limits Ties to Europe's Trade," *The New York Times*, November 2, 1949, 1.
[81] OEEC, "Statement by the Secretary General to the Council on 2nd June 1950 on the Need for Preparing a Programme of Further European Economic Expansion," June 1, 1950, FO 371/86975, TNA.
[82] Acheson and Nitze are quoted in the Princeton Seminars, October 10, 1953, Acheson Papers, reel 1, track 2, Box 97, 6, 3, Truman Library.

interpretation of the events as they unfolded, however. That may have been true in 1953 and 1954, but in 1949 Nitze was of the belief that the crisis was extremely dire and Acheson was "scared to death" by it. It is in this context that we need to understand their actions. The stage was set for NSC 68.[83]

[83] The fact that the dollar gap would still exist after the Marshall Plan terminated is well documented in the British archives. See, for instance, the numerous documents in FO 371/86974 and FO 371/82955, TNA. Among other things the documents show that some U.S. leaders, including Senator Arthur Vandenberg, were desirous of forming a commission under Averell Harriman's leadership to study the issue. Authors who have noted that the Marshall Plan failed to achieve its goals include LaFeber, "NATO and the Korean War," 461–477; Gabriel Kolko and Joyce Kolko, *The Limits of Power: The World and United States Foreign Policy, 1945–1954* (New York: Harper and Row, 1972); and Block, *The Origins of International Economic Disorder.*

6

The Origins and Development of NSC 68

> What we work toward must be on a higher plane than a solution of the Russian problem. That happens to be a major irritation in the side of western civilization today but that may be a benefit, because it may make us think. It is an abnormal power relationship which we have to deal with today.
>
> George Kennan, June 13, 1950

> The purpose of NSC-68 was to so bludgeon the mass mind of "top government" that not only could the President make a decision but that the decision could be carried out.
>
> Dean Acheson, 1969

NSC 68, and the rearmament program that it spawned, fundamentally altered the course of the Cold War. The Cold War certainly had begun as early as 1946–1947, but it did not become the rigid standoff that characterized it for the roughly forty years after 1950 until the advent of NSC 68. NSC 68 was a point of departure for the United States in its relations with the Soviet Union and virtually the entire world. It marked the point at which the country, under the guidance of the multilateralists in the Truman administration and their private colleagues, gave up any and all pretense of cooperating with the Soviet Union and took the position that only unbridled power in its own hands – hegemony – could secure the kind of world that would allow the United States itself to function along liberal capitalist democratic lines, a world defined in terms of multilateralism by those committed to multilateralism. In this hegemonic enterprise, NSC 68 played a major, even the preeminent, role. It, thus, matters a great deal why NSC 68 was created. This chapter explores those reasons.

160

The Origins and Development of NSC 68

To fully comprehend the origins of NSC 68 the focus must necessarily be on its principal authors – Secretary of State Dean Acheson and Director of the Policy Planning Staff (PPS) Paul Nitze. NSC 68 was their project from beginning to end. They formulated it, they constructed it, and they tried with all their might to ram it through to fruition. And, they did so, over and above the lawful mandate handed down to them by the president. Hence, their motivation for creating NSC 68 is what matters most in unraveling the reasons why, in fact, it was created. As we will see, these two men were so invested in finding a solution for the dollar gap that it is difficult to believe that the formulation of NSC 68 was not intimately connected to the dollar gap and the impending end of the Marshall Plan in 1952. Although the evidence that will be presented in making this case is largely circumstantial, it is enormously compelling. The story necessarily begins with the breakdown of U.S. foreign policy that occurred in 1949, throwing it into a tailspin.

The Breakdown of U.S. Foreign Policy

For U.S. foreign policymakers, 1949 began on a high note. The Marshall Plan had been inaugurated in April 1948, and the first shipments of aid had gone out in May. A month later, the Soviets blockaded West Berlin by cordoning off the roads and railway lines running from western Germany to the great capital city. This action on the part of the Soviets led to the famed Berlin airlift, which probably did more to enhance the prestige of the United States and Britain, and harm that of the Soviet Union, than any other single act since the end of the war. Another major achievement occurred in April 1949 when the North Atlantic Treaty Organization (NATO) was formed by ten western European nations, the United States, and Canada, although as yet it remained a treaty in name only, lacking, as it did, military might.[1] In May 1949, the Federal Republic of Germany, a separate West German state, was born. This move was a triumph in that the multilateralists had long been convinced that such a state was a necessity against those states and individuals, foreign and domestic, who were adamantly opposed to its creation. However, it was also a triumph because the United States had managed to make its creation seem a

---

[1] Lawrence Kaplan, *NATO and the United States: The Enduring Alliance* (Twayne Publishers, 1988); Melvyn Leffler, *A Preponderance of Power: National Security, the Truman Administration, and the Cold War* (Stanford, California: Stanford University Press, 1992), 208–218; Chester Pach, *Arming the Free World: The Origins of the United States Military Assistance Program, 1945–1950* (Chapel Hill, North Carolina: University of North Carolina Press, 1991).

162   *NSC 68 and the Political Economy of the Early Cold War*

defensive measure against a recalcitrant Soviet Union.[2] Still, another great achievement was the implementation of the Mutual Defense Assistant Program (MDAP). Although the act only allotted $1.3 billion for the first year of the program, it represented a significant victory for the multilateralists. Not only would it provide some military aid to allies, more importantly it would assure the western Europeans that the United States was committed to their security and help instill confidence in them to take the necessary steps toward political and economic integration, which was deemed essential to overcoming the dollar gap.[3] Finally, the United States was winning the Cold War. To say as much does not mean, of course, that it was driving the Soviet Union back to its prewar borders; it was not. However, in the contest for the hearts and minds of men, in 1949 the United States clearly had the upper hand.

U.S. leaders, therefore, had much to be confident about in early 1949. But shortly it all began to unravel. First came the British crisis, which, as we have seen, made clear that the Marshall Plan would not overcome the dollar gap, stopped multilateralism dead in its tracks when the British refused to integrate economically and politically with the continent, and created problems with the French over the integration of West Germany into the western European community.[4] Japanese problems also became acute during this same period. The Japanese dollar gap, which became severe in 1949, in some respects represented an even greater challenge than the British debacle because no ERP-type program existed for Japan and the Truman administration did not feel it had any chance of getting Congress to fund one. The Japanese were getting restless. Unemployment was running high, and social unrest was simmering just below the surface. Some outlet for Japanese production had to be found to secure the survival of capitalism and democracy there. Otherwise, Japan might begin looking to China and the Soviet Union for its trade.[5]

Domestic politics complicated matters. Congress, which controlled the purse strings of U.S. foreign policy, had made clear its intention to

---

[2] For information on the division of Germany, see Carolyn Eisenberg, *Drawing the Line: The American Decision to Divide Germany, 1944–1949*, passim; Leffler, *A Preponderance of Power*, 151–157, 201–202, 277–286.

[3] Pach, *Arming the Free World*, is the definitive study.

[4] See Chapter 5.

[5] The problems associated with Japan's dollar gap are well covered in William Borden, *The Pacific Alliance: United States Foreign Economic Policy and Japanese Trade Recovery, 1947–1955* (Madison, Wisconsin: University of Wisconsin Press, 1984), 19–142; and Andrew Rotter, *The Path to Vietnam: Origins of the American Commitment to Southeast Asia* (Ithaca, NY: Cornell University Press, 1987), 35–48, 127–140.

The Origins and Development of NSC 68

cut Marshall Plan funding if the recipient nations did not take further steps toward integration. Paul Hoffman's October 31 speech before the Organization for European Economic Cooperation (OEEC), examined in Chapter 5, aimed precisely at driving this point home to the Europeans. With Britain's formal announcement not to integrate, Congress began to grow restless. Yet, as William Foster, deputy director of the Economic Cooperation Administration (ECA), argued, the issue was pure politics. At congressional hearings on the matter, the Congress was "not really making a careful economic investigation but, in the main, [was] making political speeches about how ECA [i.e., Marshall Plan] aid is developing competition with our own industries." Such was the nature of the problem with Congress; it was less interested in finding out the facts than scoring political points. Hoffman did manage to eke out an agreement among the European nations to slash intra-European tariffs by 50 percent in an attempt to stimulate more intra-European trade. This agreement hardly constituted economic integration as either the administration or Congress envisioned it. However, the move did pacify Congress momentarily, but there was no guarantee that such pacification would last.[6]

Then, as if cast in a Greek tragedy, the United States was hit with the news that the Soviet Union had detonated an atomic device, presumably a bomb. Within days the president was told of the findings – the U.S. atomic monopoly had been broken. However, as we have seen, U.S. officials did not view Soviet possession of the bomb as increasing the chances for war. Rather, what the bomb did was enhance the Soviet Union's political clout. For instance, now when it called for the destruction of all atomic weapons and international control of atomic energy, as it had been doing since the bombings of Hiroshima and Nagasaki, it did so as an equal – one of only two known nations in possession of atomic power. As the Central Intelligence Agency (CIA) put it, "Moscow's current campaign to prohibit the use of atomic weapons and to attach a moral and legal stigma to their use is enhanced by the fact that the USSR can pose as willing to accept the same restrictions that it demands of other countries." The United States

---

[6] U.S. State Department, *Foreign Relations of the United States* (hereinafter *FRUS*), *1949* 4 (Washington, D.C: U.S. Government Printing Office, 1976): 438–440; William Foster to Harriman, June 16, 1949, Averell Harriman Papers, Marshall Plan, General Correspondence – William Foster, Box 266, Library of Congress, Washington, D.C. (hereinafter LC), 2; Harold Callender, "Hoffman Demands Action by Europe on Economic Unity," *The New York Times*, November 1, 1949, 1; Felix Belair, Jr., "Marshall Aid End Threatened by U.S.," *The New York Times*, November 1, 1949, 22; Harold Callender, "Cripps Limits Ties to Europe's Trade," *The New York Times*, November 2, 1949, 1.

refused to negotiate, however, weakening its prestige and enhancing the Soviet Union's.[7]

U.S. foreign policy also came under attack in Germany, "the football of international politics," as one commentator put it.[8] The battle over Germany's future came to a head in late 1949 when the Soviet Union established an East German state to counter the West German state created a few months earlier by the western allies. Unification was preached by East and West as the ultimate goal, and it is fair to say that no one at the time, especially the Germans, envisioned that Germany would be divided for some forty years. However, U.S. leaders would not tolerate any unification that included Soviet cooperation, short of the Soviet Union abandoning its claims on any say in Germany's future.[9] The establishment of an East German government and the subsequent call for unification, the removal of foreign troops, and economic self-support for Germany, which at least on the surface reflected the Soviet commitment to an independent Germany, boosted the Soviet Union's position.[10] And it put the United States on the defensive, especially because the U.S. plan for Germany was not fully enunciated. Truman administration officials were determined to make West Germany into a thriving capitalist state, to include its remilitarization. However, the fragile nature of the western European alliance prevented them from making their intentions fully public. France remained leery of German reconstruction, as did most of Germany's victims in WWII. France continued to push for dismantling of German factories and insisted on control, if not out right annexation, of the Saar. These French demands took place at a moment when U.S.

[7] Truman to Acheson, January 31, 1950, *FRUS*, 1950 1 (Washington, D.C.: U.S. Government Printing Office, 1977): 142; Central Intelligence Agency, "The Effect of the Soviet Possession of Atomic Bombs on the Security of the United States," June 9, 1950, *Declassified Documents Reference System* (Farmington Hills, Mich.: Gale, 2009), CK3100443766, 2–3; David Holloway, *Stalin and the Bomb: The Soviet Union and Atomic* Energy (New Haven, Ct.: Yale University Press, 1994), 231–252; James Reston, "Washington is Wary of a 'Peace Offensive': Russia is Believed to Have Effective Propaganda Weapon, Whatever the Value of Her New Military Weapon," *The New York Times*, September 25, 1949, 3(E).

[8] Study Group on Aid to Europe (hereinafter SGAE), October 31, 1949, Council on Foreign Relations (CFR), 30, Public Policy Papers, Department of Rare Books and Special Collections, Princeton University Library (hereinafter PUL), 1. The comment is Edward Mead Earle's.

[9] See Eisenberg, *Drawing the Line*, passim; Thomas McCormick, *America's Half-Century: United States Foreign Policy in the Cold War and After* (Baltimore, Maryland: Johns Hopkins University Press, 1994), 2nd edition, 64–67.

[10] Kathleen McLaughlin, "Soviet Zone Forms New German State as Rival to Bonn," *The New York Times*, October 8, 1949, 1.

The Origins and Development of NSC 68

officials were determining that both of these policies had to be abandoned if multilateralism were to become a reality in western Europe. The one justification for the United States' continued policy toward Germany – necessary until they could build support from France and other nations for a rebuilt West Germany – was Soviet obstinacy. But now the Soviets were calling the United States' bluff, and it had no answer. U.S. leaders continued to point the finger at the Soviets, a policy that was increasingly losing its teeth. As *New York Times* diplomatic correspondent James Reston noted, "Ten public protests [of Soviet moves] in a month make a record, but after a while, as one of Mr. Acheson's own supporters observed today, they sound slightly like a stuck whistle." Increasingly, the Cold War rationale was appearing impotent.[11]

The problem was exacerbated by the fact that the Germans were getting restless. Four years after the war, Germans on both sides were beginning to feel more confident, worrying U.S. leaders about the rise of "ugly German nationalism."[12] What was to stop the Germans from unifying on their own? Neither the United States nor the Soviet Union, nor France especially, wanted that to occur. Yet, it was the United States that held out against Soviet calls for unification without explaining what otherwise was to be done.[13]

All told, in the fall of 1949 the Soviet Union made significant political gains, what U.S. officials, and the press in their wake, derisively called a "peace offensive." It was a peace *offensive* in the sense that U.S. officials argued publicly that Soviet efforts to reach reconciliation were merely a smokescreen for darker motives. However, not everyone was certain that this interpretation was correct. Charles Bohlen, the reigning Soviet-Russian expert in the state department along with George Kennan, noted that he "did not agree with those who explain the Soviet peace propaganda on the grounds of exuberant confidence in the Kremlin." He felt "rather that the Russians may actually be concerned enough to mean it." For most U.S. officials, nonetheless, this contention was too uncomfortable to contemplate. To do so would be to assign blame for international

---

[11] Drew Middleton, "Soviet Said to Gain Lead in Germany," *The New York Times*, October 8, 1949, 4; Drew Middleton, "Eastern German State is Challenge to West," *The New York Times*, October 9, 1949, 5(E); Drew Middleton, "Two States Competing for German Loyalties," *The New York Times*, October 16, 1949, 4(E); James Reston, "U.S. Diplomatic Talk Tough, but Its Effects Stir Doubts," *The New York Times*, October 27, 1949, 9.

[12] Minutes of the 148th Meeting of the Policy Planning Staff (PPS), October 11, 1949, *FRUS, 1949* 1 (Washington, D.C.: U.S. Government Printing Office, 1976): 402.

[13] SGAE, October 31, 1949, CFR, 30, PUL, 1.

166   NSC 68 and the Political Economy of the Early Cold War

discord on the United States. Still, the very phrase "peace offensive" reflects the uneasiness they felt.[14]

The "loss" of China was yet another setback. The administration had tried to explain away whatever failures it had committed in China's impending fall to the Communists in a White Paper written in the summer. A Communist victory in China could not have been prevented, the paper said. The United States had tried to find a workable solution, but the Nationalist regime was corrupt. As Melvyn Leffler remarks, "[A]s a source of historical research, the *White Paper* was impressive; as a tool for influencing opinion, it failed." The "China lobby," a mixture of Republican senators and representatives, viciously attacked it. They charged that there were Communists in the State Department who had actively worked to undermine the Nationalist regime, months before Senator Joe McCarthy, whose name would become forever attached to the phenomenon known as McCarthyism, began leveling his allegations. Although the administration stood its ground by blocking new aid for China, the attack only added to its woes. When China and the Soviet Union signed a treaty of friendship and mutual support in February 1950, the administration appeared impotent.[15]

The combined effect of all these various problems – Soviet political advances enhanced by its development of atomic capabilities, the British sterling-dollar crisis, the breakdown of economic integration for Europe, the German question, Japan's dollar gap, and the "loss" of China – threw U.S. foreign policy into disarray. In the fall of 1949, the United States suddenly found itself on the defensive in the Cold War, or so its leaders believed.

New York Times European correspondent C. L. Sulzberger captured the dilemma in a series of articles written in October 1949. "In Europe one frequently hears, even from the greatest admirers of the United States," Sulzberger wrote on October 19, "the view that the American Government is overwhelmed by the world problems now facing it and for which it has no previous historical experience." Europeans were

---

[14] 6th Meeting of the PPS, January 18, 1950, Record Group 59, General Records of the Department of State (RG 59), Records of the Policy Planning Staff, 1947–1953, Minutes of Meetings, 1947–1952, Box 32, National Archives II, College Park, Maryland (NAII), 2.

[15] Leffler, *A Preponderance of Power*, 291–298, quote on 296; Walter LaFeber, *America, Russia, and the Cold War, 1945–1996* (New York: McGraw-Hill, 1997), 8th ed., 84–89; Thomas G. Paterson, *Meeting the Communist Threat: Truman to Reagan* (New York: Oxford University Press, 1988), 54–75.

The Origins and Development of NSC 68

troubled by the seeming inconsistency between stated American goals and the means for achieving them. Sulzberger cited the recent debacle over devaluation of the British pound as one example. "In France," he wrote, "it is asserted by many that the United States did not realize how much was involved in this step, with the result that the American attitude appeared to be fumbling and inconsistent." Europeans were confused by the policy-making process in the United States. It appeared that the State Department was often at odds with the ECA in its policy toward Europe and that this left Europeans feeling unsure of American commitments. For instance, Sulzberger noted, "It is asked: Is the United States only now facing the fact that the Marshall Plan alone will not solve the world dollar crisis? Is it facing it yet? When the Marshall Plan terminates will the United States cease foreign aid?"[16]

Sulzberger listed four areas in which U.S. foreign policy troubled the Europeans. Europeans wanted to know what exactly the United States expected the Soviet Union to do. Did the United States expect the Soviet Union to retreat back behind its pre-war borders? That seemed highly unrealistic. They also wanted to know how the United States envisioned eastern Europe. Would it become a "bloc of agrarian Socialist regimes?" If not, then what? They were equally concerned that U.S. leaders seemed not to grasp the very diverse nature of Europe and wondered how they could possibly envision a "United States of Europe." Finally, they were confused by a foreign policy that allowed Portugal into NATO but kept Spain, then under the dictatorship of Franco, out.

Sulzberger noted that he "has heard statesmen contend that United States policy makers are sometimes not fully aware of the basic issues posed today and, for that reason, they are occasionally placed at a disadvantage." He cited the following as an example:

Economically speaking, it is the United States and its allies that require an "empire" today – not in the old fashioned sense but in terms of commerce and economy. The underpopulated and insufficiently industrialized Soviet Union has no such basic need. Yet the current political contest is paradoxically in reverse, with the United States leading those who seek to prevent Russia from acquiring an empire she does not need and could not absorb. If this fundamental is accepted in Washington, should it not be realized that something like the Marshall Plan is necessary as a permanent facet of national policy in the American interest rather than a temporary means of halting Soviet expansionism? ... Should Americans not realize that not only must they permanently increase their purchases from

---

[16] C. L. Sulzberger, "U.S. Policy Brings European Queries," *The New York Times*, October 19, 1949, 17.

areas where they have political interest but also that it may be necessary to recognize that some form of permanent "pump priming" is required?

What the Europeans were looking for, Sulzberger concluded, was for the United States to take "positive stands." One unnamed diplomat noted: "Until the United States Government is fully conscious of its fundamental political objectives in positive terms rather than the limited conception of merely halting Soviet aggression, it cannot truly work to attain its aspirations."[17]

As the foregoing demonstrates, in the fall of 1949 U.S. foreign policy was losing its steam. Its economic program was falling to pieces and now its political one – wedded to the Cold War – was in danger of unraveling. Roving ambassador for the Marshall Plan Averell Harriman admitted as much in a meeting with the U.S. ambassadors in western Europe in October 1949. "One of the most important psychological developments in the last year in western Europe had been the abatement of the fear of Soviet aggression," he argued, which "had been brought about by the *progress* of the Marshall Plan, the *decline* in influence of Communist parties and the development of the Western Union security framework through the negotiation of the North Atlantic Treaty [Organization] and the passage by Congress of MAP [the Military Assistance Program]."[18] These are striking comments by Harriman. It did not seem to matter that U.S. efforts had actually lessened the Soviet threat. What was troubling to him was the "abatement of the *fear* of Soviet aggression," which apparently mattered more than actual threats posed by it.

Some five months later, Dean Acheson made a similar observation and was also thinking of a way out:

If we look back two years to 1947, it could be seen that there were a number of dynamic steps which had been initiated, including Secretary Marshall's speech and the birth of ERP, the development of [NATO], [and] the establishment of the West German Government. These had all represented forward steps and considerable progress had been made in advancing the Western cause through these steps. They seem now to have lost their momentum and we seem to have slowed down to a point where we are on the defensive while the Soviet [*sic*] are apparently showing more confidence. We could not hold our position defensively, we would slip backwards. It was, therefore, necessary to find some new idea or new step which would regain the initiative. The economic incentives which were the basic of ERP seem to have lost their vitality and we were engaged in discussions

[17] Ibid., quotations in the original.
[18] Meeting of U.S. ambassadors at Paris, October 21–22, 1949, *FRUS, 1949* 4: 478 (emphasis added).

The Origins and Development of NSC 68

of such things as the [European] payments union. While this was no doubt of some importance, the successful working out of a payments union would have no popular appeal, there would be no holidays or torch-light parades in celebration of a payments union.[19]

Acheson was well immersed in the development of NSC 68 by the time he made these comments, but they make the point. Something grand was needed. The setting was readied for NSC 68.

The Origins of NSC 68: The October 11 Meeting of the Policy Planning Staff

The problems bearing down on U.S. foreign policymakers in the summer and fall of 1949 and their relation to the origins of NSC 68 come into sharp relief in a meeting of the PPS held on October 11, 1949, a meeting in which Acheson played a key role. This meeting has garnered significant attention from scholars, but the real significance of it has been missed. For, a careful analysis of this meeting's minutes reveals, not only that NSC 68 was born at the meeting, but that the dollar gap laid at the heart of it.

The meeting was convened to discuss "the world situation."[20] George Kennan, then-director of the PPS, began the meeting by laying out the "major issues" confronting the United States in the world. "The situation is high-lighted by the differences between the East and the West," he stated. "It is the most serious of all individual factors, although it is not the sum total of our difficulties." He believed that "both sides have somewhat over-extended lines and are attempting to consolidate their positions." As to Soviet aggressiveness, he noted "the best evidence available to us indicates that the Russians are not planning to start a war but that they are, on the contrary, too preoccupied with [Yugoslavian leader Josep Broz] Tito and the Far East."

The most important question for the United States, Kennan advanced, was: "Are we holding our own?" In addressing that question, Kennan laid out the many problems confronting U.S. foreign policy in the fall of 1949 in the following order: (1) the British crisis and the problems it posed for European economic integration and for the reintegration of West Germany with the continent, which is to say, his focus was the

---

[19] Memorandum of Conversation, March 7, 1950, *FRUS, 1950* 3 (Washington, D.C.: U.S. Government Printing Office, 1977): 1629.

[20] 148th Meeting of the PPS, October 11, 1949, *FRUS, 1949* 1: 399–403.

dollar gap; (2) the problems associated with Japan's position in the world and its mounting dollar gap; (3) the end of the U.S. atomic monopoly occasioned by the Soviet's acquisition of atomic power; and (4) the Communist assumption of power in China. On China he noted that the "problem is not one primarily of Russians but of the basic relations of Americans with 'Asiatics,'" reflecting the sentiment among most top officials that the Communist victory in China did not necessarily spell greater Soviet-Chinese cooperation. On the Soviet bomb, Kennan remarked that he had written an article that he hoped to have published in *Reader's Digest* under the title: "Is War with Russia Inevitable?" a question that he answered with a resounding no.[21]

At this juncture, Acheson interjected, in obvious frustration: "We need our own analysis of what is happening and where we are heading, an analysis made independently of economists." Paul Nitze, deputy director of the PPS but shortly to replace Kennan as its head, added, "Economists in general are leery of making projections into the future, as they felt it was a very difficult field in which to predict the future and that their professional reputations were at stake." As these comments imply, Acheson and Nitze clearly did not want to be constrained on spending. Then Acheson made the following, crucial, observation, the significance of which largely has been missed by historians:

What is needed is a thorough study of the history of the last 35 or 40 years. During that time we have been holding a concept that if something "abnormal" happened, it was a temporary thing and that we would shortly return to "normality"; whereas, in actuality, during that entire period the realities of the situation confronting us forced us to do nothing but "abnormal" things.... The prevailing interpretation of this concept is to the effect that we must end this 35 or 40 year program of abnormality by 1952.... Unless we face up to what we want, decide on how to get it, and take the necessary action the whole structure of the Western World could fall apart in 1952.

To which Kennan responded, "The Western World need not necessarily collapse simply because we stopped financing it but that perhaps the main strain might be felt in this country unless we can decide how we can swallow our own surpluses." Nitze, disagreeing, replied, "We might not have to spend $5 billion a year abroad annually but we will probably have to spend something." Marshall Plan aid, or some other type of funding, Nitze was saying, would have to continue beyond 1952.[22]

---

[21] It is published in both the State Department *Bulletin*, February 20, 1950, 267, and *Reader's Digest*, March 1950.
[22] 148th meeting of the PPS, October 11, 1949, *FRUS, 1949* I: 401.

The Origins and Development of NSC 68   171

What makes these comments so significant, and what historians have
failed to recognize, is that in them lay the origins of NSC 68, origins that
clearly are grounded in the dollar gap. As to the latter, this is easy to demonstrate. What has made this an oft-quoted document is Acheson's comment about the Western world collapsing in 1952. Obviously, a comment
of this sort substantiates that Acheson was not only stressed out about
the situation that the United States faced but that the year 1952 held
particular significance. But what was it about this year that held such
significance? The only viable answer is that 1952 was the end year for
the Marshall Plan, which leads only to the conclusion that when Acheson
spoke of the Western world collapsing he was talking about this poten-
tiality in the context of the dollar gap. Kennan had listed all the various
problems that the United States faced at that time, including the Soviet
acquisition of atomic power and the Communist victory in China. The
year 1952 had no significance for these other problems, but it did for
the dollar gap. Moreover, Kennan's immediate response to Acheson, that
perhaps the Western world would collapse "unless we can decide how we
can swallow our own surpluses," makes clear that Kennan understood
Acheson's comments as relating to the dollar gap. While this evidence
does not prove unequivocally that the dollar gap lay at the heart of NSC
68, it does demonstrate unequivocally that the dollar gap had become a
primary concern of Acheson's by October 1949, so much so that he worried about the Western world collapsing if it were not overcome.[23]

What is less obvious is how this interchange connects to NSC 68. It
is Acheson's directive to conduct a study of the last thirty-five or forty
years that leads to this conclusion. First, taking thirty-five and forty years
off of 1949 leaves dates of 1909 and 1914, years well in advance of the
Communist victory in Russia. Acheson was hardly one to mistake dates;
he used those years to denote the period prior to World War I before the
global economy entered a period of high instability, a period in which the
dollar gap also first arose as an international problem. Second, certainly
it is not coincidence that the opening lines of NSC 68 begin: "Within the
past thirty-five years ... "[24] A "thorough study of the history of the last
35 or 40 years" was specifically what Acheson asked for at this meeting

---

[23] In *A Preponderance of Power*, Leffler at one point argues that 1952 signaled the "point
of maximum danger" for a Soviet attack in an apparent attempt to make sense of
Acheson's comment. However, Leffler's evidence for that claim is from the summer and
fall of 1950, long after NSC 68 had been submitted to the president so it has no bearing
on Acheson's comments from October 1949. Leffler, *A Preponderance of Power*, 370
and footnote 28 on the same page.

[24] NSC 68, *FRUS, 1950* 1: 237.

172   NSC 68 and the Political Economy of the Early Cold War

of the PPS.[25] Finally, what happened to this proposed study if NSC 68 is not it? There is no other such study extant that fits the criteria. Given the seeming desperation with which Acheson ordered it, he is not likely to have let it go by the wayside.[26] That said, it is not being argued here that the decision to rearm was made at this meeting of the PPS. That came only as events developed. What is being argued is that this meeting marked the starting point for the study that would culminate in NSC 68. And it shows that the event that precipitated the study was the impending end of the Marshall Plan in 1952, that is, the dollar gap.

The meeting did not end there. After the exchange described in the previous paragraphs, the participants next took up the fact that the Russians had broken the U.S. atomic monopoly and what this reality meant for U.S. strategic planning. Kennan was of the mind that because the Russians now had the bomb, "neither total annihilation nor complete surrender of the enemy is possible" and that "limited rather than total warfare should be our objective." He also suggested that, given the changed environment, conventional weapons may no longer be of much use. Here, Nitze interjected that, on the contrary, "this fact might make conventional armaments and their possession by the Western European nations, as well as by ourselves, all the more important." It might, he continued, even require a suppression of consumer goods in order to produce armaments and that the Europeans could produce such armaments if they devoted 20 percent rather than 5 percent of their national economies to the endeavor. Acheson argued that "we must examine these problems from the point of view of what peoples and governments *will* do rather than what they *can* do." Acheson went on to say that the Soviet achievement meant there might have to be consideration of "international control of atomic energy" but that such a decision would eliminate the "fear of retaliation by atomic bombing against orthodox aggression." Kennan said that the U.S. military has been basing its plans on use of the bomb in the event of war, which he felt was in error because the president had sole responsibility for using the bomb. He also argued strenuously against using atomic bombs against Soviet cities, which would likely only "stiffen the courage and will to resist of the Russian people." If, he suggested, it was decided in advance that atomic

[25] 148th meeting of the PPS, October 11, 1949, *FRUS, 1949* I: 401.
[26] Leffler argues that in the fall of 1949 "Acheson prodded Nitze to develop a program to close the dollar gap," but he never tells us what came of this program. We do know, however, that Nitze subsequently developed NSC 68. See *A Preponderance of Power,* 313, 316.

The Origins and Development of NSC 68

bombs would not be used against the Soviet Union, perhaps an agreement not to use them would be prudent.

Acheson then made the following observation: "[I]f for a variety of reasons we wish to agree with the Russians not to use the bomb such a decision would make rather awkward a request of Congress for additional appropriations to make more bombs which we weren't going to use; by January more military assistance funds will be required; ECA [Marshall Plan funding] will be up before Congress again and ... it is going to be much more difficult to put through than before." Nitze then added, "In our planning for the future we must *not* assume that 1952 is an automatic cut-off date for foreign assistance." Acheson then set Christmas as a target date for coming up with answers to these questions and said he was going to spend two mornings or afternoons with the PPS working on solutions for them. With that the meeting adjourned.

However, for all of that, a careful analysis of these minutes reveals that Acheson's and Nitze's focus remained on the dollar gap. First is Nitze's preoccupation with conventional weapons and his suggestion that if the western Europeans contribute more of their national incomes to conventional armaments production they could produce such weapons. A ratcheting up of conventional armaments would be a major component of NSC 68. Second is the issue of whether there should be international control of atomic energy. As we will have occasion to see, Acheson shuttled Kennan off to study this issue while he and Nitze began to formulate their plans for rearmament. Third, Acheson's concern that agreeing with the Soviets to the non-use of atomic bombs might create problems with Congress over future Marshall Plan aid indicate just where his priorities lay. Clearly, the Marshall Plan mattered more to him than that the Soviets now possessed the bomb. Finally, there is Nitze's observation that 1952 need not necessarily end U.S. extraordinary assistance abroad. NSC 68 would ensure that such assistance in fact would not end.[27]

All told then, what we see at this meeting of the PPS is Acheson's (and Nitze's) deep concern for the dollar gap in the context of the impending end of the Marshall Plan in 1952. When Acheson talked about the "Western world collapsing in 1952" he meant that the dollar gap would still exist in 1952 when the Marshall Plan ended. Furthermore, it demonstrates that the Soviet acquisition of the atomic bomb and the Communist victory in China were not the primary concerns in late 1949 as the writing of NSC 68 was about to get underway, at least not by those who would conduct and execute the writing of it.

[27] 148th meeting of the PPS, October 11, 1949, *FRUS, 1949* 1: 402–405.

The Origins of NSC 68: Nitze's Dollar Gap Memorandum

The evidence mounts that the dollar gap was at the heart of NSC 68 when we shift our focus to Paul Nitze. Nitze was among those assigned the task of producing the study of the "last 35 or 40 years" that Acheson called for at the October 11, 1949, meeting of the PPS described in the last section. Interestingly, on November 1, 1949, we find Nitze attending a Council on Foreign Relations study group devoted to finding a solution for the dollar gap.[28] Seeking such a solution, Nitze turned to a trusted ally.

The purpose of the study group was stated at the outset by Frank Altschul, chairman of the group. "On the assumption that the Marshall Plan will not achieve what was expected of it by 1952," Altschul explained, "the first question that arises is whether 'some new highly imaginative and more broadly inclusive program cannot be developed'" to ensure that American aid continues to flow abroad after 1952. It was important to work out a plan now, Altschul noted, rather than in a presidential election year when the political environment would be overheated. "One thing that needs to be considered," Altschul explained, "is whether we are looking for a program that will help us win the cold war, or whether we are going to be more ambitious and try to find one that will end the cold war." Nitze interjected that "the economic problems of the dollar gap, European rehabilitation and the development of backward areas would

[28] For evidence of Nitze's work on the dollar gap and the economic situation more generally see, for example, 119th Meeting of the PPS, July 29, 1949, RG 59, Records of the PPS, 1947–1953, Minutes of Meetings, 1947–1952, Box 32, NAII; 121st Meeting of the PPS, July 29, 1949, ibid.; 122nd Meeting of the PPS, August 1, 1949, ibid.; 123rd Meeting of the PPS, August 2, 1949, ibid.; 1st Meeting of the PPS, August 8, 1949, ibid.; 126th Meeting of the PPS, August 11, 1949, ibid.; 7th Meeting of the PPS, August 16, 1949, ibid.; "Implications of the Sterling Area Crisis to the U.K. and the U.S.," August 18, 1949, *FRUS, 1949* 1: 806, fn.1; 134th Meeting of the PPS, September 7, 1949, RG 59, Records of the PPS, 1947–1953, Minutes of Meetings, 1947–1952, Box 32, NAII; "Points on European Integration," October 18, 1949, RG 59, Records of the PPS, 1947–1953, Country and Area Files – Europe, Box 27, NAII; 1st Meeting of Study Group on Economic Policy (hereinafter SGEP), November 1, 1949, Office Files of Gordon Gray as Special Assistant to the President (hereinafter Gray Papers), Record Group 286, Records of the Agency for International Development (RG 286), Council on Foreign Relations – Study Group Reports, Box 6, Truman Library; Nitze to Webb, November 16, 1949, RG 59, Records of the PPS, 1947–1953, Country and Area Files – Europe, Box 27, NAII, and accompanying document "Outline of Work Program on Western European Economic Integration," [n.d.], ibid. See also the chronological file of Robert Tufts, RG 59, Records of the PPS, 1947–1953, PPS Members, Chronological File – Robert W. Tufts, Box 52, NAII. Tufts was Nitze's assistant as head of the PPS and worked extensively on NSC 68.

The Origins and Development of NSC 68 175

continue, cold war or no cold war," an important observation because it
points up the fact that the dollar gap crisis was a problem independent
of the Cold War. Altschul agreed, but he believed that the Cold War exacerbated the dollar gap, because in its absence East-West trade would be
more prolific and pressures in Southeast Asia less critical. On this point,
Nitze disagreed. In his estimation, the dollar gap was a problem independent from that posed by communism.[29]

Altschul then opened the floor to Nitze, who set the agenda for the
evening's discussion. "Let us assume that our objective is a working economic scene for the free world," Nitze began. "Such a scene, or condition,
will have to satisfy two criteria." The first was that the U.S. economy had
to continue operating "normally," that is, free of government controls.
The second was that the rest of the world had to be in a position to operate alongside the first. "That means there cannot be a basic defect in the
system such as the present American export surplus." The best way to
ensure this was, as he put it, to "lick the problem of the dollar gap."

Nitze believed that it was impossible to bring equilibrium in trade
between the dollar and nondollar area at the present level of U.S. exports,
which stood at $13 billion, a figure he thought "abnormally high." He
believed that an export amount of $10 billion was more feasible. That level,
however, would still constitute a dollar gap of around $4 billion, he noted,
because the nondollar area sold to the dollar area around $6 billion annu-
ally. Nitze argued that a narrowing of the gap by about $2 billion could
be achieved through such means as stockpiling, export of agricultural surpluses, and through Point Four aid to underdeveloped areas. However, it
is noteworthy that Nitze placed most emphasis on stockpiling, which was
solely a domestic expenditure, because he felt that Point Four aid could not
possibly amount to more than $500 million annually. Of the remaining $2
billion, he said: "The problem that remains is not only to fill the rest of the
gap but to provide a logical framework for various kinds of measures which
may make each of them more acceptable to Congress and the public."[30]

Altschul felt that Point Four's emphasis on "development" ought to be
more fully utilized because "such measures should be easier to put across
to the American people who will feel they are getting something for their
money instead of just handing it out to fill preexisting deficits." Provost
of Columbia University and Council member Grayson Kirk noted that

---

[29] 1st Meeting of the SGEP, November 1, 1949, Gray Papers, RG 286, Council on Foreign
Relations – Study Group Reports, Box 6, Truman Library, 1, emphasis added.
[30] Ibid., 1–2.

176   *NSC 68 and the Political Economy of the Early Cold War*

"checking the spread of communism" would "improve the chances of getting such a program adopted, whereas Congress and the public may be less interested in the development of areas not so directly threatened by communism."[31]

All members of the group agreed that lowering or even removing altogether the American tariff would be wise policy, especially from a political standpoint, because Europeans often pointed to the United States' high tariff when balking on adopting multilateral policies. The group was less enthusiastic about European integration as an immediate solution, though they felt it was a necessary long-term objective. ECA chief Paul Hoffman's speech before the OEEC on October 31, 1949, in which he argued for the creation of a United States of Europe, was not feasible, Altschul argued. The hope was futile anyway, noted the economist John Kenneth Galbraith, because "if Marshall Plan aid is expected to end in 1952, and if it is expected not to solve Europe's dollar problem by that time, the logical course for each European government is to work toward some degree of autarky by 1952. And that is what is actually happening, especially in agriculture." Galbraith added: "This is very bad from the point of view of the European economy as a whole, and for the prospects of American exports."[32]

The group debated whether the dollar gap was the proper framework for tackling the problem. Altschul, especially, "was not altogether convinced that Mr. Nitze's emphasis on the dollar gap was correct." Rather, he felt that "the dollar gap was a symptom of the underlying difficulty, not the thing itself." Others agreed but felt that the "balance of payments had the virtue of providing a concrete framework and a series of problems which actually had to be faced." "If this approach were taken," economist William Diebold noted, "the [Study] Group would at some point arrive at a clearer picture of what the basic problem is than if it tried to tackle this difficult subject directly."[33]

The British crisis came up for discussion as well. Thomas K. Finletter, corporate lawyer soon to be appointed Secretary of the Air Force, noted that "there is a short-run crisis as well as a long-run crisis." "How is Britain to get through the next year?" he asked. "There is a considerable danger of another sterling crisis with a further drain on reserves and a possible disintegration of the sterling area." As to the impending crisis of 1952, Finletter stated that "all studies showed a probable gap

---

[31] Ibid., 3.
[32] Ibid., 3–4.
[33] Ibid., 4.

The Origins and Development of NSC 68   177

of considerable size in Europe's dollar balance at that time." He believed some program had to be devised to reverse the trend, but he questioned whether the CFR was the proper place. "Only if the [Study] Group could have access to the facts of the case," he suggested, "would its 'imaginative thinking' have any practical value."[34]

The group left off by agreeing to hold meetings on the subject into the next spring. The group would attack the problem in the following manner: "Going on the hypothesis that the Marshall Plan is not enough, what else do we have to do to leave the world where we hoped it would be by 1952 when the Marshall Plan was originally set out? How do we make the world less vulnerable than if we did nothing but carry out the Marshall Plan?" Nitze added that "the aim had to be to find an adequate solution, not just a series of palliatives." "The world economy now works only because of American gifts," he emphasized. "That is what we have to get away from," Altschul added.[35]

At the next meeting of the study group, Altschul raised objection to Nitze's suggestion that the United States strive for an export level of only $10 billion, which would mean a reduction in the level it was then exporting. Altschul believed that "restoring the European economy cannot be solved without a growth in world trade in general." A decline in U.S. exports, at any rate, would represent a step backward not forward. If the United States needed to increase its imports then the U.S. economy had to grow, not retard. Nitze seems to have been persuaded by Altschul's argument. He said: "The [American] export surplus is now supported by United States grants and loans to the net amount of $5.3 billion which just about covers the deficit. Congress will certainly not be satisfied with this type of arrangement for the future, so the question arises as to what policy the U.S. can follow in order to remain a creditor. The only sound way to remain a creditor is through growing imports." A way out of the dollar gap had to be found that increased imports into the United States while maintaining growth in the American economy. The dilemma was how to achieve it.[36]

Nitze stopped attending the CFR study group on the dollar gap after the December 1, 1949, meeting. By then he had been appointed to succeed George Kennan as chief of the PPS, which may explain that decision. Meanwhile, he produced a paper on the dollar gap that is of great

[34] Ibid.
[35] Ibid., 5.
[36] 2nd Meeting of the SGEP, December 1, 1949, Gray Papers, RG 286, Council on Foreign Relations – Study Group Reports, Box 6, Truman Library, 1.

178   *NSC 68 and the Political Economy of the Early Cold War*

importance for understanding his mindset on the dollar gap in the crucial months in which NSC 68 was formulated, a paper that, incidentally, this author has never seen cited before. In it, he wrote:

> The [dollar] gap will be bridged. If nothing else is done, it will be forcibly reduced to tolerable size by cutting of United States exports of goods and services concurrently with the tapering off of extraordinary financial assistance. This would mean acceptance by this country of a low level of international trade in goods and services, with adverse effects on our domestic and foreign policy objectives. Domestic and foreign production would be reduced; American exports, i.e., foreign purchases of American goods and services, would fall and become subject to increasingly onerous restrictions designed to safeguard foreign monetary reserves; the competitive system would find it increasingly difficult to function; standards of living would drop; and employment here and abroad, especially in export industries would suffer. The chances for restoration of currency convertibility and adherence to liberal trading principles by foreign countries would be very poor in any foreseeable future under these circumstances, and the economic isolation of the United States would be a hard fact.[37]

It is not clear for whom this paper was intended, but the importance of it cannot be overstated. Not only does it offer, in candid detail, how threatening the dollar gap crisis was perceived to be by multilateralists in the Truman administration such as Nitze and put at the heart of that crisis the man who shortly would become the primary author of NSC 68, but these very same sentiments found their way into NSC 68. Certainly, this is hardly coincidence.[38]

As the foregoing demonstrates, Acheson and Nitze, the principal authors of NSC 68, were deeply concerned about the dollar gap crisis in the fall of 1949. And with good reason. Over the course of the fall, it became obvious that the long-term and short-term solutions to the dollar gap being contemplated by the State Department, the CFR, and other institutions were inadequate for meeting the crisis. Any long-term solution to the dollar gap required that the United States import more goods. However, Nitze, through his discussions with the CFR, came to believe that developing a program to increase imports would take four to five years "of very intensive effort."[39] Such a time frame was simply far

---

[37] Paul Nitze, "A Program for Resolving the Balance of Payments Problem of the United States," Gray Papers, RG 286, Working Papers; Executive Departments; Department of the Interior-General-Working Papers-Miscellaneous, Box 22, Department of State, Folder 2, Truman Library, 4–5.

[38] NSC 68, *FRUS, 1950* 1: 279–281.

[39] Nitze, "A Program for Resolving the Balance of Payments Problem of the United States," Truman Library, 8.

The Origins and Development of NSC 68 179

too long given the current crisis, and even then there was no guarantee that it would work. For one thing, there was significant opposition from Congress and the American people to reducing tariffs. An even greater problem, perhaps, was the lack of demand in the United States for foreign goods. Even if the tariff were lowered, there was no market in the United States for many of the goods foreign nations produced.

The short-term solution to the dollar gap – that dollar assistance would have to continue beyond the Marshall Plan's scheduled ending date of 1952 – was equally inadequate. That such aid had to continue was not the issue. The problem was that Congress could not be counted on to come up with more funds. Given Congress's penchant for cutting ERP allotments at the slightest hint of provocation on the part of the ERP nations, there was little hope that Congress could be convinced to extend the Marshall Plan. Even so Acheson, Nitze, and others believed they could not wait until 1952 to test congressional waters. What if Congress failed to act in 1952, a presidential election year, when the crisis would be upon them?

The breakdown of U.S. foreign policy in the latter half of 1949 brought the crisis to a head. Action was needed immediately. The dollar gap was breaking apart the fragile unity keeping the United States and western Europe tied together. Britain already had announced plans not to integrate economically with the continent and was moving ever closer toward autarchy. West German reindustrialization was being hampered by French reluctance to accept a rebuilt West Germany without British participation in a western European economic union. West Germans were increasingly being courted by the East, and unless something was done quickly to give the West Germans faith in following the United States, they were likely to unite with the East on their own and go neutral in the Cold War or maybe even side with the Soviet Union. The Soviet Union was making political advances and was threatening to neutralize the Cold War, the actual problem occasioned by its acquisition of the atomic bomb. Japan's dollar gap was threatening the loss of Japan, as China had been similarly "lost." The multilateralists' ability to control events was rapidly slipping away. Their second chance to reorder the world economy according to multilateralist dictates was going the way of Versailles.

No similar alarm was expressed over the Soviet atomic explosion or the Communist victory in China, not in the way that tradition holds, as "hammer blows" that shocked and frightened U.S. officials. In fact, as we have seen, Truman responded to the news of these events by asking for a reduction in military spending, a position endorsed, albeit somewhat begrudgingly, by virtually all top officials, military or otherwise.

Moreover, Acheson and Nitze, as late as December 1949, were calling a Soviet military strike a "tertiary risk." Yet, out of all of this NSC 68 emerged. Put aside for a moment that NSC 68 talked in such dire terms about the "Kremlin's design for world domination" and "God-less communism." Given what we know, how could NSC 68 – in the absence of no other program[40] – not have been aimed at the dollar gap and all the attendant difficulties it was causing U.S. plans for the postwar world? It was the dollar gap, not the Soviet Union, that presented the greater crisis in 1949. The Soviet Union was containable; the dollar gap was not. It is in this context that the origins of NSC 68 must be understood.

The Origins of NSC 68: The Emerging Consensus on a Military-Economic Solution

Why rearmament to overcome the obstacles presented by the dollar gap and the general breakdown of U.S. foreign policy such as occurred throughout 1949? The answer is that NSC 68 developed out of existing programs and policies and the emerging consensus on a military-economic solution to the dollar gap crisis where no other solution presented itself.

In a July 14, 1948, memorandum Averell Harriman, scion to the E. H. Harriman empire and Truman's newly appointed special representative in Europe for the Marshall Plan, stressed the need to offer military assistance to western Europe (actually the Western Union, consisting of Britain, France, and the Benelux countries), even if only in token amounts, as a means of capitalizing on the already increased morale generated by the first shipments of Marshall Plan aid. Harriman argued that "maintaining and strengthening the will to resist in Europe should be fundamental in our policy [in] the coming months. This requires not only effective implementation of ERP but active encouragement of the idea that we intend to help rebuild military defense against outside aggression." Confidence, in fact, had been growing, Harriman noted, and the western Europeans, with continued U.S. support, could resist "internal and external aggression." Nonetheless, pessimism ran deep. "On the continent ... the almost universal comment is that 'Western Europe will be overrun by the Russians, eventually the US will defeat Russia and liberate Western Europe, but in

---

[40] Acheson did form a committee in February 1950 to study the dollar gap problem under the direction of former Secretary of the Army Gordon Gray. The reasons for this committee are analyzed later in this chapter.

The Origins and Development of NSC 68

the meantime most of the better people, and therefore, their civilization will have been destroyed.' Appeasement psychology, like isolationism in the US, is not deeply buried." Harriman was "concerned over the possibility of a reversal of the upward trend of determination in Europe unless we give some concrete evidence of support." An offer of military aid would have an "incalculable morale effect," he suggested.[41]

Very early on, however, Harriman came to understand military aid to western Europe as involving economic factors as well, as in August 1948 when he discussed rearmament in terms of the "inter-relationship of political and military matters with economic matters and the importance of political and military considerations as bearing upon what can be done in the economic field."[42] By November those ideas had crystalized further. On November 11, 1948, Colonel Charles H. "Tick" Bonesteel weighed in on the matter in a memorandum that further expanded Harriman's ideas. Bonesteel by this time was working under Harriman. "The European Recovery Program," Bonesteel wrote, "is aimed at restoring individual economic confidence, thus, among other things, arresting and defeating Communist internal aggression. Military support, primarily to the Western Union, can begin the restoration of national confidence and remove the present numbing fear of external aggression. Neither ERP nor military support, however, can achieve success without the other. Furthermore, both must be so correlated and so balanced as not to overstrain the American economy nor the progress toward economic recovery in Europe."[43]

Others were thinking along the same lines as Harriman and Bonesteel. In May 1948, only one month after the first ERP shipments left for Europe, Frank Lindsay of the ECA suggested to Allen Dulles, future director of the CIA, that the CFR head a study group on economic aid to Europe in light of the fact that the dollar gap would still exist in 1952, after the Marshall Plan ended, and that something needed to be done about it. Dulles then wrote to Paul Hoffman, chief of the ECA, to solicit his opinion. Hoffman replied in the affirmative, and the CFR agreed to the endeavor. However, by the time the group began meeting in January 1949, it had become a study of economic *and* military aid to Europe. The records of the CFR do

---

[41] Harriman memorandum, July 14, 1948, Harriman Papers, Marshall Plan: Policy planning, 1948–1950, Box 272, LC.

[42] Thomas K. Finletter to Harriman, August 31, 1948, Harriman Papers, Marshall Plan, General Correspondence – Thomas K. Finletter, Box 266, LC, 2.

[43] Bonesteel memorandum, November 11, 1948, Harriman Papers, Box 272, Marshall Plan: Policy planning, 1948–1950, LC.

182   *NSC 68 and the Political Economy of the Early Cold War*

not reveal why, but the change is noteworthy. One of its most important conclusions, delivered a year and a half later, was that the United States needed to "ti[e] our military and economic help together in a common program," a position endorsed by both Harriman and Kennan when they attended a meeting of the group on April 24, 1950.[44]

In January 1949, Paul Nitze, in his capacity as deputy to the assistant secretary of state for economic affairs, conducted a fact-finding mission to western Europe. The goal of the mission was to "obtain information and any studies already made concerning production capabilities of the Western Union countries, the balancing of military requirements against potential productive capabilities, and the determination of implications of present and future military requirements to ERP." In his report, Nitze made the suggestion that "if the portion of assistance so linked is made available in dollars rather than in military aid items, it would cover the dollar cost of increased imported raw material requirements resulting from their increased military budgets and any decrease in export potentialities resulting from diversion of manpower," an early indication of precisely the way NSC 68 would operate.[45]

While in London, Nitze met with Harriman and Bonesteel, at which time they discussed the examination Nitze was undertaking. Before the meeting Harriman had received word that the Western Union Supply Board (WUSB) was preparing its own report on what contribution it could make to rearmament.[46] Harriman was angry that the WUSB had reached such a high stage of planning without consulting with him or the ECA. Careful planning had to go into rearmament on any scale lest it conflict with the objectives of the Marshall Plan. Production for consumption and infrastructure was not to be sacrificed for rearmament. Excess productive capacity had to be available for the program to work. Harriman wanted himself appointed U.S. representative to the WUSB rather than a civilian official from the Defense Department, as was being contemplated. This because, as Harriman put it, the "position ... is directly concerned

---

[44] Frank Lindsay to Allen Dulles, May 1, 1948, SGAE, CFR, 30, Box 242, PUL; Allen Dulles to Paul Hoffman, June 15, 1948, ibid.; Hoffman to Dulles, June 22, 1948, ibid.; Digest of the Sixteenth Meeting of the SGAE, April 24, 1950, CFR, 31, Box 243, PUL, 15–17.

[45] Paul Nitze to the Foreign Assistance Steering Committee, January 31, 1949, *FRUS, 1949* 1: 56–57; Paul Nitze, "The Development of NSC 68," *International Security* 4 (Spring 1980): 170–174.

[46] The Western Union was the initial effort at creating a collective security apparatus for western Europe. It consisted of Britain, France, the Netherlands, Belgium, and Luxembourg.

The Origins and Development of NSC 68

with the economic situation." He added, "I feel [the] time has come when I should be brought into developments and activity [concerning] Western Union rearmament. Otherwise we are likely to be working unwittingly at cross purposes."[47]

Meanwhile, planning for the Military Assistance Program got under- way. Devised less to ward off a Soviet military advance (because there was not fear of one) than to instill confidence in the western Europeans so that the Marshall Plan could work to its intended conclusion, the MAP started out small.[48] For fiscal year 1950, U.S. officials asked for an appropriation of $1.5 billion. However, from the beginning, U.S. officials viewed the MAP as a vehicle for funneling dollars to western Europe out- side of the ERP. In a letter from Acheson to Lewis Douglas, U.S. ambassa- dor to Britain, Acheson quoted a report written by the National Advisory Council on International Monetary and Financial Problems (NAC), to wit: "The NAC is of the opinion that the proposed military assistance program for fiscal 1950 might appropriately include provision for some dollar financing of the costs of a limited program of incremental defense output in the recipient countries. The Council calls attention to the neces- sity of minimizing conflict with the objectives of ERP by limiting [the] extent to which such output places demands upon resources in ERP countries which could otherwise be used for increasing output of essen- tial goods for European consumption, capital development or exports."[49] Translated: It might be possible for the United States to provide the fund- ing for WU nations to produce weapons, in the process transferring dol- lars to those nations that they otherwise would not get. No wonder that Acheson became upset in the summer of 1949 by Truman's request for reduced military spending for fiscal year 1951, for military spending was no longer solely about defense but a new paradigm increasingly being referred to as "national security." Acheson responded by asking Nitze, whose expertise was in *economic* affairs, to develop closer ties with the defense establishment with the aim of reversing Truman's decision. Moreover, he pushed to keep the MAP firmly under the control of the State Department.[50]

[47] Harriman to Lovett, January 9, 1949, Harriman Papers, Marshall Plan – Military – Defense, 1949–1950, Box 271, LC.
[48] This point is argued in Pach, *Arming the Free World*, 201–206, 219.
[49] Acheson to Douglas, March 12, 1949, *FRUS*, 1949 4: 195.
[50] Paul Y. Hammond, "NSC 68: Prologue to Rearmament," in *Strategy, Politics, and Defense Budgets*, eds., Warner R. Schilling, Paul Y. Hammond, and Glenn Snyder (New York, 1962), 287; "Why the Military Assistance Program Should be Administered by the State Department," July 25, 1949, *FRUS*, 1949 4: 359–361.

NSC 68 and the Political Economy of the Early Cold War

By the fall of 1949, Harriman also had begun thinking of a new direction for U.S. foreign policy, one that blurred the lines between the economic and the security realms. Harriman was particularly frustrated by western Europe's failure to integrate politically and economically. That frustration was clear at a series of meetings held in October 1949 with the U.S. ambassadors to western Europe. Economic and political union was not working out, he argued. The Europeans were proving too stubborn. Nationalism still held great sway in the Old World. Then he made the telling observation that perhaps western European integration, which was essential to overcoming Europe's dollar gap, "might best be made not from the purely economic or the purely political standpoint but the standpoint of *security* which was the most important thing both with us and the Europeans." Harriman perceived British recalcitrance in taking greater strides toward economic integration with the continent, which was "the basic principle of cooperation upon which the ERP was presented to and supported by the U.S. Congress," as particularly bothersome. For the United States, he argued, British resistance meant that the "US [had to] find some areas for participation [in western Europe] in order to accelerate the movement [toward integration] and give confidence to Europeans." Such a way, he wagered, could be done in the name of security. "The Atlantic Pact concept should be the umbrella under which all measures agreed upon should be taken," Harriman implored. "Security, and not economic integration or political integration, should be the point of departure of our policy."[51] Lest the import of Harriman's comments be missed, the goal, Harriman was saying, was economic and political integration, but because those endeavors were not working in and of themselves to achieve the desired end, the administration would resort to using "security" instead. This, *not* because security had become more critical; in fact, as we have seen Harriman did not believe that it had (even though, by then, the Soviets had acquired the atomic bomb). Understanding Harriman's approach is of great importance for it demonstrates that when Truman administration officials evoked the term "security" to justify or press for some desired objective, especially from late 1949 on, they did not necessarily mean security in terms of military defense. Rather, they were practicing a form of doublespeak.[52]

[51] Meeting of the U.S. Ambassadors at Paris, Friday, October 21, 1949, *FRUS, 1949* 4: 489, 494 (emphasis added). See also the Sixteenth Meeting of the SGAE, April 24, 1950, CFR, 31, Box 243, PUL, 13–17, in which Harriman was a participant.

[52] In *A Preponderance of Power*, Leffler cites a Bureau of the Budget memorandum from April 14, 1950, which he calls "one of the most important memoranda written on the

The Origins and Development of NSC 68

Tracy Voorhees, under secretary of the army in 1949 and early 1950, waged a one-man campaign to link economic and military aid together to overcome the dollar gap. Voorhees' idea was to "create dollar markets by production of maximum amount of equipment and supplies in Europe, and so make one dollar of aid do two dollars' work." It is not known how early Voorhees' views found their way into the administration. Voorhees had the ears of R. C. Leffingwell and General Eisenhower, both of whom served on the Council on Foreign Relations' Study Group on Aid to Europe. According to Voorhees, they both concurred with his assessment "of linking military aid to economic aid and making full use of the counterpart funds," which were western European currencies equivalent to the amount of Marshall Plan aid that were put into special accounts for use at a later date. His report on the matter found its way to Harriman via Secretary of the Army Gordon Gray, who mentioned that it also had been seen and approved by General Omar Bradley, chairman of the Joint Chiefs of Staff (JCS); General James H. Burns, military advisor to the secretary of defense; and Vannevar Bush, the esteemed doctor of physics. President Truman read Voorhees' report on March 22, 1950, and a memorandum dated April 10, 1950, from Voorhees to Acheson arguing the same points is in State Department files. The letter was addressed to "Dear Dean," suggesting that the two were fairly close and, therefore, that Acheson

dollar gap," in an effort to prove that the dollar gap was of secondary concern to political and security objectives. The memorandum was written to be passed on to Gordon Gray who was heading a commission to study the dollar gap problem. The relevant quote from the memorandum is the following: "Foreign economic policies should not be formulated in terms primarily of economic objectives; they must be subordinated to our politico-security objectives and the priorities which the latter involve" (317). This evidence might be persuasive were it not for the fact that, long before this memorandum was written, Harriman and others in the administration had already decided that "security" would be the primary means going forward to accomplish the goals of European integration and combating the dollar gap. Furthermore, a cover note accompanying the memorandum suggests it was written by Walter Salant, economist for the Council of Economic Advisors, who worked closely on the dollar gap in 1949 and 1950 and was sympathetic to the views of administration officials such as Harriman. Although I do not have direct evidence to support this contention, it is entirely plausible, and, in fact, likely, that Salant understood the new policy and wrote the memorandum to influence policy precisely in that direction. It is also worth noting that the quote can be interpreted in more than one way. Just because it says that "foreign economic policies should not be formulated in terms primarily of economic objectives" does not mean economic objectives were not primary. It just means that they should not be framed in those terms. The entire problem with the so-called "national security thesis" is laid bare by this reality.

186   *NSC 68 and the Political Economy of the Early Cold War*

would have read it.[53] Voorhees was intimately connected with Gordon Gray, who in early 1950 would be appointed to lead a commission on the dollar gap. Tellingly, in early 1950, both Gray and Voorhees resigned their posts as secretary and under secretary of the army, respectively, after becoming disgruntled with Defense Secretary Louis Johnson's persistent emphasis on lowering military spending.[54]

Thus, the idea of combining military and economic aid into a single package, both to contribute to the defense of western Europe and to the dollar gap problem, was on the table as Acheson and Nitze contemplated how to "end this 35 or 40 year program of abnormality by 1952." It would not have required a fit of genius to realize that a more expanded military program could accomplish both ends and a whole lot more.

The Development of NSC 68: Two Proposals

After the October 11, 1949, meeting of the PPS, preliminary work on a "study of the last 35 or 40 years" began in the PPS. This apparently took the form of many "position papers" on various subjects, which were ultimately turned over to Kennan who was to write the final report.[55] Acheson makes note of this in *Present at the Creation* when he remarks that "by October the Policy Planning Staff had started to work on a reappraisal of our position, inquiring initially whether the situation did not require a renewed attempt on our part to get international control of atomic energy." And further that "the Policy Planning Staff, and George Kennan in particular, had been at work on an approach to international control of the atomic race, a study which George completed after he left the Planning Staff."[56] The importance of these developments should not be missed. What appears to have occurred is that, as work went forward

---

[53] Tracy Voorhees, "Dollar Gap Study," October 20, 1950, Tracy Voorhees Papers, Alexander Library, Rutgers, New Brunswick, New Jersey (hereinafter AL). Voorhees, "Proposal to Correlate Economic Aid to Europe with Military Defense," October 20, 1950, Voorhees Papers, AL. "A Proposal for Strengthening Defense Without Increasing Appropriations," March 21, 1950, Harriman Papers, Marshall Plan, Military – Defense, Policy Planning, 1948–1950, Box 272, and accompanying cover letter from Gray to the Secretary of Defense, March 22, 1950, LC; Tracy Voorhees to Acheson, April 10, 1950, *FRUS*, 1950 3: 48.

[54] Tracy Voorhees to President Truman, February 14, 1950, Voorhees Papers, AL.

[55] 4th Meeting of the PPS, January 13, 1950, RG 59, Records of the PPS, 1947–1953, Minutes of Meetings, Box 32, NAII, 2.

[56] Dean Acheson, *Present at the Creation: My Years in the State Department* (New York: W. W. Norton, 1969), 345–46.

The Origins and Development of NSC 68

on the study of which Kennan was in command, Acheson and Nitze were already leaning in a different direction – toward rearmament – which they knew Kennan would not support. Ernest May, for instance, notes that "Acheson ... picked Nitze" to replace Kennan as head of the PPS because "Kennan did not share Acheson's belief that containment required substantial military forces" (Kennan apparently believed that the Soviet Union could be contained with two or three well-trained marine divisions). Thus, it would appear that this preliminary study focusing on international control of atomic energy was eventually shuttled off to Kennan while Acheson and Nitze formulated a different plan – the plan for rearmament – in other, decidedly secret, quarters. This turn of events also helps explain Acheson's increasing dependence on Nitze, which would ultimately end in Nitze replacing Kennan as head of the PPS.[57]

Meanwhile, the issue that caught Washington's attention most was not the study that Acheson wanted done but the decision to build the H-bomb. The issue was highly contested. The "Super," as it was often called, had several strong advocates, among them the preeminent scientists Edward Teller, Luis Alvarez, and Ernest Lawrence, but it had far more antagonists. After the General Advisory Committee of the Atomic Energy Commission studied the issue in October 1949, they resoundingly voted not to pursue it, a position shared by Atomic Energy Commission Chief David Lilienthal. When President Truman appointed the Special Committee of the NSC on November 19, 1949, to study the issue, he brought together three individuals with conflicting views. The committee consisted of Acheson, Johnson, and Lilienthal. Of the three, only Johnson was firmly behind the project. Acheson was undecided, and Lilienthal was thoroughly opposed. This, after the Soviets had obtained the atomic bomb.[58]

Prior to the seating of the committee, however, Acheson received a major breakthrough in his effort to get the study he wanted. On November 1, 1949, Lilienthal paid Acheson a visit at the State Department. His mission was to turn over to the State Department the decision on whether

---

[57] Ernest May, "Introduction: NSC 68: The Theory and Politics of Strategy," in Ernest May, ed., *American Cold War Strategy: Interpreting NSC 68* (New York: Bedford Books, St. Martin's Press, 1993), 8; John Lewis Gaddis and Paul Nitze, "NSC 68 and the Threat Reconsidered," *International Security* 4 (Spring 1980): 171.

[58] Robert Oppenheimer to Lilienthal, October 30, 1949, *FRUS, 1949* 1: 569–73; Truman to the Executive Secretary of the NSC Sydney Souers, November 19, 1949, *FRUS, 1949* 1: 587–95. There is some discrepancy here between the record and Acheson's memory. In *Present at the Creation*, Acheson says this occurred on November 10, 1949.

to proceed with the H-bomb. At the meeting, Lilienthal made clear his opposition. Acheson, too, expressed his reservations about it, calling attention to the fact that the political dimensions of the decision were virtually insufferable. How could they not go forward, Acheson wondered? Congress would eat the president alive if they did not. But, importantly, Lilienthal believed that the decision on the H-bomb was essentially a foreign policy question and that what was required was, as Acheson put it, a "thorough review of our whole foreign policy" in order to make the proper decision. Although Lilienthal could not have known it, this handover was music to Acheson's ears. As he explains in his memoir, "Immediately after my talk with Lilienthal, I met with the whole Policy Planning Staff, all of whom recognized the far-reaching consequences of the even broader decision that now faced the President." A new impetus, what historian Marc Trachtenberg has called a "window of opportunity," had suddenly opened up.[59]

It is in this context that Nitze's well-known consultation with leading scientists on the efficacy of pursuing the H-bomb should be understood. After the November meeting between Acheson and Lilienthal, Nitze embarked on a crusade of sorts to get approval for the H-bomb. He met first with Robert Oppenheimer, who had led the atomic bomb program at Los Alamos during WWII. Oppenheimer was thoroughly opposed to building the H-bomb on both technical and moral grounds. He next talked to Robert LeBaron, one of the liaison officers Nitze had cultivated in the Pentagon. LeBaron suggested he talk to Edward Teller, a Hungarian exile who would go on to claim the mantle "father of the H-bomb," a mantle of which he was apparently very proud. Teller expressed overambitious enthusiasm for the project. He not only believed it should be undertaken but that it had to be lest the Soviets get one first. Nitze went with Teller, ignoring entirely all evidence that countered Teller's claims, including his scientific explanation for how the bomb would work, which in the long run proved incorrect. The point here is that Nitze clearly was convinced even before he embarked on his crusade that development of the H-bomb

---

[59] Marc Trachtenberg, "A 'Waiting Asset': American Strategy and the Shifting Nuclear Balance, 1949–1954," in Marc Trachtenberg, History and Strategy (Princeton, New Jersey: Princeton University Press, 1991), 101. Trachtenberg writes that "the whole concept of 'windows' ... was not an abstract, academic construct, artificially imposed on historical reality.... The impact of this whole way of thinking on actual policy was enormous." I do not cite Trachtenberg because I absolutely agree with him, although I agree U.S. officials saw things in terms of "windows." However, our conceptions of those "windows" are very different. Acheson, Present at the Creation, 346.

The Origins and Development of NSC 68   189

should go forward, and he merely sought out and found the support he needed. Nitze's zeal in this matter is hard to understand. In the literature he appears among State Department officials virtually singularly committed to pursuing the H-bomb, whereas most top officials remained torn over the issue. Nothing in his background up to that time, especially given that most of his work in government from the onset of WWII had been in the economic realm, paints him as a hawk. Even as late as December 1949 he would be calling the Soviet military threat "tertiary."[60] Furthermore, Nitze went on to base his own claim for the decision to rearm on his belief that nuclear weapons were becoming obsolete as a result of the break in the atomic monopoly.[61] The H-bomb, once built, would not remain a U.S. monopoly for long. So, why the enthusiasm?

Nitze biographer David Callahan offers a possible explanation. From the time in which Nitze took an active interest in the H-bomb, Callahan argues, he never argued that the bomb should be built. Rather, he argued that work should go forward on whether it was possible to build such a bomb. If, after such a study, it should prove untenable, then the project could be dropped and, likely, it could be assumed the Soviets would be no closer than the Americans to possessing the Super. According to Callahan, Nitze, in fact, hoped that the feasibility study would prove that building it was impossible. If Callahan is correct, then it is entirely plausible that Acheson and Nitze saw the decision on the H-bomb – again, not to build it but to examine whether it could in fact be built – as crucial to obtaining what they really wanted, which was a complete reexamination of U.S. foreign policy objectives. In other words, they had come to the conclusion that the decision on the H-bomb was absolutely critical to securing the review, which explains why Nitze was so eager to find support for pursuing the H-bomb, even though he was not, it would appear, really in favor of it.[62]

As these events were transpiring, a wholesale cleaning out of those who would oppose increased military spending was taking place. On November 1, 1949, Edwin Nourse resigned as chief economic adviser to the president and was replaced by Leon Keyserling, although initially only on a temporary basis. There must have been a great sigh of relief from Acheson when he received the news. Nourse and Keyserling disagreed over the ability of the economy to handle larger military outlays.

---

[60] 171st Meeting of the PPS, Dec 16, 1949, *FRUS, 1949* 1: 414.
[61] Nitze's Commentary, in May, *America's Cold War Strategy*, 105.
[62] David Callahan, *Dangerous Capabilities: Paul Nitze and the Cold War* (New York: Harper Collins), 73–91.

Nourse thought it could not, at least, not without great harm to the domestic economy; Keyserling thought it could, and in fact believed it might actually benefit the economy. With Nourse out and Keyserling in, a major obstacle to rearmament was removed. Not surprisingly, shortly thereafter Nitze began meeting regularly with him, receiving his assurance that the economy could handle a $40-billion-a-year military budget. Then, on January 1, 1950, Kennan was replaced by Nitze as head of the PPS. It would be crude to call Kennan a thorn in the side of Acheson by this time, but it would not be off mark. Kennan offered, in his many and characteristically thoughtful memorandums on the issues confronting the administration in 1949 and 1950, a powerful counterpoint to Acheson's and Nitze's position on the need for rearmament. NSC 68 would never have been written if Kennan had remained head of the PPS. With him out and Nitze in, another great obstacle to rearmament was dissolved. However, the axing spree would not end here, as we will see later.[63]

Meanwhile, work continued on the decision to build the Super, although "work" is not the best way to describe it. As Acheson tells it, the special committee of the NSC only met twice – on December 22, 1949, and on January 31, 1950. The meeting of December 22, in Acheson's words, "turned into a head-on confrontation between Louis Johnson and David Lilienthal and ... produced nothing either new or helpful to the President."[64] Because Johnson was already on board, the issue was up to Acheson and Lilienthal. Certainly, by December Acheson had made up his mind in favor of the Super, because by then he had already decided on a more comprehensive appraisal of U.S. foreign policy goals. Lilienthal was the hold out. He objected to the H-bomb primarily on moral grounds, which made his opposition all the worse. When all roads seemed to point to building it as the only logical conclusion, he lamented that those charged with making the decision – meaning himself, Acheson, and Johnson – were simply not wise enough to see any alternatives.

Whereas the H-bomb decision remained somewhat stalled, the NSC moved ahead with its decision to undertake a reexamination of national security requirements. There was initially no connection between the NSC study and the one Acheson was aiming to conduct. It was the job of the NSC to reexamine the nation's national security situation as

---

[63] Benjamin Fordham, *Building the Cold War Consensus: The Political Economy of National Security Policy, 1949–1951* (Ann Arbor, Michigan: University of Michigan Press, 1998), 25–48; Acheson, *Present at the Creation*, 347–348.

[64] Acheson, *Present at the Creation*, 348.

The Origins and Development of NSC 68

circumstances warranted, and the Soviet bomb and Communist victory in China clearly warranted such a reexamination. On January 5, 1950, NSC Executive Secretary Admiral Sydney Souers directed the NSC to do just that.

As December became January, the H-bomb decision hung in limbo, with Lilienthal seemingly unable to commit himself one way or another. This prompted Johnson to fire off a letter directly to the president, apparently spurring the committee to action. Although Johnson's "unilateral" move was in violation of committee decorum, the president did wish to move forward as he was receiving increasing pressure from Congress and the press to make a decision.[65] The special committee of the NSC met on January 31 in the office of Admiral Souers. Acheson produced a draft of a paper he had written based on his discussions with Lilienthal. The paper recommended that the United States "investigate the H-bomb, defer decision on production pending investigation, and immediately inaugurate a review of foreign and military policies."[66] Johnson was unhappy with the paper because it delayed decision on production until after the feasibility of the project could be ascertained, which could have taken years. The whole approach pained Lilienthal to a considerable degree. He believed "authorizing investigation and research while a review of our policies was going on ... would extinguish whatever faint hope there might be of finding a way to prevent development of the weapon."[67] However, Lilienthal agreed to sign the recommendation on the condition that he be allowed to present his views to the president. Once this was agreed

[65] According to David Alan Rosenberg, the president had decided to endorse the feasibility of building the hydrogen bomb as early as January 19 after considering a JCS paper of January 13 that did the same. David Alan Rosenberg, "American Atomic Strategy and the Hydrogen Bomb Decision," *Journal of American History* 66: 1(June 1979): 83. Rosenberg goes on to argue that the top military brass became convinced in February 1950 that the Soviet Union might well have been engaged in trying to develop an atomic weapon since 1943 and, therefore, that it might have been further along the path to developing a hydrogen bomb than U.S. officials believed. To make his case he cites a memorandum written by Brigadier General Herbert B. Loper, and sent to Military Liaison Committee to the Atomic Energy Commission Chairman Robert LeBaron, in which Loper makes precisely that "hypothetical case." Space does not permit a full analysis of Loper's memorandum and its impact, but it is certainly of no small significance that LeBaron was the primary Defense Department representative involved in the PPS's writing of NSC 68. This participation was largely concealed from Secretary of Defense Louis Johnson, who was against increased military spending. It is fair to say that LeBaron was on the side of Acheson and Nitze for increased military spending. The Loper memorandum, and its promotion by LeBaron, should be considered in this light.
[66] Acheson, *Present at the Creation*, 348.
[67] Ibid., 349.

to, the three men, along with Admiral Souers, presented it to the president. After he read the recommendation, Acheson told him Lilienthal wanted a chance to speak. Lilienthal began his discourse when the president abruptly cut him off. He had made up his mind. The work would go forward. Proposal one had now been given official sanction at the highest level.

Later that same day, Truman was presented with proposal two, the review of national security Acheson had wanted for a long time. The directive, which served as the basis for NSC 68, called for a "reexamination of our objectives in peace and war and of the effect of those objectives on our strategic plans, in light of the probable fission bomb capability and possible thermonuclear bomb capability of the Soviet Union." Truman approved it as well. Thus, proposal two was now approved. At this juncture, then, three studies were on the table – the decision to test the feasibility of building the H-bomb, the reappraisal Truman ordered, and the reappraisal already underway in the NSC, the latter of which was not part of the president's orders for that day but nonetheless forms a part of the story. As Hammond notes, however, the effect of the president's directive on the study Acheson wanted and got was to replace the NSC study with the study to be conducted, at Truman's order, with the study group under the agency of Acheson and Johnson.[68]

From here we learn from Hammond that Acheson "delegated the responsibility assigned him in the President's letter for reappraisal to the [PPS]." Hence, Paul Nitze was put in charge of the study. To assist him, Nitze brought from the PPS Robert Tufts, who would in fact do most of the actually writing on NSC 68 and who is most responsible for the language contained in it, John Davies, Robert Hooker, and Carlton Savage. Not mentioned by Hammond were two other members of the PPS staff who contributed to the study – George Butler and Harry Schwartz. Johnson turned to Major General James H. Burns who, Hammond writes, was "the only Defense Department official authorized to maintain contacts with the State Department." As for the JCS, that august body assigned the U.S. Air Force member of the JSC to the project. This was Major General Truman H. Landon, who had served on the NSC subcommittee devoted to the H-bomb problem. But Landon's appointment, Hammond asserts, in no way suggested that either the JCS or the Defense Department was in agreement with the project. As Hammond explains, "since he formally represented only the views of an advisory staff, no

---

[68] Truman to Acheson, January 31, 1950, *FRUS, 1950* 1: 142.

The Origins and Development of NSC 68

commitment by the Defense Department prior to approval by JCS or the Office of the Secretary of Defense (OSD) could be inferred from his participation in and support of the group's work."[69] In addition to these individuals, two other officials from Defense participated, partly because Burns was in ill health and could not devote full time to the project. These men were Najeeb E. Halaby, Burns' assistant in his capacity as director of the Office of Foreign Military Affairs, and Robert LeBaron, who was the chairman of the Military Liaison Committee to the Atomic Energy Commission. James Lay, executive secretary of the NSC staff, along with Everett Gleason, also attended in order to lend NSC support to the study. Secretary of Defense Johnson, who supported Truman's commitment to reduced military spending, was left out of the loop. With this, the study group got underway.[70]

The Development of NSC 68: The Issue of Timing

At this juncture, it is necessary to ascertain whether the decision to rearm came before or after Truman's directive of January 31, 1950. The issue matters because if it came after, then such would present fairly strong evidence against the notion that the dollar gap played any role in the origins of NSC 68. If, however, it can be shown that the decision to rearm had been made before the president's directive, then the thesis of this study, that the dollar gap played a central role in the origins of NSC 68, is significantly bolstered.

If one were to take *Present at the Creation* at face value, one would have to conclude that the decision to rearm only came through the reappraisal. This impression is the one Acheson leaves. The context for this assessment comes from the H-bomb decision, which, as we have seen, troubled him and Lilienthal a great deal. As Acheson described it, at the January 31 meeting of Acheson, Lilienthal, Johnson, and Souers, Lilienthal expressed his continued reticence over building the H-bomb. Acheson displayed some sympathy for Lilienthal's position but ultimately dismissed it as inadequate. Then, in his attempt to give Lilienthal, who Acheson admired greatly, his fair due, he remarked that "much that [Lilienthal] said was appealing, and in our later review we were strongly persuaded toward increased conventional capability."[71] This would imply that the idea for

---

[69] Hammond, "NSC 68," 297.
[70] For inclusion of Butler and Schwartz, see Callahan, *Dangerous Capabilities*, 102.
[71] Acheson, *Present at the Creation*, 349.

194   *NSC 68 and the Political Economy of the Early Cold War*

rearmament came through the reappraisal and not before it, almost as if it had been Lilienthal's idea and his alone. However, this appears to be another case of Acheson being uncharacteristically modest. For, the evidence suggests that the decision to rearm was made prior to the president's directive and that the directive was sought out to provide the basis for a decision already made.

Most of the evidence for this contention we have already chronicled. It is found in the State Department's unhappiness with Truman's cuts in military spending against the majority opinion that they were acceptable. It is found in Acheson's pushing Nitze to develop ties with the Defense Department and with his successful move to put the MAP under the direction of the State Department. It is found in the different opinions Nitze and Kennan had over how best to pursue containment and Acheson's increasing gravitation toward Nitze's belief that it would take more than two marine divisions, as Kennan believed. And, it is found, ultimately in the decision to replace Kennan with Nitze as head of the PPS.

There is other evidence as well. There is, for instance, the peculiar "epiphany" that Nitze experienced after the president gave his directive. As he began to assume leadership of the PPS in December 1949 (he officially took over on January 1, 1950), Nitze's comments with regard to the Soviet Union reveal a man who did not believe it posed a military threat of any great significance. On December 16, 1949, Nitze is recorded saying that "a total war started deliberately by the Soviets is a tertiary risk."[72] Also, in a memorandum written three days later, Nitze noted that "the most immediate risks facing the security of the free world and ultimately of the U.S. are in the ideological, economic, and political aspects of the cold war."[73]

However, on February 2, 1950, three days after Truman issued his directive, Nitze had abruptly changed his tune. Asked at a meeting of the PPS about his opinion on the chances for war, he remarked that "it seemed considerably greater than last fall." Then, in a paper drawn up on February 8, 1950, titled "Recent Soviet Moves," Nitze concluded that these moves "reflect not only a mounting militancy but suggest a boldness that is essentially new – and borders on recklessness." He further pointed out that, although the events of the fall do not suggest that "Moscow is preparing to launch in the near future an all-out military attack on the

---

[72] 171st Meeting of the PPS, Dec 16, 1949, *FRUS, 1949* I: 414.
[73] Memorandum from the Secretary of State, December 20, 1949, *FRUS, 1949* I: 615; Nitze to Acheson, December 19, 1949, ibid., 611–612.

The Origins and Development of NSC 68

West," they reveal "a greater willingness than in the past to undertake a course of action, including a possible use of force in local areas, which might lead to an accidental outbreak of general military conflict." He concluded, "Thus the chances of war through miscalculation is increased."

But what new evidence produced between December 19, 1949, and February 2, 1950, did Nitze have that would have changed his mind regarding the Soviet threat? He does not cite any. The benefit of hindsight has not produced any. In fact, as we have seen, during this period the Soviets launched their so-called peace offensive aimed at securing international control of atomic energy and reaching agreements over Germany. Whereas U.S. officials might be excused if they did not accept Soviet overtures, Soviet moves hardly constituted "a mounting militancy" that "borders on recklessness." Clearly, the assertion was contrived. A more likely reading of the document is that Nitze wrote it as a primer for the study group to begin its work on the task at hand. But, importantly, the starting point for asking that question was not whether a more heightened Soviet threat based on "recent Soviet moves" existed, but simply that it did. Nitze here provided the assumption behind the study to be undertaken, that massive rearmament was necessary, not a serious analysis of what was actually required. He was committed to rearmament already. Now that he had presidential approval, he had the license to make his case. Moreover, because he was already committed to rearmament, that meant he had to push the Soviet button. Hence the production of "Recent Soviet Moves."[74]

Then there is how quickly the report came together after the president's directive of January 31. Ernest May notes that the committee put together by Nitze to handle the president's directive "produced a first draft in a matter of weeks."[75] If, as Acheson implied in his memoir, the decision to rearm came only through the study group's work, it is doubtful that the work could have proceeded so quickly to a decision to rearm. The study group would have debated what the response should be, not merely spent its time producing a paper of a decision that was made in advance, as appears was the case. By the time work began on the paper, the issue was not what was to be done but how best to sell it to the president. That could only be so if rearmament was an option already on the table.[76]

---

[74] Paul Nitze, "Recent Soviet Moves," February 8, 1950, *FRUS, 1950* 1: 145–148.
[75] May, "Introduction," *Interpreting NSC 68*, 11.
[76] The work of the committee is documented in *FRUS, 1950* 1: 126–200.

One final proof that rearmament had been decided on before the president issued his directive is the way in which the project was produced and by whom. The official directive ordered by President Truman to investigate the state of U.S. military preparedness in light of the Soviet atomic achievement, issued on January 31, 1950, stipulated that the study would involve both the State Department and the Defense Department; it was to be a joint effort. But that is not what happened. Instead, the development of NSC 68 was carried out in utmost secrecy within the bowels of the State Department headquarters. Dean Acheson and Paul Nitze commandeered the study to the Policy Planning Staff, in essence hijacking it. This says volumes about the origins of NSC 68. As we have seen, U.S. officials, including foremost the president himself, did not view the Soviet acquisition of the atomic bomb or the Communist victory in China as particularly dire events. Truman wanted to cut military spending, not raise it. Secretary of Defense Johnson was on board with Truman. Acheson and Nitze knew he would never go for rearmament, so he was kept out of the project. But why would they do that if they did not already know ahead of time what the report was going to argue?[77]

All told, it appears that Acheson and Nitze had decided on rearmament prior to the directive and that the directive was the stamp of approval they needed to carry out their agenda. Although not definitive proof, such evidence bolsters the case that NSC 68 had its origins in the dollar gap, for what other reason would Acheson and Nitze have for wanting rearmament? If one were to argue because of the Soviet threat, that would mean Acheson and Nitze were alarmed by that threat to the point of rearmament when virtually no one else felt the same way, a rather awkward argument to make and one not supported by the evidence.

The Development of NSC 68: Drafting the Document

Although NSC 68 technically fell under the jurisdiction of the National Security Council, it was devised and constructed by the PPS entirely at the direction of Acheson and Nitze.[78] Writing in 1989, Nitze described the process by which NSC 68 was formulated:

---

[77] Memorandum of Conversation, March 22, 1950, *FRUS, 1950* 1: 203–206; Acheson, *Present at the Creation*, 373–381.

[78] See Walter Iaascson and Evan Thomas, *The Wise Men: Six Friends and the World They Made, Acheson, Bohlen, Harriman, Kennan, Lovett, and McCloy* (New York: Simon Schuster, 1986), 56–57, 482–485; Borden, *Pacific Alliance*, 43–44.

The Origins and Development of NSC 68

The writing of NSC 68 fell almost entirely to the Policy Planning Staff.... Practically everyone on the staff participated in one way or another to make it a joint effort from start to finish.... After becoming director of the [PPS], I joined Secretary Acheson every morning in his small staff meeting room or dropped by his office, which was adjacent to mine, to check with him on important developments. Thus, Acheson stayed current on what the group was doing."[79]

Left out of the process were officials whom Acheson and Nitze knew were opposed to large defense expenditures. As we have already seen, Johnson and virtually the entire Defense Department staff were left out; so were Russian experts George Kennan and Charles Bohlen. Although Kennan was the father of the "containment" policy he had always been of the mind that the Soviet Union would not wage war to achieve its objectives unless provoked. His mind had not been changed by events in the fall of 1949. "There is little justification for the impression that the 'cold war' by virtue of events outside of our control, has suddenly taken some drastic turn to our disadvantage," Kennan wrote in one of his last memorandums to Acheson before leaving the State Department. With such a view, it was not likely that Kennan would be useful to the study group. Bohlen was of similar opinion, so he, too, was left out.[80]

As the drafting of NSC 68 occurred, experts outside of the PPS were brought in to analyze the paper. These included Wall Street financier and long-time friend of Acheson, Robert Lovett, the wizard of Los Alamos Robert Oppenheimer, eminent nuclear physicists Henry D. Smyth and Ernest O. Lawrence, President of Harvard James Conant, and President of the Rockefeller Foundation Chester Barnard. The men were chosen from a much larger list of possible witnesses. The initial idea was to consult with Conant and Oppenheimer individually and then meet with groups of nonscientists "with the dual objective of getting reactions from these men and instilling in them a sense of confidence that the Government is studying this subject deeply and thoroughly."[81] However, this plan fell through and, in the end, the six individuals just mentioned were chosen for independent consultation. If the experience of Oppenheimer was the norm, none of the men were given much time to study the document. Oppenheimer was allotted at most one hour and a half "to absorb it"

---

[79] Nitze, "NSC 68," 94.

[80] Kennan to Acheson, February 17, 1950, *FRUS, 1950* 1: 160–167; PPS Meeting, January 18, 1950, RG 59, Records of the PPS, 1947–1953, Minutes of Meetings, Box 32, NAII.

[81] Memorandum by Harry Schwartz, February 23, 1950, RG 59, Records of the PPS, 1947–1953, Chronological File 7: 1950, Box 34, NAII.

198   NSC 68 and the Political Economy of the Early Cold War

before sitting down with Nitze and others to discuss it.[82] As expected, all of the experts endorsed the report. As political scientist Benjamin Fordham has pointed out, "The purpose of the consultation process was the cultivation of sympathetic individuals who were in a position to influence public and elite opinion, not to rewrite the report."[83]

The Gray Commission: A Backup Plan

Meanwhile, Acheson officially organized a commission under retiring Secretary of the Army Gordon Gray to study the dollar gap problem and make recommendations to the president on ways to overcome it. In this regard Acheson offered his most succinct analysis of the dollar gap crisis extant, which he sent to President Truman on February 16, 1950.

We are now exporting about $16 billions of goods and services. We are importing only $10 billions of goods and services. Of the difference of about $6 billions, $5 billions is being paid for by foreign assistance. In short, about a third of our exports is being financed by grants. At the end of ERP [the Marshall Plan], European production will have been restored and substantial recovery achieved. This will be a tremendous accomplishment. But the problem of payment for American goods and services will remain. The countries of the free world will still require from us a volume of exports which they will not be able to pay for if their exports to the United States remain at present levels. Put in simplest terms, the problem is this: as ERP is reduced, and after its termination in 1952, how can Europe and other areas of the world obtain the dollars necessary to pay for a high level of United States exports, which is essential both to their own basic needs and to the well-being of the United States economy? This is the problem of the "dollar gap" in world trade.[84]

What is significant about this evidence is that it offers irrefutable proof that top U.S. officials, including the president, knew that the dollar gap would still exist in 1952, after the Marshall Plan's termination, and that it concerned them greatly.

Reference to the Gray Commission is found in NSC 68:

The Executive Branch is now undertaking a study of the problem of the United States balance of payments and of the measures which might be taken by the United States to assist in establishing international economic equilibrium. This is a very important project and work on it should have a high priority. However, unless such an economic program is matched and supplemented by an equally

---

[82] Memorandum by Schwartz, February 24, 1950, ibid.
[83] Fordham, *Building the Cold War Consensus*, 42.
[84] Acheson to Truman, February 16, 1950, *FRUS, 1950* 1: 834–835.

The Origins and Development of NSC 68

far-sighted and vigorous political and military program, we will not be successful in checking and rolling back the Kremlin's drive.[85]

However, there is reason to suggest that the Gray Commission was set up less to find a solution to the dollar gap than to give added reinforcement to a policy that had already been decided on but had yet to win Congress' or the American people's approval – to extend foreign economic assistance beyond 1952. Philip Trieze, a member of the Commission, believed that

the Gray Commission ... was set up, presumably, to endorse a decision which the administration wished to make, and that was to continue the Marshall plan for a longer period. I think the conclusion had been arrived at that Europe was not going to be sufficiently recovered by the end of the Marshall plan to justify ending it, and, therefore, the essential task of the Gray Commission was looked upon as setting forth a full-scale justification for a view which was already well along toward being accepted.[86]

Acheson was taking no chances. The Gray Commission would provide justification for increasing foreign economic aid beyond 1952 and for striving toward greater imports to close the dollar gap regardless of what came of the rearmament plan. However, the Korean War changed the nature of the Gray Commission. After the war broke out and it became clear that war-related spending would reestablish the triangular trade pattern of the pre-WWII days and effectively nullify the need to reduce tariffs, as the commission had determined was necessary, Gray dropped the idea of putting pressure on Congress to reduce tariffs and instead called for increased foreign *military* aid and public investment in Third World countries, much as NSC 68 did.[87]

The Development of NSC 68: The Review

On March 22, 1950, Acheson, Nitze, and other members of the study group met with Secretary of Defense Johnson to review what was supposed to be the joint State-Defense reappraisal of national security requirements. Johnson, it will be recalled, was kept out of the study, despite the president's directive. Johnson was given only a brief time to

---

[85] NSC 68, *FRUS, 1950* 1: 278–279.

[86] Philip Trieze, Oral History, May 27, 1975, Truman Library, 23. The British saw it this way as well. See "The Gordon Gray Report," Foreign Office 371/86975, UR 1015/36, The National Archives, Kew, England, United Kingdom (hereinafter TNA).

[87] Gordon Gray, *Report to the President on Foreign Economic Policies* (Washington, D.C.: U.S. Government Printing Office, 1950), 38–41, passim.

NSC 68 and the Political Economy of the Early Cold War

review the study. What he saw made him fume. Because the study called for greatly increased military spending, which Johnson was adamantly opposed to, he refused to consider it. The meeting ended abruptly when Johnson stormed out. Acheson records in *Present at the Creation* that he was appalled by Johnson's behavior and was not surprised when several years later Johnson had a brain operation. Truman, who was kept abreast of the group's work and knew the general contents of NSC 68 before formally receiving it, was livid. He ordered Acheson to press on, which he and the PPS did.[88]

As NSC 68 neared completion, it was sent to several high-ranking members of the State Department for their perusal. They were ordered to make comments on it and send them immediately to the secretary of state.[89] Nitze, in a remarkable distortion of the facts, claimed at the time that everyone was in agreement with the findings of NSC 68.[90] This claim is simply untrue, as there were some officials highly critical of the report. Not only that, but a fair hearing of their views reveals that they offered a more accurate accounting of the actual Soviet threat than NSC 68 provided.

Some did agree with the paper wholeheartedly. Assistant Secretary of State for Public Affairs Edward Barrett, for instance, judged that it did a "magnificent job of analyzing the problem." He further suggested, in one of the more memorable memoranda associated with the origins of NSC 68, the following:

> If and when this whole project is approved by the President, the public education campaign must obviously receive the most careful study.... The first step in the campaign is obviously building up a full public awareness of the problem. This might take three months or it might require no more than ten days. My hunch is that it will be nearer ten days. We must be sure that the Government is in a position with positive steps to be taken just as soon as the atmosphere is right.... In other words, we should have at least the broad proposals for action well in hand before the psychological "scare campaign" is started.

Clearly, Barrett was thinking of a war scare akin to the war scare of 1948, which aided passage of the Marshall Plan. Barrett's "hunch" that "it will be nearer ten days," makes that clear. This was a man comfortable with

---

[88] "Procedural Steps for Getting Approved Paper to the President," April 3, 1950, RG 59, Records of the PPS, 1947–1953, Chronological File 7: 1950, Box 34, NAII, 2.

[89] Memorandum by Under Secretary of State James Webb, March 30, 1950, *FRUS, 1950* I: 210.

[90] "Comments on State-Defense Staff Study," April 6, 1950, RG 59, Records of the PPS, 1947–1953, Chronological File 7: 1950, Box 34, NAII.

The Origins and Development of NSC 68   201

the techniques of war scares. John Hickerson, assistant secretary of state for United Nations affairs, equally expressed great support for NSC 68. His only caveat, which is an important one for how the program actually developed, was that the United States' allies get on board as well and share equally in the "sacrifices" that would be necessary to carry out the program.[91]

However, others expressed thorough rebuttals. Willard Thorp, assistant secretary of state for economic affairs, for instance, took issue with the draft's thesis that "the USSR is steadily reducing the discrepancy between its overall economic strength and that of the United States." Thorp stated: "I do not feel that this position is demonstrated, but rather the reverse.... The actual gap is widening in our favor." He pointed out that the United States' economy increased twofold over the Soviet Union's economy in 1949. Steel production in the United States outpaced steel production in the Soviet Union by two million tons, and stockpiling of goods and oil production far exceeded Soviet amounts. Furthermore, "if one compares the total economic capacity [of the two countries]," Thorp wrote, "*the gap is so tremendous that a slight and slow narrowing would have little meaning.*" As for Soviet military investment, Thorp opined: "I suspect a larger portion of Soviet investment went into housing."[92]

Raymond Hare, acting assistant secretary of state for Near Eastern, South Asian, and African affairs, questioned the report's emphasis on Soviet expansion. "Are we yet certain that the Soviet venture in China will strengthen the U.S.S.R. to the extent now feared? Have we, in fact, adequately explored the question of whether there may not be a critical point in Soviet expansion beyond which the benefits to the U.S.S.R. will turn to disadvantage?" Hare wondered.[93] Charles Bohlen, the Soviet expert who was kept out of the writing of NSC 68 but was involved in the review, had similar thoughts. He wrote: "It is open to question whether or not, as stated [in the report], the fundamental design of the Kremlin is the domination of the world."[94]

After Truman read the report he asked for analysis of the costs involved. Acheson and Nitze deliberately had left cost figures out of the report because they believed these would distract people from supporting the program. No wonder, given that they envisioned a program costing at least

---

[91] Edward Barrett to Acheson, April 6, 1950, *FRUS, 1950* I: 225–226; Hickerson to Acheson, April 5, 1950, ibid., 216-217.
[92] Willard Thorp to Acheson, April 5, 1950, ibid., 218–220, emphasis added.
[93] Hare to James Webb, April 5, 1950, ibid., 220–221.
[94] Bohlen to Nitze, April 5, 1950, ibid., 221-225.

202   *NSC 68 and the Political Economy of the Early Cold War*

$50 billion a year. An ad-hoc committee was set up to study the issue. There the dissension continued. William Schaub of the Bureau of the Budget took especial exception to NSC 68. If, as the paper stated, the main struggle was ideological, Schaub wondered, why were the programs and policies being considered for this ideological war "subordinated to programs of military strength; in fact, the only program dealt with in any detail is the military program." Schaub also complained about the terms "free world" and "slave world." "While it is true that the USSR and its satellites constitute something properly called a slave world, it is not true that the U.S. and its friends constitute a free world." In case of point, he wrote:

> This free world vs. slave world treatment obscures one of the most difficult problems we face – the fact that many peoples are attracted to Communism because their governments are despotic or corrupt or both. And they are not going to become the friends of a major power simply because of that power's military strength. Rather, their friendship is to be had at the price of support of moves which will improve or, failing that, replace their present governments.

In a particularly astute observation, Schaub noted: "The U.S. is stronger militarily and economically in relation to the USSR than was the case just before World War II. We hardly gave Russia a second thought then. What makes for the difference today?" Nor did Schaub buy the argument that the Soviet Union was closing in on the United States' military capabilities.

> It is hard to accept a conclusion that the USSR is approaching a straight-out military superiority over us when, for example, (1) our Air Force is vastly superior qualitatively, is greatly superior numerically in the bombers, trained crews and other facilities necessary for offensive war; (2) our supply of fission bombs is much greater than that of the USSR, as is our thermonuclear potential; (3) our Navy is so much stronger than that of the USSR that they should not be mentioned in the same breath; (4) the economic health and military potential of our allies is, with our help, growing daily; and (5) while we have treaties of alliance with and are furnishing arms to countries bordering the USSR, the USSR has none with countries within thousands of miles of us.[95]

As these documents prove, Nitze was wrong. There were dissenting views on NSC 68, and cogent ones at that.

Which, then, is more accurate – the dissenting views or NSC 68? On April 25, 1950, the Joint Intelligence Committee of the U.S. embassy in Moscow issued a report on Soviet capabilities and intentions. The

[95] William Shaub, Deputy Chief of the Division of Estimates, Bureau of the Budget, to James Lay, Executive Secretary of the NSC, May 8, 1950, ibid., 298–306. Shaub was one of those economists Nitze lamented about at the October 11, 1949, meeting of the PPS noted earlier in this chapter.

The Origins and Development of NSC 68

first section of the report concerned military matters. Noting that the Communist victory in China and the Soviet acquisition of atomic capability had been "counter-balanced" by the establishment of NATO and passage of the MDAP, the report stated that "net relative military capabilities of the Soviet-satellite and free western worlds have changed but slightly during the last year." Although it was believed that the Soviets had the capacity to take over western Europe, gain a foothold in the Middle East, and even attack South Korea, "Soviet-satellite forces would everywhere have weak and overextended supply lines." The report's conclusion was, "From a military point of view, the Soviets are not prepared to launch hostilities and carry an actual war against the West to successful conclusion in the immediate future." In a section of the report on economic concerns, it was acknowledged that the Soviet economy had grown stronger over the course of the last year and that the Soviet Union was capable of continued efforts in the Cold War. Nonetheless, the report found that it was "unlikely that [the Soviets] expect to be economically prepared for a long drawn-out, global conflict before one or more decades." Under a section of the report examining "military disadvantages accrued by the Soviet Union," there appears this notable comment shedding light on Soviet capabilities. "With the return to the United States and Great Britain of ships which had been lent to the Soviets during World War II, the Northern Fleet was greatly reduced in strength." Under "Evaluation of Soviet Intentions," we find that "probably the Soviets are even less ready for war now than they let appear. Their protestations of peaceful intent[96] are likely motivated in part by real weaknesses on the economic front." Finally, toward the end of the report this dose of reality appears: "Even if the production goals announced by Stalin in 1946 (to be reached in 1960) were achieved, the Soviets would still be far behind the *present* economic strength of the United States.... The Soviet shortage of petroleum alone should greatly hamper them in a prolonged war."[97] This intelligence assessment was written on the same day that President Truman, according to Acheson, made NSC 68 the official policy of the United States.

Denouement: The Korean War

On April 7, 1950, Truman formally received NSC 68. The long effort by Acheson and Nitze to force a change in U.S. military spending had

---

[96] This is in reference to the so-called peace offensive that the Soviets embarked on beginning in late 1949.

[97] "USSR, 1947–50," Harriman Papers, Box 271, LC, emphasis and brackets added.

reached a critical stage. Now what was needed was the president's approval of the program. Years later, Acheson would write in his memoir that "NSC 68 was designed to so bludgeon the mass mind of 'top government' that not only could the President make a decision but that the decision could be carried out," which may explain its hyperbolic language, but also suggests that the authors believed they had to sell the president on a rearmament program that he was not inclined to support. Indeed, Truman proved to be a tough sell. Although according to Acheson he approved the program on April 25, in fact what he did was to approve it for further review of the costs.[98] That analysis, as we have seen, carried out by an ad-hoc committee set up for the task, proved difficult, as several members took exception with the paper's arguments. Meanwhile, Truman made no effort to prepare the country for an increase in military spending, if indeed he intended to do so, even saying in a May 4 speech that military spending would be lower next year than it was the current year.[99] As late as June 5, Secretary of Defense Louis Johnson told Acheson that defense spending was not set to increase in the next fiscal year.[100] Furthermore, Nitze, one of the principal authors of the document, left for vacation on June 7 convinced the rearmament program was dead. It was only with the outbreak of the Korean War on June 25, 1950, that Truman changed course and began implementing rearmament. Even so, he did not officially approve NSC 68 until September 30, 1950, and it was not until after the Chinese intervention in the Korean War in the first week of November 1950 that NSC 68, under the revised NSC 68/4 of December 15, 1950, became fully operational. In fact, Truman declared a "national emergency" on December 16, often viewed as the culminating event in the implementation of NSC 68. This chain of events has led some scholars to argue that it was the Korean War, rather than NSC 68 itself, that instigated the massive rearmament program; a point that, if true, would seem to greatly diminish NSC 68's importance and, in that sense, any relevance it may have had for the dollar gap crisis.[101]

[98] Acheson, *Present at the Creation*, 374. In fact, after weighing the evidence it would appear that Acheson is simply in error here in claiming that NSC 68 became "national policy" on April 25.

[99] Truman Press conference, May 4, 1950, *Public Papers of the Presidents, Harry S. Truman, 1945–1953* (hereinafter *PPP*), http://www.trumanlibrary.org/publicpapers/index.php?pid=728&st=&st1=.

[100] Memorandum of Telephone Conversation between Acheson and Johnson, June 5, 1950, Reel 2, Official Conversations and Meetings of Dean Acheson, 1949–1953 (University Publications of America Frederick, Maryland, 1980).

[101] See for instance William Steuck, "The Soviet Union and the Origins of the Korean War," in Kim Chull Baum and James Matray, eds., *Korea and the Cold War: Division,*

The Origins and Development of NSC 68

The issue, however, is far more complicated than such a scenario suggests. To begin, Truman had been kept abreast of the writing of NSC 68 while it was ongoing. When Secretary of Defense Louis Johnson, who was not kept abreast of it, first read it and stormed out of the meeting on March 22, Truman was livid and told Acheson to press on, evidence that Truman was aware of the report's general contents and nominally supportive of it.[102] Furthermore, although it is true that Truman suggested in his May 4, 1950, press conference that military spending would actually decrease even further, he was, in fact, very ambiguous about the issue, suggesting on May 15 that military spending might go up, and refusing to comment either way in a May 25 press conference.[103] Then, at the meeting of the Foreign Ministers of the United States, Britain, and France held in London in May 1950, Acheson made a startling announcement – the United States would provide economic assistance to western Europe beyond 1952. The announcement was startling because no program for providing such assistance was in the works. Acheson pointed to the Gordon Gray commission, organized in February to study the dollar gap problem, as evidence that the United States was fully aware of the issue and was working on it. However, there was no guarantee that the promise could be carried out, unless, that is, Acheson believed that NSC 68 had been approved and would go forward.[104] That he believed so is further borne out by his conversation with Louis Johnson of June 5, 1950, noted directly above. Although it is true that Johnson argued in the conversation that military spending would not increase, Acheson remained firm that it would and, it is fair to say, he was far more in tune with Truman's thinking than Johnson was.

Truman also removed Frank Pace, director of the Bureau of the Budget and an advocate of the increasingly arcane idea of balanced budgets, and replaced him with Frank Lawton, who took a decidedly less critical view of that issue. There is also evidence that Truman was prepared to go public with an endorsement of NSC 68, although the paper itself was to

---

Destruction, and Disarmament (Claremont, California: Regina Books, 1993), 111–112; Robert P. Newman, "NSC (National Insecurity) 68: Nitze's Second Hallucination," in Martin J. Medhurst and H. W. Brands, eds., *Critical Reflections on the Cold War: Linking Rhetoric and History* (College Station, Texas: Texas A&M Press, 2000), 55–94.

[102] Acheson, *Present at the Creation*, 373–374.

[103] Truman Radio Address, May 15, 1950, *PPP* http://www.trumanlibrary.org/publicpapers/index.php?pid=757&st=military&st1=; The President's News Conference, May 25, 1950, http://www.trumanlibrary.org/publicpapers/index.php?pid=770&st=&st1=.

[104] Acheson to Acting Secretary of State James Webb, May 9, 1950, *FRUS, 1950* 3: 1014–1015; Statement by the Secretary General to the O.E.E.C., June 2, 1950, FO 371/86975, TNA.

206 NSC 68 and the Political Economy of the Early Cold War

remain classified. He did not do so only because the report on costs had not been completed.[105] Finally, in June 1950, before the outbreak of the Korean War, Truman appointed Averell Harriman to be special assistant to the president to coordinate Cold War policy among the various cabinets, but particularly between State and Defense, which, the reader will recall, had a falling out over NSC 68. There appears to be little reason that Harriman would have been appointed to this newly created post if, in fact, NSC 68 was dead.[106]

Truman was torn over NSC 68, neither wholly behind nor wholly against it. He wanted what it seemed capable of offering – a great surge in U.S. power on the global stage to salvage U.S. foreign policy from the quagmire it had become – but was leery of the costs involved both because he believed it would be politically difficult to get through Congress and his own belief in balanced budgets and limits on government spending that he could not easily surrender. Indeed, he was not "bludgeoned" by NSC 68's hyperbolic rhetoric, despite Acheson's claim. He had seen it before, and had even been a participant in it in the Clifford-Elsey report, in the meeting with Congress that led to the Truman Doctrine, and in the "war scare" of 1948, among others. Certainly, he knew that the Soviets were weak compared to the United States and that they were not likely to engage in an all out military offensive any time soon, even given the Soviet Union's acquisition of the atomic bomb, which, as we have seen, did not cause Truman any great alarm. Because NSC 68 discusses the dollar gap in considerable detail, he also understood that it was about more than the Soviets alone. It is probable that he would never have gone in for the roughly $50 billion annual program that Acheson and Nitze wanted, but it appears that he was prepared to do something. Nonetheless, he was trapped in the world of American politics and felt ill-equipped to act. Other presidents in similar circumstances have faced no less.

It appears likely, then, that in the two months between April 25, when he approved NSC 68 for further review, and June 25, when the Korean

[105] Fordham, Building the Cold War Consensus, 59–62.
[106] James Reston, "Truman Appoints Harriman Special Foreign Affairs Aide," The New York Times, June 17, 1950, 1; Walter Trohan, "Think Harriman Will Take Over Acheson's Post," The Chicago Tribune, June 18, 1950, 10; Acheson, Present at the Creation, 410–411; Leffler, A Preponderance of Power, 313, 363. Leffler's treatment of the Harriman appointment is marred, particularly on page 363 of his book, when he makes it appear as though the appointment was made after the outbreak of the Korean War, when, in fact, it was done prior to it. It is of great significance for understanding the origins of NSC 68 that the appointment was made prior to Korea when no possible knowledge that the war would occur was known.

The Origins and Development of NSC 68

War began, he was buying time. He vacillated in his public speeches because the stakes were so high, the issues too fraught with emotion. The situation was complicated by the fact that, despite having broken the U.S. atomic monopoly and signed a treaty of friendship and mutual support with Communist China, the Soviets were not stirring up trouble and, in fact, were pressing the issue of international control of atomic energy. The administration, it might well be argued, was paralyzed. And then the Soviet Union did what it had so often done before – it came to the administration's rescue.

On June 25, 1950, North Korean forces stormed across the 38th parallel dividing North from South Korea in an attempt to unify the country under communist rule. At the time, Truman was vacationing in his hometown of Independence, Missouri. Although the United States had pulled its troops out of South Korea on June 29, 1949, appearing in effect to have abandoned the fledgling nation, when Acheson contacted him via telephone both men agreed that the United States had to take a stand. Intervention was yet to be formalized, especially as to ground troops, which they hoped to avoid, but they agreed that the United States could not declare itself protector of the free world and let such a flagrant violation of a nation's sovereignty go unchallenged. As the historian William Stueck writes, "To the United States, the Korean conflict became a struggle for credibility, to prove that the liberal democracy of people unused to sustained effort abroad could rise to the challenge of international communism."[107]

Domestic politics also played an important role in the decision to intervene. Since the congressional elections of 1946, in which the Republicans won a majority in both houses for the first time in years, the Republicans had been tireless critics of Truman's foreign and domestic policies. When Truman unexpectedly won the presidential election of 1948 and the Democrats took back both houses of Congress, their pressure on him only mounted. One consistent argument they proffered was that the administration had neglected Asia in its foreign policy and had, therefore, contributed to the "loss" of China. The Soviet acquisition of atomic power in the summer of 1949 also proved fodder for Republican attacks on the administration, which they claimed it could have prevented, although they offered no proof as to how. By then, Senator Joseph McCarthy had

---

[107] William Stueck, *The Korean War: An International History* (Princeton, New Jersey: Princeton University Press, 1995), 43, passim. See also James Matray, *The Reluctant Crusade: American Foreign Policy in Korea, 1941–1950* (Honolulu, Hawaii: The University of Hawaii Press, 1985), 226–252.

begun his campaign to root out alleged communists in the government, which touched off a "red scare" that cast the administration as "soft" on communism. When the Korean War broke out, Republicans wasted no time in blaming the Democrats for it, claiming they had been naive in the face of the Soviet threat going back to Yalta and Potsdam. Republicans did not pressure the administration to intervene, and many were opposed. Rather, they used the war to pull political punches. Nonetheless, the pressure to intervene was overwhelming lest the administration give credence to the Republicans' charges.[108]

Whereas issues of credibility and the pressures of domestic politics clearly played crucial roles in the decision by Truman and Acheson to come to South Korea's aid, so did NSC 68. With the outbreak of the war, Truman found the political will he needed to give it his full endorsement. Although he did not formally do so until September 30, his actions from June 25 onward indicate that he had accepted NSC 68. This fact is borne out by the dramatic shift the administration's foreign policy took as a result of Korea. Handed a seemingly irrefutable example of Soviet aggression, U.S. leaders determined to milk it for all it was worth. They would push through a peace treaty with Japan, one that would fully ensconce it within the United States' orbit; greatly expand the U.S. troop presence in Europe; demand West Germany's rearmament, which was the final obstacle to bringing West Germany into the western community as a full-fledged nation; ask for more robust military aid for allies; and embark on the long-term military buildup, all of which were called for in the document. Would the administration have chose to intervene in Korea if NSC 68 had not been at stake? It certainly appears likely. However, it cannot be denied that NSC 68 was an added incentive to take a stand.

For the members of the administration who had worked so tirelessly to bring NSC 68 to fruition, the Korean War could not have come at a more opportune time. Tradition holds that the outbreak of the Korean War proved the thesis of NSC 68 correct, thereby giving Truman the political will to push the militarization program through Congress.[109] But

---

[108] Leffler, *A Preponderance of Power*, 343–344, 368; Stueck, *The Korean War*, 41–42; Stephen Pelz, "U.S. Decisions on Korean Policy, 1943–1950: Some Hypotheses," in Cumings, *Child of Conflict: The Korean-American Relationship, 1943–1953* (Seattle, Washington: University of Washington Press, 1983), 93–132.

[109] Leffler, *A Preponderance of Power*, 361–371; John Lewis Gaddis, *Strategies of Containment: A Critical Appraisal of Postwar American National Security Policy* (New York, 1982), 112–113; Samuel J. Wells, "Sounding the Tocsin: NSC 68 and the Soviet Threat," *International Security* 4:2 (Fall 1979): 116–158; Matray, *The Reluctant Crusade*, 226–227, 256.

The Origins and Development of NSC 68

that interpretation could not be further from the truth. Although it is correct that the Korean War paved the way for Truman to fully endorse NSC 68, the war did not actually prove that NSC 68's thesis was valid. NSC 68 exaggerated the Soviet threat to the nth degree, turning the Soviet Union into a Hitlerian-like nation with an insatiable desire to expand and conquer. To argue that the Korean War proved the thesis of NSC 68 correct would be to accept NSC 68's depiction of the Soviet threat as accurate.

Furthermore, it also would be to accept that administration officials viewed the Korean War as reflecting a new Soviet militancy that presaged a more general Soviet offensive, particularly on western Europe, one that they were deeply disturbed and even frightened about, which is supposed to explain why they pushed so hard for rearmament. But this interpretation also has no basis in reality. Although it is fair to say that administration officials believed that the Soviet Union was behind the attack, they were quick to realize that it did not represent a new Soviet push either for the conquest of western Europe or for world domination. For instance, the NSC, in a paper drawn up on July 1, 1950, only days after the attack, concluded that "in causing the attack to be launched in Korea, the Kremlin did not intend to bring about a general war or to involve the USSR in a showdown with us." Kennan and Bohlen, the State Department's foremost Russian experts, drew similar conclusions. On June 30, Bohlen argued that "he saw no evidence that [the North Korean attack represented proof] that the Russians had changed their traditional tactic of probing for soft spots" and sought, rather, to avoid any direct conflict with United States forces. On August 8, Kennan contended that "the Soviet Communists did not launch the Korean operation as a first step in a world war or as the first in a series of local operations designed to drain U.S. strength in peripheral theaters."[110]

Moreover, rather than being disturbed by the outbreak of the war, administration officials welcomed it. Understanding this reality is of

---

[110] NSC 73, "Note by the Executive Secretary to the National Security Council to the Position and Actions of the United States with Respect to Possible Further Soviet Moves in Light of the Korean Situation," July 1, 1950, *FRUS, 1950* 1: 331–341; Memorandum of Conversation, June 30, 1950, *Foreign Relations of the United States, 1950* 7 (Washington, D.C.: U.S. Government Printing Office, 1976): 258; Kennan to Acheson, August 8, 1950, *FRUS, 1950* 1: 361. We now know that the North Korean leader Kim Il Sung pushed and prodded Stalin into backing the attack and that Stalin only reluctantly did so and that strategic reasons played a far greater role than exporting communist revolution through force. On this argument, see Sergei N. Goncharov, et al., *Uncertain Partners: Stalin, Mao, and the Korean War* (Stanford, California: Stanford University Press, 1993), 130–167; Geoffrey Roberts, *Stalin's Wars: From World War to Cold War, 1939–1953* (New Haven, Connecticut: Yale University Press, 2006), 364–370.

extreme importance because it demonstrates conclusively that NSC 68, and not the Korean War, was the force behind the rearmament program and that Korea merely paved the way for its implementation. Evidence from the Princeton Seminars proves this point conclusively. The Princeton Seminars were a series of discussions held among top officials in the Truman administration and their underlings in 1953 and 1954 to put down for posterity their view of what the administration had faced and what it had accomplished (they were so named because they took place at Princeton's Institute for Advanced Study, then under the leadership of George Kennan). Among the participants were Acheson, Nitze, Harriman, Kennan, and Oppenheimer. The topics advanced were wide-ranging and covered many aspects of the Truman administration's triumphs and travails. Not surprisingly, a great deal of attention was devoted to NSC 68, demonstrating how important it was to administration officials. It is when the discussion turns to the problems these officials encountered in getting Truman to accept NSC 68, that, in fact, he might not approve it and the rearmament program would fail, that it becomes apparent that the Korean War was, for these officials, more of a blessing than a calamity. "We were sweating it," recalled Edward Barrett (he who upon first reading NSC 68 suggested that a "psychological 'scare campaign'" was needed to gain public support for the program), "and then – with regard to NSC 68 – thank God Korea came along."[111] Acheson weighed in as well, stating that "Korea came along . . . [and] created the stimulus which made [for] action."[112] These were comments about a war that, at the time they were made, had taken the lives of more than 33,000 Americans and an untold number of Koreans, Chinese, and U.N. forces.

The implications are clear – NSC 68 is what mattered to these officials, even to the point that war was worth it if it helped make it happen. This is why it is so important that the motivations behind NSC 68 are fully understood.

---

[111] Princeton Seminars, October 10, 1953, Dean Acheson Papers, Princeton Seminars Reading Copy III, Box 97, folder 1 – Acheson, reel 2, track 2, 15, Truman Library.
[112] Ibid., 3.

7

The Political Economy of Rearmament

> Recent events have already made clear to a large part of Congress that the old ERP concept – i.e., economic aid for four years to achieve dollar viability – is to a considerable extent obsolete. The current dollar position of the sterling area, the fact that rearmament of the continental countries is inconsistent with rapid further improvement in their balances of payments, and the fact that certain countries (Austria, Greece, Italy) would, apart from rearmament, continue to require dollar assistance after 1952, have made the principal objective of ERP legislation (dollar viability in 1952) largely irrelevant as a basis for U.S. economic aid to Europe.
>
> H. Van B. Cleveland, November 1950

> [E]xperience has demonstrated that the economic and technical side of foreign aid enjoys less popularity with the Congress than the military side.
>
> A. G. Vigderman to John Ohly, July 1951

> The Congress will do anything in the world that the uniform services want them to do.
>
> Dean Acheson, October 1953

The Korean War broke the logjam on NSC 68. First, the decision to intervene in the war was made. Then, on July 19, 1950, Truman went before Congress and asked for a $10 billion supplement to the military budget and announced his intention to ask for greatly expanded military spending, including military assistance for foreign nations.[1] This request should be seen as the beginning of NSC 68's implementation despite the fact that

---

[1] Special Message to the Congress Reporting on the Situation in Korea, July 19, 1950, *Public Papers of the President, Harry S. Truman, 1945–1953*, http://www.trumanlibrary. org/publicpapers/index.php?pid=822&st=&st1=.

work on the paper continued for months and, indeed, under varying titles for years.[2] For instance, the National Security Council acknowledged in August 1950 that the initial appropriations put forth in the president's July 19 message to Congress, "constitute[d] an initial implementation of the long-term United States build-up."[3] Hence, the fact that Truman did not officially approve NSC 68 until September 30, or fully implement the program until December 15, is of little consequence. The implementation of NSC 68 began on July 19.

Subsequently, U.S. military spending shot up from the low figure of $13 billion that Truman had proposed for fiscal year 1951 to more than $58 billion, a fourfold increase. In fiscal year 1952 military spending neared $70 billion, inclusive of foreign military and economic aid. In fiscal year 1953 military spending fell to a little more than $50 billion, but, thereafter, U.S. military spending would never again dip below $42 billion annually.[4] Thus did NSC 68 usher in a new era of military spending in United States history, one that would see it adopt a permanent semi-war economy with all that such an economy entails in terms of allocation of resources, government spending, research and development, greatly expanded military forces in being, and the propaganda necessary to carry such a program through.[5] By the end of his second term as president in 1961, Dwight D. Eisenhower would be warning the nation against the creation of what he called a "military-industrial complex." Eisenhower's warning, however, was too late. It had already been created.[6]

NSC 68 was designed to accomplish many things. It sought to ensure the survival of the nascent global economy that was born in the wake of

---

[2] NSC 68 went through a number of revisions. NSC 68/4 of December 14, 1950, is generally accepted as the final version adopted by the government, but it came under review both as NSC 73 and as NSC 135 in later years.

[3] Interim Report by the National Security Council, August 22, 1950, Record Group 59, General Records of the Department of State (RG 59), Records of the Policy Planning Staff relating to State Department participation in the NSC, 1935–1962 (PPS/NSC), Box 24, National Archives II, College Park, Maryland (hereinafter NAII).

[4] Doris M. Condit, *History of the Office of the Secretary of Defense, Volume II, The Test of War, 1950–1953* (Washington, D.C.: U.S. Government Printing Office, 1988), 241, 259, 284, 304, 422.

[5] Michael Sherry, *In the Shadow of War: The United States since the 1930s* (Yale, 1995); Michael Hogan, *A Cross of Iron: Harry S. Truman and the Origins of the National Security State, 1945–1954* (Cambridge, United Kingdom: Cambridge University Press, 1998); Kenneth Osgood, *Total Cold War: Eisenhower's Secret Propaganda Battle at Home and Abroad* (Lawrence: Kansas: University of Kansas Press, 2006).

[6] Dwight D. Eisenhower, "Farewell Address," January 17, 1961, *Public Papers of the Presidents of the United States: Dwight D. Eisenhower, 1953–1961* (Washington, D.C.: U.S. Government Printing Office, 1961).

The Political Economy of Rearmament 213

WWII and that was breaking apart under the weight of the dollar gap. It sought to hold together the fragile western alliance that was fragmenting due to economic dislocation and pressure from the Soviet Union and internal Communists. It sought to bolster the United States' military might above and against the Soviet Union's. It sought to establish West Germany as a full-fledged member of the western European community. Above all, it sought to put the United States into a state of such preponderant power – what Dean Acheson called "total diplomacy" – that it could not be challenged by any one or combination of powers, economically, politically, or militarily (and by this he meant not just such obvious enemies as the Soviet Union, but the United States' allies as well). In this, NSC 68 was nothing less than the means through which the United States assumed hegemony over the "free world," much as the British had done in the nineteenth century. Key to this achievement, however, was not military might or political stewardship, although these were important, but economic supremacy. As Thomas McCormick has argued: "Economic supremacy is the indispensable base of hegemony, for all other forms of power are possible with it and no others possible, for very long, without it."[7] It was the potential loss of that supremacy, occasioned by the dollar gap crisis, that posed the gravest threat in the time period in which NSC 68 was developed and implemented.

The domestic effects of NSC 68 were considerable, both in terms of political economy and of culture. We remember the 1950s for a lot of things, not least of which is the Cold War atmosphere that gave us fallout shelters, "duck and cover" lessons for school children, Cold War-themed movies and television shows, rock and roll songs that spoke of death from hydrogen bombs, a revival of patriotism that bordered on the religious, a religious revivalism that was overtly patriotic, the stark conformity that came with doing one's part to fight communism, and, of course, unbridled prosperity that seemed to prove capitalism's supremacy over communism. In all of these aspects of the domestic side of the Cold War, NSC 68 – or massive rearmament – played a crucial, if not always obvious, role. Crucial because rearmament on the scale of NSC 68 would never have been accepted by the American people without a major propaganda campaign aimed at convincing them, as NSC 68 put it, that "the cold war is in fact a real war in which the survival of the free world is at stake."[8]

---

[7] Thomas McCormick, *America's Half-Century: United States Foreign Policy in the Cold War and After* (Baltimore, Maryland: The Johns Hopkins University Press, 1994), 2nd edition, 5.

[8] NSC 68 quoted in Ernest May, ed., *American Cold War Strategy: Interpreting NSC 68* (New York: Bedford Books, 1993), 81.

Not always obvious because very few people understood (or understand) the way in which rearmament contributed to postwar prosperity at home. As important as that story is, however, the focus here is on rearmament abroad and how it helped overcome the dollar gap internationally and paved the way for the emergence of that global economy that was the primary objective of the multilateralists.[9]

Thus far, the objective of this study has been to delineate the role that the dollar gap played in the origins of NSC 68. This concluding chapter will focus on how rearmament actually worked to alleviate the dollar gap problem. As we will see, virtually all of the solutions that were discussed among public and private elites as being necessary for overcoming the dollar gap but for which there was neither time, given the impending end of the Marshall Plan in 1952, nor the political will to carry out, were implemented through rearmament. These include increasing western European productivity; providing a vehicle for continued economic aid after 1952; aiding western European economic, and to a lesser extent political, integration; securing West Germany's integration into the western European community as a full-fledged member; restarting triangular trade; and keeping western Europe fully ensconced in the U.S. camp. Truman administration officials also came up with additional ways to shuttle dollars to western Europe through offshore procurement, base and airfield construction, and stationing troops abroad. They were able to pursue these endeavors because they were no longer about the dollar gap but were, in the changed circumstance, about security. As a result, the dollar gap and all its potential problems were obviated.

The dollar gap did not go away; the structural problems that caused it were not fixed until the 1960s. Rather, rearmament prevented the "Western World" from collapsing in 1952, as Dean Acheson had fretted

---

[9] A number of fine monographs have broached the subject of culture and political economy in the early Cold War. See Elaine Tyler May, *Homeward Bound: American Families in the Cold War Era* (New York: Basic Books, 1999), second edition; Hogan, *A Cross of Iron*; Paul Pierpaoli, Jr., *Truman and Korea: The Political Culture of the Early Cold War* (Columbia, Missouri: The University of Missouri Press, 1999); Laura McEnaney, *Civil Defense Begins at Home: Militarization Meets Everyday Life in the Fifties* (Princeton, New Jersey: Princeton University Press, 2000); Ann Markusen, *The Rise of the Gunbelt: The Military Remapping of Industrial America* (New York: Oxford University Press, 1991); Roger W. Lotchin, *Fortress California, 1910–1961: From Warfare to Welfare* (New York: Oxford University Press, 1992); Rebecca S. Lowen, *Creating the Cold War University: The Transformation of Stanford* (Berkeley, California: University of California Press, 1997). Much more work needs to be done in this area, and it is my hope that this book will help with that endeavor by demonstrating how intricate were the connections between militarization and postwar prosperity in saving the global economy from collapse.

The Political Economy of Rearmament

about at the important meeting of the Policy Planning Staff on October 11, 1949 (chronicled in Chapter 6), and made it unlikely that any such collapse would occur in the future, as the United States assumed the role of guarantor and protector of the "free world."[10] To be sure, rearmament greatly enhanced western Europe's defense capabilities such that the Soviet Union, if it were harboring plans to invade (it was not), would have had to think twice before doing so. However, as the reader will see, Truman administration officials were entirely cognizant of the ways in which rearmament also worked to alleviate the dollar gap, offering final proof that one of the major aims of NSC 68, if not the major aim, was overcoming the dollar gap and its attendant difficulties.

Increasing Western European Productivity

As we saw in previous chapters, the key solution to western Europe's dollar gap was increasing western European productivity. Western European productivity had not kept pace with the United States' phenomenal productivity rates over the course of the twentieth century, multilateralists in the administration believed, due to an insufficiently developed intra-European market in both goods and labor, outdated production and distribution techniques, unmodernized plant and equipment, lack of a competitive ethos, and cultural mores against mass consumption, filtered through two world wars and a major depression. If the dollar gap were ever to be overcome, these "deficiencies" had to be corrected. However, the countries of western Europe, to include Great Britain, did not have the political will, the psychological motivation, or the resources to pull it off. The Marshall Plan, instituted to keep U.S. imports flowing into western Europe while the Europeans rebuilt their economies, prevented potential disaster but, as we have seen, was not sufficient to orchestrate the long-term changes that were deemed necessary.

This dilemma found its solution in the military assistance programs that the Truman administration instituted beginning in 1949 with the Military Assistance Program (MAP), which by the time it was implemented had become the Mutual Defense Assistance Program (MDAP), followed by the International Security Affairs Committee (ISAC), and culminating in the Mutual Security Program (MSP), the primary program aimed at increasing western European productivity and, by virtue

[10] See Chapter 6.

of that, stanching the dollar gap through military assistance. Over and above the MSP, of course, was NSC 68; and it is important to stress that the MSP likely never would have existed absent NSC 68. From the start these programs were about more than military assistance for defense purposes but were aimed at overcoming the dollar gap. Nonetheless, the ways in which they operated to alleviate the dollar gap developed incrementally, before receiving formal institutionalization in the MSP. The history of their development and implementation removes any doubt that administration officials used rearmament to counteract the dollar gap and save multilateralism. We begin with the MAP.

The MAP was designed, ostensibly, to begin the process of bolstering the defense capabilities of western Europe, exclusive of West Germany, against would-be aggressors. It was viewed as a natural counterpart to the Marshall Plan, the one aiding economic recovery and the other military security, although economic recovery was deemed most important and received priority. However, when the MAP was conceived in the summer and fall of 1948, as we saw in Chapter 6, it was less for actual security per se than as a way of instilling confidence for continued efforts toward economic recovery. The actual military aid items offered were to be mere tokens.[11] Military assistance was, from the beginning, viewed by top officials in terms of what political and economic gains it could achieve. By the spring of 1949, U.S. officials such as Acheson, Nitze, and Harriman had developed the idea that military assistance could be a vehicle for economic aid under a different label, namely, security.

The first MAP legislation went to Congress on July 25, 1949. One billion dollars in military aid was asked for western Europe and $314 million total for Greece, Turkey, Iran, the Philippines, and Korea. Next, the MAP made its way through Congress where it encountered stiff resistance from Republicans, one of whom complained that it made the president "the number one war lord on earth."[12] After a tough fight that almost saw the program cut in half, both houses of Congress approved it. According to Acheson, what broke the deadlock was President Truman's announcement of September 23, 1949, that the Soviets had exploded an atomic device. As Acheson put it, "once again the Russians had come to the aid of an imperiled nonpartisan foreign policy." Finally, on October 6,

---

[11] Harriman memorandum, July 14, 1948, Averell Harriman Papers, Marshall Plan: Policy planning, 1948–1950, Box 272, Library of Congress, Washington, D.C. (hereinafter LC); Charles H. Bonesteel memorandum, November 11, 1948, ibid.

[12] Quoted in Dean Acheson, *Present at the Creation: My Years in the State Department* (New York: W. W. Norton, 1969), 309.

The Political Economy of Rearmament

1949, the MAP was given official sanction when President Truman activated it as the Mutual Defense Assistance Program (MDAP).[13]

The MDAP was devised primarily to aid western Europe in building up its defense forces. Nonetheless, evidence that the MDAP was, from the beginning, intricately connected to the dollar gap crisis is not hard to find. Consider, for instance, a telegram Acheson sent to the U.S. embassy in Britain dated November 2, 1949. At issue was procurement for the transfer of military equipment to the Western Union countries. How was said equipment to be paid for? Here is how Acheson explained it: "Belgium and [the] Netherlands [would] receive from [the] US, and transmit to [the] UK, dollars to pay dollar costs involved in UK production of aircraft components, [and the] US [would] require [the] UK to justify costs involving MAP financing. Dollar materials and tools [would] then be provided to [the] UK." Although this specific issue was aimed at offering a *possible* solution to the payments dilemma, it displays how U.S. officials conceived of ways in which military aid could work to accomplish other ends.[14]

Further evidence that the MDAP paid attention to how such aid also could work to alleviate western Europe's dollar gap problem can be found in records pertaining to the Additional Military Production program (AMP). The AMP was the first program sponsored under the MDAP. It was, in effect, an interim program until the MDAP could get up and running. One hundred million dollars was allotted for it, which was all that Congress would allow until the North Atlantic Treaty Organization (NATO) countries, that is, the western European nations minus West Germany, submitted an integrated defense plan and the president approved it. It was designed to enhance production in the NATO countries of certain specified military items above planned outlays from the previous fiscal year. The idea was that the AMP would be paid for primarily out of local currencies or supplied as end-item transfers from the United States (end-items consisted of finished military goods that could be provided by the United States in lieu of dollars). If these avenues proved inadequate to meet the specified goals, however, then U.S. financing might be granted, as was usually the case.[15]

[13] Ibid., 307–313; *Foreign Relations of the United States* (hereinafter *FRUS*), *1949* 1 (Washington, D.C.: U.S. Government Printing Office, 1976): 398.

[14] Record Group 59, General Records of the Department of State (RG 59), Records of the Mutual Defense Assistance Program (MDAP), William Harry Bray, Jr., Records, Subject Files Relating to Policy and Program Development, 1948–1951 (hereinafter Bray Records), Foreign Activities, Box 12, NAII.

[15] Memorandum for the President, January 3, 1950, *Foreign Relations of the United States* (hereinafter *FRUS*), *1950* 3 (Washington, D.C.: U.S. Government Printing Office,

An example of AMP in action is "Italy AMP No.3" from March 23, 1950. The request was for aid to help the Italian Army manufacture 9mm cartridges for Italian submachine guns. The report began by recommending that U.S. aid should be granted. It noted that the project would bolster Italian ammunition stores, would not conflict with the terms of the Italian peace treaty, would not cause "political repercussions," that is, conflict with the Italian Communists, and required very limited funding, only $23,260. The next section dealt with the military aspects of the project. Here the deficiencies in existing stores and planned stores was noted, and a shortage of 7,500,000 rounds was determined to exist. The report then turned to the economic aspects of the project. It is here where we begin to see how rearmament and the dollar gap interplay. The report noted that the "sum requested is small and will have no impact on the local economy." It further stated that "the project does not involve diversion of power, labor, materials, or equipment to the detriment of the civilian economy." This last fact was important because U.S. leaders feared that if the standard of living suffered as a result of rearmament, the political will to carry out the rearmament program would dwindle. Then, in the last sentence of the economic section, the report stated: "It is our opinion ... that the project will be beneficial to the extent that it will give employment to a number of people."[16] Although it is not being questioned that the Italians in fact needed this ammunition, this bit of evidence, obscure as it is, goes a long way in showing how U.S. leaders conceived of AMP aid both in terms of rearmament and with an eye to the dollar gap. For, here we see that military aid for something seemingly as innocuous as submachine gun bullets also helped the Italian unemployment situation. And the benefits did not stop there.

The final section of the report concerned production. What is important here is that the report named a specific company that should be awarded the contract. The company in question was the Bombrini-Parodi-Delfino company, an ammunition manufacturer. Whereas the report stressed that the company was amply suited for the task, what this evidence more importantly demonstrates is that U.S. military aid consciously targeted specific companies for aid, which not only helped them to survive but, in many instances, to modernize as well, which put them in a better position

1977): 2; "Additional Military Production: Definitions and Procedures," December 24, 1949, Bray Records, Military, Box 17, NAII.

[16] "Embassy Project Report – Italy AMP No.3," March 23, 1950, Bray Records, Military, Box 17, NAII.

The Political Economy of Rearmament   219

to produce for the consumer market once recovery had fully occurred. When it is recognized that some of these companies went on to become household names worldwide – such as FIAT – one begins to understand how rearmament helped fuel a world of consumption, what was deemed the primary means for overcoming the dollar gap.

Many documents concerning the AMP exist in the archives. In each, sections pertaining to the recommendation and then the military, economic, and production aspects of a given AMP project are provided. Sometimes the order of the sections changes, but the basic contours are the same. What we see in this evidence is that the United States used military spending as a form of "pump-priming." Although such methods did nothing to directly alleviate the dollar gap problem, which was primarily a problem of insufficient dollar earnings in western Europe, they did help the European unemployment problem, which improved the standard of living and kept the western Europeans on board with the United States, a crucial factor in any effort to overcome the dollar gap.

The AMP was merely a beginning point for the MDAP, but it began the process whereby military spending was utilized to accomplish goals related to finding a solution for the dollar gap. Meanwhile, the MDAP became more fully operational after President Truman approved NATO's integrated defense plan on January 27, 1950. According to the Mutual Defense Assistance Act of 1949, of the $1 billion pledged for western Europe, half, made available in cash, could go to direct purchases to be made by June 30, 1950, and half for securing contracts to acquire military goods and services, also by June 30, 1950, although the contracts did not have to be filled by that point.[17] Nonetheless, from the beginning, the MDAP was viewed as too small to be really effective, whether for building adequate defense forces for western Europe or for aiding with the dollar gap. Clearly, a much broader program was needed.[18]

Initial Problems

Desires are one thing; fulfilling such desires quite another. Administration officials had determined that rearmament was necessary, but convincing others came with a host of problems, ones that were not overcome

---

[17] "A Fact Sheet" – The Mutual Defense Assistance Program, April 1950, John Ohly Papers, Foreign Aid Files, Forms of Military Aid – Military Assistance – General MDAP, Box 106, Harry S. Truman Library, Independence, Missouri (hereinafter Truman Library).

[18] This fact is most apparent in the Bray Records and the Records of the Policy Planning Staff, Country and Area Files, 1950–1951, NAII.

easily. One obstacle was Congress, which made clear, and the administration had to promise, that any military buildup in western Europe would not be a one-way street. The western Europeans would have to contribute to the rearmament effort as well. The problem was that the NATO nations' budgets already were pushed to the limit. This meant that any contributions made to rearmament, unless otherwise financed, would have to come at the expense of the economic recovery. However, that was politically unfeasible. For, the western European masses, plagued by decades of war and reduced standards of living, simply would not trade economic recovery for security. This reality led to a less than enthusiastic response on the part of some of the western European countries to even pursue rearmament, leading to the awkward circumstance in which U.S. officials often found themselves pushing for rearmament for western Europe more than the western Europeans themselves, even though they faced the Soviet threat directly. For instance, Harriman complained to Truman after a meeting with Winston Churchill and Anthony Eden in April 1950 that the two Britons expressed "a curious lack of appreciation of the attitude of the Kremlin since 1945," while a telegram from the State Department to the U.S. embassy in Rome from December 1950 fretted that the Italian commitment to rearmament was hampered by "two premises: (a) disbelief in [the] likelihood of war; [and] (b) necessity [of] subordinating rearmament expenditures to [the] stability of [the] lira."[19] If rearmament was to be useful, a way had to be found to help the NATO nations finance rearmament without cutting into the economic recovery effort; no easy task, especially given Congress's penchant for attacking the administration's foreign economic aid programs. In the long run, as we will see, this requirement would work in the administration's favor, but that is to get ahead of the story.

Still another problem was integrating production on the continent for maximum effectiveness. Here, the issue was western European political and economic integration, which, the reader will recall, also was deemed essential for overcoming the western European dollar gap. However, as with the dollar gap, the integration solution ran into serious problems. The NATO countries proved resistant to integration that would destroy national sovereignty, whether for security or to overcome the dollar gap.

---

[19] See, for instance, the discussion of East-West trade found in Harriman's papers, "East-West Trade, 1948," Box 271, LC; the discussion of East-West trade found in *FRUS, 1950* 3: 1–1346, passim; Harriman to Truman, March 13, 1950, Harriman Papers, Marshall Plan, Truman Correspondence, Box 268, LC, 5; Department of State to the embassy in Rome, December 2, 1950, Bray Records, Box 63, NAII, 3.

The Political Economy of Rearmament

Also, the British continued to resist anything but a military union with the continent, and even this commitment was weak, which dampened enthusiasm for the idea on the continent.

Finally, serious conflict arose over what the U.S. contribution to the European rearmament program would be. The western Europeans, because of the political problems posed by rearming, were reluctant to come up with firm figures for their contribution without knowing what the U.S expenditure would be. They did not want to get into a situation where they had pledged more than their economies could stand on the premise that the United States would foot the bill, only to have the U.S. renege or come in at too low of a figure. However, Congress was proving resistant without knowing what the western European contribution would be. The result was a stalemate.[20]

Beginnings of the Offshore Procurement Program

As a result of these problems, thinking began to change. Neither the MDAP nor the AMP were designed to provide dollar payments to the western Europeans to cover the dollar gap. The idea of utilizing these programs for that purpose was discussed in the formative stages of both programs but was thought politically impossible and so was kept out at that point. Acheson, in particular, came out against any such proposal.[21] However, that view underwent revision as work on the MDAP stalled throughout the spring of 1950. One result was the beginnings of the Offshore Procurement Program (OSP). In March 1950, months prior to the outbreak of the Korean War, Harriman and Bonesteel began formulating the idea of using offshore procurement to build military arms and equipment both as a means of "making Europe physically strong" and of funding the "dollar problem." Bonesteel suggested this new approach in a letter dated March 29, 1950, to John Ohly, deputy director of the MDAP and destined ultimately to become head of the OSP. Prior to sending the letter, Bonesteel sent a draft of it to Harriman for his comments. It is worth quoting at length.

"This letter," began Bonesteel, "concerns some long-range thinking on the future of MDAP, European military production, and, in fact,

[20] Information pertaining to these issues can be found in European Coordinating Committee, "MDAP Information Activity," May 6, 1950, and NATO, FEC. (50) D-12, May 3, 1950, Harriman Papers, Box 270, LC.

[21] Acheson to London, November 2, 1949, Bray Records, Foreign Activities, Box 12, NAII, 4. See also "U.S. Financing of Infrastructure Costs," June 6, 1950, ibid.

the whole scope of our military and economic policies *vis-à-vis* Western Europe." Bonesteel then proceeded to outline the problem of rearmament given the state of the world at that time.

Western Europe has long been known as the "work shop of the world," dependent, however, for a large part of its raw materials and food on overseas trade and supplies. The physical productive capacity of Europe today is perhaps higher than ever before, but world economic and political dislocations are making it well nigh impossible for Western Europe to be self-supporting at the standards of life which politically and sociologically are necessary today. The "dollar problem," disruption of triangular trade, the rise of nationalism in Southeast Asia with the inevitable concommitant [*sic*] of desires for national self-sufficiency, the problem of industrialized Japan – not to mention Communism, the loss of China, and the possible subversion in Southeast Asia – all tend to leave Western Europe with an industrial production potential which it cannot sustain unaided.

The "Dilemma of Defence" so excellently expounded in the London *Economist's* lead article of last December 15 is very real and not by any means easily solvable. It arises from the fact that the necessary increases in military budgets in Europe – necessary to achieve appropriate military strength in being – must come very largely from sacrifices in the field of individual social security expenditures. The exaggerated emphasis on social security in Europe has had a long evolution, which, politically, will be extremely difficult to reverse, if indeed this is either feasible or desirable.

At the same time, Bonesteel stated, "the US economy with its enormous industrial production and equally great agricultural and raw material production (now producing surpluses) is unlikely to be able to bear the major burden of providing as end items the majority of the overseas European military requirements, particularly when the needs for economic and military assistance to other parts of the world are taken into account." Given these problems, Bonesteel then posed what he called the "$64 question – what do we and the Western Europeans do to find a feasible solution to the problem of making Europe physically strong while preserving her economic stability, and not wrecking her own strength"? He then set out his "solution."

The essence of the approach I want to suggest is that an important segment of European productive capacity be utilized, with American aid, to produce most of the arms required for Europe's re-strengthening. In other words, a vastly broader approach to the problem of "additional military production" [AMP] in Europe. At present we are working on the basis of a few million dollars worth of assistance to AMP under the caveat of not jeopardizing economic recovery. The results are discouraging and there is little broad incentive involved. Can we not enlarge the present concept of AMP to relate it to very substantial increases of European military production with American economic and military assistance, both direct

The Political Economy of Rearmament

and indirect, permitting utilization of European productive capacity within a coordinated working out of the future economic and political as well as the military policies of the US vis-à-vis Europe?

Bonesteel drew attention to the fact that much of European labor was being directed toward output for export "in the effort to get foreign exchange to buy both industrial raw materials and food." Diverting labor to military production, *absent* U.S. funding, was thus virtually impossible. "These conditions will be aggravated by the cessation of Marshall Aid," he added. "Somewhere in this maze of economic factors, I believe, there is a pattern which if followed through might indicate a method of applying total American assistance to Europe so as to greatly benefit both military production and the economic situation of Europe in the future." It would also, Bonesteel suggested, aid the U.S. economy with its "surpluses of food, cotton, tobacco, and ... other raw materials."[22]

To make the point crystal clear, what Bonesteel was suggesting in this memorandum was that the United States essentially pay western Europe in dollars to build military goods. Such payments would aid in western Europe's military buildup but also would enhance its productivity, which, as he implied, was underutilized, and, perhaps most importantly, alleviate its dollar gap, especially *once Marshall Aid ended*. Bonesteel's memorandum was widely circulated at high levels. It clearly demonstrates that U.S. officials were cognizant of the ways military spending could be used for purposes other than security. Such uses would not be forgotten once the military buildup outlined in NSC 68 got underway.

The Buildup Begins

With the outbreak of the Korean War, the push for military assistance was on. Immediately after the war began, MDAP Director John Ohly prepared a memorandum for Acheson, certainly at Acheson's request, justifying an increase of $5.2 billion in military assistance, the vast majority of it for western Europe. The requested amount for the second year of the MDAP already on the table was $1.2 billion, which, Ohly argued, should be immediately approved. He then argued for an additional $4 billion in new obligational authority, "which would clearly be required under

---

[22] Bonesteel to Harriman, March 13, 1950, Harriman Papers, Marshall Plan, Military – Defense, General, 1949–1950, Box 271, LC (parentheses in original). The actual letter was sent to Ohly on March 29, 1950. It is in *FRUS, 1950* 3: 36–40. Acheson knew of Bonesteel's letter. See Acheson to Ohly, May 3, 1950, Harriman Papers, Box 270, LC.

224 NSC 68 and the Political Economy of the Early Cold War

an expanded or accelerated assistance program for Western Europe but which, if not so required, could be utilized by U.S. forces." Truman then went to Congress with the request. He did so in two increments. On July 26 he asked for the $1.2 billion for the second year of the MDAP. Five days later he requested the other $4 billion.[23] These amounts were a dramatic increase from the $1.3 billion allotted for the MDAP for fiscal year 1951 and began the process whereby "mutual security" assistance would, in the main, replace economic assistance as the chief means for overcoming the dollar gap.

On July 22, the United States asked the NATO countries to supply figures for their projected rearmament costs. This, too, represented a decisive new turn reflective of the changed circumstances brought on by the adoption of NSC 68 and the war in Korea. As we have seen, initially work on the MDAP had gone slow in part because the NATO countries could not agree on financing rearmament. Once that it was clear that greatly increased funds would be available, U.S. officials wanted action.[24] The request asked the NATO countries to provide answers by August 5, 1950, an amazingly quick turnaround for such sensitive national information. Not surprisingly, obtaining such information proved difficult, as financial and logistical arrangements had not been worked out. When the figures came in on August 5, they were far less than U.S. officials hoped. The NATO countries proposed a combined increased military program of $3.5 billion, which, according to U.S. calculations, fell short by roughly $4 billion over three years. Nonetheless, the NATO countries did pledge publicly their determination to proceed with rearmament subject to working out the arrangements, a significant step in itself.[25]

Expectations

From the beginning, U.S. officials expected great things from the rearmament program as it pertained to the dollar gap. For instance in France, U.S. officials expected that rearmament "would entail attack on major social

[23] "Memorandum for the Secretary of State," [July 1950], Ohly Papers, Foreign Aid File: Subject File, 1950–1968, MDAP FY 1951 and FY 1951 Supplemental, Box 161, 19, Truman Library; Lewis Wood, "2d-Year Arms Aid Signed by Truman," *The New York Times*, July 27, 1950, 7; C. P. Trussell, "Arms Aid is Rushed on Huge New Scale," *The New York Times*, August 2, 1950, 1.

[24] "Ways and Means to Achieve Increased Defense Efforts on the Part of the Other NAT Countries," July 22, 1950, Bray Records, Policy, Box 57, NAII.

[25] Sept 7, 1950, Bray Records, Military, Box 23, NAII; Douglas to Acheson, August 5, 1950, Bray Records, Policy, Box 59, NAII.

The Political Economy of Rearmament 225

inequities, fiscal weaknesses, lack of entrepreneurial aggressiveness, and other impediments to revival of traditional French spirit." With regard to Germany, they believed it would pave the way for West Germany to rejoin the western European community of nations as a full-fledged member, combining its rearmament and reindustrialization. "If Germany does become [a] partner in defense, many of the restrictions that now limit its economy would presumably be removed. In that event … the great possibilities of the German economy for expansion could be realized." Given that Germany's future lay at the heart of the Cold War conflict, and, therefore, was a political "hot potato" of the first rank, this was some hopeful thinking. Then there was Italy. As we have seen, Italy had both an immense unemployment problem as well as a production capacity problem. Too many Italians were unemployed, and much of Italy's industrial plant was underutilized. Rearmament, U.S. officials believed, could work to cure both of these ailments.[26]

U.S. officials also envisioned rearmament as a vehicle for spreading dollars to the world via circuitous routes, well-known as triangular trade. An Economic Cooperation Administration (ECA) cablegram from August 4, 1950, made the case succinctly. The issue was how to increase NATO countries' dollar earnings in light of the Korean War. Wanting to ensure that the balance-of-payments problems posed by rearmament, that is, the increased cost of raw materials, would not require the United States to provide aid solely for that purpose, the cable stated that "we are more interested than ever in maximizing European dollar earnings." It then put forward the following benefits that the rearmament program could provide for that effort: (1) That "there will be an opportunity for [NATO countries] to sell much more to us than they are now doing"; (2) That "there will be more dollars in third areas that may be earned by [the NATO countries] than have been anticipated in the past"; and (3) That, "the U.S. market should be protected against inflation by larger [NATO country] exports to the U.S., whether of necessities or luxuries."[27]

Continued Problems

Nonetheless, problems continued to plague the rearmament program abroad. In the fall of 1950, the western European countries supplied the

---

[26] U.S. embassy in Paris to ECA administrator, August 16, 1950, Bray Records, NAII.
[27] Paris to the ECA Administrator, August 4, 1950, Bray Records, Policy, NSC 68, France, July–October 1950, Box 60, NAII.

United States with their new plans for rearmament. In general, they fell short of what U.S. officials wanted. The same difficulties noted in the previous section continued to plague them, with new ones thrown in as well. In the first instance, despite the outbreak of the Korean War and propaganda efforts by the United States to use the war to generate a greater concern for security, the western European governments continued to feel severe pressure from their own peoples over rearmament versus recovery. "If it becomes generally believed that the United States is insisting on an excessive proportional effort in Europe which would have drastic effects on the local economies – as is being suggested by the Bevan 'insurrectionists' in England – and if, at the same time, U.S. arrangements implied in past NATO planning to provide substantial amounts of military equipment did not seem to be met, there could be widespread dissatisfaction among segments of the European public," stated a paper prepared by the executive group working on the presentation of the Mutual Security Program to Congress.[28] Another angle to this problem was supplied by U.S. Ambassador to Belgium Charles Murphy. Discussing Belgian rearmament, but with clear implications for the rest of western Europe, Murphy remarked at a meeting of the International Security Affairs Committee (ISAC) that "Belgian experience over the past years makes the armament idea repugnant."[29] If the United States was willing to fund the bulk of rearmament, then the issue was largely moot and the western Europeans would do whatever the United States wanted.

This first problem led to a second one: Congress would not support extensive military assistance if the western Europeans were not shouldering an adequate share of the rearmament burden. However, the western European countries' budgets were already pushed to the limit and suffering extreme dollar shortages. A vicious cycle was thus begun. Any expanded effort toward rearmament would have to come at the expense of their civilian recovery efforts, a politically difficult path, but the idea was that the United States would pick up the tab. In

---

[28] "The Implications of Substantially Delayed Deliveries of MDAP End-Items," May 1, 1951, Bray Records, NSC 68, NAT Area, Box 59, NAII; Minutes of Meeting, International Security Affairs Committee (ISAC), February 16, 1951, RG 59, Executive Secretariat, Subject Files Relating to the ISAC, 1951–1952, Box 3, NAII, 11. Aneurin Bevan was the British Minister of Labour in 1951, a position from which he resigned in April of that year due to the rearmament policies of the Labor government.

[29] Memorandum of Meeting, April 3, 1951, ISAC, Box 3, NAII, 4. A more thorough discussion of this issue is found in Outline, October 18, 1951, Records of the PPS, Country and Area Files, Box 32, and passim, NAII.

The Political Economy of Rearmament

fact, the western Europeans saw the rearmament program less in terms of rearmament for the sake of rearmament against a determined foe than they did as the "ticket" to U.S. aid, which they needed for other purposes. U.S. leaders understood this all too well. However, Congress demanded a higher level than the western Europeans were willing to expend without knowing what the United States would offer; and U.S. officials could not provide that information without commitments from the western Europeans.[30]

France provides a good example. The French were fairly eager to accept rearmament aid, although not for reasons that U.S. officials necessarily wanted. U.S. officials sought to cast rearmament as aimed solely at the aggressive agenda of the Soviet Union. The French, however, did not view the Soviet Union with near the alarm that U.S. officials would have liked. "The great danger in Europe was Germany and not the Soviet Union," French President Vincent Auriol told Acheson during one of their conversations, words Acheson most certainly did not want to hear.[31] The French hoped rearmament also would aid them in putting down the resistance from Ho Chi Minh's forces in Indochina. To this end – the recolonization of Vietnam – they eagerly sought military assistance. A program of $240 million was worked out for the first six months of 1951, most of it going into AMP. At any rate, France's problem was not unemployment or lack of capacity per se, although these played a role, it was a problem of financing. The French could not afford to increase their rearmament program without risking serious inflation absent U.S. aid.[32] Thus it was that France became the initial focal point of the OSP. "The economic impact of the French program might be eased by the judicious use of offshore procurement for components, materials, and production equipment needed for the French projects which are not readily available in France," a report from October 1950 noted.[33] The French had hoped that OSP would begin immediately but perceived congressional opposition

---

[30] The history depicted here is derived from the Bray Records, Boxes 1–65, NAII. See also Memorandum of Meeting, March 30, 1951, ISAC, Box 3, NAII, 4.

[31] Princeton Seminars, March 14, 1954, reel 7, track 1, 11–12, Dean Acheson Papers, Box 98, Truman Library. See also Frank Costigliola, *France and the United States* (New York: Twayne Publishers, 1992), 58–117.

[32] U.S. Ambassador to France Bruce to Acheson, July 28, 1950, Bray Records, Policy, NSC 68, France, July–October 1950, Box 60, NAII; Bruce to Acheson, September 16, 1950, ibid.; "The French Proposals for Financing European Rearmament," October 3, 1950, ibid.

[33] Bray to Kerr, October 5, 1950, ibid.

228   *NSC 68 and the Political Economy of the Early Cold War*

made that impossible.[34] At that juncture, U.S.-French relations over rearmament underwent severe strain. The French cut back its own rearmament effort without informing U.S. officials. For their part, U.S. officials continued to be noncommittal on the amount of aid or when it would be available, although they did tell the French that they planned to ask Congress for "legislation involving the 'marriage' of the ERP and the MDAP."[35] By April 1951, the U.S. ambassador to France believed a "very damaging crisis in French-American relations" was on the horizon if the United States did not immediately release the remaining funds pledged for the first six months of 1951.[36]

There was a third problem as well. Even if the United States had been in a position to cover the entire cost of western European rearmament, there was a danger in doing so. If the United States somehow could supply the bulk of the costs of rearmament, there was fear that the western Europeans would then get lazy, as it were, and merely rely on the United States to fund the cost of rearmament. In a cable to Acheson, U.S. Ambassador to Britain Lewis Douglas explained that

In administering aid programs, it is of course elementary that there is always a difficult line to be drawn between the point at which (A) inadequate US aid may discourage constructive Eur[opean] action and the point at which (B) softness on our part may encourage postponement of essential and difficult decisions which Eur[opean] Gov[ernmen]ts may inevitably face. There is still a lag between the US sense of urgency and determination to get on with the job and corresponding Eur[opean] attitudes. The Eur[opean] Gov[ernmen]ts are aware of this, and also know of our concern over the econ[omic] stress and psychological and polit[ical] difficulties with which they are beset. Consequently, they are understandably tempted by the attractive possibility that, if they hesitate long enough, we may be moved by sympathy and impatience to step in and pick up the check.... To the extent that this were to be done, it w[ou]ld result in inadequate utilization of Eur[opean] resources and an excessive drain on those of the US. This c[ou]ld have serious polit[ical] repercussions at home.[37]

---

[34] U.S. Ambassador to France Bruce to Acheson, July 28, 1950, ibid.; Bruce to Acheson, September 16, 1950, ibid.; "The French Proposals for Financing European Rearmament," October 3, 1950, ibid.; Joint State-Defense-ECA telegram, November 1, 1950, Bray Records, Policy, NSC 68, France, November 1950–January 1951, Box 61, NAII; Paris to the MAP, November 7, 1950, ibid.

[35] "Agreed Minute of Discussions on Economic Questions by the US-French Economic Working Group," January 29–30, 1951, ibid.

[36] Bruce to Acheson, April 18, 1951, ibid.

[37] London embassy to Acheson, April 11, 1951, Bray Records, Policy, NSC 68, NAT Area, Box 59, NAII. See also "To: SUSREP MPSB London England," July 8, 1950, Bray Records, Policy, NSC 68, April–November 1950, Box 57, NAII, a portion of which reads: "We must be careful [to] avoid taking attitudes which c[ou]ld encourage our European allies

The Political Economy of Rearmament

At issue here was ensuring that rearmament actually aided in boosting European production. If rearmament had been the sole goal, it would have been easier to just provide the western European nations with military equipment manufactured in the United States, although it is far from certain that Congress would have approved such a measure. Nonetheless, that never was the sole goal.

Then there was the problem of West Germany. The Truman administration had determined long before 1950 that West Germany had to be rebuilt and integrated into the western European alliance. U.S. officials argued publicly that this was necessary for the defense of western Europe, if not the United States itself. Privately, however, economic and political factors crept into their discussions. As NSC 68 stated it, "The movement toward economic integration does not appear to be rapid enough to provide West Germany with adequate economic opportunities in the West."[38] The fear was that West Germany, unable to satisfy its needs in concert with the West, would opt to go neutral in the Cold War or even side with the East. Some Germans were advocating exactly that.

It is in this context, rather than solely in terms of security, that the decision was made to rearm West Germany. The idea was that West Germany would be integrated into NATO, at one and the same time providing it with a measure of sovereignty while circumscribing its ability to break free from the West. The economic potential and raw resources of West Germany could then be brought to bear on western Europe's recovery and, most importantly, be kept out of the Soviet's sphere. The problem was that few of the western European nations agreed with the United States on this score. Germany had been the primary aggressor in Europe in WWII. All of its neighbors had suffered the brunt of the German assault. Few of them trusted it or wanted to see it rebuilt.

For this reason the administration initially did not make its wishes about West Germany known. But the Korean War, like with so much else, opened the door for the United States to begin talking publicly about West German rearmament. However, when it did so in a September 1950 meeting of the NATO countries, the problems mounted. France was adamantly against any plan to rearm West Germany. It promised to be an obstacle every step of the way, demanding concessions, hemming and

---

to relax their own efforts in [the] belief that US [is] 'now thoroughly alarmed [by the events in Korea]' and will make entire add[itiona]l finan[cial] and econ[omic] effort required to build up collective security."

[38] NSC 68, *FRUS, 1950* 1: 260.

230 NSC 68 and the Political Economy of the Early Cold War

hawing, and obfuscating the process. The Soviet Union, too, made known its opposition. A December 5, 1950, Policy Planning Staff memorandum argued that war between the United States and the Soviet Union would be the likely result if the United States pursued such plans. West Germany, in fact, would not begin rearming until 1955.[39]

Meanwhile, the dollar gap continued to plague western Europe. ECA projections for France, Italy, the Netherlands, and Britain from March 1951 determined that significant dollar gaps would exist for all of them in 1952.[40] In fact, the rearmament program initially exacerbated the dollar gap because it caused a spike in prices for raw materials. The western Europeans subsequently became spooked about how much they would be asked to provide toward the rearmament effort.[41] Given this, it might be fairly argued that the rearmament program did the opposite of what it intended to do with regard to the dollar gap. This would be misleading, however. In actuality, the inflation caused by rearmament worked precisely in the United States' favor. Although the rise in prices was likely an unintended consequence of the turn to rearmament, it sparked the need for even more U.S. aid to western Europe, which, in turn, forced Congress' hand and kept western Europe more deeply wedded to the U.S. side.

The International Security Affairs Committee

The various problems described in the previous section would find their solution in the Mutual Security Program (MSP), although it would be misleading to argue that the MSP resulted solely from those problems. Truman approved what would become the MSP on December 19, 1950, and by October 1951 the program was up and running, not surprisingly with Averell Harriman at its head; Harriman had been immersed in the

---

[39] NSC 68, quoted in May, *Interpreting NSC 68*, 49; the PPS staff to Nitze, December 5, 1950, PPS, 1947–1953, Country and Area Files, 1950–1951, Box 28, NAII; Robert G. Hooker to Nitze, July 11, 1951, ibid. See also Carolyn Eisenberg, *Drawing the Line: The American Decision to Divide Germany, 1944–1949* (Cambridge, United Kingdom: Cambridge University Press, 1996).

[40] "Primary Comments on ECA Projections for France," March 27, 1951, Bray Records, NAT, NSC 68, Box 59, NAII; "Primary Comments on ECA Projections for Italy," March 27, 1951, ibid.; "Primary Comments on ECA Projections for Netherlands," March 27, 1951, ibid.; "Primary Comments on ECA Projections for UK," March 27, 1951, ibid.

[41] ECA chief to Paris embassy, Sept 28, 1950, Bray Records, Policy, NSC 68, April–November 1950, Box 57, NAII; "The Italian Economic Position Before and After June 1950," Bray Records, Policy, NSC 68, Italy, Box 63, NAII.

The Political Economy of Rearmament

dollar gap problem since at least 1948 and had, as roving ambassador for the Marshall Plan, suggested in October 1949 that "security" justifications should replace economic or political ones in securing western European integration because the latter simply were not working. However, in its practical dimensions the MSP was the culmination of what first Harriman as far back as 1948 and then Acheson and Nitze in NSC 68 saw as crucial to overcoming western Europe's dollar gap – combining military and economic aid into a single program.

The beginning point for the MSP as an actual program was the creation of the International Security Affairs Committee (ISAC) in December 1950. The interdepartmental committee, "a new office with a far broader mission and much more far-reaching responsibilities than the conduct of the [MDAP]," was created essentially to facilitate the development of the MSP. A program of mutual security aid had been decided on, but what precisely it would look like had not been determined. Representatives from State, Treasury, Defense, the ECA, the Executive Office of the President, the Bureau of the Budget, the NSC, the JCS, and other interested agencies participated in the committee. If the committee could not agree unanimously on a given issue, it could appeal to the Cabinet level through the Foreign Mutual Aid Coordinating Committee or directly to the president. Thomas Cabot, head of the Cabot Corporation, a multinational chemical company, was instated as its director.[42]

The primary objective of the ISAC was to find the means to expand the capacity of western European nations to produce military goods for the rearmament effort. In this regard, it sought to (1) "Expedite military production and procurement thus minimizing the time lag before European-produced material is available to defense forces"; (2) "Expand the production base for European rearmament"; (3) "Overcome the protectionist obstacles now hindering the placement of contracts with the most efficient European producers"; and (4) "Introduce U.S. technological skills at an early stage in order to improve the quality and efficiency of European-[produced] material."[43] A key way NSC 68 worked to overcome the dollar gap is made evident here. The ISAC was saying that merely ensuring the defensive capabilities of western Europe was not enough. Western Europe needed to be

---

[42] "Organization to Administer the Mutual Security Act," June 11, 1951, Ohly Papers, Foreign Aid File, Subject File 1950–1968, Draper Committee, Organization – ISA, Box 127, 5, Truman Library.

[43] Harlan Cleveland memorandum and accompanying report, May 28, 1951, ISAC, Box 2, NAII.

sufficiently rebuilt to carry a defense production burden commensurate with the determined needs of western European defense. Hence, plants had to be expanded and modernized; comparative advantage had to be applied within Europe; production had to increase; and old ways of thinking about production and consumption, as well European economic integration, had to be broken down – all of which had also been deemed essential for overcoming the dollar gap long before the Soviet acquisition of atomic power, the Communist victory in China, or the Korean War.[44]

ISAC was of primary importance because it set the groundwork for expanding the use of three measures that up to that time had been used only minimally toward the rearmament effort – offshore procurement, use of counterpart funds for "rearmament" purposes, and production of end-items in Europe.[45] Although these programs were in some sense distinct, they all sought the same end – to increase the productivity capacity of western Europe and other countries while providing a vehicle for continued dollar assistance to cover the dollar gap. They were interconnected because they were designed to promote the latter three of these measures – stimulating end-item production in western Europe. End-item production referred to the process whereby western Europe would be given the materials to finish the production of military goods and equipment. If the United States had wanted merely to aid in the defense of western Europe, it could have produced all end items at home and merely transferred them to western Europe. That is certainly how Congress saw the issue, as it would aid U.S. industries in addition to aiding the rearmament effort abroad. However, that was not the goal. The goal was to both contribute to rearmament and to find a solution for the dollar gap. For instance, as an ISAC report from October 1951 noted: "It is recognized that one effect of providing a European country with dollars to finance the production or procurement of equipment is to increase the amount of dollars available to that country – that is, to provide some relief for a dollar balance of payments deficit.... It is assumed that in most cases a large proportion of the dollars going into the European country as payment for military items would be available for relief of the dollar balance of

[44] Memorandum to Thomas Cabot, August 6, 1951, ISAC, Box 2, NAII. One segment of this memorandum reads: "The European countries ... must be made to realize the time limitation, namely that this procurement is primarily for 'pump priming' purposes."

[45] See ISAC D-14/2, August 6, 1951, ISAC, Box 2, NAII; on end-item production, see ISAC D-14/1, July 6, 1951, ibid.

The Political Economy of Rearmament

233

payment."[46] Or, as Najeeb Halaby, a member of the ECA and a contributor on NSC 68, put it: "In the final analysis, from an economist's viewpoint, our end-item aid is economic aid."[47] There is much in the ISAC records that bears out the relationship between rearmament and the dollar gap crisis, and the end result of the ISAC was the MSP, in which all that the ISAC recommended actually was carried out.

Two other aspect of ISAC's work are worth mentioning. ISAC was influential in shaping public opinion both at home and abroad. On several different occasions in 1951, it sponsored visits of western European journalists and other prominent citizens to the United States to witness the U.S. defense effort. It also sponsored travel to western Europe for U.S. journalists to see the MDAP at work. The idea was that influential citizens would pass on the good word to wider audiences in their respective countries.[48] In addition, the ISAC possessed a propaganda arm designed to "achieve public backing of our foreign policy in Europe and to answer criticisms that Europe (NATO) is not or will not pull its own weight."[49] Head of this propaganda effort was none other than Edward Barrett, who, as we saw in Chapter 6, on reading NSC 68 for the first time in March 1950, suggested that the administration engage in a "scare campaign" to get the program through. He got his wish. The effort was carried out on film, radio, television, and through the printed media. One example was the creation of the film *U.S. Arsenal of Democracy*, the stated purpose of which was "to show the strength and determination of the U.S. to participate in and back up the joint effort." Other suggested films included one "on the subject of European integration," one "on trainees," and another "along the line of strength through unity and productivity in which would be projected the American concept of productivity in a manner which would show what this theme translated in European terms could mean to Europe as a whole within, possibly, two years."[50] Newsreel production, with the cooperation of the "five major American newsreel" companies, occupied the ISAC as well. Topics included "U.S. Fourth Division Prepares to Join European

---

[46] ISAC D-14/3a, "Report of the Working Group on Off-Shore Procurement," October 4, 1951, ISAC, Box 1, NAII.
[47] Memorandum of Meeting, April 3, 1951, ISAC, Box 3, NAII.
[48] ISAC, "Chronology of Events Relating to International Security Affairs and the Mutual Defense Assistance Program," December 7, 1951, ISAC, Box 1, NAII.
[49] C. Tyler Wood to ISAC Information Working Group, March 19, 1951, ISAC, Box 5, NAII.
[50] ISAC Public Information Committee D-2/1, May 24, 1951, ISAC, Box 5, NAII.

234 *NSC 68 and the Political Economy of the Early Cold War*

Defense," "Transfer of Two U.S. Destroyers to Italian Navy," "U.S. Planes Sent to Indo-China," "U.S. Speeds Tank Production," and the like.[51] The Mutual Broadcasting System was also enlisted in the effort. "The Mutual Broadcasting System is very interested in broadcasting reports in the actual voices of our Chiefs of Mission and other U.S. officials in the NATO countries (Eisenhower, Spofford, McCloy, Handy, Katz, and Batt) on the state of the nation to which they are assigned," noted a paper in the ISAC. The report concluded that "these would be broadcast on Mutual's 500 odd stations."[52]

The Mutual Security Program

On May 24, 1951, President Truman asked Congress for approval of the Mutual Security Program (MSP).[53] He asked for $6.25 billion for military assistance and $2.25 billion for economic assistance. Also in May he signed the last military supplemental for fiscal year 1952 of $6.25 billion. On June 26, 1951, the House Foreign Affairs Committee began hearings on the MSP. The joint Senate Foreign Relations-Armed Services Committee followed on July 26.[54] Of course, the hearings were anything but smooth going. For instance, in the Senate hearings William Foster, head of the ECA, received a lashing from Senator Tom Connally when he mentioned that economic aid would be needed for Asia. Connally, losing his temper, shouted at Foster: "You were put in here to take care of Europe. Now you're chasing out to southeast Asia."[55] As was its prerogative, the Congress took an ax to the president's request despite much pleading from administration officials. When the Mutual Security appropriations bill was enacted in October 1951, roughly $1 billion had been slashed from the original request. Still, the MSP was destined to be the program through which the dollar gap was overcome and multilateralism secured.[56]

The MSP was the logical development of the desire to intertwine economic and military aid, long the goal of the multilateralists in and out of government. Its accomplishments are as fascinating as they are troubling.

---

[51] ISAC/PIC D-3, March 23, 1951, ibid.

[52] C. Tyler Wood to ISAC Information Working Group, March 19, 1951, ibid.

[53] In this section the Mutual Security Program (MSP) is used interchangeably with the Mutual Security Agency (MSA), which administered the program.

[54] ISAC, "Chronology," ISAC, Box 1, NAII.

[55] C. P. Trussell, "Taxpayer Squeeze in Rising Aid Costs Arouses Connally," *The New York Times*, July 31, 1951, 1.

[56] William White, "$7.328 Billions Foreign Aid Voted; Optional Item for Spain Included," *The New York Times*, October 21, 1951, 1.

The Political Economy of Rearmament   235

Nonetheless, the MSP has been poorly understood. No history of it has ever been written.[57] Because the program highlighted the word "security," moreover, it has been viewed generally as a program aimed solely at security, that is, the national defense. Thus, demonstrating how the MSP worked to overcome the dollar gap opens an entirely new understanding of what U.S. foreign policymakers were trying to accomplish in and through NSC 68.

To make sense of how the MSP used military spending to overcome the dollar gap and all the attendant difficulties associated with it, we can turn to the Public Advisory Board of the Mutual Security Agency (MSA), which ran from October 1951 to March 1953. The board was made up of such leading citizens as George Meany, secretary-treasurer of the American Federation of Labor; Allan B. Kline, president of the American Farm Bureau Federation; Orin Lehman, a New York banker;[58] Sarah G. Blanding, first female president of Vassar College; Eric A. Johnston, president of the Motion Picture Association of America; Herschel D. Newsom, master of the National Grange; Robert H. Hinckley, vice president of the American Broadcasting Company (ABC); Jonathan W. Daniels, editor of *The Raleigh* (North Carolina) *News and Observer*; George H. Mead, chairman of the Mead Corporation (maker of the Pee Chee All Season Portfolio beloved of school children for decades and now, sadly, a relic); and James G. Patton, president of the National Farm Union.[59] The board issued monthly reports during its tenure, which offer a wealth of information about what the MSP accomplished. As far as this author has been able to determine, these reports have remained in obscurity until now.[60]

The reports follow a general format. On the inside cover of each volume some specialized issue is discussed. For instance, the October and December 1951 volumes devote this page to "grain for India," whereas the March 1952 volume examines "strategic materials development projects." Next, the volumes usually address some other problem in more

---

[57] Chester Pach's book on the MAP, *Arming the Free World: The Origins of the United States Mutual Security Program, 1945–1950* (Chapel Hill, North Carolina: University of North Carolina, 1991) ends in 1949, long before the MSP came on the scene.

[58] Not to be confused with Orin Lehman of Lehman Brothers and a U.S. senator from 1949 to 1957.

[59] "Truman's Study of Foreign Trade Meets Mixed Praise and Criticism," *The New York Times*, July 15, 1952, 29; "Trade Inquiry Set; Policy Challenged," *The New York Times*, August 22, 1952, 10.

[60] When I first encountered them in the stacks of the Alexander Library on the Rutgers New Brunswick campus, they were wrapped in twine seemingly as old as the booklets themselves. Clearly, no one had looked at them in years, if ever.

depth. For example, the April 1952 volume examines "controls for economy in procurement," and the June 1952 volume devotes this section to "defense support ... supply program for Western Europe." Each volume then turns to a section called "European Operations." Here, the reader is confronted with various graphs, charts, slogans, and drawings depicting the MSP at work in western Europe. This section is followed by a "statistical appendix" of the projects funded for western Europe. Here is presented a very detailed breakdown of exactly where and on what the money was spent. Next, in each volume, comes the section "Far East Operations," which proceeds along the same lines as the section on western Europe. Occasionally, the volumes will address other issues as well, such as the "Spanish Aid Program."

Therefore, we can learn a lot about how the MSP operated to aid in overcoming the dollar gap through these reports. For example, under "Industrial Projects Approved," which is a section found in each volume, we find that military assistance to western Europe helped pay for the following: (1) Manufacturing: iron and steel production, petroleum refining, automotive products, chemicals production, pulp and paper production, and cement production, among other things; (2) Raw materials extraction: potash mining, coal mining, iron mining, and oil drilling; and (3) Transportation, communication, and utilities: power facilities, communications, roads, air transport, waterways and harbors, railroads, and fishing fleets. Under "Industrial and Informational Media Guaranties," we find that military assistance spent on "industrial investment" went to petroleum refining, machinery and equipment, watches and clocks, consumer goods, building materials, and vegetable seed cultivation. As to "informational media," the report lists that military assistance went toward motion pictures, periodicals, books, and newspapers.

In some cases these can be broken down even further. For instance, in the "statistical appendix" for the October 1951 volume, we get a more detailed analysis of what "manufacturing projects" entailed. In a section titled "machinery and equipment" are listed the following items as paid for through military assistance from the United States: earth moving equipment, sewing machine parts, drill chucks, dictating machines, regulating instruments, metalworking machinery, miners safety lamps, mine car loading equipment, metal spraying equipment, machine parts, material loading equipment, and road building machinery. Under "transportation equipment" are listed diesel trucks and railway equipment. Under "consumer goods" are found low-cost books, soluble coffee, cooking, lighting, heating appliances, public technical and education books, and talon zippers.

The ways in which rearmament helped restart triangular trade also are laid out. Under "Strategic Materials Development Projects," military assistance was paid to Norway and Germany for aluminum, Jamaica for bauxite, Southern Rhodesia for railway improvement, French Morocco for lead-zinc, Northern Rhodesia for copper-cobalt, French Equatorial Africa for industrial diamonds and copper-lead-zinc, New Caledonia for chrome, Portuguese Africa for port improvement, Belgian Congo for tin, and Italy for zinc-cadmium.[61] "Technical Assistance" was another avenue for the MSP. Under this program, which eclipsed the ineffective Point Four program, dollars went to cover the costs of technical training to improve industrial and agricultural productivity, public administration, manpower utilization, transportation and communication, development of overseas territories, marketing, and tourism.[62]

The volumes often focus on a specific issue. An example is "European Industrial Projects" from January 1952. The section begins by telling us that "expansion and modernization of Europe's capital plant are essential for defense support and economic strength" and that the MSA has "aided nearly all sectors of Western Europe's industrial economies." The report then turns to specifics. With regard to steel production, we find the following: "With the aid of over $67 million in equipment and supplies authorized under industrial projects in this field, France will be able to produce a balanced quantity of steel products, eliminating many of the surpluses and critical shortages which now exist." On Italy, the report stated that the "development of the steel-making facilities of the FIAT Company is another important step in building up the economic and defensive strength of Italy. The FIAT plant is one of the major European facilities capable of immediate conversion to production of military-type vehicles." For Britain, the MSA helped build a new steel plant that "not only increase[d] production" but left a "substantial export surplus." In Austria, MSP funds helped build a "new blooming mill ... which ... is capable of rolling about 40,000 tons of steel per month on a two-shift basis."

---

[61] Mutual Security Agency, *Monthly Report for the Public Advisory Committee* (hereinafter MSA), October 31, 1951 (Washington, D.C.: U.S. Government Printing Office, 1951), 26, 29.

[62] MSA, December 31, 1951, 16.

238   NSC 68 and the Political Economy of the Early Cold War

This particular report addresses electric power production as well. In France, "MSA ... extend[ed] dollar aid to three thermal plants" including the "Arrighi power plant, near Paris, serving a vital industrial area where aircraft, machine tools, motor vehicles, and other equipment for France's rearmament program are produced." In Turkey, military assistance helped construct "a new 185-mile transmission line, with necessary transformers and substations" for the Izmit-Istanbul region. In Italy, the MSA helped fund "eleven new steam-electric generating installations capable of producing 720,000 kilowatts."

Transportation and communication also came in for consideration. In Turkey, MSA funds contributed to "improv[ing] and maintain[ing] the 15,000-mile national road system[,]" which has "reduced travel time between principal cities and [has] connected hitherto relatively inaccessible rich agricultural and mineral resource areas with markets and seaports by means of all-weather highways." In France, the MSA provided partial funding for the commercial aviation industry. The report stated the reason: "Grossly inadequate transportation of all types has been a serious deterrent to development of France's overseas territories.... Improved air transport between France and her territories and within the territories will contribute materially to the productivity of these areas and will earn more foreign exchange through the accommodation of large numbers of tourists." The MSA also aided France in "better[ing its] telephone and telegraph services ... and to increase the efficiency of [its] postal-checking system, the principal channel for transfers of funds within the French economy."[63]

That U.S. officials understood that the MSP would aid in building up western Europe's productive capacity for eventual *civilian* manufacture is clear. For instance, the April 1953 Advisory Board report noted the following: "Steel consumption is an accurate guide to a nation's standard of living as well as to its ability to produce modern arms and munitions. The same pieces of equipment are used to produce the structural shapes and plates for bridges and buildings as are used to manufacture similar items for tanks and armament. The same plant and equipment used to manufacture automotive body sheets can be used to manufacture the components of weapons carriers, military vehicles, and airplanes." The report went on to discuss how the MSP was helping France's USINOR corporation build two mills at Denain and Montataire for "supplying important quantities of cold-reduced sheets – an essential component

---

[63] MSA, January 31, 1952, 10–17.

of armament products." Those items also were useful for production of civilian goods. "The hot-and cold-strip rolling mill facilities being built in Lorraine, by SOLLAC (a merger of nine leading iron and steel firms) are even larger than USINOR," stated the report. "Located in the heart of France's richest iron ore region, the ... mills are designed to turn out products of the type needed for manufacture of jeeps, military trucks, and armored vehicles."

One of the primary goals of the MSP was to aid in western Europe's modernization of its plant and equipment, seen long before Korea as necessary to overcoming the dollar gap. Italy provides a good example. In pre-war Italy, the Advisory Board's report noted, "Over 200 plants [were] manufacturing iron and steel [prior to the war], many of them small and medium-sized companies using obsolete equipment and operating inefficiently.... Postwar efforts have aimed to: (1) replace obsolete equipment with modern installations; (2) concentrate production in a few large plants; [and] (3) specialize production in various plants." Here, we are seeing how the United States sought to "Americanize" western European industry through the MSP. For instance, with regard to upgrading electrical power sources in Britain, the report noted that "the greater part of the *dollar-financed* plants have modern, efficient, and reliable, American-designed thermal units of a type not heretofore installed in European plants" (emphasis added). The extent of this transformation becomes clear from what follows: "Designed to burn a low grade of fuel previously considered of little commercial value, these MSA-aided projects are of particular importance to the European economy because they increase thermal power generation without a proportionate increase in the use of high cost fuels which in many cases would have to be imported. Furthermore, MSA-aided plants have been installed in locations of critical need and have greatly stimulated European interest in the economic advantages of such equipment."

Another area of the April 1953 report helps us to understand the depth to which the MSP, and by virtue of that, rearmament more generally, operated to maintain the status quo with regard to western Europe's continuance of colonialism. "MSA has financed several projects to supply France with aircraft and equipment to help meet increasing demand for air passenger and freight transportation." We might find it interesting that "air passenger and freight transportation" were national security issues, but it is what follows that is of significance. "Grossly inadequate transportation of all types," the report stated, "has been a serious deterrent to development of France's overseas territories." The report goes

240   *NSC 68 and the Political Economy of the Early Cold War*

on to say that "one company receiving MSA-financed transport planes operates the only commercial air line in Indochina. Improved air transport between France and her territories and within the territories will contribute materially to the productivity of these areas and will earn more foreign exchange through the accommodation of larger numbers of tourists."[64]

The March 1952 report of the Advisory Board featured an exposé on the use of counterpart funds. These funds derived directly from the ERP (Marshall Plan) nations and worked in the following manner: The United States would provide western Europe with selected dollar goods free of charge. The recipient country then would be required to place into a special account its currency equal to the amount of the grant aid, with said currency being derived from the firms that imported the dollar goods. Once the currency was in the special account, 95 percent of it could be used, with United States approval, for infrastructure development, primarily, but sometimes for other uses as well, such as debt retirement. The remaining 5 percent was to be used by the United States for administrative costs, information programs, and whatever other uses the United States deemed necessary. Counterpart, then, allowed western Europe to devote precious resources to infrastructure and other needs that otherwise likely would have gone elsewhere for necessary imports. The very existence of counterpart funds gave the United States a great degree of leverage over the recipient nation's economy.

Prior to the development of the MSP, the United States forbade western Europe from using the counterpart funds for rearmament. The thinking was that such use would hamper the economic recovery for which the ERP was designed. Although there was truth to this claim, the decision had political dimensions as well. If ERP funds were diverted from economic recovery to any other purpose, then the program would fall prey to the charge, plied mostly by the Soviet Union, that the ERP all along was an American (i.e., capitalist) ploy to enslave western Europe. Throughout 1950, U.S. leaders resisted all attempts by interested parties to open up counterpart funds for rearmament. The ERP had to remain focused on economic recovery and nothing else.[65]

Under the MSP, counterpart was opened up in ways that allowed infrastructure development to be considered under the rubric of rearmament

---

[64] MSA, April 30, 1953, 1–17.

[65] "Proposed FY 1952 Foreign Assistance Program, Title I, Europe, Chapter IV, Principles and Policies for Administration of U.S. Aid Program for Title I Countries," Ohly Papers, MDAP FY 1952, Box 162, Truman Library, 85–86.

The Political Economy of Rearmament   241

in ways that were impossible under the Marshall Plan. It would not be incorrect to argue that the MSP broke the logjam on counterpart. Under the Marshall Plan, the counterpart idea did not go as planned. Although the reasons are complex, it can be said that the institutional bases for utilization of counterpart simply did not exist. Decisions on where and for what purpose the money would be spent bogged down in details over what constituted a legitimate use of counterpart. As a result, counterpart funds under the Marshall Plan languished to a degree. Under MSP, they exploded. Virtually overnight it became acceptable for counterpart to be used for the "rearmament" program. It is as if rearmament gave counterpart a *raison d'être*.

As the March report indicates, the counterpart funds contributed to the development of the following enterprises: electric, gas, and power facilities, transportation and communication, manufacturing, agriculture, and mining. Let's first take up electrical power. The report stated that "about one-fourth of the counterpart funds released to stimulate production has been used in the expansion and modernization of electric, gas, and power facilities. A contributing factor to Western Europe's present high level of electric power output – more than double prewar – is the additional capacity financed in part with counterpart funds." The report added that "this greatly enlarged output is now a vital factor in supporting the defense program of the European NATO countries and Germany." Manufacturing provides another good example. "Western European industries which have benefitted most from the use of counterpart funds through expansion and modernization of their facilities are those engaged in the production of primary metals, machinery, pulp and paper, chemicals, and basic textiles." On mining, the report stated: "The short supply of coal in Western Europe has at times necessitated costly imports of coal from the United States. Counterpart funds have been used to modernize mines and boost *indigenous* production to meet European needs." The report also noted that under counterpart "the equivalent of $2,450 million has been released for monetary and financial stabilization" and "$1,162 million ... for other purposes." Among these latter were "housing, relief projects, payments to German exporters, tourism, and public buildings." To reiterate, there is a logical explanation for how all of these enterprises contributed to defense, but it needs to be kept in mind that they also helped overcome the dollar gap.[66]

---

[66] MSA, March 30, 1952, 6–7, emphasis added.

The Offshore Procurement Program

The offshore procurement program (OSP) was but one facet of the MSP, but it deserves to be singled out for further examination because of the unique way it functioned in overcoming the dollar gap and because it bears out succinctly that U.S. leaders understood it that way. From the beginnings of the MAP something akin to the OSP had been on the table. A minor OSP project was in fact instituted as part of the MDAP.[67] However, U.S. officials initially moved cautiously in expanding the program. They feared that Congress would never go in for it, not without a heavy fight. The goal of the OSP was to pay foreigner countries to build armaments for the United States and western Europe, both for those nations that built the armaments and for transfer to other NATO countries, including U.S. forces in western Europe. The objective was clear – to provide western Europeans further means to earn dollars with the aim of correcting balance-of-payments deficiencies.

John Ohly headed the OSP from its inception in the fall of 1951 until the Truman administration left office. His work on offshore-type aid had begun much earlier, however, in connection with the MDAP.[68] Ohly discussed the OSP in an oral interview recorded in 1971. His frankness in describing the OSP and its role in the dollar gap crisis are striking and deserve lengthy quotation.

[J]ust as the Marshall plan [*sic*] economic aid program was scheduled for gradual phase-out and the American Congress was pressing for reductions in foreign aid, there was a new desperate need for the infusion of dollars in Europe in order to enable the NATO countries to engage in a large and rapid military build-up without suffering a disastrous collapse of their economies and, as a result of such collapse, the devastating political consequences that the Marshall plan [*sic*] had been launched to prevent.

It was under these circumstances that offshore procurement came to be considered an ideal device for the massive transfer of dollars to the European countries that might be capable of producing military equipment on a large scale for MDAP (and, to some extent, for U.S. forces as well), ideal not only because *it permitted the Executive to avoid increased requests for the increasingly unpopular*

---

[67] Theodore Tannenwald to Harriman, September 8, 1950, Harriman Papers, Truman Administration, Special Assistant, MDAP, 1951, LC; U.S. Financing of Infrastructure Costs, June 6, 1950, Bray Records, Foreign Activities, Infrastructure, 4–12–50/8–15–51, Box 12, NAII.

[68] Spofford to Ohly, July 19, 1950, Bray Records, Policy, NSC 68, April–November 1950, Box 57, NAII. This letter is dated the same day that Truman requested steep increases in military spending in response to the outbreak of the Korean War.

The Political Economy of Rearmament 243

economic aid programs but also because one end result would be the provision of the military end-items for which the funds used to finance these contracts had been appropriated. Thus, in a very real sense, the funds so used served a dual purpose – to provide foreign exchange necessary to sustain Europe's economic recovery while at the same time providing for the production of the military equipment that Europe's growing military forces required.[69]

Translated: offshore procurement became a substitute for economic aid. As the Congress had become increasingly "allergic" to such aid, the OSP made it possible to get dollars to western Europe, Japan, and other nations without calling it economic aid.[70] It was all too successful in this endeavor, as Ohly makes plain in this telling remark:

The importance of the *economic* effects of placing off-shore procurement contracts became so great that the level of such contracts that were to be placed off-shore during each of several years was determined ... by the Director for Mutual Security *on the basis of economic considerations and before the Department of Defense had finally refined its annual end-item programs and reached any conclusions of its own* with regard to the locus of procurement of the items likely to be included in such programs.[71]

Whereas the OSP clearly did serve a dual purpose – aid for defense and for the dollar gap – given such evidence it certainly cannot be argued that the economic aid aspects of it were merely accoutrements to the military aid aspects. In fact, it is quite possible that the reverse was true.

On the surface, OSP projects appear as straightforward military contracts dispersed throughout Europe for the aim of building adequate defense forces to protect western Europe from a Soviet military assault. The unsuspecting investigator into such contracts would have next to no reason for thinking that they were anything but what they purport to be. Thus, we do not learn much from the contracts themselves, even though such contracts are abundant in the archives.[72] Much more insightful is how those who understood the program discussed it. For instance, an

---

[69] John Ohly oral history, Truman Library, 92–94, emphasis added.
[70] Minutes from MAAC meeting, December 11, 1951, Ohly Papers, Box 160, Truman Library; Coolidge to Cabot, July 9, 1951, Ohly Papers, Truman Library.
[71] Ohly oral history, 92–94, emphasis added.
[72] See, for instance, RG 59, Records Relating to the Mutual Security Assistance Program, Military Assistance Coordination Division, Western European Country Files, 1952–1956 (hereinafter MSAP), Box 1 and 2, NAII. It is unfortunate that space does not permit a more detailed analysis of the OSP contracts located in these sources. Among some of the items contracted for using OSP funds were: aircraft, ammunition, minesweepers, textiles (such as blankets, socks, denim trousers and blouses, etc.), agricultural products, pharmaceuticals (including cocaine), technical films, and radios.

ECA report from April 1953 noted the following: "OSP ... provides much-needed *dollar exchange and stimulates general economic activity. The latter is significant in France because business in general, and in the metal-working industries in particular, appears to be slacking. By indirectly providing employment, OSP also contributes to political stability. In this connection, it is noteworthy that there has been no difficulty with labor with respect to OSP orders in France."[73] Furthermore, a telegram from the foreign office to British Prime Minister Winston Churchill, while he was sailing aboard the *Queen Mary*, shows that the British understood the OSP as related to the dollar gap as well. "The Americans are definitely interested in the idea of buying British Centurion tanks as an off-shore purchase for the equipment of European NATO countries, and could possibly be persuaded to allocate to the British Army some of the tanks which they bought from us. *To that extent we should be getting both tanks and dollars.*"[74]

Then there is this MDAP report from November 1950. It demonstrates that U.S. leaders also saw OSP as a means of boosting consumption in western Europe, one of the primary objectives for overcoming the dollar gap. "It is recognized that a full utilization of resources in the defense effort will generate increased demand for consumer goods and imports. Accordingly, off-shore procurement by the United States will be utilized to alleviate this demand to a limited extent by providing free dollars."[75] There is no doubt that OSP aided in the rearmament effort, but U.S. leaders and their European counterparts understood it as serving other means as well.

Base and Airfield Construction and Garrisoning U.S. Troops Abroad

There were two other ways that the Truman administration conjured up for shuttling dollars to western Europe – base and airfield construction and garrisoning U.S. soldiers abroad in massive numbers. These ways for contending with the dollar gap would likely not even be believable if it were not for Dean Acheson's penchant for hubris. Speaking retrospectively in 1954 about the Truman years as part of the Princeton Seminars,

---

[73] "Country Team Study on French Defense Production and OSP," April 17, 1953, RG 59, MSAP, Box 1, NAII, 38 (emphasis added).
[74] Foreign Office to Prime Minister on Board R.H.S "Queen Mary," January 26, 1952, FO 371/100175, TNA (emphasis added).
[75] "Basic Off-Shore Procurement Procedures," Nov. 13, 1950, MDAP, Bray Records, Policy, File 12.0720, Box 36, NAII.

The Political Economy of Rearmament

a series of colloquiums held among former members of the Truman administration in 1953 and 1954, Acheson talked of what he called an "incredibly complicated and confused" scheme for shuttling dollars to France. He recalled how the administration

> would place procurement orders in France and we would see that amounts spent through the infrastructure and the [U.S.] air force funds on the production of airfields, so that greater numbers of [U.S.] forces would be brought into France and more dollars would be spent in paying those forces, so that the balance of payments problem which went along with their budgetary problem would be solved.[76]

What is "incredibly complicated and confused" here is Acheson's discourse, not the program itself, although one might assume that Acheson is stumbling over his words because of what an incredible admission it is. Nonetheless, it is clear from his comment that the Truman administration used military spending, including the stationing of troops overseas, as a means for overcoming the dollar gap.

That Acheson was not simply engaging in a bit of that famous bravado when he made this claim is clear from a letter from William Draper, Jr., special representative in Europe, to President Eisenhower from June 1953, written on the occasion of the former's retirement from that office. The point of the letter was to provide his thoughts on the political, economic, and defense problems facing the United States in Europe, but he also had this to say:

> Five years ago commercial exports and services from the dollar area exceeded exports and services from the European Payments Union Area (to include the sterling bloc) by over five billion dollars. This commercial dollar gap has been greatly reduced, and is currently not over two billions a year. ... During this calendar year extraordinary dollar expenditures in Europe by the United States (nearly one billion of military and construction spending by our troops, another billion of economic aid expenditures, and a half billion in payments for off-shore procurement deliveries) will more than close the 1953 commercial gap.[77]

The British archives offer further proof that aid for airfield construction served as a way for the British to earn dollars to close the dollar

[76] Princeton Seminars, March 14, 1954, Acheson Papers, reel 6, track 1, Box 97, 10, Truman Library.
[77] William Draper, Jr., to President Eisenhower, June 5, 1950, *Declassified Documents Reference System* (Farmington Hills, Mich.: Gale, 2009), CK3100188849, 4.

246 *NSC 68 and the Political Economy of the Early Cold War*

gap. For instance, one memorandum noted the following: "More recently the Americans have proposed to expand the [airfield] construction programme by adding further items estimated to cost about £55 million. They have offered to pay the whole of this themselves, provided that we will pay half the increased cost of the original programme. Their proposal would enable us to earn a substantial sum in dollars."[78] Another, reporting on a discussion held among U.S. and British officials, had a Mr. Tuthill of the U.S. embassy "stress[ing] that the American objectives were identical to our own, namely to make an early contribution towards the airfields construction programme to give us help with our balance of payments."[79]

The ISAC records also shed light on this type of aid. A lengthy report from the ISAC dated October 16, 1951, tells the tale. The report concerned the "status of [the] negotiations re defense expenditures" then taking place between the United States and its western European allies. The report detailed in separate sections each nation's progress with respect to the issue at hand. Our interest here is on the section pertaining to Denmark.

First, the document spells out the progress of negotiations undertaken thus far in regard to mutual security between the United States and Denmark. In other words, it analyzes what the Danes had accomplished and not accomplished in this direction. It calls attention to such aspects of the Danish program as their commitment to honor previous pledges with regard to rearmament; Denmark's "establishment of 3 infantry divisions and 2 armored regiments ... in addition to ... 2 more regimental combat teams"; the development of a "night-fighter squadron, to cost some 25 million kroner ($3.5 million)"; providing a brigade to General Eisenhower, then NATO commander, for Germany; and that no further commitments on Navy and Air Force could be expected.

The document then turns its attention to the current state of negotiations, remarking, "Since the 1950/51 aid amount was allotted no formal negotiations have been held with the Danes. It has been ECA's intention to reopen such negotiations as soon as the pending foreign aid legislation is enacted." Next, it turns to the issue of the "main obstacles" blocking the way toward further commencement of the mutual security program with Denmark. These are (1) "their touchiness about possible infringements of

---

[78] "Construction of air fields in the United Kingdom for the United States Air Force," [1952], FO 371/100156, TNA.
[79] "United States Air Fields in the United Kingdom," [1952], FO 371/100156, TNA.

The Political Economy of Rearmament

their sovereignty"; (2) "inertia that has permeated the armed forces, and particularly the general staff, as a result of 100-year-old pacificist traditions in Denmark"; and (3) "the feeling that their economic problems are insurmountable and uncontrollable."

For our purposes, the final paragraph dealing with the Danish in this section of the report contains an important message: "The first two obstacles have diminished over the past two years, and will probably continue to do so. With respect to economic problems, however, the Danes seem determined to be as sticky as possible on this point. However, there are many actions that they could take, even without further ECA aid, that would directly improve their situation. Not least of these is a greatly expanded productivity drive and *a strong attempt to obtain food and textile contracts from the U.S. Army in Europe.*"[80] To be sure, this provides but one example of this type of aid, but it was a practice repeated throughout western Europe, especially as the U.S. military presence there grew following the implementation of NSC 68.

One of the main achievements for the defense of western Europe under NSC 68 was the garrisoning of four divisions of American troops, a number that by 1955 had increased to five. All told in the decade of the 1950s, more than three million troops were stationed in western Europe, a number that held firm in the 1960s, dipped to just below three million in the 1970s, and shot back up to more than three million in the 1980s before dropping off with the end of the Cold War in the 1990s.[81] The influx of such a huge number of servicemen and women and their families was something akin to hitting the jackpot for western Europe, at least insofar as its ability to earn dollars was concerned. Two articles from *The New York Times* from 1957 demonstrate this fact concretely. The articles focus on West Germany, but the implications for all of western Europe are clear. One of the articles noted that there were 250,000 troops in Germany at that time and that housing and garrisoning them and their families required huge facilities, all of which include "schools, hospitals, shopping centers, theaters, clubs, playing fields, and gymnasiums," and no doubt the materials and local labor to build and staff them. The article then went on to discuss the fact that, with such a large influx of G.I.s,

---

[80] "Status of Negotiations re Defense Expenditures," October 16, 1951, RG 59, Executive Secretariat Subject Files Relating to the ISAC, 1951–1952, Box 1, NAII, emphasis added.

[81] Tim Kane, Ph.D., *Global U.S. Troop Deployment, 1950–2005* (Washington, D.C.: The Heritage Foundation, 2006), http://www.heritage.org/Research/Reports/2006/05/Global-US-Troop-Deployment-1950–2005

there were bound to be frictions between them and their hosts, and no doubt there were. However, the article pointed out, "the German population has been educated by its Government to understand that the survival of West Germany ... depend[s] entirely on the continued presence of United States military power." Then it noted that "there is also the economic factor. A large amount of money is spent every year by United States servicemen for West German goods and services and by the United States military establishment for direct procurement on the German market. The amount of dollar expenditures runs into hundreds of millions annually and plays an important role in Germany's balance of payments with dollar area countries."[82]

The other article in the same edition of the paper more directly addressed the issue of tensions among G.I.s and Germans. The story focused on an area of Kaiserslautern, a city with a very large G.I. presence, known as Steinstrasse, "a shabby street winding through a rundown section of this garrison town" that has earned the reputation as "the most notorious army bordello district in Germany." The focus of the article was an incident that had occurred in the past, which is not of interest to us. What is of interest is the picture it paints of the role of the American G.I. as human "pump primer" for the West Germany economy. "Each night hundreds, and pay-day nights thousands of American servicemen used to swarm into the Steinstrasse area," the article explains, "overflowing twenty-three seedy cabarets and providing a livelihood to 3,000 prostitutes. In Birdland, the New York Bar and similar 'American' establishments, German musicians pounded out synthetic jazz while waiters served up cheap wine at a \$1.50 a glass." Then the military put the area off limits, however, leading to a most interesting reaction. "The off-limits order, issued at the Mayor [of Kaiserslautern]'s request, brought forth a spate of new citizens' committees. These committees demanded redress for the injury done to Steinstrasse businessmen [by the decree]." So "on Nov. 13 the Army command revoked the original off-limits order and declared Steinstrasse open to servicemen again from 7 A.M. to 7 P.M." The article goes on to say that "the Kaiserslautern experience is not unique." As a case in point, it noted that "there are 135 United States military installations in southern Germany, and similar minor crises have flared and faded at other places."[83]

[82] M. S. Handler, "The G.I. Abroad: He Learns to Coexist," *The New York Times*, December 30, 1957, 1.

[83] Arthur J. Oslen, "Incident Flares and Fades," *The New York Times*, December 30, 1957, 4.

The Political Economy of Rearmament

It is an amazing thing to think about. All those G.I.s stationed in France, in Italy, in Germany, in the Netherlands, in Great Britain, in Denmark, and elsewhere, spending their dollars in beer halls, brothels, ballrooms, bistros, and just about everywhere else imaginable, were unbeknownst to them (although not to U.S. leaders) overcoming the dollar gap and helping to forge a multilateral world order.

Other Achievements

In addition to the military assistance programs, and such efforts as the Offshore Procurement Program and utilizing troops as pump primers, rearmament helped initiate a number of other policies that Truman administration foreign policy officials and other elites had deemed necessary to overcome the dollar gap in their deliberations throughout 1949 and 1950. What could not be accomplished purely on economic and political grounds could be achieved through rearmament.

Maintaining Economic Aid beyond 1952

As we saw in Chapter 4, U.S. officials were aware even as the Marshall Plan began operating that economic assistance would be necessary beyond 1952, the year the Marshall Plan was scheduled to end. Although they did not share this information with either the U.S. Congress or the American people, this knowledge was a rather frank assessment that the dollar gap would require long-term and far-ranging solutions. In the meantime, the United States would have to continue funding the dollar gap, lest the western world "collapse." The problem, of course, was that Congress could not be counted on to provide continued aid beyond 1952. As we saw in Chapter 3, achieving passage of the Marshall Plan in 1948 was no easy task and the Truman administration resorted to initiating a war scare to get it through. Not only that, but each year Congress reviewed the program and made cuts where it thought appropriate often to the dismay of administration officials. Thus, administration officials were very apprehensive that Congress would provide further economic aid. Of course, we will never know what would have happened. Administration officials did not wait around to find out. Instead, rearmament came to the rescue.

Rearmament obviated the need to ask Congress for economic aid on its own merits and made it necessary for the western Europeans'

250   NSC 68 and the Political Economy of the Early Cold War

rearmament programs. Here is how one of the architects of the OSP put the matter in July 1950:

> The most urgent problem before the United States is no longer how to close the "dollar gap" on the assumption that the present modest scale of rearmament will continue and that the free nations will devote themselves to the achievement of the fullest possible measure of self-support by 1952. The most urgent problem is to determine the maximum contribution which the free nations can make toward the mutual defense, measured by their industrial resources and manpower; and then to determine the amount of aid which the United States must furnish to make such optimum contribution possible.[84]

Western European countries had needed U.S. economic assistance to cover the dollar gap. However, with NSC 68 and the Korean War the United States had begun pushing the western Europeans to rearm. Their budgets were already pushed to the hilt, however. Rearmament, if it were to happen, therefore, would have had to come at the expense of economic recovery, and the people of western Europe would not stand for it. So, went the argument, the United States would have to provide economic aid for the rearmament programs. The fact of the matter is, though, that the dollar gap still remained. And it would still remain after 1952, making economic aid a continuing necessity. Nonetheless, rearmament stopped Congress dead in its tracks. Very few congressmen or women were willing to vote down appropriations tied to rearmament. Thus did economic aid continue year in and year out as part of mutual security aid.

Western European Integration

It will be remembered that one of the key solutions to ending the dollar gap that administration officials and other elites pondered in 1949 and 1950, chronicled in Chapter 4, was western European political and economic integration, to include bringing West Germany in as a full-fledged member. The idea behind such integration was that it would spur a "United States of Europe," by which they really meant a multilateral economy in Europe in which trade barriers would disappear, comparative advantage and regional specialization would trump national economies, labor and currency flow obstructions would be eradicated, and productivity as well as consumption thereby enhanced. Without such integration it was believed, at least by U.S. officials, that western Europe

---

[84] Tracy Voorhees to Gordon Gray, July 17, 1950, Truman Administration, Special Assistant, Harriman Papers, Box 302, LC, 2.

The Political Economy of Rearmament   251

simply would not be able to produce at a high enough rate to overcome the dollar gap at the level of production the United States was capable of and deemed necessary to secure its own prosperity and free market system. Given that situation, the western Europeans would have had no choice but eventually to cut their trade with the United States, as indeed the British began to do in the summer of 1949. They would have had, thus, to pursue some form of autarchy and/or likely develop closer ties with the Soviet bloc. Europe itself certainly would have fragmented, with Great Britain clinging to Imperial Preference and the continent left open to German or Soviet domination. Either way, western Europe would be turning its back on multilateralism, dooming it. However, as we saw, the Europeans were not ready for such integration. The political will was not there, and the nationalism remained too strong.

In this environment, Truman administration officials seized on security as the means through which to achieve western European integration absent economic and political motivations alone to achieve that goal. It is in this context that the formation of the North Atlantic Treaty Organization, signed by ten European nations plus the United States and Canada, was formed in April 1949. NATO was not devised solely to promote western European integration in order to tackle the dollar gap, nor was it devised solely to defend against Soviet aggression. It was, rather, devised to give the western Europeans some cause around which to integrate their economies and find common political ground, especially with regard to West Germany, which was becoming increasingly restless. As Leffler has written, "The Truman administration supported the Atlantic alliance *primarily* because it was indispensable to the promotion of European stability through German integration."[85]

In July 1950, a step toward integration was achieved with the establishment of the European Payments Union (EPU). The EPU was designed to enhance intra-European trade by making the currencies of the seventeen Marshall Plan countries convertible. Because Britain was a signatory, the union also included the sterling area, a major advancement given Britain's opposition to integration just months earlier. Another step toward integration occurred with the formation of the European Coal and Steel Community (ECSC) in April 1951. This organization, comprised of West Germany, France, Italy, Belgium, Luxembourg, and the Netherlands,

---

[85] Melvyn Leffler, *A Preponderance of Power: National Security, the Truman Administration, and the Cold War* (Stanford, California: Stanford University Press, 1992), 282, emphasis added.

abolished customs duties on these products among the member nations and sought to create a "single, free and competitive market that is to expand production, assure employment and raise living standards."[86] Then, there was the European Defense Community proposed in October 1950 in response to the United States' call for West German rearmament.

What role did NSC 68 play, then, in western European integration? Although each of these institutions reflected moves toward integration, they were encumbered with difficulties. The EPU had the greatest initial success, but the ECSC almost never materialized and in early 1952 it was still plagued with problems. Not until May 1953 did the first steel produced by the community roll off the production line.[87] As for the EDC, it never did become a reality, as the French refused to accede to West German rearmament. This is where NSC 68 came in. Given the tenuous nature of these institutions, NSC 68 gave teeth to NATO as a means of securing integration until such a time as those institutions could become viable. Here is how *The New York Times* explained the situation:

Western European integration, preached incessantly by United States officials for three years as a means of increasing production by reducing or eliminating national trade barriers, gathered notable momentum in spite of great obstacles in 1951.

It acquired a double motive – economic and defensive – and it proceeded so to speak on two levels: that of the economic cooperation slowly developed under the Marshall Plan, and that of defensive planning, which was more rapidly developed after the Korean war and stimulated greater rearmament efforts.

On the first level were the consistent and largely successful efforts to make the European payments plan work as a means of financing intra-European trade by ensuring convertibility of European currencies, and the proposals for collective action by Governments to check inflation while expanding production.

On the second level were the efforts, notably by the Temporary Council Committee of the North Atlantic Treaty Organization, to attain a better coordinated and more serious program for building up armed forces in Western Europe in the three years ending June, 1954. *This entailed both military and economic integration.*[88]

True western European economic integration was not achieved until the Treaty of Maastricht, signed in 1993, forming the European Community.

---

[86] "History is Made in Paris," *The New York Times*, April 19, 1951, 30.
[87] "Problems of Unity," *The New York Times*, January 31, 1952, 26; Harold Callender, "First 'European' Steel Cast; Single Market Starts Today," *The New York Times*, May 1, 1953, 1, quotations in original.
[88] Harold Calendar, "Integration Drive Gaining Momentum," January 3, 1952, *The New York Times*, 47, emphasis added.

The Political Economy of Rearmament

Political unity still remains elusive. Meanwhile, NATO not only continues to function but has begun absorbing former Eastern-bloc countries.

West German Integration

The problem of Germany had plagued U.S. foreign policy officials long before the end of WWII. Disagreements existed among those who believed a revitalized Germany was crucial to western European economic recovery and, thus, to overcoming the dollar gap, and those who believed that Germany should never again be allowed to develop heavy industry and armaments capability. Under Truman, the former officials won out, but they faced many obstacles in pushing their plans for Germany. For one thing, hardly anyone else agreed with them. Although the British generally could be counted on to side with the United States, the Soviet Union, France, and just about all of Germany's neighbors – who had suffered the brunt of German aggression – wanted to see Germany kept weak. Even the first U.S. plan for postwar Germany, Joint Chiefs of Staff document 1067, called for as much. Truman administration officials, therefore, had to walk a thin line as they set about with their plans to revitalize Germany.

The story of how they did so has been well told. By 1950, the Federal Republic of Germany (West Germany) had been created and its reindustrialization was moving forward. However, due primarily to French opposition, West Germany retained second-class status within the western European community, which prevented it from reaching its full productive potential and thereby aiding western European economic recovery. Furthermore, the West Germans were getting restless. U.S. officials feared that West Germany might strike off on its own and push for reunification with East Germany and either into a position of neutrality or alignment with the Soviet bloc if its full incorporation into the western bloc was not achieved. "The movement toward economic integration does not appear to be rapid enough to provide Western Germany [sic] with adequate economic opportunities in the West," NSC 68 noted. There was, too, always the possibility that German aggression would reassert itself if Germany went it alone. The Department of Defense was particularly concerned with this potential outcome.

The answer to the multifaceted dilemma that was West Germany, implied more than stated directly in NSC 68, was West German rearmament. The goal, as Thomas McCormick has aptly stated it, was to "restore some sense of [West] German national grandeur, but within a

254   *NSC 68 and the Political Economy of the Early Cold War*

collective framework that would not threaten the security of Western Europe but keep German political-economic leaders committed to the American rules of internationalism." This, McCormick correctly notes, "two months before the Korean War."[89] The war, as with so much else, paved the way for West German rearmament or, at least, to having open and frank discussions about it. With Korea serving as proof of Soviet aggression, administration officials were able to tell the British and the French that their goal was West German rearmament. Putting the pressure on, they made the stationing of four U.S. divisions in Europe contingent on British and French acceptance of it. To make the idea more palatable, they offered additional military assistance. The French, nonetheless, protested that it was too soon for West German rearmament. They contended that the Soviet Union had no interest in war and that rearming West Germany would be unnecessarily provocative.

It is in this context that the French proposed the European Defense Community (EDC). An all-European force distinct from NATO, the EDC was France's attempt to get out from under U.S. control. It was to include twelve German units and four British divisions, the latter so as to ensure that West Germany would not dominate on the continent. More than anything, however, the EDC aimed at slowing West German rearmament. As Melvyn Leffler has written, the creation of such an institution "presupposed the creation of a federated Europe into which the European members would merge a great deal of their sovereignty," a process that "would take years."[90] Truman administration officials deplored the EDC but could not publicly admit as much. Thus, they simply moved ahead with their plans to strengthen NATO on the basis of NSC 68, to include integrating a rearmed West Germany into the western European community as a full-fledged member, while paying lip service to the EDC. In the end, they won out. In December 1954, France accepted West Germany's inclusion into NATO, and West Germany went on to become the "workshop" of Europe that administration officials had planned all along.

Restarting Triangular Trade

Although this aspect of the rearmament program is touched on under the MSP, it deserves further comment. Rearmament also aided in

---

[89] McCormick, *America's Half-Century*, 106.
[90] Leffler, *A Preponderance of Power*, 390.

The Political Economy of Rearmament

overcoming the dollar gap by getting dollars into "third areas" that would ultimately find their way back into the NATO countries' hands. This goal was accomplished primarily through the stockpiling of raw materials, deemed "necessary" in light of the Communist attack on Korea. Without dismissing that as a necessity, it should be remembered as argued in Chapter 4, that such a "scheme" was believed to be one way to end the dollar gap long before anyone had to contemplate what a U.S. response to war between North and South Korea would be. The problem then was that there was no incentive. Rearmament under NSC 68 proved to be that incentive. In the end, the Korean War proved to be the impetus, but the effect was all the same. Stockpiling purchases by the United States restarted triangular trade and went a long way toward overcoming the dollar gap. The key example is natural rubber. Due to the United States' stockpiling effort, "United States purchases of natural rubber quadrupled between 1949 and 1951, making the product America's second most valuable import," notes historian Andrew Rotter in his superb study of the origins of U.S. involvement in Vietnam. Because a great portion of the rubber came from British Malaya, "by early 1951, Malaya's export surplus was more than $1.1 billion and climbing." In light of this, "American dollars were now more accessible to the British," writes Rotter, "who needed only to sell more extensively to their colony" in order to close the dollar gap between Britain and the United States. This effort applied to Japan and western Europe as well. For instance, administration officials often forced Southeast Asian suppliers of raw materials to purchase industrial goods from Japan, thus putting dollars in Japanese hands for purchases in the United States. "In certain situations," noted Director of the Bureau of the Budget Frederick Lawton, "stockpiling was a partial substitute for foreign aid." Or, as Averell Harriman, put it: "Some of us wanted to get some political and economic judgements brought into the stockpiling purchasing."[91]

Restarting triangular trade was essential to overcoming the dollar gap. Although the initial spike in the cost of raw materials caused by rearmament was a setback for the western Europeans, because it increased the costs of their recovery effort and the rearmament program and caused a momentary inflationary rise on their domestic fronts, over time it

---

[91] Andrew Rotter, *The Path to Vietnam: Origins of the American Commitment to Southeast Asia* (Ithaca, New York: Cornell University Press, 1987), 207; Princeton Seminars, October 10, 1953, Acheson Papers, reel 1, track 2, 14, Box 97, Truman Library.

Keeping Western Europe in the United States' Camp

Finally, rearmament kept western Europe fully wedded to the United States, thereby preventing the dissolution of the global economy. The major fear of an enduring dollar gap, especially after the end of the Marshall Plan in 1952, was that the western Europeans would, through no choice of their own, move out of the U.S. orbit into either neutrality or closer ties with the Soviet Union, either of which would have certainly meant autarchy. As a result, the nascent global economy would fragment, not unlike the 1930s. Through rearmament, the United States in effect merged its economy with western Europe, making it virtually impossible for it to pursue either course. However, disturbing as the prospect of neutrality was, what U.S. officials really feared was that western Europe might look east for its trade. If that occurred, then the United States would likely lose western Europe as a trading partner as well as political and military partner, ensuring the isolation of the United States to the western hemisphere.

U.S. officials had reason to be concerned. Prior to Korea and NSC 68, the effort to prevent any potential closer association between western Europe and the Soviet Union came in the form of blocking East-West trade as much as possible on the grounds of security. However, U.S. officials found that the western Europeans were not as enthusiastic as they had hoped about stopping East-West trade. Repeatedly, western Europeans ignored the restrictions U.S. leaders imposed on such trade. More than that, as economic conditions worsened throughout 1949 and into 1950, western Europeans had no choice but to look eastward. For instance, an ECA memorandum from the summer of 1950 noted that "German industrialists are becoming increasingly inclined to deal with Eastern Europe, including East Germany, rather than the West." This was something of which to be truly afraid.[92] Rearmament opened an opportunity to prevent

---

[92] U.S. embassy in Paris to ECA administrator, August 16, 1950, RG 59, Bray Records, NAII.

The Political Economy of Rearmament

this from occurring, and U.S. policymakers seized on it. This policy, more than anything else, explains why U.S. officials often appear in the evidence more eager for western European rearmament than the western Europeans themselves, who allegedly would most benefit from the rearmament.

In this, the United States essentially forced rearmament on the western Europeans. It was a matter of accepting military/economic aid under rearmament or nothing. Great Britain provides a key example. At the end of 1950, Britain announced that it was terminating Marshall Plan aid two years early. For all appearances Britain had licked the dollar gap and was on the way to full recovery. But that was not the case at all. On October 6, 1950, the ECA delivered an aide memoire to Britain proposing "an almost complete cessation of ECA aid." According to a November 27, 1950, MDAP memorandum, the memoire had "induced a state of profound shock among Britain's planners," apparently by the fact that they had failed to offer a reply. As a result, Britain, the memorandum said, was "pulling back" and seeking "a new approach," one that would emphasize common defense efforts. In other words, the United States had forced Britain to accept rearmament in lieu of Marshall Plan aid. The British had little choice but to accept this offer. When the British announced that they were terminating Marshall Plan funding early, then, it was not because they wanted to; they were given little choice.[93]

Given this, some scholars have characterized the defensive umbrella the United States constructed via NSC 68 not as the "containment" of the Soviet Union but of its allies. There is much to be said for this argument. The extent to which the United States extended its power over its allies in respect to (1) economic and fiscal policies, including tariff levels, currency convertibility, taxation and inflation rates, the nature and extent of investments, and the ratio of social to military spending; (2) military policies, including the size, composition and disposition of military forces, and terms of any military draft; and (3) foreign policies, especially those concerning political and economic relations with the Soviet Union, the People's Republic of China, and any other area outside the control of the United States, is indeed striking.[94] To occasion this remarkable

---

[93] Bray to Ohly, "UK Production Programs and Defense Efforts," November 27, 1950, RG 59, Bray Records, MDAP, NSC–NAT, Box 59, NAII. A report developed in the ISAC put it this way: "The assumption implicit in discussions and documents relating to aid in 1952 are that there must be economic aid in the traditional form – that such aid should be conditional – for example, on agreement by countries that they will reach certain levels of defense effort," ISAC D-14/3, October 1, 1951, ISAC, Box 2, NAII.

[94] Frank Kofsky, "Did the Truman Administration Deliberately Prolong the Korean War?," unpublished paper in the author's possession.

development, the United States essentially integrated its economy with those of western Europe and Japan, in the first instance, and then coaxed others on board through generous economic and technical aid. Here is how Acheson described this process with regard to France, but with clear implications for other nations as well. The administration, he remarked, went about

> using the whole NATO business as an instrument of foreign policy in and of itself to get the French to do internal French things. That I have always thought was an aspect of NATO which was quite overlooked, and a very powerful one, because in connection with doing NATO business, steps forward in NATO, and in connection with NATO meetings and discussions, you could quite properly intervene very seriously in French internal affairs, because they weren't [any longer] French internal affairs, they were NATO internal affairs. And the French budget and the French attitude toward Germany and everything else became a matter of common concern.[95]

In this manner, the United States "contained" western Europe and its other allies even as it sought to rebuild them into viable trading partners. Through methods such as these, wholly impossible absent the rearmament program that was NSC 68, the nascent global economy that the multilateralists in the Truman administration were so determined to create was saved.

---

[95] Princeton Seminars, December 11, 1953, Acheson Papers, reel 2, track 2, Truman Library, 6.

Conclusion

The rearmament program known as NSC 68 accomplished its goals, although the effort to establish a multilateral, global economy certainly did not end with NSC 68. Nonetheless, through it the immediate crisis of the postwar era – the impending end of the Marshall Plan in 1952 with the dollar gap still in existence – was overcome and the groundwork laid for that "liberal global economic regime" of which James Baker spoke so glowingly before the Rotary Club in 1994.[1] Furthermore, NSC 68 ensconced western Europe, Japan, and many other nations under the U.S. defense umbrella, thereby keeping the "free world" intact when it was otherwise poised to splinter. The United States would not face economic isolation in the western hemisphere, as Paul Nitze had so feared, after all. Nor did the "Western World" collapse in 1952, as a distraught Dean Acheson had predicted if the dollar gap were not overcome. For these multilateralists, military spending, under the auspices of NSC 68, proved the right medicine. Yet, we must ask, was it worth it?

In 1951, the basic assumptions of Soviet intentions as laid down in NSC 68 underwent review as part of a new NSC paper series titled NSC 114. In this context, Soviet expert Charles Bohlen offered two particularly damaging analyses of Acheson's and Nitze's pet project. Both are worthy of quoting at length. The first was from September 25 and was written in response to a memorandum Nitze had authored on September 22 making the case that the analysis of Soviet intentions found in NSC 68 was essentially accurate. Bohlen's stinging critique is sobering, to say the least:

---

[1] See the Introduction of the present study.

259

260   *Conclusion*

The ... issue ... is whether or not the NSC 68 analysis of the Soviet Union is sufficiently accurate to serve as a guide for U.S. Government interpretation of Soviet actions and for an estimate of probable future Soviet moves. My entire position is that it is not; that it is not a true picture of how the Soviet Union operates insofar as I have observed and studied it. Furthermore, I contend that Soviet actions since April 1950 do not fall harmoniously within the analysis of NSC 68. It must be recalled that NSC 68, the master paper on the Soviet Union, was completed less than three months before the Soviet Union took its most important single action since the close of hostilities, i.e., Korea. Yet NSC 68 would not set anybody's mind to think of the probability of such type action on the part of the Soviet bloc. In fact, as I read it, it rather tends to the thought that isolated actions of this character are less rather than more likely in the light of the general Soviet design. Furthermore, it seems to me that the significance of Korea and Chinese intervention particularly has been analyzed in light of NSC 68 rather than as checks to determine the validity of the general thesis.[2]

The October 9 memorandum continues this critique of NSC 68.

[NSC 68] totally ignores, except for one brief phrase on page 20, the role of the Soviet internal situation in Soviet policies and actions. I believe there is powerful evidence in the history of the Soviet Union to show that the internal situation is the single greatest controlling force in its foreign policy; yet this is virtually ignored in the entire [NSC] 68 series, and anyone reading this paper would inescapably conclude that the opportunity, risk and the strength of its opponents are the only factors controlling and affecting Soviet actions. No attempt whatsoever is made to analyze the great body of Soviet thought in regard to war between states or the even more elementary fact that any war, whether the prospect of victory be dim or bright, carries with it major risks to the Soviet system in Russia. The fact of war alone, its attendant mobilization, added strain on an already strained economy, exposure of Soviet soldiers to external influences, the entire problem of defection, the relationship of party to Army, the question of the peasantry and many other factors, which I am convinced are predominantly present in Soviet thinking on any question of war, are either ignored or treated as insignificant.[3]

Bohlen apparently was not against the military buildup that constituted NSC 68 and believed that, in Soviet actions and intentions, there was justification for it. His complaint was that NSC 68 had badly, even recklessly, stated them. Nonetheless, Bohlen's comments certainly give us pause to consider the question of whether it was all worth it.

---

[2] Memorandum from Counselor Charles "Chip" Bohlen to Secretary of State Dean Acheson, September 25, 1951, *Foreign Relations of the United States* (hereinafter *FRUS*), *1951* 1 (Washington, D.C.: U.S. Government Printing Office, 1979): 177–178.

[3] Policy Planning Staff Memorandum, September 22, 1951, *FRUS, 1951* 1 (Washington, D.C.: U.S. Government Printing Office, 1979): 172–175 (this is written by Nitze); Bohlen to Acheson, October 9, 1951, ibid., 180–181.

Conclusion

261

Acheson, also gives us plenty of reason to ponder this question. In his famed memoir *Present at the Creation*, not only did he remark that NSC 68 was designed to "bludgeon the mass mind of top government," a telling admission that raises the issue of whether the authors of NSC 68 were attempting to dupe the president (if so, they did not succeed), but he also said the following in describing what the document's argument sought to accomplish:

> The task of the public officer seeking to explain and gain support for a major policy is not that of the writer of a doctoral thesis. Qualification must give way to simplicity of statement, nicety and nuance to bluntness, almost brutality, in carrying home a point. It is better to carry the hearer or reader into the quadrant of one's thought than merely to make a noise or to mislead him utterly. ... If [in writing NSC 68] we made our points *clearer than truth*, we did not differ from most other educators and could hardly do otherwise.[4]

Given this sentiment, expressed by one of the principle authors of NSC 68, we certainly have reason to ask whether NSC 68 was, in fact, worth it.

If the argument put forward in the foregoing chapters is accurate, the *primary* threat facing the United States in the immediate postwar era was not the Soviet Union but a world torn to shreds by two world wars and a major depression in between that caused a structural imbalance in the global economy. The Soviet Union could have retreated back behind its borders and closed itself off from the global economy, much as it had done before being brought by force into world affairs by Hitler's attack, and the problems posed by this imbalance, most notably in the form of the dollar gap, still would have existed and been in need of correcting if multilateralism were to succeed. This observation is not merely conjecture on my part. American leaders said as much, as when Dean Acheson noted before Congress in 1950, as he was at the same time in the throes of writing NSC 68, that "even if there were no Russia, if there were no communism, we would still face very grave problems in trying to exist and strengthen those parts of the free world which have been so badly shaken by the war and its consequences, the two wars and the consequences of both of them;"[5] or as in NSC 68 when the authors argued that "even if there were no Soviet Union we would face the great problem of the free

---

[4] Dean Acheson, *Present at the Creation: My Years in the State Department* (New York: W. W. Norton, 1969), 375 (emphasis added).

[5] Dean Acheson, quoted in U.S. Senate, Senate Committee on Foreign Relations, *Reviews of the World Situation, 1949–1950* (Washington, D.C.: U.S. Government Printing Office, 1975), 108.

262   *Conclusion*

society, accentuated many fold in this industrial age, of reconciling order, security, the need for participation, with the requirement of freedom."[6]

There were alternatives to multilateralism pushed by responsible, thinking individuals well versed in international affairs. The progressive internationalists' push for international economic planning on a regional basis, coupled with U.S.-Soviet cooperation, was one such alternative. A garrison state centered on the western hemisphere and guarded by a strong air force and navy, rather than an expensive standing army, was another. Harry Truman's labor-friendly Fair Deal was yet another. These alternatives were anathema to the multilateralists, however. For them, failure to reestablish a multilateral, global economy was simply unfathomable. They saw WWII as their "second chance" to create such an economy, and they were not going to squander it. Not the U.S. Congress, not the American people, not the dollar gap, not the Europeans, not the Communists – no one and no thing was going to stand in the way of seeing the project fulfilled. And that might not have been a problem if only the world economy were not so broken. The fact is that it was broken to the point at which constructing that economy on free-market principles alone, that is, letting multilateralism works its alleged magic all on its own, proved impossible. Thus, they turned to using non-free-market, or state, solutions to cope with the crisis, with deleterious consequences.

In analyzing these consequences, we can identify three aspects to the problem. One is the consequences incurred by creating an exaggerated depiction of the Soviet threat to cajole Congress and the American people into supporting the administration's foreign economic goals. Another is the consequences that inhered from using militarization as a pump priming agent, in this case to overcome the dollar gap. Finally, there are the consequences that accrued from the very devotion to multilateralism itself.

Consequences of Creating an Exaggerated Depiction of the Soviet Threat

In order to get Congress and the American people to support the administration's foreign economic policies, the multilateralists adopted a strategy of conjuring up an exaggerated depiction of the Soviet threat. This image emerged in and through the administration's battles with Congress to fund the economic aid programs that the administration formulated to cope with the dollar gap and keep their dream of multilateralism alive.

---

[6] NSC 68, *FRUS, 1950* (Washington, DC: U.S. Government Printing Office, 1975), 1: 262–263.

Conclusion 263

It painted the Soviet leaders as people who were hell-bent on the world-wide spread of communism and would stop at nothing until their goal was met. To be sure, administration officials were not alone responsible for the image. It was encouraged by the media, popular pundits, academics, clergy, and members of Congress, among others. These groups, in turn, benefitted in their own way by these actions. But the administration's use of the image at crucial moments to push its agenda, namely, during the debates on the British loan, the Greco-Turkish aid bill, and the Marshall Plan, and in attempting to gain support for the rearmament program that was at the heart of NSC 68, lent heavy weight to the image's acceptance by the majority of Americans. Whereas the fear mongering involved in this domestic political game probably had little bearing on actual East-West relations, it backed the administration into a corner such that it had little choice but to live up to its claims, which had the effect of discouraging cooperation with the Soviet Union and contributing to the origins of the Cold War. Three incidences during the Truman years bear out this reality: discounting of the Soviets' "peace offensive" in 1949–1950, sabotaging of the Korean peace talks in 1951, and rejecting Stalin's apparently sincere effort to arrive at a peace treaty for Germany in 1952. The fact is that by then the administration had no interest in ending the Cold War. It was serving its interests too well. Subsequent administrations followed a similar path. Furthermore, it helped fuel the postwar red scare that gave the United States loyalty oaths, government lists of subversive organizations, and McCarthyism, each of which did far more harm than good. To this day, most Americans still believe in the image, which contributes to a false sense of their nation's place in the world and justifies the United States' continued role as global hegemon with all of the consequences that have followed therefrom.

The Consequences of Using Rearmament to Overcome the Dollar Gap

Using rearmament to overcome the dollar gap had a number of devastating, long-term consequences. One was the unnecessary militarization of the Cold War. To be sure, by the time NSC 68 went to the president tensions between the two nations were already high and the Soviet Union had reversed its demilitarization efforts and had begun modestly rebuilding its military. The emphasis here, however, needs to be on the word modestly, for it was not engaging in any way in the kind of arms buildup NSC 68 ascribed to it. It was, indeed, NSC 68 that was responsible for the subsequent arms race that came, perhaps more than anything else, to symbolize the Cold War, especially in regard to nuclear weapons. As this study has shown, there was plenty of opposition to building the hydrogen bomb. Furthermore, if his biographer is correct, Nitze only wanted the hydrogen bomb for what it could do to mobilize the administration to pursue conventional rearmament. He hoped that studying the feasibility of building the "Super" would, in fact, turn out to be in the negative. A similar case could be made for Acheson. If true, then the conclusion that must be drawn is that Nitze and Acheson were willing to gamble with the hydrogen bomb in order to get what they really wanted – a reexamination of overall national security so that they could push through massive rearmament to contend with the dollar gap. The problem with that gamble, of course, is that the H-bomb did prove to be feasible. The Americans exploded their first hydrogen bomb in November 1952; the Soviets followed with theirs in August 1953. Thereafter, each side pursued nuclear weapons stockpiles with a vengeance. This effort included years of nuclear weapons testing and the ever present possibility of a nuclear war occurring either deliberately or by accident. As we have dismantled many of these weapons since the end of the Cold War, finding a place to store the nuclear material has become a trying task. At the same time, nuclear proliferation remains a searing issue in international affairs, as India, Pakistan, Iran, and North Korea have developed the capacity to create nuclear weapons, with potentially devastating consequences for the world.

A further consideration is the extent to which militarization actually worked. On the one hand, the methods Truman administration officials devised to cope with the dollar gap crisis through the use of military spending might well be considered ingenious. Stationing more troops abroad so they would spend dollars in the local economies; paying nations in dollars to build weapons that otherwise could have been produced in the United States; reconfiguring economic aid as necessary for security so that it could continue beyond 1952; using rearmament to restart triangular trade; using the notion of "mutual security" to rebuild the western European infrastructure as well as to achieve its integration and keep it wedded to the United States – these were all amazing feats of diplomacy. And they can be considered to have worked to an extent. They did prevent western Europe from breaking away from the United States. They did help achieve European economic growth; by 1958 the western Europeans were largely able to earn all the dollars they needed to trade with the United States. In effect, multilateralism, so long the goal of U.S. policymakers, was saved as a result of NSC 68.

Conclusion

On the other hand, we know from subsequent developments that the use of what has been termed "military Keynesianism" to bring about this historic transformation was fraught with negative consequences. For one, military spending was unable to promote economic development in the third world, with the result that by the late 1950s and early 1960s, one of the most pressing issues was how to stimulate economic modernization in those countries with the results far from satisfactory. Furthermore, the use of military "pump priming" to cover the dollar gap and enhance western European economic recovery ultimately led, by the end of the 1950s, to the United States running dangerous balance-of-payments deficits. By then the United States had sent so many dollars abroad through military expenditures that, in effect, the western European countries became saturated with them. Then, as their dollar reserves stabilized, they began converting those dollars to gold. The year 1958 was the first that the United States saw a major drain on its gold reserves since it had become a creditor nation in the wake of World War I. By the early 1960s, the United States was running balance-of-payments deficits of $3 billion and $4 billion. In addition, western Europe and Japan had by the late 1950s began to recover, such that these countries were able to earn the dollars they needed on their own, even as the United States continued to spend huge sums on the military apparatus it had created abroad.

There was, too, the fact that military spending at high levels, whereas it can serve as a temporary stimulus to economic growth, in the long-run will prove a drain on the domestic economy of the nation pursuing it. This occurs because military spending is not profit-generating but must be derived from taxes, taxes that must be paid by the productive elements of society. It also steers investment into military industries rather than civilian sectors. Military Keynesianism may have kept a certain kind of economy afloat, but it did not eradicate poverty, well proved by Michael Harrington's *The Other America*, the influential 1962 critique of American society that found that a significant number of Americans lived below the poverty line at the end of the 1950s. Nor has it to this day. Furthermore, once such spending becomes embedded in an economy in the form of a military-industrial-academic complex, it is almost impossible to jettison it, as too many entities (not least Congressmen and women who want military contracts steered to their districts) become reliant on it. All of these things happened to the United States as a result of the adoption of NSC 68 in the summer of 1950.

Another consequence of rearming to overcome the problems posed by the dollar gap was that NSC 68 militarized U.S. foreign policy to the

266   *Conclusion*

point at which American officials tended to believe that military intervention was the only way to resolve foreign policy problems. Recall the
words of Robert Blackwill, discussed in Chapter 1, in which he contends
that the ideas of NSC 68 most certainly became pervasive not only within
the Truman administration but in subsequent administrations as well.
Specifically, he mentions the administrations of Kennedy, Carter, and
George H. W. Bush, demonstrating, at least in his view, the *long-term*
influence that NSC 68 had on the nation's foreign policy. As this study
has shown, there is no reason to suggest that his analysis is incorrect.

Beginning in 1953, the United States began undertaking covert actions
to overthrow or support the overthrow of undesirable governments all
over the world. Arbenz in Guatemala, Mossadiq in Iran, Lumumba in
the Congo, Castro in Cuba (this one failed), Diem in South Vietnam,
Sukarno in Indonesia, Nkrumah in Ghana, and Allende in Chile are just
some of the more known. Military interventions occurred in Vietnam,
Cambodia, Laos, Indonesia, the Dominican Republic, Haiti, Lebanon,
Grenada, Panama, and Iraq, to name just some. To be certain, these
interventions were not solely the result of NSC 68. The point is that, in
the process of militarizing the Cold War, NSC 68 fomented a mentality
within government circles and among the military brass that, as the document itself said, "the cold war is a real war in which the survival of the
free world is at stake." This militarized "us versus them" mentality made
it virtually impossible not to wage Cold War and see the world in black
and white terms, a way of seeing the world that has not ended along with
the Cold War.

Consequences of Multilateralism

We need as well to consider the consequences of pursuing a policy of
multilateralism without which none of the problems mentioned in the
previous section would have occurred. That, in fact, is the first point. If
the multilateralists had not been so unshakeably committed to creating
a multilateral world order, or if they simply had not come to power, the
consequences likely never would have occurred. If the United States had
truly adhered to the Yalta and Potsdam Accords on Germany, these consequences may have been avoided; instead, the United States trampled all
over them and sought to rebuild WWII's most virile antagonist. Certainly,
there was reason to try to adhere to the accords. Initially, per agreements
made at Yalta, Germany was to be kept permanently in a weakened state
so that it could never again threaten its neighbors. The process called

Conclusion 267

for the denazification, the decartelization, and the deindustrialization of Germany. Germany unquestionably deserved such punishment. However, driven by the determination to establish a multilateral, global economy, the multilateralists in the administration came to the conclusion, even before the war was over, that Germany had to be rebuilt so that it could serve as the "workshop" of Europe, the largest producer and consumer in the region whose vitality would strengthen the economies of all western European countries. This, then, would allow western Europe to participate in the larger global economy as a partner. But in pursuing such a position, the multilateralists were essentially telling the Soviet Union – a U.S. ally during the war and the nation that both suffered the most damage at the hands of the enemy and inflicted the most damage on the enemy – that its concerns and interests did not matter. Not only that, but that they were going to rebuild the enemy that had just pulverized their country twice in thirty years! Of course, the multilateralists were wont to come out and admit this fact outright. Hence, they surreptitiously went about the process of rehabilitating western Germany, all the while blaming the Soviets for the division of the country into east and west spheres. In the process, Soviet leaders, Stalin of course first among them, felt betrayed and disrespected and determined to press their control of their sphere in eastern Europe ever more tightly, which only contributed to even more Cold War tensions.

Much the same occurred over Japan. The situation was somewhat different there because the Soviet Union had been kept out of postwar decision making on Japan. Initially, the U.S. plan for Japan was similar to Germany – it was to be punished for its war activities and forcibly weakened so that it could never again threaten its neighbors. Again, the situation changed as the multilateralists came to believe that Japan had to become the "workshop" of Asia, especially as it became clear that China, which was succumbing to communist domination, could not play that role. The decision to rehabilitate Japan could hardly have provided succor to Stalin and other Soviet leaders. Although the two nations had remained at peace during the war, except at the end when the Soviets declared war on Japan on August 8, 1945, per the Yalta agreement, they were longstanding enemies. The Russo-Japanese War of 1904–1905, which the Japanese won, hardly had been forgotten by the Soviets. Furthermore, Stalin believed that the Japanese would rise up again and that war between the Soviet Union and Japan was a very real possibility, although not probably for twenty years. Thus, Soviet leaders certainly looked on the American decision to rebuild Japan with trepidation.

This critique raises the issue, then, of whether there would have ever even been a Cold War if the multilateralists had not gained ascendancy in the Truman administration. This argument is an old one but has not (and probably never will be) settled. It usually revolves around the question of whether FDR's untimely death, and Truman's sudden rise to the presidency, resulted in a radical departure from FDR's soft policy toward the Soviet Union that resulted in the Cold War. There are those historians who insist that, indeed, FDR's death brought to the White House a man who had limited knowledge of foreign affairs, was given to black-and-white understandings of how the world worked, had no real interest in working with the Soviets, and was overly influenced by anti-Soviet advisors whom Roosevelt had kept at arm's distance. Hence, the argument goes, Truman took a harder line with the Soviets than FDR ever intended, and the result was a hardening of tensions leading to the Cold War. Others insist that Truman attempted to continue Roosevelt's policy of cooperation with the Soviets subject to his, and his aides' understanding of what Roosevelt intended, which was not always easy to figure out (and is still not), but that the Soviets proved to be entirely uncooperative and hostile.

I want to suggest that all the wrangling over whether there was a "reverse course" does not really matter, however interesting it may be from a historical standpoint. We can never know for certain what FDR would have done in relation to the Soviets had he lived. All we can deal with is what did happen. And what did happen is that, under Truman, the multilateralists became the dominant voice in the foreign policy establishment, and they were determined to push their agenda at all costs. In that situation, the only way the Cold War likely could have been avoided would have been for the Soviet Union to retreat back to its pre-war borders (it probably could have kept the Baltic states and its Polish acquisitions, however). Anything short of that meant confrontation, for the multilateralists would not settle for a middle ground. Furthermore, they would stop at nothing to see their goal fulfilled, even when the measures called for posed a direct threat to the Soviet Union, real or perceived.

To be sure, the Soviets were committed to certain objectives that they would not give way on either. However, these were objectives that their allied partners had largely agreed to at the various conferences at which they met. The one major Soviet breach of the wartime agreements was, arguably, its failure to comply with the Declaration on Liberated Europe; but it has been well demonstrated in this study and elsewhere that the Declaration was for the most part political window dressing designed for domestic consumption. Furthermore, as the Soviet expert Geoffrey

Conclusion

Roberts has argued, Stalin viewed the Declaration more as anti-fascist in its intent and did not see the establishment of communist, pro-Soviet governments in states such as Poland, Rumania, and Bulgaria as undemocratic.[7] Moreover, in other eastern European states he did allow free elections, thus abiding by the Declaration.

It was the United States, under the guiding hand of the multilateralists, that broke the Yalta accords on Germany, the single most important issue over which the Cold War broke out. Even so, as this study (and others) has shown, it was not the Soviet Union but the problem posed by getting Congress to fund foreign economic aid to cope with the dollar gap that gave birth to the notion, mostly for domestic political consumption, that the Soviet Union was determined to conquer the world and had to be stopped. The Soviet Union's *actual* behavior mattered little in this political game. Then, when the multilateralists' entire agenda seemed on the verge of implosion, they opted to escalate the Cold War through massive rearmament and to expand American power abroad to save it from that fate. So the question persists: Was it worth it?

This historian's answer is that it was not. It is an impossible task to investigate the past for what might have been. We can never know what would have happened to the global economy or the economies of the United States, western Europe, Japan, and other countries of the world, if NSC 68 had never been implemented. We will never know if world trade would have closed down as a result or if the western Europeans and the Japanese would have adopted communism and formed an alliance with the Soviet Union. Perhaps, they would have simply formed autarchies and made the best of it. What would have happened to the United States? Would it have been forced to adopt some kind of state economic planning that curtailed the "free enterprise" system? Would it have become

---

[7] See Geoffrey Roberts, *Stalin's Wars: From World War to Cold War, 1939–1953* (New Haven, Connecticut: Yale University Pres., 2006), 242, 296–299. Critics will protest that I have ignored Stalin's breach of the Yalta agreement on Poland, which was the initial issue on which the Grand Alliance began to splinter. It is true, of course, that Stalin suggested at Yalta that Polish elections might be held within a month and that they were not. It is also true that Stalin initially balked at broadening the Soviet-puppet Lublin government to include Poles from abroad (the London Poles) and domestic non-Lublin Poles. But far too much has been made of this issue in assigning blame to the Soviet Union for starting the Cold War. The fact of the matter is that, after the Americans and the British held their ground in the negotiations over Poland, Stalin eventually gave way in allowing for a more inclusive provisional Polish government. The Poles themselves then formed that government and on July 5, 1945, Truman recognized it. Thereafter, he apparently never thought much about it.

a garrison state centered on the western hemisphere and defended with a massive navy and expanded air force? Both of those scenarios were an anathema to the multilateralists who controlled foreign policy, but that does not mean that they were not potentially better policies than the militarization option. Both were in fact pushed by various factions between 1945 and 1950, the latter in the so-called Great Debate of 1951. We will never know.

At the same time, it can be fairly argued that the economy it did help create – that "liberal global economic regime" – gave us a world of consumption unseen in the annals of human history, one that, whatever faults can be found with it, did contribute substantially to an improvement in the standard of living of most Americans and many other people as well; a world that, it seems likely, would not have been possible absent NSC 68. However, even if that is true, it must be acknowledged then that it was not the free enterprise system that brought this about, at least not it alone, but a militarized form of social spending, which should give anyone reading this book who thinks free-market capitalism is the world's greatest benefactor and socialism its worst detractor pause to think otherwise.

Still, given the costs as outlined in this conclusion, it does seem that the route chosen – that of militarization – was either the best or the most enlightened one. Certainly, it is quite possible that there would have been no Cold War. Critics will insist that the Soviets were the antagonists, but I think Geoffrey Roberts has it more correct when he asserts that "Stalin … did not want a cold war with the west and hoped for continued negotiations with Britain and the United States about the postwar peace settlement."[8] Roberts does not believe that the Soviets were blameless in starting the Cold War, nor is that the argument of this study. The Soviet leaders, Stalin of course primarily, had specific issues that they simply were unwilling to give up, not least security from a potentially revived Germany. To be sure, Truman administration officials similarly had goals that they would not relinquish. For the Soviets, however, those goals were a matter of life and death, occasioned by the experience of suffering two crushing invasions from Germany in the space of thirty years. For the Americans, those goals were to preserve the free enterprise system at home by establishing multilateralism abroad. The result was a long, drawn out Cold War.

[8] Roberts, *Stalin's Wars*, 24.

Select Bibliography

Manuscript Collections

Library of Congress, Washington, D.C.

Averell Harriman Papers
Paul Nitze Papers

Rare Book and Manuscript Library, Columbia University, New York City, New York

Frank Altschul Papers

Harry S. Truman Memorial Library, Independence, Missouri

Dean G. Acheson Papers
Eben A. Ayers Papers
George Elsey Papers
Gordon Gray Papers
Charles S. Murphy Papers
Edward G. Nourse Papers
John H. Ohly Papers
Walter Salant Papers
Harry S. Truman Papers
President's Secretary's File
Records of the National Security Council
Record Group 286, Records of the Agency for International Development
White House Central File
Confidential File
General File
Official File
Oral History Collection
Dean G. Acheson, Oral History, June 30, 1971
Richard M. Bissell, Oral History, July 9, 1971
Joseph D. Coppock, Oral History, July 29, 1974

W. John Kenney, Oral History, November 29, 1971
Leon H. Keyserling, Oral History, May 3, 10, and 19, 1971
Frederick J. Lawton, Oral History, June 17 and July 9, 1963
John M. Leddy, Oral History, June 15, 1973
Paul Nitze, Oral History, June 11 and 17, and August 4, 5, and 6, 1975
John H. Ohly, Oral History, November 30, 1971
Edwin Noel Plowden and Douglas Allen, Oral History, June 15, 1964
Walter Salant, Oral History, March 30, 1970
Isaac P. Stokes, Oral History, July 3, 1973
Willard Thorp, Oral History, July 10, 1971
Philip Trieze, Oral History, May 27, 1975
C. Tyler Wood, Oral History, June 18, 1971

Special Collections, Alexander Library, Rutgers, The State University of New Jersey New Brunswick, New Jersey

Tracy Voorhees Papers

Unpublished U.S. Government Documents

National Archives of the United States II, College Park, Maryland
Record Group 59, General Records of the Department of State
Decimal Files
Charles Bohlen Papers
Charles Bonesteel Papers
Records of the International Security Affairs Committee
Records of the Mutual Defense Assistance Program
Records of the Policy Planning Staff
Records of the Office of the Executive Secretariat
Records of William Bray
Record Group 218, Records of the Joint Chiefs of Staff
Record Group 273, Records of the National Security Council

Seeley G. Mudd Manuscript Library, Princeton, New Jersey

Records of the Council on Foreign Relations
Study Group on Aid to Europe, Records of Groups
Study Group on the Dollar Gap, Records of Groups
David Lilienthal Papers

Foreign Archives

The National Archives, Kew, England, United Kingdom
Records of the Foreign Office
Records of the Prime Minister
Record of Cabinet Meetings

Select Bibliography 273

Published U.S. Government Documents

Congress

House
Committee on Foreign Affairs. *The Mutual Security Program.* 82nd Cong., 1st
Sess. Washington, D.C.: U.S. Government Printing Office, 1951.
*Selected Executive Session Hearings, 1951–1956, Volume 15: European
Problems.* Washington D.C.: U.S. Government Printing Office, 1980.
To Amend the Economic Cooperation Act of 1948: Part One. 81st Cong., 2nd
Sess. Washington, D.C.: U.S. Government Printing Office, 1950.
To Amend the Economic Cooperation Act of 1948: Part Two. 81st Cong., 2nd
Sess. Washington, D.C.: U.S. Government Printing Office, 1950.

Senate
Committee on Foreign Relations. *Hearings on the North Atlantic Treaty
Organization.* 81st Cong., 1st Sess. Washington, D.C.: U.S. Government
Printing Office, 1949.
Mutual Security Act of 1951. 82nd Cong., 1st Sess. Washington, D.C.: U.S.
Government Printing Office, 1951.
Mutual Security Act of 1952. 82nd Cong., 1st Sess. Washington, D.C.: U.S.
Government Printing Office, 1952.
Mutual Security Act of 1953. 83rd Cong., 1st Sess. Washington, D.C.: U.S.
Government Printing Office, 1953.
Reviews of the World Situation: 1949–1950. Historical Series. 81st Cong., 1st
and 2nd Sess. Washington, D.C.: U.S. Government Printing Office, 1974.
Committee on Appropriations. *Analysis of the Gray Report.* Washington,
D.C.: U.S. Government Printing Office, 1951.

Executive Branch

Department of State. *Bulletin.* March 1950.
Foreign Relations of the United States: 1947. Vol. III. Washington, D.C.: U.S.
Government Printing Office, 1972.
Foreign Relations of the United States: 1948. Vol. III. Washington, D.C.: U.S.
Government Printing Office 1974.
Foreign Relations of the United States: 1949. Vol. I. Washington, D.C.: U.S.
Government Printing Office, 1976.
Foreign Relations of the United States: 1949. Vol. IV. Washington, D.C.: U.S.
Government Printing Office, 1975.
Foreign Relations of the United States: 1950. Vol. I. Washington, D.C.: U.S.
Government Printing Office, 1977.
Foreign Relations of the United States: 1950. Vol. III. Washington, D.C.: U.S.
Government Printing Office, 1977.
Foreign Relations of the United States: 1950. Vol. VII. Washington, D.C.: U.S.
Government Printing Office, 1976.
Foreign Relations of the United States: 1951. Vol. I. Washington, D.C.: U.S.
Government Printing Office, 1979.

274   *Select Bibliography*

Council of Economic Advisors. *Economic report of the President transmitted to the Congress, 1949–1955.* Washington, D.C.: U.S. Government Printing Office, 1949–1955.

Gray, Gordon. *Report to the President on Foreign Economic Policies.* Washington, D.C.: U.S. Government Printing Office, 1950.

Public Papers of the Presidents of the United States: Dwight D. Eisenhower, 1961. Washington, D.C.: U.S. Government Printing Office, 1961.

Public Papers of the Presidents of the United States: Harry S. Truman, 1947. Washington, D.C.: U.S. Government Printing Office, 1963.

Public Papers of the Presidents of the United States: Harry S. Truman, 1950. Washington, D.C.: U.S. Government Printing Office, 1963.

Other Published Primary Sources

Mutual Security Agency. *Monthly Report for the Public Advisory Committee.* October 1951-March 1953. Washington, D.C.

Official Conversations and Meetings of Dean Acheson, 1949–1953. Frederick, Maryland: University Publications of America, 1980.

Declassified Documents Reference System. Farmington Hills, Michigan: Gale, 2009.

Newspapers and Periodicals

Business Week
Chicago Tribune
Fortune
Life
Los Angeles Times
New Technology Week
New York Times
Reader's Digest
Time
Times Union
Toronto Sun
U.S. News and World Report
Washington Post
Weekly Standard

Secondary Sources and Memoirs

Acheson, Dean. *Present at the Creation.* New York: W. W. Norton, 1969.

    Morning and Noon: A Memoir. Boston, Massachusetts: Houghton Mifflin, 1965.

    Power and Diplomacy. Cambridge, Massachusetts: Harvard University Press, 1959.

    This Vast External Realm. New York: W. W. Norton and Company, 1973.

    "'Total Diplomacy' to Strengthen U.S. Leadership for Human Freedom." Department of State. *Bulletin.* March 20, 1950.

Select Bibliography

Adams, Fred. *Economic Diplomacy: The Export-Import Bank and America Foreign Policy, 1934–1939.* Columbia, Missouri: University of Missouri Press, 1976.

Adler, Les K. and Thomas G. Patterson, "Red Fascism: The Merger of Nazi Germany and Soviet Russia in the American Image of Totalitarianism," *American Historical Review* 75 (April 1970): 1046–1064.

Alterman, Eric. *Who Speaks for America? Why Democracy Matters in Foreign Policy.* Ithaca, New York: Cornell University Press, 1998.

American Bankers Association. Department of Economic Research. *The Cost of World Leadership: An Analysis of the United States Balance-of-Payments Problem.* New York, 1968.

Anderson, Terry. *The United States, Great Britain, and the Cold War, 1941–47.* Columbia, Missouri: University of Missouri Press, 1981.

Appy, Christian. *Cold War Constructions: The Political Culture of United States Imperialism, 1945–1966.* Amherst, Massachusetts: University of Massachusetts Press, 2000.

Axilrod, Eric. *U.S. Balance of Payments, 1946–1968.* Hong Kong: Chinese University of Hong Kong, Economic Research Centre, 1970.

Balogh, Thomas. *The Dollar Crisis: Causes and Cures.* London: Oxford University Press, 1950.

Baum, Kim Chull and James Matray, eds. *Korea and the Cold War: Division, Destruction, and Disarmament.* Claremont, California: Regina Books, 1993.

Becker, W. H. "Foreign Markets for Iron and Steel, 1893–1913: A New Perspective on the Williams School of Diplomatic History," *Pacific Historical Review* XLIV (1975): 233–248.

Beisner, Robert L. *Dean Acheson: A Life in the Cold War.* New York: Oxford University Press, 2006.

Benton, William. *This is the Challenge: The Benton Reports of 1956–1958 on the Nature of the Soviet Threat.* New York: Associated College Presses, 1958.

Berstein, Barton, J. "American Foreign Policy and the Origins of the Cold War," in Thomas Paterson, ed. *The Origins of the Cold War.* Lexington, Massachusetts; D.C. Heath and Company, 1974. 2nd ed., 89–99.

"The Truman Administration and the Korean War," in Michael Lacey, ed. *The Truman Presidency.* New York: Cambridge University Press, 1989, 410–444.

Bird, Kai. *The Chairman: John J. McCloy: The Making of the American Establishment.* New York: Simon and Schuster, 1992.

Bissell, Richard M. "The Impact of Rearmament on the Free World Economy." *Foreign Affairs* 29 (April 1951): 385–405.

Block, Fred L. "Economic Instability and Military Strength: The Paradoxes of the 1950 Rearmament Decision." *Politics and Society* 10:1 (1980): 35–58.

The Origins of International Economic Disorder: A Study of United States International Monetary Policy from World War II to the Present. Berkeley, California: University of California Press, 1977.

Bohlen, Charles. *Witness to History.* New York: W. W. Norton, 1973.

Bolton, Roger E. *Defense Purchases and Regional Growth.* Washington, D.C.: Brookings Institute, 1966.

Borden, William. *The Pacific Alliance: United States Foreign Economic Policy and Japanese Trade Recovery, 1947–1955*. Madison, Wisconsin: University of Wisconsin Press, 1984.

Boyer, Paul S. *By the Bomb's Early Light: American Thought and Culture at the Dawn of the Atomic Age*. New York: Pantheon, 1985.

Boyer, Paul S., et al. *The Enduring Vision: A History of the American People, Volume II*. New York: Houghton Mifflin, 2000. 4th ed.

Brands, H. W. *The Devil We Knew: Americans and the Cold War*. New York: Oxford University Press, 1993.

Breslin, Thomas A. *Beyond Pain: The Role of Pleasure in the Making of Foreign Affairs*. Westport, Connecticut: Praeger Publishers, 2002.

Brief, Sam Post. "Departure from Incrementalism in U.S. Strategic Planning: The Origins of NSC 68," *Naval War College Review* (March–April 1980): 34–57.

Brinkley, Alan. *End of Reform New Deal Liberalism in Recession and War*. New York: Alfred Knopf, 1995.

Brinkley, Douglas, ed. *Dean Acheson and the Making of U.S. Foreign Policy*. New York: St. Martin's Press, 1993.

Brune, Lester H. "Guns and Butter: The Pre-Korean War Dispute Over Budget Allocations: Nourse's Conservative Keynesianism Loses Favor Against Keyserling's Economic Expansion Plan." *American Journal of Economics and Sociology* 48 (July 1989): 357–372.

Buhite, Russell D. and William Christopher Hamel. "War for Peace: The Question of an American Preventive War against the Soviet Union." *Diplomatic History* 14 (Summer 1990): 367–364.

Bullock, Alan. *Ernest Bevin: Foreign Secretary, 1945–1951*. London: William Heinemann Ltd., 1983.

Bundy, McGeorge. *Danger and Survival: Choices about the Bomb in the First Fifty Years*. New York: Random House, 1988.

Caincross, Alan and Barry Eichengreen. *Sterling in Decline: The Devaluations of 1931, 1949, and 1967*. New York: Palgrave MacMillan, 2003. 2nd ed.

Calder, Lendol Glen. *Financing the American Dream: A Cultural History of Consumer Credit*. Princeton, New Jersey: Princeton University Press, 1999.

Callahan, David. *Dangerous Capabilities: Paul Nitze and the Cold War*. New York: Edward Burlingame, 1990.

Cannon, Charles Allred. *The Military-Industrial Complex in American Politics, 1953–1970*. Stanford, California: Stanford University Press, 1974.

Carpenter, Ted Galen. "United States' NATO Policy at the Crossroads: The 'Great Debate' of 1950–1951." *International History Review* 8 (August 1986): 389–415.

Cerri, Dominic. "Truman and Korea: Overcoming Domestic Enemies, the Marshaling of Tensions, and the Containment of Western Europe." M.A. Thesis. California State University, Sacramento, California, 1996.

Chace, James. *Acheson: The Secretary of State Who Created the American World*. New York: Simon & Schuster, 1998.

Chafe, William. *Unfinished Journey: The United States Since World War II*. New York: Oxford University Press, 1986.

Select Bibliography

Cherny, Robert W. *American Labor and the Cold War: Grassroots Politics and Postwar Political Culture*. New Brunswick, New Jersey: Rutgers University Press, 2004.

Clayton, James L. *The Economic Impact of the Cold War*. New York: Harcourt, Brace, and World, 1970.

Clemens, Diane Shaver. *Yalta*. New York: Oxford University Press, 1970.

Cohen, Lizabeth. *A Consumer's Republic: The Politics of Mass Consumption in Postwar America*. New York: Alfred A. Knopf, 2003.

Combs, Jerald. "The Compromise That Never Was: George Kennan, Paul Nitze, and the Issue of Conventional Deterrence in Europe, 1949–1952." *Diplomatic History* 15 (Summer 1991): 361–386.

Combs, Jerald A. and Philip A. Karber. "The United States, NATO, and the Soviet Threat to Western Europe: Military Threats and Policy Options, 1945–1963," *Diplomatic History* 22: 3 (Summer 1998): 399–430.

Condit, Doris M. *History of the Office of the Secretary of Defense, Volume II, The Test of War, 1950–1953*. Washington, D.C: Historical Office, Office of the Secretary of Defense, 1988.

Condit, Kenneth W. *The History of the Joint Chiefs of Staff: The Joint Chiefs of Staff and National Policy: Volume II, 1947–1949*. Historical Division, Joint Chiefs of Staff, Record Group 218, Records of the Joint Chiefs of Staff, National Archives II, College Park, Maryland.

Coombs, Tessa. *CNN: Cold War*. Atlanta, Georgia: Turner Home Entertainment, 1998.

Costigliola, Frank. "Broken Circle: The Isolation of Franklin D. Roosevelt in World War II." *Diplomatic History* 32: 5 (November 2008): 677–718.

"'I Had Come as a Friend': Emotion, Culture, and Ambiguity in the Formation of the Cold War." *Cold War History* 1: 1 (August 2000): 103–128.

"'Unceasing Pressure for Penetration': Gender, Pathology, and Emotion in George Kennan's Formation of the Cold War." *The Journal of American History* 83: 1 (March 1997): 1309–1339.

Awkward Dominion: American Political, Economic, and Cultural Relations with Europe, 1919–1933. Ithaca, New York: Cornell University Press, 1984.

France and the United States: The Cold War Alliance Since World War II. New York: Twayne Publishers, 1992.

Cumings, Bruce. "Revising Post-Revisionism," or "The Poverty of Theory in Diplomatic History." *Diplomatic History* 17: 4 (Fall 1993): 539–569.

"The American Century and the Third World." *Diplomatic History* 23: 2 (Spring 1999): 355–370.

The Origins of the Korean War. 2 volumes. Princeton, New Jersey: Princeton University Press, 1981, 1991.

ed. *Child of Conflict: The Korean-American Relationship, 1943–1953*. Seattle, Washington: University of Washington Press, 1983.

Dean, Robert. *Imperial Brotherhood: Gender and the Making of Cold War Foreign Policy*. Amherst, New York: University of Massachusetts Press, 2001.

Diebold, William. *New Directions in Our Trade Policy*. New York: Council on Foreign Relations, 1941.

Select Bibliography

Trade and Payments in Western Europe: A Study in Economic Cooperation,
1947–51. New York: Published for the Council on Foreign Relations by
Harper's, 1952.

Divine, Robert. *Second Chance: The Triumph of Internationalism in America*
during World War II. New York: Atheneum, 1967.

Dobson, Alan P. *US Economic Statecraft for Survival 1933–1991.* London: Taylor
& Francis, 2002.

Drew, S. Nelson, ed. *NSC-68: Forging the Strategy of Containment.* Washington,
D.C.: National Defense University, 1994.

Dubofsky, Melvyn, ed. *The New Deal: Conflicting Interpretations and Shifting*
Perspectives. New York: Garland Pub., 1992.

Eckes, Alan Jr. *A Search for Solvency: Bretton Woods and the International*
Monetary System, 1941–1971. Austin, Texas: The University of Texas Press,
1975.

Edmonds, Robin. *Setting the Mould: The United States and Britain, 1945–1950.*
Oxford, England: Clarendon Press, 1986.

Eichengreen, Barry. *Elusive Stability: Essays in the History of International*
Finance, 1919–1939. New York: Cambridge University Press, 1990.

Globalizing Capital: A History of the International Monetary System. Princeton,
New Jersey: Princeton University Press, 1996.

ed., *Europe's Post-War Recovery.* New York: Cambridge University Press,
1995.

Eisenberg, Carolyn Woods. *Drawing the Line: The American Decision to divide*
Germany, 1944–1949. New York: Cambridge University Press, 1996.

Ellis, Howard. *The Economics of Freedom: The Progress and Future of Aid to*
Europe. New York: Harper & Brothers, for the Council on Foreign Relations,
1950.

Fatemi, Nazsrollah, Thibaut de Saint Phalle, and Grace M. Keeffe. *The Dollar*
Crisis: The United States Balance of Payments and Dollar Stability. Fairleigh
Dickson University Press, 1963.

Foot, Rosemary. *The Wrong War: American Policy and the Dimensions of the*
Korean Conflict, 1950–1953. Ithaca, New York: Cornell University Press,
1985.

Fordham, Benjamin O. *Building the Cold War Consensus: The Political Economy*
of U.S. National Security Policy, 1949–1951. Ann Arbor, Michigan: University
of Michigan Press, 1998.

Fraser, Steve and Gary Gerstle, eds. *The Rise and Fall of the New Deal Order,*
1930–1980. Princeton, New Jersey: Princeton University Press, 1989.

Freeland, Richard. *The Truman Doctrine and the Origins of McCarthyism: Foreign*
Policy, Domestic Politics, and Internal Security, 1946–1948. New
York: Schocken Books, 1974.

Friedberg, Aaron L. "Why Didn't the United States Become a Garrison State?"
International Security 16 (Spring 1992): 109–142.

Gaddis, John Lewis. *Russia, the Soviet Union, and the United States: An*
Interpretative History. New York: Alfred Knopf, 1978.

"The Emerging Post-Revisionist Synthesis and the Origins of the Cold War."
Diplomatic History 7: 3 (Summer 1983): 171–190.

Select Bibliography

Strategies of Containment: A Critical Appraisal of Postwar American National Security Policy. New York: Oxford University Press. 1982.

The United States and the Origins of the Cold War, 1941–1947. New York: Columbia University Press, 1972.

We Now Know: ReThinking Cold War History. New York: Claredon Press, The Council on Foreign Relations, 1997.

Gaddis, John Lewis and Paul Nitze. "NSC 68 and the Threat Reconsidered." *International Security* 4 (Spring 1980): 164–176.

Gardner, Lloyd C. *Approaching Vietnam: From World War II through Dienbienphu, 1941–1954.* New York: W. W. Norton, 1987.

Architects of Illusion. New York: Quadrangle Books, 1970.

Economic Aspects of New Deal Diplomacy. Boston, Massachusetts: Beacon Press, 1964.

The Origins of the Cold War. Waltham, Massachusetts: Ginn-Blaisdell, 1970.

Safe for Democracy: The Anglo-American Response to Revolution, 1913–1923. New York: Oxford University Press, 1984.

Spheres of Influence: The Great Powers Partition Europe, from Munich to Yalta. New York: Ivan R. Dee Publishers, 1993.

Gardner, Richard N. *Sterling-Dollar Diplomacy Anglo-American Collaboration in the Reconstruction of Multilateral Trade.* Oxford, United Kingdom: Clarendon Press, 1956.

Sterling-Dollar Diplomacy: The Origins and Prospects of Our International Economic Order. New York: McGraw-Hill, 1969.

Glantz, Mary E. *FDR and the Soviet Union: The President's Battles over Foreign Policy.* Lawrence, Kansas: University Press of Kansas, 2005.

Goncharov, Sergei N., John Lewis, and Litai Xue. *Uncertain Partners: Stalin, Mao, and the Korean War.* Stanford, California: Stanford University Press, 1993.

Gottheil, Fred M. *Principles of Macroeconomics.* Cincinnati, Ohio: South-Western College Publishing, 1996.

Graebner, William. *Age of Doubt: American Thought and Culture in the 1940s.* Boston: Twayne Publishers, 1991.

Gray, Gordon. *Report to the President on Foreign Economic Policy.* Washington, D.C.: U.S. Government Printing Office, 1950.

Gray, H. Peter, ed. *The Dollar Deficit: Causes and Cures.* Boston: D.C. Heath and Co., 1967.

Gubin, Emil Kemair. *How to do Business Under the Marshall Plan.* Washington, D.C. 1948.

Haberler, Gottfried. "Reflections of the Future of the Bretton Woods System." *The American Economic Review* 43 (May 1953): 81–95.

Hall, Margaret. "The United Kingdom After Devaluation." *The American Economic Review* 40 (December 1950): 864–875.

Hamby, Alonzo L. *Beyond the New Deal: Harry S. Truman and American Liberalism.* New York: Columbia University Press, 1973.

Man of the People: A Life of Harry S. Truman. New York: Oxford University Press, 1995.

Harris, Seymour E., ed. *The Dollar in Crisis.* New York: Harcourt, Brace, and World, Inc., 1961.

Select Bibliography

Harvey, David. *The Condition of Postmodernity: An Enquiry into the Origins of Cultural Change*. Cambridge, Massachusetts: Blackwell, 1990.

Hearden, Patrick. *Roosevelt Confronts Hitler: America's Entry into World War II*. DeKalb, Illinois: Northern Illinois University Press, 1987.

Hearn, Charles. *The American Dream in the Great Depression*. Westport, Connecticut: Greenwood Press, 1977.

Herken, Gregg. *The Winning Weapon: The Atomic Bomb in the Cold War, 1945–1950*. New York: Vintage Books, 1982.

Hilfrich, Fabian. "George Kennan," in Ruud van Dijk, ed. *Encyclopedia of the Cold War, Volume 2*. New York: Routledge, 2008.

Hixson, Walter L. *Parting the Curtain: Propaganda, Culture, and the Cold War, 1945–1961*. New York: St. Martin's Press, 1997.

Hoffman, Paul G. *Peace Can Be Won*. Garden City, New York: Doubleday, 1951.

Hogan, Michael J. *America in the World: The Historiography of American Foreign Relations Since 1941*. New York: Cambridge University Press, 1995.

A Cross of Iron: Harry S. Truman and the Origins of the National Security State, 1945–1954. New York: Cambridge University Press, 1998.

Informal Entente: The Private Structure of Cooperation in Anglo-American Economic Diplomacy, 1918–1919. Columbia, Missouri: University of Missouri Press, 1977.

The Marshall Plan: America, Britain, and the Reconstruction of Western Europe, 1947–1952. New York: Cambridge University Press, 1987.

Holloway, David. *Stalin and the Bomb: The Soviet Union and Atomic Energy, 1939–1956*. New Haven, Connecticut: Yale University Press, 1994.

Hoover, Calvin B. "Foreign Economic Aid and Communism, *The Journal of Political Economy* 54 (February 1951): 1–13.

Horowitz, David. *Corporations and the Cold War*. New York: Monthly Review Press, 1969.

Huntington, Samuel P. "The Defense Establishment: Vested Interests and the Public Interest," in Omer L. Carey, ed., *The Military-Industrial Complex and United States Foreign Policy*. Pullman, Washington: Washington State University Press, 1968.

International Economic Policy Association. *The United States Balance of Payments: From Crisis to Controversy*. New York, 1972.

Isaacson, Walter and Evan Thomas. *The Wise Men: Six Friends and the World They Made, Acheson, Bohlen, Harriman, Kennan, Lovett, and McCloy*. New York: Simon and Schuster, 1986.

Janeway, Eliot. *The Economics of Crisis: War, Politics, and the Dollar*. New York: Weybright and Talley, 1968.

Jervis, Robert. "The Impact of the Korean War on the Cold War." *Journal of Conflict Resolution* 24 (December 1980): 563–593.

Johnson, Robert David. *The Peace Progressives and American Foreign Relations*. Cambridge: Harvard University Press, 1995.

Kane, Tim. *Global U.S. Troop Deployment, 1950–2005*. Washington, D.C.: The Heritage Foundation, 2006. http://www.heritage.org/

Select Bibliography 281

Kaplan, Lawrence. *The Long Entanglement: NATO's First Fifty Years.* New York: Praeger, 1999.

Kaufman, Burton. *Trade and Aid: Eisenhower's Foreign Economic Policy, 1953–1961.* Baltimore: The Johns Hopkins University Press, 1982.

Kennan, George. *Memoirs, 1925–1950.* New York: Bantam, 1967.

Kennedy, Paul. *The Rise and Fall of the Great Powers: Economic Change and Military Conflict from 1500 to 2000.* New York: Random House, 1986.

Killick, John. *The United States and European Reconstruction, 1945–1960.* Edinburgh, United Kingdom: Keele University Press, 1997.

Kimball, Warren. *The Juggler: Franklin Roosevelt as Wartime Statesman.* Princeton, New Jersey: Princeton University Press, 1991.

Kipping, Matthias and Ove Bjarnar, eds. *The Americanisation of European Business: The Marshall Plan and the Transfer of US Management Models.* London: Routledge, 1998.

Kling, Rob, Spencer Olin, and Mark Poster, eds. *Postsuburban California: The Transformation of Orange County Since World War II.* Berkeley, California: University of California Press, 1991.

Knight, Jonathan. "American Statecraft and the 1946 Black Sea Straits Controversy." *Political Science Quarterly* 90: 3 (Autumn 1975): 451–475.

Knock, Thomas. *To End All Wars: Woodrow Wilson and the Quest for a New World Order.* New York: Oxford University Press, 1992.

Kofsky, Frank. "Did the Truman Administration Deliberately Prolong the Korean War?" Unpublished paper.

The Truman Doctrine and the Origins of McCarthyism: A Successful Campaign to Deceive the Nation. New York: St. Martin's Press, 1995.

Koistinen, Paul A. C. *Arsenal of World War II: The Political Economy of American Warfare, 1940–1945.* Lawrence, Kansas: University Press of Kansas, 2004.

The Military-Industrial Complex: A Historical Perspective. New York: Praeger, 1980.

Kolko, Gabriel. *The Politics of War: The World and United States Foreign Policy, 1943–1945.* New York: Random House, 1968.

Kolko, Gabriel and Joyce Kolko. *The Limits of Power: The World and United States Foreign Policy, 1945–1954.* New York: Harper & Row, 1972.

Kozul-Wright, Richard and Robert Rowthorn, eds. *Transnational Corporations and the Global Economy.* New York: St. Martin's Press, 1998.

Krock, Arthur. *Memoirs: Sixty Years on the Firing Line.* New York: Funk and Wagnalls, 1968.

Kuniholm, Bruce R. *The Origins of the Cold War in the Near East: Great Power Conflict and Diplomacy in Iran, Turkey, and Greece.* Princeton, New Jersey: Princeton University Press, 1980.

Kunz, Diane B. *Butter and Guns: America's Cold War Economic Diplomacy.* New York: The Free Press, 1997.

Kuznick, Peter and James Gilbert, eds. *Rethinking Cold War Culture.* Washington, D.C.: Smithsonian Institution Press, 2001.

Lacey, Michael J., ed., *The Truman Presidency.* New York: Cambridge University Press, 1989.

LaFeber, Walter. *America, Russia, and the Cold War, 1945–1996.* New York: McGraw-Hill, 1997. 8th ed.

America, Russia, and the Cold War, 1945–1966. New York: Wiley, 1967. 1st ed.

The American Age: U.S. Foreign Policy at Home and Abroad, 1750 to the Present. New York: W. W. Norton and Company, 1994. 2nd ed.

"NATO and the Korean War: A Context." *Diplomatic History* 13: 4 (Fall 1989): 461–477.

"Technology and U.S. Foreign Relations," *Diplomatic History* 24: 1 (Winter 2000): 1–20.

Latham, Michael E. *Modernization as Ideology: American Social Science and "Nation Building" in the Kennedy Era.* Chapel Hill, North Carolina: University of North Carolina Press, 2000.

Lary, Hal B. *Problems of the United States as World Trader and Banker.* New York: National Bureau of Economic Research, 1963.

Lederer, Walter. "Major Developments Affecting the United States Balance of International Payments," *The Review of Economics and Statistics* 38 (May 1956): 177–192.

Leffler, Melvyn P. "The Cold War: What Do 'We Now Know'?" *American Historical Review* 104 (April 1999): 501–524.

The Elusive Quest: America's Pursuit of European Stability and French Security, 1919–1933. Chapel Hill, North Carolina: University of North Carolina Press, 1979.

"Inside Enemy Archives: The Cold War Reopened," *Foreign Affairs* 75 (July/August 1996): 120–135.

For the Soul of Mankind: The United States, the Soviet Union, and the Cold War. New York: Hill and Wang, 2007.

A Preponderance of Power: National Security, the Truman Administration, and the Cold War. Stanford, California: The Stanford University Press, 1992.

The Specter of Communism: The United States and the Origins of the Cold War, 1917–1953. New York: Hill and Wang, 1994.

Lens, Sidney. *The Military-Industrial Complex.* Philadelphia, Pennsylvania: Pilgrim Press, 1970.

Leslie, Stuart W. *The Cold War and American Science: The Military-Industrial-Academic Complex at MIT and Stanford.* New York: Columbia University Press, 1993.

Lippman, Walter. *The Cold War: A Study in U.S. Foreign Policy.* New York: Harper, 1947.

Lotchin, Roger W. *Fortress California, 1910–1961: From Warfare to Welfare.* New York: Oxford University Press, 1992.

Lowen, Rebecca S. *Creating the Cold War University: The Transformation of Stanford.* Berkeley, California: University of California Press, 1997.

Lucas, Scott. *Freedom's War: The American Crusade Against the Soviet Union.* New York: The New York University Press, 1999.

Lundestad, Geir. "Empire by Invitation? The United States and Western Europe, 1945–1952." SHAFR *Newsletter* 15 (September 1984): 1–21.

Select Bibliography

Mark, Eduard. "Revolution by Degress: Stalin's National Front Strategy for Europe, 1941–1947," Working Paper no. 31. Cold War International History Project. Woodrow Wilson International Center for Scholars, Washington, D.C., 1999.

"The War Scare of 1946 and Its Consequences," *Diplomatic History* 21: 3 (Summer 1997): 383–416.

Markusen, Ann, Peter Hall, Scott Campbell, and Sabina Deitrick, eds. *The Rise of the Gunbelt Economy: The Military Remapping of Industrial America*. New York: Oxford University Press, 1991.

Markusen, Ann and Joel Yudken. *Dismantling the Cold War Economy*. New York: Basic Books, 1992, 1993.

Martel, Gordon. *American Foreign Relations Reconsidered, 1890–1993*. London: Routledge, 1994.

Mastny, Vojtech. "NATO in the Beholder's Eye: Soviet Perceptions and Policies, 1949–1956." Working Paper No. 35. Cold War International History Project. Woodrow Wilson International Center for Scholars, Washington, D.C., 2002.

Russia's Road to the Cold War: Diplomacy, Warfare, and the Politics of Communism, 1941–1945. New York: Columbia University Press, 1979.

Matray, James. *The Reluctant Crusade: American Foreign Policy in Korea, 1941–1950*. Honolulu, Hawaii: The University of Hawaii Press, 1985.

May, Elaine Tyler. *Homeward Bound: American Families in the Cold War Era*. New York: Basic Books, 1999. 2nd ed.

May, Ernest, ed. *American Cold War Strategy: Interpreting NSC 68*. New York: Bedford Books, St. Martin's Press, 1993.

May, Lary. *Recasting America: Culture and Politics in the Age of Cold War*. Chicago: The University of Chicago Press, 1989.

Mazlish, Bruce and Ralph Buultjens, eds. *Conceptualizing Global History*. Boulder, Colorado: Westview Press, 1993.

McAuliffe, Mary Sperling. *Crisis on the Left: Cold War Politics and American Liberals, 1947–1954*. Amherst, Massachusetts: University of Massachusetts Press, 1978.

McCloy, John J. *The Atlantic Alliance: Its Origins and Its Future*. New York: Columbia University Press, 1969.

McCormick, Thomas J. *America's Half-Century: United States Foreign Policy in the Cold War and After*. Baltimore, Maryland: The Johns Hopkins University Press, 1995. 2nd ed.

McEnaney, Laura. *Civil Defense Begins at Home: Militarization Meets Everyday Life in the Fifties*. Princeton, New Jersey: Princeton University Press, 2000.

McLellan, David S. *Dean Acheson: The State Department Years*. New York: Dodd, Mead, and Company, 1976.

McMahon, Robert. *Dean Acheson and the Creation of an American World Order*. Washington, D.C.: Potomac Books, 2009.

Melman, Seymour. *Pentagon Capitalism: The Political Economy of War*. New York: McGraw-Hill, 1970.

Menderhausen, Horst. "Foreign Aid with and without Dollar Shortage." *The Review of Economics and Statistics* 33 (Feb. 1951): 38–48.

284 *Select Bibliography*

Miller, James Edward. *The United States and Italy, 1940–1950.* Chapel Hill, North Carolina: The University of North Carolina Press, 1986.

Mills, C. Wright. *The Power Elite.* New York: Oxford University Press, 1956.

Milward, Alan S. *The Reconstruction of Western Europe, 1945–51.* Berkeley, California: University of California Press, 1984.

Mintz, Alex. *The Political Economy of Military Spending in the United States.* London: Routledge, 1992.

Miscamble. Wilson. *From Roosevelt to Truman: Potsdam, Hiroshima, and the Cold War.* New York: Cambridge University Press, 2007.

  George F. Kennan and the Making of American Foreign Policy, 1945–1950. Princeton, New Jersey: Princeton University Press, 1992.

Moran, Theodore H. *American Economic Policy and National Security.* New York: Council on Foreign Relations Press, 1993.

Naimark, Norman. *The Russians in Germany: A History of the Soviet Zone of Occupation, 1945–1949.* Cambridge, Massachusetts: Belknap Press, 1997.

  "'To Know Everything and To Report Everything Worth Knowing': Building the East German Police State, 1945–49." Working Paper No. 10. Cold War International History Project. Woodrow Wilson International Center for Scholars, Washington, D.C., 1994.

Naimark, Norman, and Lenoid Gibianski. *The Establishment of Communist Regimes in Eastern Europe, 1944–1949.* Boulder, Colorado: Westview Press, 1998.

Nelson, Anna K. "President Truman and the Evolution of the National Security Council." *Journal of American History* 72 (September 1985): 360–378.

Newman, Robert P. "NSC (National Insecurity) 68: Nitze's Second Hallucination," in Matin J. Medhurst and H. W. Brands, eds., *Critical Reflections on the Cold War: Linking Rhetoric and History.* College Station, Texas: Texas A & M Press, 2000.

Nitze, Paul H. "The Development of NSC 68." *International Security* 4 (Spring 1980): 170–176.

  From Hiroshima to Glasnot: A the Center of Decision, A Memoir. New York: Grove Weidenfeld, 1989.

  Tension between Opposites: Reflections on the Practice and Theory of Politics. New York: Scribner 1993.

  United States Foreign Policy: 1945–1955. New York: Foreign Policy Association, 1955.

Oakes, Guy. *The Imaginary War: Civil Defense and American Cold War Culture.* New York: Oxford University Press, 1994.

Offner, Arnold. *Another Such Victory: President Truman and the Cold War, 1945–1953.* Stanford, California: Stanford University Press, 2002.

Olvey, Lee D. *The Economics of National Security.* Wayne, New Jersey: Avery Publishing Group, 1984.

O'Neill, William L. *American High: The Years of Confidence, 1945–1960.* New York: Free Press, 1986.

Pach, Chester. *Arming the Free World: The Origins of the United States Military Assistance Program, 1945–1950.* Chapel Hill, North Carolina: The University of North Carolina Press, 1991.

Select Bibliography

Parrish, Scott D. and Mikhail M. Narinsky. "New Evidence on the Soviet Rejection of the Marshall Plan, 1947: Two Reports." Working Paper No. 9. Cold War International History Project. Woodrow Wilson International Center for Scholars, Washington, D.C., 1994.

Parry-Giles, Shawn J. *The Rhetorical Presidency, Propaganda, and the Cold War, 1945–1955.* Westport, Connecticut: Praeger Publishers, 2002.

Paterson, Thomas G. *Cold War Critics: Alternatives to American Foreign Policy in the Truman Years.* Chicago: Quadrangle Books, 1971.

Meeting the Communist Threat: From Truman to Reagan. New York: Oxford University Press, 1988.

On Every Front: The Making of the Cold War. New York: W.W. Norton and Co., 1980.

Soviet-American Confrontation: Postwar Reconstruction and the Origins of the Cold War. Baltimore, Maryland: Johns Hopkins University Press, 1973.

Patterson, James T. *Grand Expectations: The United States, 1945–1974.* New York: Oxford University Press, 1996.

Pechatov, Vladimir O. "'The Allies are Pressing on You to Break Your Will...' Foreign Policy Correspondence between Stalin and Molotov and Other Politburo Members, September 1945-December 1946." Working Paper No. 26. Cold War International History Project. Woodrow Wilson International Center for Scholars, Washington, D.C., 1999.

"The Big Three After World War II: New Documents on Soviet Thinking about Post War Relations with the United States and Great Britain," Working Paper No. 13. Cold War International History Project. Woodrow Wilson International Center for Scholars, Washington, D.C., 1995.

Philips, Joseph D. "Economic Effects of the Cold War," in David Horowitz, ed., *Corporations and the Cold War.* New York: Monthly Review Press, 1969.

Pierpaoli, Paul, Jr. *Truman and Korea: The Political Culture of the Early Cold War.* Columbia, Missouri: The University of Missouri Press, 1999.

Poiger, Uta G. *Jazz, Rock, and Rebels: Cold War Politics and American Culture in a Divided Germany.* Berkeley, California: University of California Press, 2000.

Pollard, Robert. *Economic Security and the Origins of the Cold War, 1945–1950.* New York: Columbia University Press, 1985.

Pollock, Ethan. "Conversations with Stalin on Questions of Political Economy," Working Paper No. 33, Cold War International History Project. Washington, D.C., 2001.

Pomeroy, William J. *American Neo-Colonialism: Its Emergence in the Philippines and Asia.* New York: International Publishers, 1970.

Rearden, Steven. *The Evolution of American Strategic Doctrine: Paul H. Nitze and the Soviet Challenge.* Boulder, Colorado: Westview Press, 1984.

Rhodes, Benjamin D. *United States Foreign Policy in the Interwar Period, 1918–1941: The Golden Age of American Diplomatic and Military Complacency.* Westport, Connecticut: Praeger, 2001.

Roberts, Geoffrey. "Sexing up the Cold War: New Evidence on the Molotov-Truman Talks of April 1945," *Cold War History* 4: 3 (April 2004): 105–125.

286 *Select Bibliography*

Stalin's Wars: From World War to Cold War, 1939–1953. New Haven, Connecticut: Yale University Press, 2006.

Robin, Ron. *The Making of the Cold War Enemy: Culture and Politics in the Military-Industrial Complex.* Princeton, New Jersey: Princeton University Press, 2001.

Rolfe, Sidney E. *Gold and World Power.* New York: Harper and Row, 1966.

Rosen, Steven, comp. *Testing the Theory of the Military-Industrial Complex.* Lexington, Massachusetts: Lexington Books, 1973.

Rosenberg, David Allen. "American Atomic Strategy and the Hydrogen Bomb Decision." *Journal of American History* 66: 1 (June 1979): 62–87.

"The Origins of Overkill: Nuclear Weapons and American Strategy." In Norman Graebner, ed. *The National Security: Theory and Practice, 1945–1960.* New York: Oxford University Press, 1986, 123–195.

Rostow, Walter. *Stages of Economic Growth: A Non-Communist Manifesto.* New York: Cambridge University Press, 1960.

Rotter, Andrew J. *Comrades at Odds: The United States and India, 1947–1964.* Ithaca, New York: Cornell University Press, 2000.

The Path to Vietnam: Origins of the American Commitment to Southeast Asia. Ithaca, New York: Cornell University Press, 1987.

Salant, Walter, ed. *The United States Balance of Payments in 1968.* Washington, D.C.: The Brookings Institute, 1963.

Sanders, Jerry W. *Peddlers of Crisis: The Committee on the Present Danger and the Politics of Containment.* Boston: South End Press, 1983.

Schilling, Warner Roller, Paul Hammond, and Glenn Snyder, eds. *Strategy, Politics, and Defense Budgets.* New York: Columbia University Press, 1962.

Schulzinger, Robert D. *The Wise Men of Foreign Affairs: The History of the Council on Foreign Relations.* New York: Columbia University Press, 1984.

Selverstone, Mark. *Constructing the Monolith: The United States, Great Britain, and International Communism, 1945–1950.* Cambridge, Massachusetts: Harvard University Press, 2009.

Service, Robert. *Stalin: A Biography.* Cambridge, Massachusetts: Belknap Press, 2004.

Shannon, David A., ed. *The Great Depression.* New York: Prentice-Hall, Inc., 1960.

Sharlet, Jeff. "Why Diplomatic Historians May Be the Victims of American Triumphalism," *The Chronicle of Higher Education* 24 (September 1999): A19-A20.

Sherry, Michael. *The Shadow of War: The United States Since the 1930s.* New Haven, Connecticut: Yale University Press, 1995.

Shoup, Laurence and William Minter. *Imperial Brain Trust: The Council on Foreign Relations and United States Foreign Policy.* New York: Monthly Review Press, 1977.

Sklar, Martin J. *The Corporate Reconstruction of American Capitalism, 1890–1916: The Market, the law, and Politics.* New York: Cambridge University Press, 1988.

Smith, Gaddis. *Dean Acheson.* New York: Cooper Square Publishers, 1972.

Select Bibliography

Smith, Neil. *American Empire: Roosevelt's Geographer and the Prelude to Globalization.* Berkeley, California: University of California Press, 2003.

Smith, Tony. *America's Mission: The United States and the Worldwide Struggle for Democracy in the Twentieth Century.* Princeton, New Jersey: Princeton University Press, 1994.

  A Pact with the Devil: Washington's Bid for World Supremacy and the Betrayal of the American Promise. London: Routledge, 2007.

Sobel, Robert. *The Great Boom, 1950–2000: How a Generation of Americans Created the World's Most Prosperous Society.* New York: St. Martin's Press, 2000.

Stephanson, Anders. *Kennan and the Art of Foreign Policy.* Cambridge: Harvard University Press, 1989.

Steuck, William. *The Korean War: An International History.* Princeton, New Jersey: Princeton University Press, 1995.

  The Road to Confrontation: American Policy Toward China and Korea, 1947–1950. Chapel Hill, North Carolina: University of North Carolina Press, 1981.

  "The Soviet Union and the Origins of the Korean War," in Kim Chull Baum and James Matray, eds. *Korea and the Cold War: Division, Destruction, and Disarmament.* Claremont, California: Regina Books, 1993.

Trachtenberg, Marc. *A Constructed Peace: The Making of the European Settlement, 1945–1963.* Princeton, New Jersey: Princeton University Press, 1999.

  History and Strategy. Princeton, New Jersey: Princeton University Press, 1991.

  "The United States and Eastern Europe in 1945: A Reassessment." *Journal of Cold War Studies* 10: 4 (Fall 2008): 94–132.

Truman, Harry S. *Memoirs.* Garden City, New Jersey: Doubleday, 1955.

Van der Wee, Herman. *Prosperity and Upheaval: The World Economy, 1945–1980.* Berkeley, California: University of California Press, 1987.

Weathersby, Katherine. "New Findings on the Korean War." *Bulletin of the Cold War International History Project* 3 (Fall 1993), Cold War International History Project. Woodrow Wilson International Center for Scholars, Washington, D.C.

  "'Should We Fear This?' Stalin and the Danger of War with America." Working Paper No. 39. Cold War International History Project. Woodrow Wilson International Center for Scholars, Washington, D.C., 2002.

  "Soviet Aims in Korea and the Origins of the Korean War, 1945–1950: New Evidence from the Russian Archives." Working Paper No. 8. Cold War International History Project. Woodrow Wilson International Center for Scholars, Washington, D.C. 1993.

Wells, Samuel. "Sounding the Tocsin: NSC 68 and the Soviet Threat." *International Security* 4: 2 (Fall 1979): 116–158.

Wettig, Gerhard. *Stalin and the Cold War in Europe: The Emergence and Development of East-West Conflict, 1939–1953.* Lanham, Maryland: Rowman and Littlefield Publishers, 2008.

White, Stephen J. *The Culture of the Cold War.* Baltimore, Maryland: Johns Hopkins University Press, 1991.

Williams, Phil. *The Senate and U.S. Troops in Europe*. New York: Macmillan, 1985.

Williams, William Appleman. *America Confronts a Revolutionary World, 1776–1976*. New York: William Morrow, 1976.

    The Contours of American History. Cleveland, Ohio: The World Publishing Company, 1961.

    Empire as a Way of Life: An Essay on the Causes and Character of America's Present Predicament Along with a Few Thoughts about an Alternative. New York: Oxford University Press, 1980.

    The Tragedy of American Diplomacy. Cleveland, Ohio: World Publishing Company, 1959; New York: Delta Books, 1962.

Wilson, Joan Hoff. *American Business and Foreign Policy, 1920–1933*. Lexington, Kentucky: University of Kentucky Press, 1971.

Wittner, Lawrence S. *American Intervention in Greece, 1943–1949*. New York: Columbia University Press, 1982.

Wood, C. Tyler. "Problems of Foreign Aid from the Inside." *The American Economic Review* 49 (May 1959): 203–215.

Woodrow Wilson Foundation. *The Political Economy of American Foreign Policy: Its Concepts, Strategy, and Limits*. New York: Holt, 1955.

Woods, Randall and Howard Jones, "Origins of the Cold War in Europe and the Near East: Recent Historiography and the National Security Imperative." *Diplomatic History* 17: 2 (Spring 1993): 253.

Yegorova, Natalia. "The 'Iran Crisis' of 1945–46: A View from the Russian Archives," Working Paper No. 15. Cold War International History Project. Woodrow Wilson International Center for Scholars, Washington, D.C., 1996.

Yergin, Daniel. *Shattered Peace: The Origins of the Cold War and the National Security State*. New York: Houghton-Mifflin, 1977.

Zeiler, Thomas. *Free Trade, Free World: The Advent of Gatt*. Chapel Hill, North Carolina: University of North Carolina Press, 1999.

Zinn, Howard. *Postwar America: 1945–1971*. Indianapolis, Indiana: The Bobbs-Merrill Company, Inc., 1973.

Zubok, Vladislov and Constantine Pleshakov. *Inside the Kremlin's Cold War: From Stalin to Khrushchev*. Cambridge, Massachusetts: Harvard University Press, 1997.

Zunz, Oliver. *Why the American Century?* Chicago: University of Chicago Press, 1998.

Index

Acheson, Dean, 2, 74, 211, 216–217, 223, 231, 255, 259, 264
  downplays Soviet intentions in December 1949, 53
  and the Greco-Turkish aid bill of 1947, 82–84
  on importance of exports to U.S. economy, 96
  on increasing western Europe's productivity and consumption, 97–98
  NSC 68, author of, 8
  NSC 68, public discussion of before declassification, 10
  NSC 68, Truman's approval of, 11
  NSC 68, problems with the conventional interpretation, 21, 23
  October 11, 1949 meeting of the PPS, 169–173
  origins and development of NSC 68, 160–210
  and the origins of NSC 68, 160–210
  and radical schemes to end the dollar gap, 123–125
  on western European integration, 103
Additional Military Production, 222, 271–220
Africa, development of by western Europe, 117–118
Allende, Salvador, 266
Altschul, Frank, on increasing U.S. imports, 107
  on the importance of exports for the U.S. economy, 108

  on western Europe earning dollars via third countries, 118–119
Alvarez, Luis, and the hydrogen bomb, 187
Anglo-Argentine trade agreement, 139–141
Argentina, 78, 139–141
Armstrong, Hamilton Fish, on western European integration, 105
Atomic diplomacy, 74
Atomic Energy Commission, 17
Australia, 78
Austria, 43
Autarchy, 30, 43, 99, 179
  during the 1930s, 99

Baker, James, 1–2, 259
Balance of payments see Dollar gap
Ball, George, 113
Barnard, Chester, consultant on NSC 68, 197
Barrett, Edward, 210, 233
  and the review of NSC 68, 200
Base and airfield construction to overcome the dollar gap, 244–249
Belgian Congo, 237
Belgium, 154, 226
Berding, Andrew, 122
Berlin airlift, 48
Berlin blocakde, 10, 48, 161
Bevan, Aneurin, 226
Bevin, Ernest, and the British sterling-dollar crisis of 1949–1950, 147–149, 154

289

290 Index

Bilateral trade arrangements, 132, 144
Blackwill, Robert, on the long-term
  importance of NSC 68, 15, 266
Blanding, Sarah G., member of the Public
  Advisory Board of the Mutual Security
  Agency, 235
Bohlen, Charles, and Soviet weaknesses, 165
  disagrees with the depiction of the Soviet
    threat in NSC 68, 201
  on Soviet non-agressiveness, 52
  and the Soviet "peace offensive", 165
Bonesteel, Charles, 181–182
Borden, William, 3, 59
Bradley, Omar, 20, 185
Bretton Woods institutions, 35
British loan of 1946, 71, 86, 91, 263
British sterling-dollar crisis of 1949–1950,
  128–159
Brussels Pact, 152
Bulgaria, 42
Bureau of the Budget, 231
Burns, James H., contributor to NSC 68, 185
Bush, George Herbert Walker, 15
Butler, George H., 51
  contributor to NSC 68, 192
Byoir Advertising Agency, 122
Byrnes, James, 79

Callahan, David, 189
Canada, 67, 119, 131
  and the British sterling-dollar crisis of
    1949–1950, 143–150, 158
Capitalism, 30, 36, 56
Carter administration, 266
Castro, Fidel, 266
Central Intelligence Agency, 103, 181
Central Intelligence Group, 76
Chiang Kai-shek, 44
China, 51, 60, 76, "loss" of, 179, 222
  Communist victory in the civil war, 11,
    24, 173
  lack of concern for Communist victory
    in, 196
  NSC 68 and, 201
  Omar Bradley and the Communist
    victory in the civil war, 20
  Republicans and "loss" of, 207
  and treaty with the Soviet Union, 207
  weakness of, 24
China lobby, 166
Chinese Communist Party, and the
  Clifford-Elsey Report, 76

Churchill, Winston, 220, "Iron Curtain"
  speech of, 2
  and the Greek civil war, 83
  October 1944 agreement with Stalin on
    eastern Europe, 83
  use of paintings to overcome dollar
    gap, 122
Clayton, William, concern for postwar U.S.
  export surplus, 67–68
Cleveland, Harlan, 1949 report on the
  dollar gap crisis, 98–100
Clifford, Clark, 76
Clifford-Elsey Report, 76–77
Cold War, 1, 3, 5, 7, 11, 14, 16, 19, 58–60,
  73, 82, 160, 165–166, 174–175, 194,
  203, 263–264
  CNN documentary, 16
  origins, 38–57
Combined Policy Committee, 123
Communism, 1, 3, 43, 56, 107, 126
Communism, China, 24
Communist Information Bureau
  (Coniform), 45
Connally, Tom, 234
Containment, 24, 74–75
Council on Foreign Relations, 21
  Study Group on Aid to Europe (SGAE),
    102–103, 107, 110, 116, 126, 185
  Study Group on Economic Policy
    (SGEP), 107, 113, 118, 174–180
Counterpart funds, 232, 244
Creed, Charles, 121
Cripps, Stafford, 137, 144, 147–149, 153,
  155–156
Currency convertibility, 178
Czechoslovakia, 43, 49
  and the Clifford-Elsey Report, 76

Dardanelles Straits, 46
Davies, John, contributor to NSC 68, 192
Denmark, 43, 249
Depression
  of the 1890s, 33
  foreign markets necessary to prevent, 96
Despres, Emile, on western European
  integration, 104
Devaluation, of the French franc, 153
Diebold, William, 103, 105, 112
Diem, Ngo Dinh, 266
Dollar area, 128, 137, 142, 148–149
Dollar diplomacy, 74
Dollar gap, 3, 5, 25, 30, 58

Index

291

Acheson's and Nitze's concern for, 161
consequences of multilateralism, 266–270
consequences of using rearmament to
overcome, 263–266
crisis, 61–71
and the Gordon Gray commission,
198–199
and Great Britain, 134–135
greater crisis in 1949 than the Soviet
Union, 180
ignored in the history, 60
Japan and, 166
Marshal Plan fails to overcome, 162
mentioned in NSC 68, 26
and the multilateralists agenda, 262
Nitze's November 22, 1949
memorandum and, 174–180
and the origins of NSC 68, 196
origins of the Cold War, 77–87
and the political economy of
rearmament, 211–258
solutions, continued economic aid
beyond 1952, 112–114
solutions, increasing western Europe's
productivity and consumption,
97–106
solutions, radical schemes, 122–127
still in existence after 1952, 259
and West European political and
economic integration, 162
Dominican Republic, 266
Douglas, Lewis, 183, 228
and the British sterling-dollar crisis of
1949–1950, 141–154
Draper, William Jr., 245
Dulles, Alan, 103, 181

East Germany, 256
creation of, 164
Eastern Europe, 142
and the origins of the Cold War, 38–57
Economic Cooperation Administration
(ECA), 67, 93, 102, 112, 116, 120,
127, 140–141, 150, 158, 181–182
Economic integration, Western Europe,
mentioned in NSC 68, 26
Egypt, 78
and the dollar gap, 64
Eisenhower, Dwight D., and knowledge of
NSC 68, 15
as commander of NATO, 246
on increasing U.S. imports, 109

and the "military-industrial
complex", 212
on the necessity of continuing economic
aid beyond 1952, 113
Ellis, Howard, 104
Elsey, George, Cilfford-Elsey Report, 206
European Coal and Steel Community,
251–252
European Defense Community, 254
European Recovery Program *see* Marshall
Plan
Export-Import Bank, 116
Exports, importance to U.S. domestic
economy, 108, 125

Federal Republic of Germany *see* West
Germany
FIAT, 219, 237
Finland, and the Clifford-Elsey
Report, 76
Fordham, Benjamin, 4
Fordney-McCumber Tariff of 1922, 61
Foreign Affairs, 105
Forrestal, James, 72
Foster, William, and Western European
economic integration, 163
France, 44, 48, 132
and the British sterling-dollar crisis
of 1949–1950, 150, 224, 237–240,
249, 258
and German reconstruction, 164–165
Kennan's ideas for leading a western
European confederation, 122
London Foreign Ministers meeting, May
1950, 205
and West German integration, 253–254
Freeland, Richard, 3
French Equitorial Africa, 237
Fulbright, William, 114

Galbraith, John Kenneth, 176
General Advisory Committee of the Atomic
Energy Commission, 187
German Democratic Republic *see* East
Germany
Germany, 30, 37, 47, 49, 51, 53, 55,
60–61, 91, 124
East, 42
future of, 179
and the Soviet "peace offensive", 195
Stalin's 1952 peace proposal for, 263
West, 43, 48

Graham and Childes, Ltd., 121
Grand Alliance, 49
Gray, Gordon, 198–199
Gray Commisssion, 198–199, 205
Great Britain, 42, 45, 48
  and 1949 devaluation of the British
    pound, 18, 105–106, 152–153
  announces intention not to integrate
    with the continent, 163
  and the Berlin blockade, 161
  and Bretton Woods, 77
  and the British sterling-dollar crisis of
    1949–1950, 176
  and the convertibility crisis of 1947,
    83, 143
  and the dollar gap, 63, 106, 119,
    215, 228, 249
  dollar pool, 132
  and the European Payments
    Union, 251
  gold and dollar reserves, 134,
    141–142, 155
  House of Commons, discusses British
    autarchy, 148–149
  and Imperial Preference, 77
  Kennan's views on integration with the
    U.S. and Canada, 122
  London Foreign Ministers meeting, May
    1950, 205
  and the Marshall Plan, 84, 128–159
  and multilateralism, 77–79
  and the Mutual Security Program, 239
  in NSC 68, 26
  and rearmament, 257
  restricts U.S. imports in the summer of
    1949, 148
  Soviet threat and the U.S. loan, 80–81
  and sterling balances, 124
  sterling debt, 119
  U.S. loan to, 77–81
  and the U.S. recession of 1948–1949, 142
Great Depression, 29, 32, 61–62, 137
  protectionism, 30
  Soviet Union, 40
Greco-Turkish aid bill of 1947, 59, 86, 91
Greece, 81–84, 216
Grenada, 266

Halaby, Najeeb E., 233
Hammond, Paul Y., 192
Hare, Raymond, and the review of NSC
  68, 201

Harriman, Averell, 121, 168, 220–221,
  230–23
  and the British sterling-dollar crisis of
    1949–1950, 136–138
  and postwar European autarchy,
    136–138
  as special assistant to the president to
    coordinate Cold War policy, 206
  on using security to achieve political and
    economic integration, 184
Harriman, E.H., 180
Hickerson, John, and the review of NSC
  68, 201
Ho Chi Minh, 227
Hoffman, Paul, and multilateralism, 140
  and the dollar gap, 68–69
  on ending the dollar gap through
    reduced world trade, 125
  on increasing western Europe's
    productivity and consumption, 98
  and the Marshall Plan, 140
  October 31, 1949 speech before the
    OEEC, 163
  and problems of western European
    integration, 103–104
  and Western European economic
    integration, 156–158
Holland, 119
Hooker, Robert, contributor to NSC 68, 192
House of Commons, 155
Hull, Cordell, 30
Hungary, 42, 76
Hydrogen bomb (H-bomb), 264
Hydrogen bomb, hesitancy to build, 22,
  187–194

Imperial Preference, 105, 139
India, 78, 119, 150, 264
Indonesia, 266
International Bank for Reconstruction and
  Development (IBRD), 77–78
International Investment Authority, 118
International Monetary Fund (IMF), 77–78
International Security Affairs Committee
  (ISAC), 226–227, 246
International Trade Organization (ITO), 66
Iran, 216
  1945–1946 crisis, 45, 47, 55
Iron curtain, 43
Italy, 45, 211, 225, 237–239, 251
  and western European economic
    integration, 100

Index

Jamaica, 237
Japan, 30, 39, 60, 72, 109, 121, 259, 269
  and the British sterling-dollar crisis of
    1949–1950, 133
  and the dollar gap, 162, 170, 222–223
  Great East Asian Co-Prosperity
    Sphere, 62
  peace treaty with the U.S., 208
  as the "workshop" of Asia, 267
Johnson, Edward Fuller, and the hydrogen
  bomb decision, 22
Johnson, Louis, 186–187, 190–193,
    196–197, 199–200
  and anger over NSC 68, 199–200
  and the January 31, 1950 meeting with
    Truman, 22
  and Soviet weakness, 23
  and Truman's request for reduced
    military spending, 20
Joint Chiefs of Staff (JCS), 11, 185, 192–193
  rejects crash program to build the
    hydrogen bomb, 20
  and Truman's request for reduced
    military spending, 20
Joint Intelligence Committee, 85

Kaiserslautern, Germany, 248
Kennan, George, 165, 186
  on China going communist, 24
  and containment, 74–75
  and end of U.S. atomic monopoly, 24
  left out of the writing of NSC 68, 197
  on the necessity of continuing economic
    aid beyond 1952, 112–113
  non-support for rearmament, 190
  and the October 11, 1949 meeting of the
    Policy Planning Staff, 169–173
  replaced by Nitze as head of the Policy
    Planning Staff, 178, 190
  on western Europe earning dollars via
    third countries, 118
  on western European integration, 102
Kennedy administration, 266
Keyserling, Leon, 189–190
Kirk, Grayson, 175–176
Kline, Allan B., member of the Public
  Advisory Board of the Mutual Security
  Agency, 235
Kofsky, Frank, 86–87
Kolko, Joyce, 3
Korean War, 13, 19, 221, 225–226, 232,
    254–255

LaBouisse, Henry, 118
Landry, Robert P., on Soviet non-
  agressiveness, aggressive intentions,
  52–53
Latin America, and the dollar gap, 63–64
Lawrence, Ernest, consultant on
  NSC 68, 197
Lay, James, 22
  contributor to NSC 68, 193
LeBaron, Robert, contributor to
  NSC 68, 188
Leffingwell, R.C., 102, 185
Leffler, Melvyn, 24, 75, 171 n 23, 185 n 52
Lehman, Orin, member of the Public
  Advisory Board of the Mutual Security
  Agency, 235
Lend-lease, 80
Lilienthal, David
  and the hydrogen bomb decision, 22,
    187–188, 190–194
  September 20, 1949 meeting with
    Truman, 17–18
Lindsay, Frank, 181
Long Telegram, 74–76
Lubin, Isador, 111–112
Luce, Henry, 29
Luxembourg, 251

Maier, Charles, 33
Malaysia, and triangular trade, 133
Mallory, Walter, 103–106
Marjolin, Robert, 32
Marshall, George C., 84
  and the Greco-Turkish aid bill
    of 1947, 82
  and the war scare of 1948, 87
Marshall Plan, 14, 32, 64, 88, 94, 101,
    223, 240, 249, 256–257
  and the British sterling-dollar crisis of
    1949–1950, 128–159
  crisis of, 104–105, 113
  and failure for Great Britain,
    133–134
  failure to overcome the dollar gap,
    128–131
  importance to the U.S. economy, 69
  origins and passage using the Soviet
    threat, 84–87, 263
  Soviet defection demonstrates Soviet
    concerns for security and distrust of
    the West, 50
  Stalin rejects, 47

Index

Marshall Plan (*cont.*)
U.S. officials deliberately write it to keep the Soviets out, 50
and the war scare of 1948, 86–87
May, Ernest, 15
McCarthy, Joseph, 89–90, 166
McCarthyism, 166
McCormick, Thomas, 3, 44, 253–254
Mead, George H., member of the Public Advisory Board of the Mutual Security Agency, 235
Merrow, Chester, 127
Middle East, 76, 82
Military assistance, and Congress, 226
and the dollar gap, 249
for overcoming the dollar gap, 211–258
and West German rearmament, 254
Military Assisstance Program (MAP), 21, 183, 215–217
"Military-industrial-academic" complex, 13
"Military-industrial complex," Eisenhower's warning on, 212
"Military Keynesianism," 6, 265
Military spending, and the dollar gap, 211–270
U.S. increase under NSC 68, 211–212
Molotov, Vyacheslav, 72
Mossadiq, Mohammed, 266
Multilateralism, 58, 62, 70, 81, 88, 128, 140, 150, 160, 165
and British suspension of nonconvertibility, 83
postwar U.S. foreign policy, 34, 36, 37
Multilateralists, 30, 32, 34, 37, 47, 59, 66–71, 75, 94–95, 118, 179
Murphy, Charles, 226
Mutual Defense Assistance Program, 162, 203, 215–228, 231–233, 240–244, 257
Mutual Security Agency (MSA), 235, *see also* Mutual Security Program
Mutual Security Program (MSP), 215–216, 233–242

The Nation, 126
National Association of Manufactures, 125
National Security Council, 1, 2, 22, 190–193
and Truman's request for reduced military spending, 20–21
National Security Resources Board, 115
Nazi Germany, autarchy of, 62
Netherlands, 230, 251
New Deal, 33, 62, 90–91

Nissan, 109
Nitze, Paul, 101, 113, 231, 264
convinced NSC 68 will not receive approval, 204
and the Marshall Plan, 84
November 22, 1949 dollar gap memorandum, 174–180
NSC 68, importance of, 15
October 11, 1949 meeting of the PPS, 169–173
origins and development of NSC 68, 160–210
and "radical schemes" to cope with the dollar gap, 158–159
Nixon, Richard, 90
North Atlantic Treaty Organization (NATO), 84, 161, 203
North Korea, 264
Nourse, Edwin, 189–190
NSC 20/4, 14
NSC 68, 3, 5, 7, 9, 60, 127
accuracy of dissenting views, 202–203
alternative origins, 26
authors of, 160–161
and the British sterling-dollar crisis of 1949–1950, 159
conventional interpretation, 15, 17
and the dollar gap, 180
dollar gap mentioned in, 71
effects of, 211–270
emerging consensus on a military-economic solution, 180–186
and George Kennan, 190
in the historiography, 15
importance of, 14
Korean War and the origins of, 203–210
mentions China, 11
Nitze's false claims about, 200–202
October 11, 1949 meeting of the PPS and the origins of, 169–173
origins and development of, 160–210
point of departure for the Cold War, 160
and the political economy of rearmament, 211–258
problems with the conventional interpretation, 16, 21, 23, 25
review of, 199–204
summarized, 11
and U.S. hegemony in the postwar era, 160
NSC 73, 209 n 110
Nurske, Ragnar, 109

Index

295

October 11, 1949 meeting of the PPS and the origins of NSC 68, 169–173
Offshore Procurement Program (OSP), 221–223, 227, 242–244, 250
Ohly, John, 221, 242–243
Oppenheimer, Robert, consultant on NSC 68, 197
  Princeton Seminars, 210
Organization of European Economic Cooperation (OEEC), 103, 127, 150, 156–157, 176
Ottawa Agreements, on Imperial Preference, 105

Pakistan, 152
Panama, 266
Patton, James G., member of the Public Advisory Board of the Mutual Security Agency, 235
Philippines, 132
  and the dollar gap, 64
Point Four Program, 115–116
Poland, 40, 43
  and the dollar gap, 64
Policy Planning Staff (PPS), 2, 102, 118, 123, 188, 215
  and the devlopment of NSC 68, 196–198
  Nitze succeeds Kennan as head of, 177–178
  October 11, 1949 meeting, 169–174
  and the origins of NSC 68, 192
Portugal, 54
Potsdam Accords, 48, 266
Potsdam conference, 38
Preventive war, against the Soviet Union, 23
Princeton Seminars, 157–159, 210, 244
Protectionism, 34

Rabi, Isidor, 110
Rayburn, Sam, 80
Reagan revolution, 1
Rearmament, 3, 6
  and the dollar gap, 160–210, 218–222, 230
  and inflation, 230
  political economy of, 211–258
  program, 2
  and West Germany, 229–233
Reciprocal Trade Agreements Act (RTAA), 62
Reparations, 50
Republicans, and economic nationalism, 36

Rhodesia, 237
Roberts, Geoffrey, 43, 50, 268–270
Roosevelt, Franklin D., 36, 72
  Declaration on Liberated Europe, 41
Rotter, Andrew, 3
Rumania (Romania), 40, 42
Russia see Soviet Union
Russo-Japanese War of 1904–1905, 267

Savage, Carlton, contributor to NSC 68, 192
Schaub, William, and the review of NSC 68, 202
Senate Committee on Foreign Relations, on China going Communist, 25
Smith, Walter Bedell, 50
Smoot-Hawley Tariff of 1930, 61
Snyder, John, and the British sterling-dollar crisis of 1949–1950, 147, 156
Socialism, 33, 45
Souers, Sydney, and the hydrogen bomb decision, 22
South Africa, and the dollar gap, 64
South America, 138
Soviet bloc, 64
Soviet threat, 30, 53, 56
  and the British loan of 1946, 80–81
  and the Marshall Plan, 84–87
  used by the Truman administration, 77–91, 269
Soviet Union, 2, 4, 24, 150
  and acquisition of the atomic bomb, 163–164, 170
  atomic weapons, 4
  and the Berlin blockade, 161
  and Bohlen's critique of NSC 68, 259–260
  compared to threat of dollar gap, 93
  depicted in NSC 68, 11–13
  and the dollar gap crisis, 71
  and end of Lend–Lease aid, 78
  foreign policy gains, 179
  and Japan, 162
  Kennan's belief that it was easily containable, 187
  Military capabilities viewed as week, 203
  and the multilateralists dismisall of its interests, 267–268
  Nitze regards Soviet threat as tiertiary, 194
  not the cause of the Marshall Plan, 84–87

Index

Soviet Union (*cont.*)
NSC 68, alternative origins, 26
NSC 68 and the Korean War, 207–209
origins of the Cold War, 39–60
"peace offensive" of, 263
and postwar Japan, 267
postwar power, 29, 37
problems with the conventional
interpretation, 18, 23, 25
Schuab criticizes NSC 68's depiction
of, 202
"socialism in one country", 62
Thorp criticizes NSC 68's depiction
of, 201
Truman and NSC 68 and, 206–207
in the Truman's directive for NSC 68, 10
and the unification of Germany, 165
war destruction of, 38, 40, 60
weakness of, 24
Spaak, Paul-Henri, 156
Spain, 54
Stalin, Joseph
1952 peace proposal for Germany, 263
and the Berlin blockade, 48
Clifford-Elsey Report, 76
and the communization of eastern
Europe, 42, 45
and crises in Iran and Turkey, 45, 47
and the Czechoslovakian coup, 49
and the Declaration on Liberated
Europe, 41
"election" speech of, 39
and the Greek civil war, 83
lack of support for Chinese
Communists, 44
lack of support for French and Italian
Communists, 45
meeting with Harry Hopkins, May
1945, 72
postwar objectives, 55
security concerns, 41
and Tito, 44
uninterested in a cold war with
the West, 270
Steelman, John R., 115
Stein, Harold, on the necessity of
continuing economic aid beyond
1952, 113
Steinhardt, Laurence A., 48–49
Sterling area, 124, 139–140, 145, 154–155
Sterling balances, 124

Stueck, William, 207
Sukarno, 266
Sweden, and the dollar gap, 64

Taft, Robert, 111
Tariffs
inter-European, 163
U.S., 106, 179
Tehran conference, 38
Thorez, Maurice, 45
Tito, Josep Broz, 44
Trachtenberg, Marc, 42
Treaty of Maastricht, 252
Truman, Harry S., 262–264, 268
accepts Soviet domination of Eastern
Europe, 41
and the British sterling-dollar crisis of
1949–1950, 151
and the dollar gap, 66–67
and end of U.S. atomic monopoly, 19
and JCS order 1067, 48
and the military buildup, 214–215, 230
and the Mutual Defense Assistance
Program, 217
NSC 68, implementation of, 14
NSC 68, presented to, 10
NSC 68, problems with the conventional
interpretation, 17, 19, 21
and the origins of NSC 68, 179–180,
192–194, 203–210
and the Point Four Program, 149
and reductions in stockpiling, 115
and the Soviet acquisition of atomic
power, 216
Truman Doctrine, 2, 14, 82–84, 206, 220
Tufts, Robert, contributor to NSC 68, 102
Turkey, 81–82, 216, 1946 crisis, 46, 55

United Nations, 28, 46
United States, ambiguity and frustration
over the Soviet threat, 71–77
and the Berlin blockade, 161
and British autarchy during the 1930s,
131–134
and the British loan of 1946, 77–81
and British toys to aid the dollar gap, 121
and counterpart funds, 120
and the creation of West Germany,
161–162
and devaluation of the British pound,
152–153

and development in backwards areas, 117–119
and the dollar gap, 93, 97, 99, 106, 232
economic nationalists, 35
effects of NSC 68 on, 14
exports, 3
and foreign markets necessary for prosperity, 107–108
foreign policy, 2, 3
foreign policy officials, 6
as global power after WWII, 29
and hegemony, 160, 213
hyper-productivity of in the postwar era, 109
and increasing western European production and consumption, 97–106
and the Industrial Revolution, 98–99
and lack of need for European imports, 110
and the "loss" of China, 25, 166
multilateralists, 33
and need to increase imports, 106–112
New Deal, 62
in NSC 68, 11, 13, 17, 27
origins of the Cold War, 39, 42, 48, 53, 55, 57, 58–59
origins of the Cold War, conventional interpretation, 45
and passage of the Marshall Plan, 84–87
postwar power, 62s
and a postwar U.S. depression, 108–109
and preventing West European neutrality, 256–258
and productivity, 215
progressive internationalists, 36
and radical schemes for closing the dollar gap, 125–127
and rearmament, 221, 233
and recession of 1948–1949, 135
sale of British toys in to aid the dollar gap, 121
and the Soviet Union's acquisition of atomic power, 163–164
and sterling balances, 119
and stockpiling to aid the dollar gap, 115
and union with Britain and Canada, 122–123
and use of military spending to overcome the dollar gap, 223
and use of military spending to overcome the dollar gap, 236

and West European integration, 250–253
and Winston Churchill's paintings to aid the dollar gap, 122
U.S. armed forces, stationing abroad to overcome the dollar gap, 244–249
U.S. Congress, 261–263, 265
and British autarchy, 146
and the British loan of 1946, 79–81
cuts Marshall Plan funding for 1950, 153–154
and the dollar gap, 175–180
and the Gray Commission Report, 199
and the H-bomb decision, 188
and influence on U.S. foreign policy, 35–36
and international control of the atom bomb, 173
knowledge that Marshall Plan would fail to end the dollar gap hidden from, 92
and the Marshall Plan, 47, 129, 149, 157, 242
and the Military Assistance Program, 216
and the military buildup, 217, 224, 232
and the Mutual Security Program, 234
and the Offshore Procurement Program, 243
and passage of the Military Assistance Program, 168
resists dollar gap explanations on their own merits, 95
and the Soviet threat, 59
and stockpiling, 115
under the Articles of Confederation, 33
and western European economic integration, 101–103, 156–157
U.S. House of Representatives, and the British loan, 80
Committee on Foreign Affairs, 93–94, 100, 108, 125
U.S. Senate, Committee on Foreign Relations, 68

Vandenberg, Arthur, 80
Vietnam, 255
Vigderman, A.G., 211
Viner, Jacob, 108, 119
Vinson, Fred, 79
Vorys, John M., 95

298   *Index*

Wallace, Henry, 88
War scare of 1948, 200
Watergate scandal, 90
Webb, James, 156–157
West Germany, 213–214, 225–230, 241,
    253–254
    and the British sterling-dollar crisis of
      1949–1950, 162
    creation of, 164
    and NSC 68, 14
    U.S. policy toward, 164–165
Western Europe, and continued economic
    aid beyond 1952, 112–114
    and the dollar gap, 67–69, 92–93, 97, 105
    and east-west trade, 126–127
    economic integration, 100–106

    and Germany, 124
    lack of products to sell to the U.S., 110
    and lowering U.S. tariffs, 110–112
    and the Marshall Plan, 84–87
    necessity of remaining tied to
      the U.S., 126
    and radical schemes for closing the
      dollar gap, 122–127
    and the Soviet threat, 72
Williams, John, 107
World War II, 13, 29, 35, 37, 47, 213,
    253, 262

Yalta, 266
Yalta Accords, 72, 266
    conference, 38, 41, 83

Lightning Source UK Ltd.
Milton Keynes UK
UKOW04f0257050118
315588UK00001B/38/P